lonely
planet
OF TRAVEL

COLORADO

**Rocky Mountain National Park
& Northern Colorado**
p112

Boulder, p84

**Vail, Aspen &
Central Colorado**
p144

DENVER, p48

**Mesa Verde &
Southwest Colorado**
p204

**Southeast Colorado &
the San Luis Valley**
p252

Liza Prado, Aimee Heckel, Christopher Pitts

CONTENTS

Plan Your Trip

The Guide

Cliff dwellings, Mesa Verde National Park (p210)

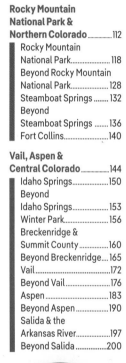

Union Station (p56), Denver

RIGHT: EGROY/SHUTTERSTOCK ©, LEFT TOP: SOPOTNICKI/SHUTTERSTOCK ©, LEFT BOTTOM: JON OSUMI/SHUTTERSTOCK ©

View of Pikes Peak (p263) from the Garden of the Gods (p259)

SNEHIT PHOTO/SHUTTERSTOCK ©

Million Dollar Hwy (p226)

COLORADO
THE JOURNEY BEGINS HERE

When I moved to Denver, I thought of it as a one-, maybe two-year whim to live someplace new. Fifteen years later, I'm still here and have no plans to leave. I'd only been to Colorado once before, a brief stopover on a cross-country road trip. But after I moved here, those snowcapped mountains pulled me in hard and fast. Anytime I looked west, they were there: a constant in the city's everchanging landscape, a reminder that time is long and slow, a promise of adventure hidden within. And with each passing year, the mountains have lived up to their promise, revealing landscapes I'd never imagined in Colorado – red-rock canyons, towering sand dunes, high desert mesas. And hot springs! So many hot springs. Even after 15 years, Colorado has the power to surprise me. I have no doubt, 15 years from now, I'll feel exactly the same way.

Liza Prado, writer

@liza.prado @ThisIsLizaPrado

Liza is a corporate lawyer turned travel writer. She has authored over 50 guidebooks.

My favorite experience is driving the Million Dollar Hwy (p226), the winding road taking me past the soaring San Juans, the glittering lakes, the golden aspens. It is magnificence incarnate.

WHO GOES WHERE

Our writers and experts choose the
places that, for them, define Colorado

CHRISTOPHER JACKSON/SHUTTERSTOCK ©

Rocky Mountain National Park (p118) is a microcosm of everything I love about Colorado: otherworldly nights in the high country watching the dancing lights of distant thunderstorms, spine-tingling adventures up gorgeous granite peaks, and crisp fall days, when the aspens blaze gold and the eerie sound of bugling elks carries across the valleys.

Christopher Pitts

www.christopherpitts.net

Christopher is the author of over two dozen Lonely Planet guides, as well as the forthcoming novel Wild Goose Pass.

LITTLENYSTOCK/SHUTTERSTOCK ©

They call it the 'Boulder bubble' for a reason: the city of **Boulder** (p84) is like nowhere else on Earth. This quirky university town stretches out below the stunning Flatiron rock formations and is a convenient Colorado travel hub for its straight shot to Denver and some of Colorado's best outdoor adventures, including nearby ski towns, tons of trails and Colorado's brewery scene. Boulder is artsy, highly educated and, well, just plain unique – in the best way.

Aimee Heckel

@heckela
@Aimeemay

Aimee is a writer about travel and fitness, as well as the author of a book about Colorado day trips by theme.

Glenwood Springs
Hot springs with Rocky Mountain views (p191)

Breckenridge
Epic skiing and mountain-town charm (p160)

WYOMING

UTAH

NORTHWEST COLORADO

Dinosaur National Monument
Dinosaur bones everywhere (p139)

Dinosaur National Monument

Dinosaur

Yampa River

State Forest State Park

Walden

Steamboat Springs

Continental Divide

Meeker

NORTHERN MOUNTAINS

Lake Granby
Granby

Winter Park

Glenwood Springs

Vail

Frisco

Beaver Creek

Breckenridge

Basalt

Leadville

Independence Pass
Quintessential Rocky Mountain drive (p194)

Fruita

Grand Junction

Colorado River

Palisade

Grand Mesa National Forest

Independence Pass

Aspen

Fairplay

Colorado National Monument

Gunnison River

Delta

Paonia

Crystal

Maroon Bells

Crested Butte

Twin Lakes

Arkansas River

Buena Vista

SOUTHWEST COLORADO

Black Canyon of Gunnison National Park

Blue Mesa Reservoir

Gunnison National Forest

Gunnison

Salida

Ridgway

SAN LUIS VALLEY

Ouray
Ice climbing in the San Juan Mountains (p222)

Ouray

Lake City

Continental Divide

Telluride

Canyons of the Ancients National Monument

Rico

Silverton

Rio Grande National Forest

Rio Grande

South Fork

Del Norte

Monte Vista

San Juan Mountains

Cortez

Mancos

Weminuche Wilderness

Alamosa

Mesa Verde National Park

Durango

Pagosa Springs

Conejos

ARIZONA

Mesa Verde National Park
Ancient cliff dwellings and sacred sites (p210)

Weminuche Wilderness Area
Vast wilderness and wildlife hot spot (p221)

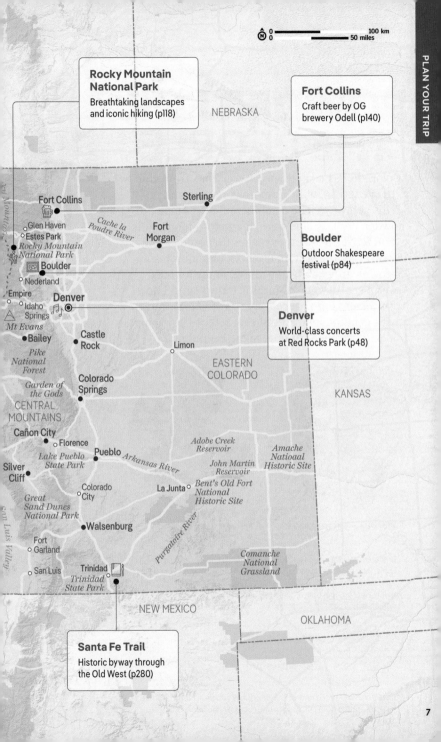

Rocky Mountain National Park

Breathtaking landscapes and iconic hiking (p118)

Fort Collins

Craft beer by OG brewery Odell (p140)

NEBRASKA

100 km
50 miles

Boulder

Outdoor Shakespeare festival (p84)

Fort Collins

Sterling

Glen Haven

Estes Park

Cache la Poudre River

Fort Morgan

Rocky Mountain National Park

Boulder

Nederland

Empire

Denver

Idaho Springs

Mt Evans

Denver

World-class concerts at Red Rocks Park (p48)

Bailey

Castle Rock

Limon

Pike National Forest

Garden of the Gods

EASTERN COLORADO

KANSAS

CENTRAL MOUNTAINS

Colorado Springs

Cañon City

Florence

Adobe Creek Reservoir

Amache Natioaal Historic Site

Lake Pueblo State Park

Pueblo

Arkansas River

John Martin Reservoir

Silver Cliff

Colorado City

La Junta

Bent's Old Fort National Historic Site

Great Sand Dunes National Park

Walsenburg

Purgatoire River

Comanche National Grassland

Fort Garland

San Luis

Trinidad

Trinidad State Park

San Luis Valley

NEW MEXICO

OKLAHOMA

Santa Fe Trail

Historic byway through the Old West (p280)

7

POWDER FOR THE PEOPLE

Colorado has a ski town for everyone, from chic to cheap(ish), with glamorous resorts and no-frills getaways. The combination of champagne powder, endless blue skies, mammoth mountains and a live-to-ski ethos makes Colorado skiing and riding the stuff of legend. Colorado's resort towns are equally appealing, many founded over a century ago as mining outposts and now transformed into welcoming resort communities, with genuine history and character to go along with excellent dining, nightlife and more.

Ski Pass vs Lift Ticket

Available in various prices, the Epic, Ikon or resort-specific passes and multipacks are typically a better deal than regular lift tickets, which can top $200/day.

BYO Boots

If there's one piece of personal gear to bring, make it your boots – rentals rarely fit as well, and aching feet can ruin your day.

Après-Ski

Ski towns have turned end-of-the-day drinks into an art form. 'Après' specials range from pub grub to fine cocktails, ski boots optional.

BEST SKI TOWN EXPERIENCES

Have it all in **Breckenridge** ❶ – the best combination of epic skiing, genuine mountain town charm and easy access from Denver. (p160)

Get your glam on in **Aspen** ❷, a stylish star-studded mountain town with world class skiing and riding to boot. (p183)

Prepare to be stunned by the sheer beauty of **Telluride** ❸, an iconic town and ski resort deep in the gorgeous San Juans. (p229)

Soak at one of the local hot springs after a day of pitch-perfect tree skiing at down-to-earth **Steamboat Mountain Resort**. ❹ (p135)

Enjoy **Crested Butte** ❺, the last great ski town in America and a small-but-mighty resort with Colorado's steepest inbound run. (p242)

Great Sand Dunes National Park (p265)

ADRENALINE RUSH

Some travelers need more than to simply admire Colorado's natural wonders: they want to engage with them, to scale, hike, bike and raft them. And the state is perfectly happy to oblige, with a virtually endless supply of high-adrenaline adventures to be had throughout Colorado's wilderness, whether it's summertime or the depths of winter.

Cover Up

The sun shines hard in Colorado, both summer and winter. Slather on sunscreen, wear your hat and shades, and don't forget the SPF-infused lip balm.

Nature Always Wins

Avalanches kill more people in Colorado than any other state, and all adrenaline sports – climbing, biking, rafting – have inherent dangers. Know your limits.

BEST ADVENTURE SPORT EXPERIENCES

Brace yourself for the icy splash, roaring waves, and hoot-hollering of your rafting buddies as you descend through **Browns Canyon ❶**. (p198)

Keep your balance as you sandboard down the shifting (and surprisingly steep!) sandscape of **Great Sand Dunes National Park ❷**. (p265)

Test your climbing skills – and finger strength – on the beautifully veined cliffs of **Black Canyon of the Gunnison National Park ❸**. (p234)

Swing that ice axe, set those crampons and you'll reach the top of the gorgeous blue ice walls of **Ouray Ice Park ❹**. (p224)

Let it rip on over 450 miles of mountain biking trails in **Crested Butte ❺**, with gorgeous scenery and options for riders of all levels. (p242)

EPIC DRIVES

For mind-blowing drives, you've come to the right place. Colorado has over two dozen nationally designated Scenic & Historic Byways, and several more that aren't on the official list but should definitely make yours. Some will take all day, while others are short hops to lonely mountain passes; all are sure to leave you speechless but smiling.

Car Rentals

Save cash by booking your car rental at an off-airport location – a cab ride can typically save about 20% on airport taxes and fees.

The I-70

On weekends, the I-70 can move at a snail's pace, packed with metro-Denverites headed to and from the mountains. Travel midweek to avoid the traffic.

Weather Alerts

Check for weather alerts before you set out – roads can close! If you're headed to the mountains, carry a set of auto-socks and have provisions.

BEST DRIVING EXPERIENCES

Enjoy outrageous alpine vistas on **Trail Ridge Rd ❶**, in Rocky Mountain National Park, the highest continuously paved road in North America. (p121)

The views are priceless on the **Million Dollar Hwy ❷**, 25 miles of hairpin turns along the incomparable Uncompahgre Gorge between Silverton and Ouray. (p226)

Drive back in time on the **Gold Belt Scenic Byway ❸**, an unpaved former stagecoach road that winds along sheer cliffs and through piñon tree forests. (p276)

Go exploring along the top of the **Top of the Rockies Scenic Byway ❹**, crossing iconic Independence Pass, three national forests and historic Colorado towns. (p179)

Go for the gold (and orange and red) on **Kebler Pass ❺**, where a dense aspen forest makes for a spectacular fall drive. (p241)

INDIGENOUS AMERICANS

Numerous tribes trace their lineage to present-day Colorado, including Cheyenne, Arapaho, Apache, Pueblo and especially the Ute. The Ute are a large and diverse tribe, composed of numerous bands and spanning centuries. They traditionally lived in the mountains, where much of their mythology is centered, and have two reservations in southwestern Colorado today. Several locations around the state honor and illuminate the experience of Utes and other Native tribes in Colorado, from ancient sights to modern-day celebrations.

Sacred Sites

Remember that places like Mesa Verde and Chimney Rock are not just archaeological sites or tourist attractions; they are sacred ground to several modern-day tribes.

Unexpected Places

Some non-Native museums have excellent and informative displays on Native American life, history and art, including Denver Art Museum (pictured) and History Colorado.

Reservations

Colorado has two established tribal nations: the Ute Mountain Ute Reservation and the Southern Ute Reservation, both located in the state's southwest corner.

OUR PICKS

❹

❷   ❸

❺
❶

BEST INDIGENOUS EXPERIENCES

Tour the incredible ancient cliff dwellings at **Mesa Verde National Park ❶**, including scaling wooden ladders and plying stone paths. (p210)

Delve into the history and culture of the Ute Tribe, Colorado's primary indigenous group, at Montrose's **Ute Indian Museum ❷**. (p241)

Commemorate the horrors inflicted on Cheyenne and Arapaho people at the **Sand Creek Massacre National Historic Site ❸**. (p281)

Enjoy traditional Native dances, music and story-telling at the **Denver March Powwow ❹**, one of the country's largest. (p76)

Travel hallowed ground at **Canyon of the Ancients ❺**, a visually and spiritually powerful area containing over 6000 ancient structures. (p215)

Denver Art Museum (p66)

THE CREATIVES

Seen as more athlete than artist, Colorado isn't an obvious place for a flourishing arts scene. But by some alchemy of its natural beauty, scrappy history and rich ferment of local and transplanted talent, Colorado is deeply artistic. The perfect summer weather, too, has allowed for outstanding cultural events and performances to be taken outdoors.

Street Art

Urban art is booming in Colorado, its alleys and underpasses gleaming with amazing aerosol art. Don't miss Street Wise Boulder and Denver's Art RiNo, both marquee events.

First Fridays

Denver and Boulder host fun First Friday events where galleries and art studios stay open late, and the sidewalks fill with a party atmosphere.

BEST ART & CULTURAL EXPERIENCES

Rock out at **Red Rocks Park & Amphitheater ❶**, arguably the world's best and most scenic natural amphitheater and concert venue. (p81)

Be inspired at **Denver Art Museum ❷**, with an impressive Native American art collection and fabulous permanent and visiting exhibits. (p66)

Test your limits at the **Aspen Art Museum ❸** known for its three floors of edgy, contemporary installations and where admission is always free. (p188)

Admire the excellent Latin American and Colonial art collection, and much more, at the **Colorado Springs Fine Arts Center ❹**. (p260)

Catch a show at the **Denver Performing Arts Complex ❺**, with 10 different venues and everything from opera to comedy. (p57)

THE OLD WEST

There's something captivating about the Old West: the sheer number of Western movies are proof enough. The reality of that era was less cinematic: fortunes were lost, mining camps were short-lived, and innumerable Native people were displaced and killed. Learning about their true histories makes Colorado's Old West sites all the more evocative and memorable.

Ghost Town Visits

Treat Colorado's ghost towns as you would any historic site: be careful not to damage the structures and leave artifacts where you find them.

Pan for Gold

Learn firsthand how tough it is to pan for gold – and have some fun too! – at mines-turned-tourist-attractions in Idaho Springs, Breckenridge and Silverton.

Mining Towns

Colorado owes its beginning to mining. Many modern-day mountain towns like Breckenridge, Aspen and Telluride (and most ghost towns) started out as mining camps.

BEST OLD WEST EXPERIENCES

Geek out on traditional log cabin construction at **Frisco Historic Park ❶**, whose grounds include a museum and several genuine log structures. (p167)

Imagine yourself as a 19th-century silver miner in **Ashcroft Ghost Town ❷**, a scenic collection of abandoned wooden homes and structures outside Aspen. (p187)

Retrace the **Santa Fe Trail ❸**, with stops at the fascinating Bent's Old Fort and wrenching Sand Creek Massacre National Historic Sites. (p280)

Ride the rails on the historic **Durango & Silverton Narrow Gauge Railroad ❹**, an impossibly scenic nine-hour round-trip journey to Silverton, with jaw-dropping mountain vistas. (p218)

Feast your eyes at Denver's **American Museum of Western Art ❺**, a remarkable and copious collection of paintings depicting Western life and landscapes. (p59)

CHEERS!

Coloradans love them a good IPA, the hoppier the better. But as home to the Great American Beer Festival, and with 400 breweries and counting, Colorado's tap list runs deep: stouts, ales, wheats, lagers and more. You can also find terrific locally brewed sours and ciders, plus local creations like Green Chile Ale and, recently, marijuana-infused seltzers. And of course, the state has been making fine wine longer than craft beer, especially riesling and cabernet sauvignon.

Mega Batch Beer

If you must drink a Big Beer, make it a Coors, which is brewed in-state. It'll sting locals a little less.

High-Altitude Wineries

Located 4000ft to 7000ft above sea level, Colorado's wine country is the highest in North America and second only to Argentina in the world.

Acronym 101

Vocab lesson! IBU = International Bitterness Units, a bitterness scale.
ABV = alcohol by volume (the higher, the stronger).
IPA = India Pale Ale, a bitter hoppy style.

BEST DRINKING EXPERIENCES

Drink some history at **Odell ❶**, the first craft brewery in the state's capital of craft brewing, Fort Collins. (p141)

Buy beer with purpose! **Upslope ❷** in Boulder makes exceptional beer while supporting good causes like Trout Unlimited. (p109)

Try something unique at **Our Mutual Friend ❸**, a Denver fave known for its artsy style and eclectic brews. (p74)

Drive, bike or book a pedicab to visit the friendly wineries along the Palisade **Fruit and Wine Byway ❹**. (p251)

Don't miss **Ska Brewing ❺**, a laid-back Durango brewery with BBQ and live music to pair with its tasty suds. (p217)

Telluride Bluegrass Festival (p231)

FESTIVAL FUN

Coloradoans know how to throw a festival. Some are low-key and local, while others draw massive international crowds. Many festivals are focused on food and music, but there are plenty of off-the-wall ones as well. No matter what's being celebrated, festivals are a fun way get to know the town and the people hosting it.

Sold Out

Many ticketed festivals, like the Great American Beer Festival and the Telluride Bluegrass Festival, require tickets and can sell out in minutes. Plan accordingly.

Wacky Festivals

Not every festival is about beer or wildflowers: Colorado has some far-out festivals celebrating everything from frozen guys to headless chickens. Save the date!

BEST FESTIVAL EXPERIENCES

Brush up on your Beethoven for the **Aspen Music Festival ❶**, with over 400 classical musical events over an eight-week season. (p187)

Get thee to the University of Colorado at Boulder for the summertime **Colorado Shakespeare Festival ❷**, which stages performances in an outdoor amphitheater. (p98)

Have a cold one with 60,000 drinking buddies at the **Great American Beer Festival ❸**, the largest and hoppiest beer festival in the US. (p56)

Experience a true field of dreams at the **Wildfower Festival ❹** in Crested Butte, with tours and workshops on all things flowery. (p243)

Fly away to the **Telluride Bluegrass Festival ❺**, where banjo and guitar music fills this impossibly scenic San Juan Mountain town. (p231)

SOAK IT UP

Colorado is a soaker's paradise, with countless natural hot springs throughout the Rocky Mountain region. Rain and snow seep deep into the earth and resurface in sublime pools, steaming and infused with healing minerals. From remote backcountry pools to steam-enveloped luxury resorts, Colorado has a healing, natural hot spring with your name on it.

❶
❸
❷
❹
❺

BEST HOT-SPRINGS EXPERIENCES

Soak it up at famous **Strawberry Park Hot Springs ❶** in Steamboat, set beside a rushing mountain stream with acres of wilderness surrounding you. (p135)

Reward yourself with a soak at the gorgeous **Conundrum Hot Springs ❷**, located at the end of a long wildflower-filled hike near Aspen. (p188)

Enjoy views of the Colorado River and Rocky Mountains from one of 16 different pools at **Iron Mountain Hot Springs ❸** in Glenwood Springs. (p191)

Find the perfect pool at **Orvis Hot Springs ❹**, a clothing-optional hot springs in a peaceful garden-like setting outside Ridgway. (p232)

Pamper yourself at **The Springs Resort & Spa ❺** in Pagosa Springs, fed by the Mother Spring, the world's deepest known geothermal spring. (p220)

Water Temperatures

The water temperature at most public hot springs is 95°F to 110°F. Some scorchers top 120°F, while family pools average 80°F to 90°F.

Naked Soaking

Prepare to see naked people at hot springs. It's not a given but it's common at resorts and in the wild.

Safety First

Soaking is a safe and beneficial pastime, but a few rules apply: stay hydrated, cool off every 20 minutes, and, if you're pregnant, consult your doctor first.

HAPPY TRAILS

Colorado is justly famous for its hiking. For mountain adventure, there are alpine lakes, wildflower-strewn valleys, and the country's highest concentration of fourteeners (over 50 in all). For something more horizontal, there are high desert mesas, slot canyons and grassland vistas. And everywhere, excellent trails and wildlife abound. Naming the best hikes in Colorado is like ranking the greatest sunsets. But here goes, with an eye toward showcasing the state's impressive variety in terrain and difficulty.

Come Prepared

Weather conditions can change quickly, especially in high country. Carry layers, a hat and plenty of water, and don't rely on cell service for maps.

Tread Lightly

Help protect Colorado! Heed fire bans, stay on trails, bury your poop and pack out your trash. And please, don't scratch your name onto rocks or trees.

Gray Clouds

Afternoon lightning above the timberline is a real danger, especially in the summer. Start summit hikes early so you'll be off exposed ridgelines by noon.

BEST HIKING EXPERIENCES

Hike your heart out at **Glacier Gorge Trailhead ❶**, jumping-off point for iconic hikes like Lake of Glass and Flattop Mountain in RMNP. (p123)

Brave the crowds at **Crater Lake ❷**, one of the state's most beautiful short hikes despite being so busy. (p187)

Stretch your legs at **Chautauqua Park ❸**, with gorgeous Front Range views and hikes for all levels. (p106)

Circumnavigate the 'Switzerland of America' on **Ouray Perimeter Trail ❹**, a 6-mile loop through aspen groves and high meadows. (p223)

Roam through otherworldly red-rock formations on the stark and beautiful high desert trails of **Colorado National Monument ❺**. (p247)

LEFT: ZACK FRANK/SHUTTERSTOCK ©. RIGHT: MICHAEL LIGGETT/SHUTTERSTOCK ©. FAR RIGHT: KELLY VANDELLEN/SHUTTERSTOCK ©

Dinosaur National Monument (p139)

FOSSIL FEVER

Although dinosaurs dominated the planet for well over 100 million years, relatively few places in the world had the proper geological and climatic conditions to preserve their bones as fossils and their tracks as permanent evolutionary place holders. Colorado is happily near the top of that list. If you're a dinophile, you've come to the right state.

Name Change

Dinosaur, Colorado (population 243) was originally called Baxter Springs but changed its name in 1966 to capitalize on Dinosaur National Monument, located just 2 miles north.

Cartoon Inspiration

Stegosaurus, Colorado's official state fossil, has a spiky tail called a 'thagomizer.' A Denver paleontologist got the name from a *Far Side* cartoon.

BEST PALEONTOLOGICAL EXPERIENCES

Wow the kids with a visit to **Dinosaur National Monument ❶**, whose enclosed quarry wall has over 1500 dinosaur bones still embedded in it. (p139)

Play paleontologist on a half- or full-day dig in **Mygatt-Moore Quarry ❷**, part of the rewarding Trail Through Time outside Fruita. (p249)

Walk in the footsteps of giants at **Picketwire Dinosaur Tracksite ❸**, containing over 1300 prints left by allosaurs and apatosaurs strolling a prehistoric lakeshore. (p280)

Hike through **Florissant Fossil Beds National Monument ❹** where dozens of petrified tree stumps can be seen along a short nature trail. (p276)

Bone up on dinosaur basics at **Denver Museum of Nature & Science ❺**, a fun family museum and important paleontological research center and repository. (p79)

WHERE THE WILD THINGS ARE

Colorado is home to a wealth of wildlife, including moose, elk, antelope, bighorn sheep, black bear, mountain lion, cutthroat trout and bald eagles. In 2020, Colorado voters approved an initiative to reintroduce gray wolves, which were eradicated almost a century ago. Like wildlife everywhere, spotting critters is a mix of skill, timing and luck.

BEST WILDLIFE-SPOTTING EXPERIENCES

Spot moose wading through wetlands and elk grazing in high country meadows in spectacular **Rocky Mountain National Park ❶**. (p118)

Keep your eyes peeled for bighorn sheep and mountain goats on **Guanella Pass ❷**, a scenic byway close to Denver. (p165)

Treat your ears to the incredible sound-scape of birdsong in the protected wetlands of **Alamosa National Wildlife Refuge ❸**. (p269)

Just try to drag yourself away from the wild horses at **Little Book Cliffs ❹**, outside of Grand Junction. (p251)

Go wild at **Weminuche Wilderness Area ❺**, a vast and remote wildland in the San Juan Mountains that's home to elk, black bears, eagles and more. (p221)

Keep Your Distance

No selfie is worth being chased or gored. Don't approach wild animals! It's dangerous and can end in harm to the animal too.

Ask a Park Ranger

Park rangers have specific tips for encounters with big animals like moose, bears and mountain lions. In general, don't run, back away slowly and avoid eye contact.

Viewing Times

You have the best chances of spotting wildlife in the early morning or late afternoon, when they're most active. Plan accordingly!

Rocky Mountain National Park & Northern Colorado

ACROSS THE GREAT DIVIDE

Grazing elk, jewel-like lakes, wildflower meadows, majestic mountains...it's no wonder Rocky Mountain National Park is one of Colorado's most captivating destinations. Nearby Steamboat Springs adds cowboy vibe and champagne powder, while youthful Fort Collins is all about craft breweries. For an older scene – much older – there's Dinosaur National Monument.

p112

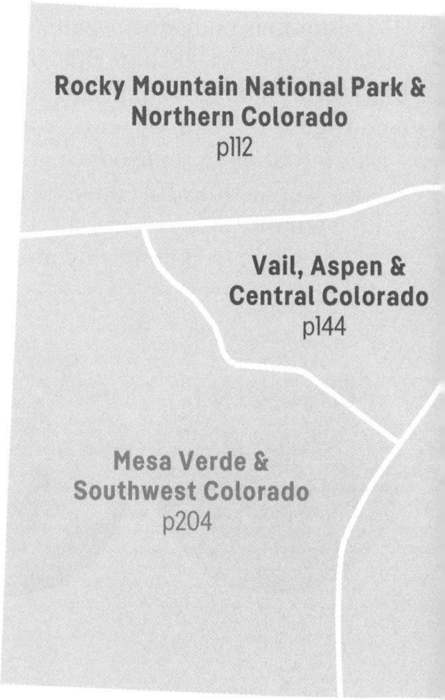

Rocky Mountain National Park & Northern Colorado
p112

Vail, Aspen & Central Colorado

LIFE AT 110%

From glamorous to historic, and fast and furious to quiet and secluded, Central Colorado is the stuff of Colorado dreams. Come here for epic mountain snow and après-ski, thrilling river runs and singletrack fun. Or bliss out in a hot spring or in the backcountry. Whatever your happy place, you're sure to find it here.

p144

Vail, Aspen & Central Colorado
p144

Mesa Verde & Southwest Colorado
p204

Mesa Verde & Southwest Colorado

HISTORY AND OUTDOOR ADVENTURE

Southwest Colorado is big, bold, and diverse. It's home to national parks, ancient cliff dwellings, epic ski areas, plunging canyons and relaxing hot springs. There are chic destinations, historic ghost towns and everything between. And yet none are exactly as you'd expect – prepare to be surprised.

p204

REGIONS & CITIES

Find the places that tick all your boxes.

Boulder

WHERE QUIRKY MEETS OUTDOORSY

A city of contrasts, ultra-liberal Boulder is known for its hippie-chic vibe and million-dollar homes. It's a party-hard college town that happens to have a vibrant art scene. And did we mention the 150-plus miles of trails or those dramatic Flatiron rock formations that look made for climbing?

p84

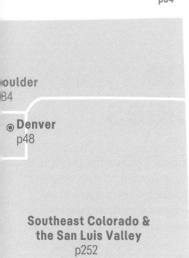

oulder
84

Denver
p48

Southeast Colorado &
the San Luis Valley
p252

Denver

URBAN, ARTSY AND SPORTY

Colorado's biggest city, Denver buzzes with activity, with numerous museums and performing arts venues plus a hopping restaurant and nightlife scene. Mix in five pro sports teams and a distinct outdoorsy ethos and the Mile High City is a destination to be enjoyed year-round.

p48

Southeast Colorado & the San Luis Valley

PIKES PEAK OR BUST

Don't be fooled by the (relative) lack of hype given Southeast Colorado. This high desert region boasts beauties like Pikes Peak, Great Sand Dunes National Park and the rushing waters of Royal Gorge. Plus, it's home to the state's second largest city, Colorado Springs, and the historic Santa Fe Trail.

p252

Brainard Lake (p131)

ITINERARIES

Big Cities & the Northern Rockies

Allow: 7 days   **Distance:** 170 miles

Denver and Boulder have genuine city appeal – museums, pro sports, nightlife – plus easy access to legit Rocky Mountain adventures. Start with the urban offerings in Denver and Boulder, then prepare to be gob-smacked by mountain peaks, alpine lakes and abundant wildlife in and around iconic Rocky Mountain National Park.

❶ DENVER ⏱ 1½ DAYS

Start off in **Denver** (p48), walk its neighborhoods and take in the museums, a traveling Broadway show or an Avalanche game. (Or all three!) Great food can be had in pretty much every corner of town, though for nightlife head to RiNo. Before leaving, take in local life at one of the city's parks or drive to Red Rocks to walk among the dramatic red sandstone formations.

🚗 *35-minute drive*

❷ BOULDER ⏱ HALF DAY

After lunch, head north to the heart of quirky **Boulder** (p84). Wander along Pearl Street Mall (pictured), shop and watch the ever-present street performers. Or see what's on at historic Colorado Chautauqua – a guided walk, a concert, a talk – or just DIY it with a hike on one of the myriad trails there, many with gorgeous views of Boulder's quintessential Flatirons.

🚗 *25-minute drive*

❸ PEAK TO PEAK HWY ⏱ 1 DAY

Bright and early, take the **Peak to Peak Hwy** (p130) to Rocky Mountain National Park. It's a winding road that takes you through the forested Indian Peak Wilderness and southern sections of the national park. Stop in the hippie town of Nederland, hike the wilderness around Brainard Lake or take in the waterfalls of Wild Basin (pictured). Pick up provisions in Estes Park.

🚗 *1-hour drive*

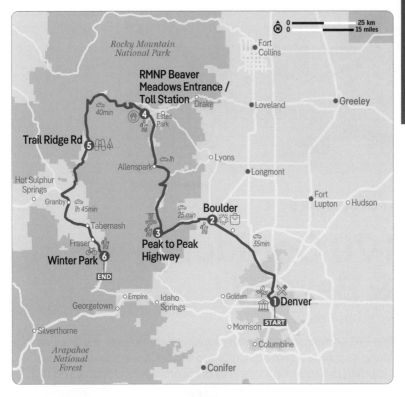

ROCKY MOUNTAIN NATIONAL PARK ⏱ 2 DAYS

Spend the next couple of days soaking in the majestic, 415-sq-mile **Rocky Mountain National Park** (p118). It has hundreds of granite peaks, shimmering alpine lakes and myriad opportunities to see wildlife. There are hiking trails of all lengths and for all level of fitness. If you're looking to lose the crowds, head to the backcountry, where hundreds of thousands of acres of wilderness await.

🚗 40-minute drive

TRAIL RIDGE RD ⏱ 1 DAY

Leave the park along **Trail Ridge Rd** (p121), the highest continuously paved road in the US, climbing steadily to a high-point of 12,183ft. The drive offers sweeping mountain vistas of pine-dotted slopes and blindingly white tundra; numerous turnoffs enable you to step out of your car to take in the magnificent views or explore tundra trails spotted with wildflowers and whistling marmots.

🚗 1¾-hour drive

WINTER PARK ⏱ 1 DAY

Spend your last day in **Winter Park** (p156), a favorite hiking and biking destination. Rent a bike in town and take your pick of singletrack trails, from mellow to intense, or check out the Trestle Bike Park at the local ski resort. For organized activities, the posh Devil's Thumb Ranch or family-friendly Snow Mountain Ranch offer horseback riding, fly-fishing, zip-lining and much more.

SEAN PAVONE/SHUTTERSTOCK ©

Breckenridge (p160)

ITINERARIES

I-70 Corridor & Beyond

Allow: 4 days   **Distance:** 138 miles

The I-70 corridor is a vital artery running right through the Rockies. Along its path are some of Colorado's most storied destinations, including the appealing towns of Breckenridge and Frisco, and the all-season juggernaut, Vail. A short jaunt from the interstate brings you to Aspen, with all its tony mountain charm.

❶ BRECKENRIDGE ⏱ 1 DAY

Begin in **Breckenridge** (p160), hiking in the surrounding mountains or having fun at the ski resort's adventure park. Afterward, pan for gold or meet sled dogs and take a summer mush being pulled on a golf cart through the forest. In the evening, stroll through town, soaking up the Victorian-era ambience; for dinner choose anything from tasting menus to pub grub.

🚗 20-minute drive

❷ FRISCO ⏱ HALF DAY

Pop into Frisco's **Historic Park** (p167) and learn about life in the Old West with museum exhibits and several original structures, including the chapel and jail. If shimmering Dillon Reservoir beckons, head to the marina and take a rental stand-up paddleboard for a spin.

🔜 *Detour: For the very fit, head to Arapahoe Basin to tackle the US's highest via ferrata. ⏱ 4–6 hours*

🚗 35-minute drive

❸ VAIL ⏱ 1 DAY

Take your pick of activities in fancy-pants **Vail** (p172): mountain bike, horseback ride, rock climb, fly fish, hike...there's even a summer amusement park. Ponder your options in the lovely (and free) Betty Ford Alpine Garden, the highest botanic gardens in the US. Fine dining before and afterward is a given.

🔜 *Detour: Enjoy a soak in the hot springs of Glenwood Springs. ⏱ 2 hours*

🚗 10-minute drive

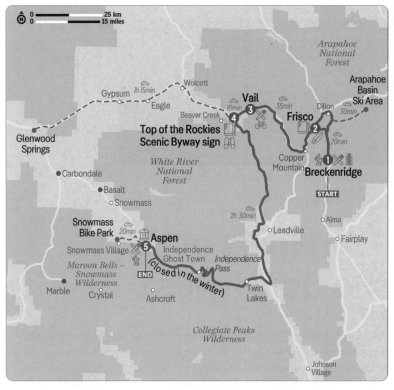

④ TOP OF THE ROCKIES
🕐 HALF DAY

Spend the morning driving to Aspen along the **Top of the Rockies** (p179) scenic byway, known for its sweeping alpine views. Stop in the historic town of Leadville for a primer on mining or continue on to Twin Lakes and the winding road up up up to the picture-perfect Independence Pass (pictured). Before arriving in Aspen, make a pit stop at Independence Ghost Town.

🚗 2½-hour drive

⑤ ASPEN 🕐 1 DAY

Enjoy **Aspen** (p183) by strolling through the historic downtown, stopping in museums, or people-watching from farm-to-table cafes. Afterward, head to the Maroon Bells Wilderness – it's quintessential Colorado – with iconic views and hikes of varying difficulty. In the evening, catch a show in the Wheeler Opera House followed by drinks at the local speakeasy.

🚲 *Detour:* For adrenaline-pumped biking, head to Snowmass Bike Park.
🕐 2 hours

The Maroon Bells (p186)

Colorado National Monument (p247)

ITINERARIES

The Heart of the Southwest

Allow: 7 days   **Distance:** 305 miles

The southwest of Colorado is truly spectacular. The itinerary starts in pleasantly low-key Grand Junction, but gets big fast: soaring cliffs, gorgeous hikes, ancient dwellings and relaxing hot springs. And you can pamper yourself in Telluride, an eye-candy town if ever there was one, deep in the San Juan mountains.

1
GRAND JUNCTION ⏱1 DAY

Base yourself in **Grand Junction** (p244), spending the morning in the dramatic red-rock landscape of Colorado National Monument; stop at overlooks along Rim Rd or take short hikes deeper into the park. In the afternoon, go wine tasting in Palisade or check out the lavender and alpaca farms. Back in Grand Junction, have dinner on Main Street, enjoying the public art all around.

🚗 1½-hour drive

2
BLACK CANYON ⏱1 DAY

Start early for **Black Canyon of the Gunnison National Park** (p234), its sheer 2000ft cliff walls a jaw-dropping sight. Take in the views at 11 spectacular overlooks, some reached via short trails off the park's South Rim Rd.

🚗 *Detour:* Make time for the Ute Indian Museum in Montrose, with well-conceived exhibits on the Ute's past and present. ⏱1½ hours

🚗 1½-hour drive

3
TELLURIDE ⏱2 DAYS

Spend a couple of glorious days in the box canyon town of **Telluride** (p229), where you can splurge on a luxe hotel or camp in town. Take your pick of breathtaking hikes surrounded by 13,000ft peaks or push your comfort zone on the Via Ferrata. Post-adventure, good food and drink abound. Time your visit for festival season...just book your tix and accommodations early!

🚗 1-hour drive

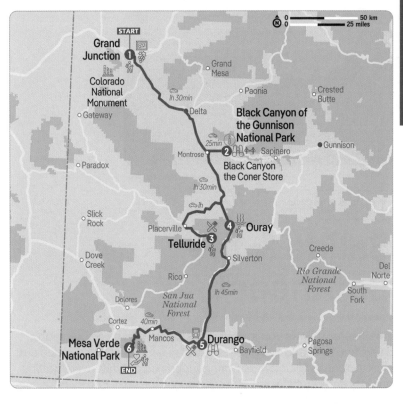

START
Grand Junction 1
Colorado National Monument
Gateway
Grand Mesa
Paonia
Crested Butte
1h 30min
Delta
Black Canyon of the Gunnison National Park
Gunnison
Paradox
25min
Montrose 2
Sapinero
Black Canyon the Coner Store
Slick Rock
1h 30min
Dove Creek
1h
Placerville 4 **Ouray**
3
Telluride
Silverton
Creede
Del Norte
Rico
Rio Grande National Forest
South Fork
Dolores
San Jua National Forest
1h 45min
Cortez
40min
Mancos
5 **Durango**
Bayfield
Pagosa Springs
Mesa Verde National Park 6
END

4
OURAY ⏱1 DAY

Enjoy hiking the alpine wonderland of **Ouray** (p222) – the 6-mile Perimeter Trail loop has several access points to choose from. Afterward, soak your tired legs in one of the town's hot springs; the historic waterpark has lots of pools, or for something quieter, try the Weisbaden vapor cave. Head out on the Million Dollar Hwy, a sinuous and steep journey over three mountain passes.

🚗 1¾-hour drive

5
DURANGO ⏱1 DAY

Stop in Durango to catch the **Durango & Silverton Narrow Gauge Railroad** (p218), a day of gorgeous vista after gorgeous vista on a 19th-century steam locomotive that cuts through the San Juan wilderness to the tiny town of Silverton. Afterward, enjoy a good dinner and brews in Durango's historic and artsy downtown corridor.

🚗 40-minute drive

6
MESA VERDE NATIONAL PARK ⏱1 DAY

Plan on a full day exploring the magnificent **Mesa Verde National Park** (p210), the best-preserved Native American archaeological site in the US and one-time home of the Ancestral Puebloans. Brimming with stunning cliff dwellings, surface sites and trails, the best way to experience it is via a ranger-led tour or two. Book online and well in advance to guarantee a spot.

ROMIANA LEE/SHUTTERSTOCK ©

Garden of the Gods (p259)

ITINERARIES

Salida & the Southeast

Allow: 4 days   **Distance:** 475 miles

This itinerary allows you to enjoy the sublime beauty of Colorado's peaks and river, and avoid the stress of major mountain passes. You'll start in appealing Colorado Springs, followed by white-water rafting one day and climbing massive sand dunes the next. End by retracing the historic Santa Fe Trail.

❶
COLORADO SPRINGS ⏱1 DAY

Spend your day in **Colorado Springs** (p262) museum-hopping, feeding giraffes at the zoo and touring the Olympic and Paralympic Training Center. Stroll through the Garden of the Gods, a spectacular park filled with red-rock formations, or head straight to mammoth Pikes Peak, a 14,000ft behemoth that you can summit by foot, car or cog railway.

🚗 *2-hour drive*

❷
SALIDA ⏱1 DAY

Get up early for rafting out of **Salida** (p197) on the Arkansas River (pictured). Depending on the season and your comfort level, you can find everything from extreme rapids to chilled-out floats. If you have energy afterward, explore the epic bike trails of S Mountain. In the evening, stroll through the pleasant redbrick downtown, filling up on elk brats and IPAs.

🚗 *1½-hour drive*

❸
GREAT SAND DUNES NATIONAL PARK ⏱1 DAY

Prepare to be awe-stricken at the otherworldly **Great Sand Dunes National Park** (p265), an undulating sea of sand bounded by jagged peaks and scrubby plains. Hike to the top of the tallest dune in North America (no easy task!), making your way down on wooden sleds made especially for sandboarding or sledding.

🚗 *2½-hour drive*

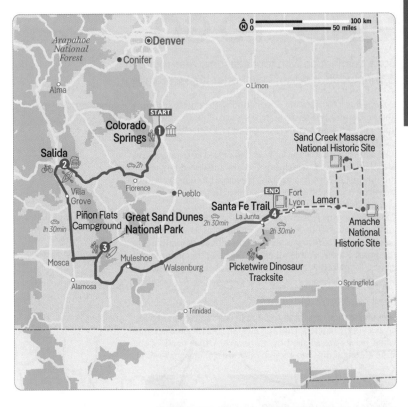

4

SANTA FE TRAIL ⏱ 1 DAY

Spend the day driving the
Santa Fe Trail (p280), making
stops to learn about the
Old West at places like the
beautifully recreated Bent's Old
Fort (pictured) and Sand Creek
Massacre National Historic Site.
Make time for a visit to Amache
National Historical Site, a WWII
Japanese internment camp.

🚗 *Detour: If time permits, visit the
Picketwire Dinosaur Tracksite to see
over 1300 dino tracks.* ⏱ *5 hours*

Sand Creek Massacre National Historic Site (p281)

WHEN **TO GO**

For a destination with four seasons, year-round sun included, it doesn't get better than Colorado.

Colorado is a four-season destination with endless sunshine and low humidity. Elevation drives much of the weather here, and with destinations from 3315ft to 14,433ft, there's lots of variation.

Winter brings snow throughout Colorado. The temperatures are relatively mild, which lures skiers and shredders to the mountains. At lower elevations, the snow often melts within a day. Spring can be unpredictable, bringing wildflowers and green landscapes, but sometimes snowstorms.

Summer means long sunny days, high daytime temperatures and temperate evenings; dramatic thunderstorms are afternoon hallmarks and hailstorms occasionally follow, especially along the Front Range. Fall is all about the changing color of the leaves. Temperatures fluctuate, and October snowstorms are possible.

Mud-Season Discounts

Accommodation rates in the mountains vary tremendously. The best deals are in late spring and late fall (aka the mud season), when prices are slashed by up to 50%. Other parts of the state see slight dips too, though rates are steadier year-round.

RIGHT: FAINA GUREVICH/SHUTTERSTOCK ©
FAR RIGHT: ED ENDICOTT/ALAMY STOCK PHOTO ©

Hailstones

⊙ **I LIVE HERE**

BIG-MOUNTAIN SKIING

Darin Pitts is an Emergency Department Staff Nurse at Denver Health in Winter Park.

'Growing up in Pueblo, most of my ski trips were to local areas. But I'll never forget my first ski trip to Silverton. I'd never experienced anything like it: guided skiing on impressively long, big, and steep lines. And the snow! It was waist deep. This was big mountain skiing. I go back with my buddies every winter now and have learned that at Silverton, every run is an adventure.'

HAIL ALLEY

Colorado's Front Range lies in the heart of 'Hail Alley,' where the nation's highest number of hailstorms occur. Take cover if one hits! In 2017, a storm of baseball-sized hail hit metro Denver, causing a record-breaking $2 billion in damages in just minutes.

Weather through the year – Denver

JANUARY	FEBRUARY	MARCH	APRIL	MAY	JUNE
❄	❄	🌧	⛅	☀	☀
Avg. daytime max: **49°F**	Avg. daytime max: **49°F**	Avg. daytime max: **58°F**	Avg. daytime max: **65°F**	Avg. daytime max: **73°F**	Avg. daytime max: **86°F**
Days of snowfall: **6**	Days of snowfall: **7**	Days of rainfall/ snowfall: **2/3**	Days of rainfall/ snowfall: **2/5**	Days of rainfall: **8**	Days of rainfall: **4**

WALKING ON SUNSHINE

Colorado boasts 300 days of sunshine each year, though some quibble with whether or not that figure should include partly cloudy days. (It does.) Whichever way you measure it, count on seeing blue skies and sun most days, even if it's between puffy white clouds.

Big Colorado Festivals

Denver's PrideFest (p66) is one of the largest LGBTIQ+ celebrations in the country, a two-day event when rainbow revelry, free performances, and joyful parades fill the city's streets and parks.
⚙ June

The revered **Colorado Shakespeare Festival** (p98) brings the Bard's works to CU Boulder's Mary Rippon Outdoor Theater on summer nights, rain or shine. Come early for pre-show talks with the artistic director.
⚙ June–August

The **Colorado State Fair and Rodeo** (p257), held since 1872, is one of the state's biggest events, a carnival combined with all sorts of competitions, concerts, parades and rodeo events.
⚙ August

Telluride Film Festival (p231) showcases indie films in venues all around its box canyon community, transforming the tiny mountain town into a cinephile paradise, red carpet included.
⚙ September

Quirky Colorado Festivals

Durango's **Snowdown** (p218) is a zany festival with a different theme each year, where costumes and eccentric events (ski kickball, any one?) coax people onto the city's wintry streets.
⚙ February

Fabulously macabre, **Frozen Dead Guy Days** (pictured right; p129) in Estes Park celebrates a cryogenically frozen Norwegian awaiting his thaw in a local Tuff Shed. Come for the hearse parade and coffin races; stay for the frozen turkey bowling.
⚙ March

Celebrating Fuita's most famous headless bird, **Mike the Headless Chicken Festival** (p249) hosts all sorts of chicken-themed events, from a 5K run in feathered costumes to a Peep-eating contest.
⚙ June

Breckenridge's raucous **Ullr Fest** (p149) celebrates the Norwegian snow god Ullr. Expect polar plunges and raging bonfires plus an annual attempt to break the world record for the longest shotski. Horned Viking helmets encouraged.
⚙ December

⊕ I LIVE HERE

SUMMER RUNNING TRAILS

Candace Gonzales is an Athlete Advocate for Rising Hearts, an Indigenous-led nonprofit dedicated to justice through movement.

'One of my favorites places to run is Turquoise Lake in Leadville. It has this beautiful single-track trail, about 8 miles long, out and back. It's so peaceful. And the lake, it's magical. It's surrounded by trees and when you look up, the mountains are all around you. The lake itself is usually really cold. After a run, I'll sometimes jump in for cold therapy training. Sometimes.'

POWDER DAYS

Thank the dry air and cold temperatures for Colorado's legendary powder snow. Low water content makes for large airy snowflakes, while cold temperatures keep them from collapsing and melting together as they pile up. The result is a blanket of snow that's light as a feather.

JULY	AUGUST	SEPTEMBER	OCTOBER	NOVEMBER	DECEMBER
Avg. daytime max: **92°F**	Avg. daytime max: **90°F**	Avg. daytime max: **82°F**	Avg. daytime max: **68°F**	Avg. daytime max: **57°F**	Avg. daytime max: **47°F**
Days of rainfall: **6**	Days of rainfall: **4**	Days of rainfall: **4**	Days of rainfall/ snowfall: **1/4**	Days of rainfall/ snowfall: **2/2**	Days of rainfall/ snowfall: **4/3**

LEFT: FRANCISCO BLANCO/SHUTTERSTOCK ©
RIGHT: JOHN SPRINGER COLLECTION/CORBIS VIA GETTY IMAGES ©

Emerald Lake Trail (p120), Rocky Mountain National Park

GET PREPARED
FOR COLORADO

Useful things to load in your bag, your ears and your brain

Clothes

Jeans and puffer jackets Casual dress rules Colorado – jeans and puffer jackets are the unofficial state uniform. In fact, pretty much the only place jeans don't work are on the slopes.

Layers Weather in Colorado can change quickly year-round, and summer evenings can be chilly too, especially in the mountains. Bring layers! A waterproof shell, fleece and warm hat are a good idea any time of the year.

Boots If you'll be hiking, bring good, broken-in hiking boots. (If they're brand new, bring moleskin padding in case you get blisters.) Likewise, if you'll be here in winter, bring warm, waterproof boots.

Manners

Use tact when talking politics. Colorado is a purple state – opinions run the gamut, and some are held especially hard and fast.

Haggling isn't common. If you're at a farmers market, though, low-key and polite bargaining is accepted.

Don't compare Colorado to the Midwest. Coloradans identify with the West, the mountains and a degree of sophistication they see as lacking in the Midwest.

Peaked hats The sun is no joke here, and the elevation makes it that much stronger. Wear a peaked hat, especially if you'll be outdoors for an extended period of time.

📖 READ

Sabrina and Corina
(Kali Fajardo-Anstine;
2019) Collection of
fictional short stories
about Latinas of
indigenous descent
living in Denver.

House of Rain
(Craig Childs; 2007)
Archaeological
travelogue about the
Ancestral Puebloans,
integrating adventure
and scholarly research.

Plainsong
(Kent Haruf; 1999)
Tale about a Colorado
farming community on
the eastern plains.

On the Road
(Jack Kerouac; 1957)
Defining work about
road-tripper culture
with Denver baked in.

Words

Après-ski (AH-pray ski) A
French term meaning 'after-
skiing,' a happy hour when
people meet up to drink
and nosh after a day on
the slopes.

Backcountry Any remote
mountain area, away from
roads, resorts, campgrounds
or other development. It's
used in conjunction with
outdoors activities (eg
backcountry skiing or
backcountry hiking).

Colorado Cologne The
skunky smell of marijuana.

Colorado Kool-Aid A can
of Coors beer.

Dispensary A place
that sells marijuana and
other cannabis products.
In Colorado, there are
recreational and medicinal-
only (prescriptions required)
dispensaries plus hybrids.

Hill Shorthand for a ski
mountain (e.g. 'A-Basin may
be small but it's a great hill').

LBS A local bike shop.

Freshies Coveted ski- or
snowboarding runs through
fresh untouched powder;
also called 'first tracks.'

Fourteener (14er) A
mountain that is higher than
14,000ft. Depending on who
you ask, Colorado has either
53 or 58 fourteeners.

420 (four twenty) Refers
to marijuana or marijuana
use. You'll see '420-friendly'
at hotels that allow pot
smoking.

Front Range Typically
means the corridor of cities
that lie along the eastern
edge of the Rockies, from
Fort Collins to Trinidad.

Peak Bagger Someone who
climbs mountains to cross
them off a bucket list, often
with a focus on epic climbs.

Western Slope The region
west of the Continental
Divide, generally Central
and Southwest Colorado.

📺 WATCH

Dear Eleanor (Kevin Connolly;
2014) Leonardo DiCaprio produced
this Sundance flick, which was
filmed on the Front Range.

Bowling for Columbine (Michael
Moore; 2002) Documentary
examining gun proliferation and
the mass shooting at Columbine
High School in Littleton.

South Park (Trey Parker, Matt
Stone and Eric Stough; 1997–
present) Animated TV satire set
in a fictional Colorado town.

The Shining (Stanley Kubrick; 1980)
Psychological horror film inspired
by the Stanley Hotel in Estes Park.

**Butch Cassidy & the Sundance
Kid** (George Roy Hill; 1969; pictured
above) Wild West classic filmed
in southwest Colorado.

🎧 LISTEN

Colorado Matters
(Colorado Public Radio;
2001–present) Six-day-
a-week radio program
and podcast focused
on the state's people
and issues.

With(in) (DU Prison
Arts Initiative/
Colorado Department
of Corrections; 2019–
present) Podcast
about prison life,
produced and hosted
by Colorado inmates.

**A Mad and Faithful
Telling** (Devotchka;
2008) Denver band with
Euro-Latin influences:
this album's thrumming
beats are made for
road-tripping.

Rocky Mountain High
(John Denver; 1972)
Hit folk rock album;
its title track is one of
Colorado's official
state songs.

LEFT: ALEXANDRALAW1977/SHUTTERSTOCK ©, RIGHT, CHATHAM172/SHUTTERSTOCK ©, FAR RIGHT: MICHAEL BERLFEIN/SHUTTERSTOCK ©.

Colorado lamb

THE FOOD SCENE

Fresh, locally grown food, combined with a culture that caters to specialized preferences, make Colorado a delicious place to eat!

A one-time meat and potatoes state, Colorado's food scene has bloomed into a celebration of the state's natural bounty. From farm-to-table fare to vegan options and everything in between, there's something for just about everyone to enjoy. Fresh produce, free-range meats and fish from the state's mountain rivers form the backbone of the local cuisine; meals are delicious, healthy and often sustainable. Colorado's thriving craft beer and distillery industries also play a major role, with most restaurants and food halls offering extensive drink menus or, at least, a couple of local brews on tap to complement their food offerings. Colorado also is home to a thriving farmers market scene, with plenty of opportunities to sample fresh, locally

grown foods. And if you're a wine lover, the state's Western Slope is ground zero for wineries and vineyards. Quickly growing into a foodie's paradise, Colorado will indulge your senses and invite you to explore the state through the flavors found within it.

Farm-to-Table Dining

Colorado takes great pride in sustainable dining, and with close to 40,000 farms and ranches in the state, there are plenty of opportunities to buy locally grown and sourced foods. There are terrific farmers markets found around the state, most bustling from May to October with rows of vendors selling fresh fruits and vegetables plus ethically produced meat like lamb and bison. The explosion of gourmet food

Best Colorado Dishes	GREEN CHILE	ROCKY MOUNTAIN OYSTERS	ELK BRATS
	Roasted chili sauce, often with pork chunks, poured over Mexican dishes.	Bull or sheep testicles, breaded and deep fried, served with dipping sauce.	Gourmet sausages, often mixed with cheddar and jalapeño.

halls, too, showcase the state's offerings with aspiring chefs testing their recipes and new concepts. And in towns like Denver, Boulder, Aspen, Telluride and Vail, auteur restaurants increasingly feature flavorful local ingredients as the new gold. Go ahead, treat your taste buds!

Alt Eating

With the lowest rate of obesity of any state, Coloradans know how to eat. They're a discerning crowd, which can make your wait in a deli line a game of patience. But, if you have a special diet or are simply a picky eater, you'll feel at home in Colorado. No one will bat an eye at any food allergies or restrictions. And it's de rigueur to find gluten-free, vegan and vegetarian items on menus in urban and tourist areas – even at local steakhouses. Many restaurants also nod to the latest food fads, so keto followers and fans of kale will do just fine.

Happy-Hour Dining

Coloradans take happy hour seriously and restaurants comply by competing fiercely and offering incredible deals. Nowhere is this more apparent than in Colorado's fine-dining establishments, which may be out of reach for many during dinner hour, but offer incredible small-plate deals

Denver omelet

during happy hour that are often cheaper than pizzerias – and far more delectable. In general, happy-hour menus are offered in pubs and restaurants from 4pm to 6pm. Go early to get a table. Weekend deals are rare, though some spots offer late-night happy hours from 10pm until closing time during the week.

FOOD & WINE FESTIVALS

Great American Beer Festival (p56) The nation's largest beer celebration brings craft beer fans to Denver to taste almost 10,000 brews, all competing for gold in 98 different categories.

Taste of Colorado (atasteofcolorado.com; pictured above) Local food vendors fill Denver's Civic Center Park at this giant event, which also features live music and artisan booths.

Food & Wine Classic (classic.foodandwine. com) An epic Aspen fest filled with tastings, cooking demonstrations and panels with celebrity chefs and beverage connoisseurs.

Pueblo Chile & Frijoles Festival (pueblo chilefestival.com) Live performances, a vibrant farmers market and roasted green chilis are hallmarks of this homegrown festival. Don't miss the chihuahua parade!

Palisade Peach Festival (p250) A celebration of Palisade's annual harvest of sweet, juicy peaches, complete with peach cooking demos, eating contests and orchard tours.

BISON BURGERS	**DENVER OMELET**	**COLORADO-STYLE PIZZA**	**COLORADO LAMB**	**GRILLED RAINBOW TROUT**
Leaner than beef burgers, though tasting almost the same.	Egg dish stuffed with bell peppers, onions, ham and cheese.	Topping-heavy pizza with a thick, braided crust made with honey.	Known for its exquisitely rich flavor, every cut is a delicacy.	Quintessential Colorado dish; the trout is often locally caught.

LEFT: GREG GARD/ALAMY STOCK PHOTO ©
RIGHT: RON NIEBRUGGE/ALAMY STOCK PHOTO ©

Horseback riding, Rocky Mountain National Park (p118)

THE OUTDOORS

Colorado's outdoors reign supreme and with so many options there's no doubt it was made for play.

Winter, spring, summer or fall, the Colorado outdoors will blow your mind. Spanning diverse geographic zones from the Great Plains to the Rocky Mountains and the desert canyons of the Colorado Plateau, there are boundless opportunities for outdoor adventure. It doesn't hurt that Colorado is home to four national parks, 11 national forests, 42 state parks and more... all totaling millions of acres of public land. Pick your adventure – whether you're an experienced outdoor enthusiast or just starting out, you'll be sure to enjoy it!

Hiking

Colorado's far-reaching and diverse trail system beckons hikers of all levels and offers year-round access to the state's impossibly beautiful landscapes.

Imagine trekking through the majestic Rocky Mountains surrounded by snowy peaks, shimmering alpine lakes and dense forests. Or the feeling of accomplishment as you summit a mountain, your heart pounding as you take in the panoramic views. Or the tranquility of hiking through meadows dotted with wildflowers or the quiet while walking through a red-rock canyon. Colorado's trails range from tidy loops through lovely landscapes to multiday backcountry routes that challenge even the most experienced trekkers. Every corner of the state has trails where you can immerse yourself in the natural beauty all around. So, grab your water bottle and some high-energy snacks, lace up your hiking boots and prepare to take in Colorado.

Adventure Sports

ROCK CLIMBING
Join locals at Boulder's **Flatirons** (p104), one of the country's most extensive and varied rock climbing areas near a city.

ICE CLIMBING
Climb (or learn to climb) on 150 routes up frozen waterfalls at the world-class **Ouray Ice Park** (p224).

VIA FERRATA
Make your way, hand over hand, across mountain on Telluride's **Via Ferrata** (p231), a spectacular and beautiful, if vertigo-inducing, experience.

FAMILY ADVENTURES

Partake in 30+ outdoor activities at the family-oriented getaway of YMCA of the Rockies - **Estes Park Center** (p129) – from horseback riding to snow tubing.

Fly over Akali Canyon – or plunge into it, headfirst – on a zip-line tour with **Zip Adventures** (p175) in Vail.

Mush a team of sled dogs or meet the pack in summertime at **Good Times Adventure Tours** (p164) just outside Breckenridge.

Ride the historic Durango & Silverton Narrow Gauge Railroad (p218) through the spectacular San Juan Mountains.

Trek with your own fuzzy alpaca at SunCrest Orchard (p250); stay afterward for a tour of the fiber mill.

Splash in Ouray Hot Springs Waterpark (p225) where geothermically heated pools make waterslides and splash pools a year-round thing.

Skiing & Snowboarding

Colorado is one of the top destinations in the country for skiing and snowboarding. Known for its high-altitude peaks, blue skies and deep champagne powder, the conditions are ideal for both sports. From cruisers and tree runs to back bowls and terrain parks, this is one of the best and most varied places to ski and snowboard in the US. In fact, some of the world's best skiers and riders are from Colorado, or have lived and trained here, including Lindsay Vonn, Mikaela Shiffrin, Red Gerard and Shaun White. With over 30 resorts to choose from – including backcountry guided-skiing at Silverton and world-renowned Vail, Aspen and Breckenridge – there really is a mountain and ski town for every sort of vacationer. Most resorts and their respective ski towns also have robust activity offerings like snowshoeing, cross-country skiing, ice skating, and sledding. Then, of course, there's always après-ski.

Mountain Biking

The state's rugged terrain, diverse landscapes and endless trails offer something for all riders – from the rocky, technical trails in Fruita and Mancos to the high-altitude singletrack in Crested Butte and Breckenridge. Many ski resorts also offer downhill riding with lift service, bermed-out mountain-bike trails and jumps included. In fact, mountain biking is so big that you can ride on dedicated bike paths from Glenwood Springs to Aspen, and from Vail to Breckenridge. Gondolas, buses and even Lake Dillon ferries also are all outfitted to tote bikes. In cities like Denver, Boulder and Fort Collins, you'll find hundreds of miles of dedicated bike trails, plus a bike-friendly culture that includes shared bike programs, plenty of bike lanes and even the occasional cruiser ride. In Colorado, mountain biking is more than just exercise: it's a lifestyle.

BEST SPOTS

For the best outdoor spots and routes, see the map on pp42-3.

Mountain biking, Crested Butte (p242)

SANDBOARDING
Sandboard down the tallest dunes in North America at **Great Sand Dunes National Park** (p265), an otherworldly sight.

RAFTING
Paddle the **Arkansas River** (p198), with everything from mellow ripples in Bighorn Sheep Canyon to white water in the Royal Gorge.

SUPING
Stand-up paddle your way around the blue waters of **Blue Mesa Reservoir** (p240), Colorado's largest body of water.

FISHING
Cast for Colorado trout in the gold-medal waters surrounding Basalt, a true fly-fishing paradise in the **Roaring Fork Valley** (p192).

ACTION AREAS

Where to find Colorado's best outdoor activities.

Skiing
1. Vail (p172)
2. Aspen (p183)
3. Copper Mountain (p168)
4. Steamboat Mountain Resort (p135)
5. Telluride Ski Resort (p230)
6. Crested Butte Mountain Resort (p242)
7. Silverton Mountain Resort (p233)

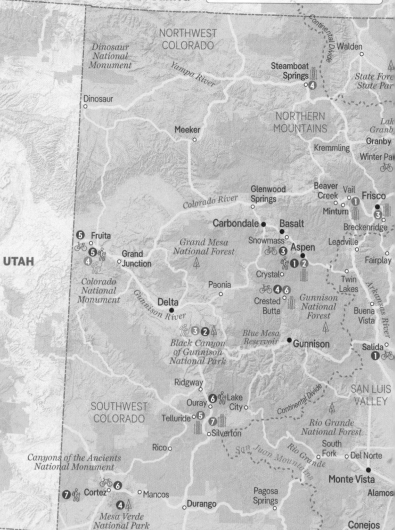

NEBRASKA

Hiking

1. Crater Lake Trail (Maroon Bells) (p187)
2. Glacier Gorge Trailhead (p123)
3. Mt Bierstadt Trail (p155)
4. Royal Arch Trail (p107)
5. Monument Canyon Trail (p247)
6. Ouray Perimeter Trail (p223)
7. McElmo Canyon Trail (p216)

Mountain Biking

1. Monarch Crest Trail (p199)
2. Trestle Bike Park (p158)
3. Rim Trail (Snowmass) (p188)
4. Lupine Loop (p242)
5. Kokopelli Trail (p249)
6. Phil's World (p216)

Fort Collins

Glen Haven

Estes Park

Rocky Mountain National Park

Cache la Poudre River

Fort Morgan

EASTERN COLORADO

derland

Boulder

Empire

Denver

Idaho Springs

Bailey

Castle Rock

Pike National Forest

Garden of the Gods

CENTRAL MOUNTAINS

National Parks

1. Rocky Mountain National Park (p118)
2. Black Canyon of the Gunnison National Park (p234)
3. Great Sand Dunes National Park (p266)
4. Mesa Verde National Park (p210)

Colorado Springs

Cañon City

Florence

Pueblo

Lake Pueblo State Park

Arkansas River

Adobe Creek Reservoir

Amache National Historic Site

John Martin Reservoir

ilver Cliff

Colorado City

La Junta

Bent's Old Fort National Historic Site

Great Sand Dunes National Park

Walsenburg

Purgatoire River

Rock Climbing

1. First or Third Flatiron (p104)
2. Lumpy Ridge (p120)
3. North Rim (p237)
4. Otto's Route (p248)
5. Red Rock Canyon Open Space (p260)

Fort Garland

San Luis

Trinidad State Park

Trinidad

NEW MEXICO

OKLAHOMA

43

LEFT: SEAN XU/SHUTTERSTOCK ©; RIGHT: GEORGIA EVANS/SHUTTERSTOCK ©

Hiking, Estes Park (p129)

COLORADO HIKING 101

Colorado hiking is an embarrassment of riches: gorgeous valleys, rugged peaks and high desert mesas, all connected by a vast network of well-maintained trails. It pays to plan ahead when it comes to hiking, and knowing the Colorado basics will put you one step closer to a hike of a lifetime.

When to Go

Trails across the state beckon day hikers from late May to early October. At lower elevations – along the Front Range and in and around Great Sand Dunes National Park and Colorado National Monument – many trails are accessible year-round. Elsewhere, with the right gear and training, you can head out on snowshoes. Contact the local ranger district to assure the trails, and the roads leading up to them, are open.

Fourteeners

Colorado has 58 mountains that top 14,000ft, more than any other state in the nation. Locals call them 'fourteeners' (also '14ers'), and many try to bag 'em all. But not all fourteeners are created equal.

Divided into four categories, they range from straightforward hikes on well-marked trails (Class 1) to steep treks that incorporate technical climbing (Class 4). There even are two you can drive up: Pikes Peak and Mt Evans. Whichever way you summit, be prepared. Check 14ers.com for up-to-date information, including routes, planning tools, peak conditions and more.

Crossing the State

Two well-maintained long-distance trails cross Colorado, offering singular opportunities to experience the state's epic alpine backcountry. Both are divided into numerous segments, making it easy to drop in for a section or to complete the trails over several seasons.

BE PREPARED

- Take time to acclimatize to the altitude, especially if you're coming from sea level – take it slow the first few days.

- Bring layers, including a windbreaker, fleece and warm hat. Weather conditions can change quickly year-round.

- Bring a trail map, compass and flashlight – don't depend on your cellphone. Pick up maps at park headquarters, ranger district offices or outdoor supply stores like REI.

- Carry plenty of water or water-purification equipment.

- Bring snacks packed with protein, carbs and electrolytes.

- Wear sunglasses and a peaked hat, and slather on sunscreen. The sun's rays are strong, even on overcast days.

- Carry wag bags.

Colorado Trail

The Colorado Trail is the state's signature trail. Known as the 'CT,' it starts at Chatfield Reservoir near Denver before winding some 567 miles to Durango. The trail passes through eight mountain ranges, six national forests, six wilderness areas and five river systems – all in all, involving 90,000ft of vertical climb, making it a spectacular and serious hike. Generally, it takes through-hikers four to six weeks to complete. The Colorado Trail Foundation (coloradotrail.org) is a great resource, offering maps and books that describe the trail in detail.

Continental Divide National Scenic Trail

The Continental Divide National Scenic Trail or 'CDT' is a 3100-mile US hiking trail that extends along the Rockies between Canada and Mexico. An 800-mile section of the CDT passes through Colorado, most of it above 10,000ft, including the highest point of the entire trail, Grays Peak (14,270ft). It joins the CT for 314 miles, most of it running through Lake County. The Continental Divide Trail Coalition (continentaldividetrail.org) has detailed information about the CDT, including maps and tips by state.

Dehydration

Colorado's dry climate makes it easy to underestimate how much water you need, especially on the trail. Dehydration will tire you out and can exacerbate altitude sickness. Drink lots of water! In general, adults need 1L of water per two hours of moderate exercise in moderate temperatures; adjust accordingly for the heat and intensity of the hike.

Wag Bags

Most hikers know to pack out whatever they pack in. In Colorado that includes human poop. Some areas offer free human waste bags or 'wag bags' at trailheads, and they are easily purchased online. Otherwise, always bury your feces at least 6in underground and 200ft from any water source, and you should still pack out your toilet paper!

STAY SAFE

- Start your hikes early and be off mountain peaks and passes by midday. In summer, afternoon rains are frequent and lightning above the timberline is a real danger. Don't hesitate to turn back if gray clouds appear – it could save your life.

- Tell someone where you're going and when you expect to be back.

- Make noise on the trail to avoid unexpected encounters with moose, bears and mountain lions (pictured).

COLORADO

THE GUIDE

Chapters in this section are organised by hubs and their surrounding areas. We see the hub as your base in the destination, where you'll find unique experiences, local insights, insider tips and expert recommendations. It's also your gateway to the surrounding area, where you'll see what and how much you can do from there.

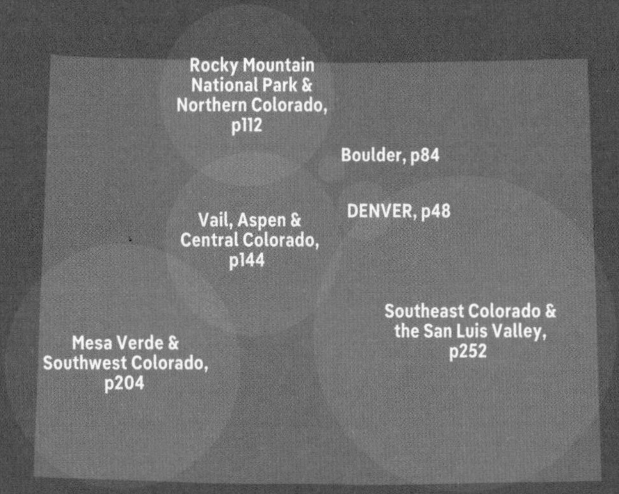

Rocky Mountain National Park & Northern Colorado, p112

Boulder, p84

Vail, Aspen & Central Colorado, p144

DENVER, p48

Southeast Colorado & the San Luis Valley, p252

Mesa Verde & Southwest Colorado, p204

Colorado Springs (p258)

ANDREW LILLIBRIDGE/EYEEM/GETTY IMAGES ©

DENVER

URBAN, ARTSY AND SPORTY

Denver has hit its stride as one of the treasures of the American West and a gateway to the Rockies.

Denver

The Mile High City has finally arrived. A cow town no more, Denver today is an urban gem, with revitalized neighborhoods, rich cultural offerings and a booming craft brewery scene. It boasts big league sports (go Broncos!) and a lifestyle where the outdoors rules. Denver is one of the US' fastest growing cities, with a mix of locals and transplants transforming it from the inside out. Denverites enjoy (and nowadays expect) first-class arts and a hopping restaurant and bar scene; they take full advantage of the city's sunny days and city parks. And who wouldn't want easy access to the country's most impressive mountain range?

Denver has seen its ups and downs, of course, all the way back to its founding in 1858. An early gold rush petered out, but the city pivoted to a supply and transportation hub for mining communities in the mountains. This brought people and wealth to Denver, some of which is still visible in the form of grand buildings and a robust parks system.

But the bubble inevitably burst, and Denver experienced a century of boom-and-bust cycles. Gold. Silver. Plutonium.

Oil. The city's fortunes were pinned on commodities and their volatile prices. By the mid-1980s, Denver had an urban center dotted with half-empty skyscrapers, dilapidated buildings and vacant lots. But the 1990s sowed the seeds that changed it all: seeing potential where others saw blight, entrepreneurs began investing in the downtown area. Artists followed. By the early 2000s, the city's core neighborhoods were being revitalized.

Today, each of these neighborhoods has a personality all its own. At the center, Downtown and LoHi have historic buildings and sights, performing arts venues and some of the best hotels and restaurants in the city. Just south and east, Golden Triangle, Capitol Hill, Cheesman Park and City Park are home to the city's museums, civic life and big green spaces. And north of downtown, Five Points and RiNo are the heart of cool, with street art and hipster nightlife. Though individual and unique, Denver's neighborhoods remain connected through history and the thread of possibility that winds its way through them all.

RADOMIR REZNY/SHUTTERSTOCK ®

THE MAIN AREAS

DOWNTOWN, LOHI & PLATTE RIVER VALLEY
Revitalized city center.
p54

GOLDEN TRIANGLE, CAPITOL HILL & CHEESMAN PARK
Museums and historic sights.
p64

Colorado State Capitol (p67)

RINO & FIVE POINTS
Urban art and nightlife.
p72

CITY PARK
Outdoor activity
and events.
p77

**RED ROCKS PARK &
AMPHITHEATER**
World-class concert venue.
p81

Find Your Way

While known for its proximity to the Rocky Mountains, Denver itself is on the plains and mostly flat. From the downtown core, most of Denver's sights, nightlife and traveler services are located within a 2.5-mile radius. If you get turned around, look for the mountains, an ever-present beacon to the west.

Red Rocks Park & Amphitheater

p81

Red Rocks Amphitheatre

WALK

Denver is a very walkable city, giving you flexibility to explore each neighborhood at your own pace. Low humidity, sun-filled days and mild weather year-round (even in winter) makes for pleasant exploring. And it's flat! Bring good walking shoes and layers.

BUS & LIGHT RAIL

Denver's public transportation system, RTD, crisscrosses the city via bus and light rail routes. It makes travel between neighborhoods easy and cheap. Single rides are $3 and unlimited day passes are just $6. Discounts available for seniors and youths; children five and under travel free.

N 0 ——————— 3 km
   0 ——————— 1.5 miles

RiNo & Five Points
p72

Downtown, LoHi & Platte River Valley
p54

Blair-Caldwell African American Museum

Coors Field

Union Station

City Park

City Park
p77

Denver Performing Arts Complex

Meow Wolf

Great American Beer Festival

PrideFest

Denver Art Museum

History Colorado Center

Clyfford Still Museum

Denver Botanic Gardens

Golden Triangle, Capitol Hill & Cheesman Park
p64

RIDESHARES

Lyft and Uber are popular ways to get around in Denver, especially at night or for destinations further afield like Red Rocks (p81) or the airport. You'll enjoy door-to-door service and avoid the hassle of driving and parking in Denver's increasingly congested streets.

FROM THE AIRPORT

Denver International Airport (DIA) is one of the country's biggest and busiest airports. It's located 24 miles east of downtown Denver, about 30 minutes by car if there's no traffic. RTD trains also run to Union Station (p56) – a sure thing any time of day.

Plan Your Days

Lace up your shoes and fill up your water bottle to explore this multilayered Western city where art, history and the outdoors intersect with craft beer and a love of sports.

Denver Botanic Gardens (p65)

Day 1

Morning

Fuel up with brekkie at **Snooze** (p60) in **Union Station** (p56). Wander through the historic station, popping into some of the boutiques. Afterward, join a guided tour of the **Museum of Contemporary Art** (p58) or catch a game at **Coors Field** (p57), whichever suits your fancy.

Afternoon

Enjoy downtime among locals, even white-water kayaking, in **Confluence Park** (p58). Stroll through the adjoining **Commons Park** (p60), making your way across the river into the hipster LoHi neighborhood.

Evening

Have tapas with skyline views at **El Five** (p60). Afterward, push past a false bookcase for post-dinner drinks at **Williams & Graham** (p63), a tiny speakeasy.

You'll also want to...

There are even more quintessential Denver spots to hit, including museums, iconic venues and sporting events, as well as lively events and parks.

HAVE A WORLD-CLASS LISTEN

Catch a concert at **Red Rocks** (p82), arguably the finest natural amphitheater in the country, even the world.

SEE A LIFE'S WORK

Take in the **Clyfford Still Museum** (p64), home to nearly all the work of the famed abstract expressionist.

TOUR A BREWERY

Visit Denver's OG brewery – **Great Divide Brewing Company** (p61) – to learn how the award-winning brews are made.

Day 2

Morning
Take an early-morning stroll past the large-scale and living art at **Denver Botanic Gardens** (p65). Afterward, walk through the famed **Cheesman Park** (p69), scoping the rolling lawns for evidence of paranormal activity. Head to **Colfax** (p80) for a tasty meal at pay-what-you-can **SAME Café** (p79).

Afternoon
Spend the afternoon learning all about the Centennial State in the excellent **History Colorado Center** (p65) or perusing the impressive collection at **Denver Art Museum** (p66).

Evening
Have a vegan bite at **City O' City** (p67) before beelining for a show at the **Denver Performing Arts Complex** (p57). Afterward, snap pics with the iconic 40ft-tall **Blue Bear** (p61).

Day 3

Morning
Spend the morning wandering through the psychedelic art installations in **Meow Wolf** (p55). Afterward, take the light rail to RiNo and find your new favorite meal at **Denver Central Market** (p75), a gourmet food hall.

Afternoon
When you've refueled, wander through the neighborhood, taking in the **murals** (p71) as you make your way to the **Blair-Caldwell African American Museum** (p73) to learn about the neighborhood's history.

Evening
At sunset, head to **Nocturne Jazz & Supper Club** (p75) for live jazz or check out RiNo's breweries, making sure you taste the lagers at **Bierstadt** (p74) and the eclectic brews at **Our Mutual Friend** (p74).

CHEER ON CHAMPS

Sport burgundy and blue, the Avalanche team colors, and catch a hockey game at **Ball Arena** (p63).

STRETCH YOUR LEGS

Explore Denver's **City Park** (p78), with 320 acres of trails, playgrounds, lakes, a zoo, science museum... even a golf course!

PARTY IN THE STREETS

Head to RiNo for **First Fridays** (p74), when galleries and studios stay open late and revelers fill the streets.

CELEBRATE COWPOKE CULTURE

Cheer on cowpokes every January at the **National Western Stock Show** (p76), an extravaganza of cowpoke life.

DOWNTOWN, LOHI & PLATTE RIVER VALLEY

REVITALIZED CITY CENTER

Present-day Downtown – Confluence Park to be exact – is where Denver started. The Arapaho people had long wintered near the river junction, but were pushed out by a surge of white settlers after gold was found in the South Platte River in 1858. The gold-seekers eventually moved into the mountains, but Denver remained an important supply town and railroad depot. Across the river, the Lower Highlands (LoHi) was historically an immigrant neighborhood, connected to downtown by bridges and streetcar lines. Throughout the 20th century, both neighborhoods went through periods of boom and bust; like many urban centers, downtown Denver was rough during the 1980s and 1990s, but slowly revived with an influx of youthful entrepreneurs (including a brewery owner named John Hickenlooper, who later served as mayor, governor and US Senator). Today, both areas, including the micro-neighborhood LoDo (Lower Downtown), are vibrant and revitalized, populated with skyscrapers and historic sites, theaters and stadiums, hipster restaurants and breweries.

TOP TIP

Avoid driving in downtown – traffic is often bumper-to-bumper and parking is scarce or expensive. Instead, travel on the Mall Ride, a free shuttle that runs the length of 16th Street Mall, a 1.25-mile pedestrian walkway with shops and restaurants that starts at Union Station (p56) and ends at Civic Center Park (p68).

Confluence Park

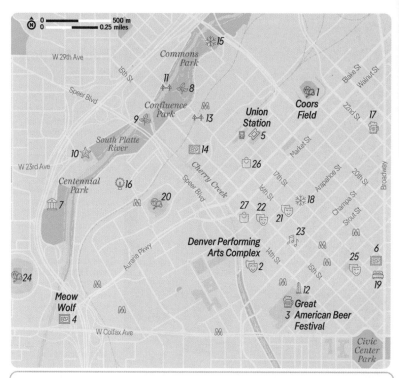

HIGHLIGHTS
1 Coors Field
2 Denver Performing Arts Complex
3 Great American Beer Festival
4 Meow Wolf
5 Union Station

SIGHTS
6 American Museum of Western Art
7 Children's Museum of Denver
8 Commons Park
9 Confluence Park

10 Downtown Aquarium
11 Highland Cable Bridge
12 I See What You Mean
13 Millennium Bridge
14 Museum of Contemporary Art Denver

ACTIVITIES
15 Denver Skate Park
16 Elitch Gardens
17 Great Divide Brewing Company
18 Southwest Rink at Skyline Park

SLEEPING
19 Brown Palace Hotel

ENTERTAINMENT
20 Ball Arena
21 Clocktower Cabaret
22 Comedy Works Downtown
23 Dazzle
24 Empower Field at Mile High
25 Paramount Theatre

SHOPPING
26 16th Street Mall
27 Larimer Square

Meow Wolf
PSYCHEDELIC ART INSTALLATION

A mind-bending, interactive art exhibit, Meow Wolf leads you through a four-story building and 70+ art installations that examine a convergence of four worlds where memories are currency. Enter dark tunnels and tipping hallways, towering spaceships and psychedelic coral reefs, and keep your eyes peeled for the live performers who somehow creep onto the scene. It's another world (er, worlds). Tickets are timed. For a nominal fee, tag on a QPASS, an ATM-like card that gives you access to hidden stories throughout the installation.

Union Station

TINY VENUES PLUS
TRAIN TICKETS

An iconic landmark, the beautifully restored Union Station is Denver's main transportation hub, used by local buses, light rail and Amtrak. But it's way more than that. Wander through the Great Hall, a waiting area and lounge with leather couches, shuffleboard and free wi-fi; swanky restaurants, lively bars and cute boutiques line its walls. Even one of Denver's best hotels – The Crawford (p59) – calls Union Station home.
In summer, head to its outdoor plaza, where you can pick up treats at its popular Saturday farmers market, while its pop-up fountain entices kids (and kids at heart) to run and play through the urban sprinklers.

Great American Beer Festival

THROW BACK CRAFT BREWS

Colorado takes its beer seriously, raising craft brewing to a high art. And with over 150 breweries in Denver, you certainly won't go thirsty in this town. If you're visiting in September, try to score tickets to the Great American Beer Festival, the largest beer festival of its kind in the US. Held in the Colorado Convention Center, the festival draws over 2000 master brewers from across the nation, with over 9900 beers vying for Best of Show medals in 98 categories ranging from American Style India Pale Lager and Classic Saison to Smoke Beer and Herb and Spice Beer. Best of all is the comradery of you and 60,000 beer buddies, all tasting outstanding brews 1 ounce at a time.

Denver Performing Arts Complex

TAKE IN A PERFORMANCE

Come to the Denver Performing Arts Complex, where you can almost bank on scoring tickets to a show. It is the nation's second-largest theater complex and occupies four city blocks in bustling downtown Denver. You'll find 10 venues connected by a sky-high glass canopy, among them the historic Ellie Caulkins Opera House (affectionately called 'The Ellie'), a luxe 2200-seat theater where both Opera Colorado and Colorado Ballet perform. Or head to the magnificent Boettcher Concert Hall, the nation's first concert hall-in-the-round, where the Colorado Symphony plays classics as well as crowd pleasers like holiday movie screenings with the score performed live.

The Arts Complex' theater wing, the similarly named Denver Center for the Performing Arts (called 'The DCPA'), has eight venues staging everything from experimental productions to Broadway musicals. If you're a theater junkie, take a behind-the-scenes theater tour with stops in dressing rooms, design studios and costume shops. The Art Complex's diverse stages often offer online discounts for kids, students and seniors, some tickets starting at just $10.

Coors Field

CATCH A GAME

This is one of the MLB's most home-run-friendly ballparks (apparently, it's the thin air), and catching a Rockies game is loads of fun...even if the home team isn't winning. It's easy with 80 home games and tickets starting at just $1 in center field (aka The Rockpile). Theme nights include freebies like trucker hats and commemorative cups; if you come around July 4, expect post-game fireworks. Tours of the stadium are offered year-round and include access to the field, club houses and mile-high seats. If you're a die-hard fan, cross the street to the National Ballpark Museum, which is jampacked with ballpark memorabilia.

PREPARE FOR THE OUTDOORS

If you're planning to play in the mountains, up-to-the-minute advice and proper gear are musts. Fortunately, the Mile High City has some excellent options.

REI

The flagship store of this outdoor-equipment super-supplier has top gear for sale and rent along the riverfront. Outdoor Recreation Information Center has an outpost with knowledgeable staff and maps.

Wilderness Exchange Unlimited

In addition to carefully selected outdoor equipment, this downtown shop has an impressive collection of quality and well-priced used gear in the basement.

Outdoors Geek

This homegrown outfitter creates packages of top gear for hiking, camping and glamping, and either ships it to you or arranges a pickup. The website also has great camping and backpacking lists.

Larimer Square (p59)

MORE IN DOWNTOWN, LOHI & PLATTE RIVER VALLEY

Museum of Contemporary Art Denver Offerings

ART THAT MAKES YOU THINK

Occupying a four-story glass box near the South Platte, **MCA Denver** was built with interaction and engagement in mind – whether the art provokes, confuses or delights, it'll always make you think. Free guided tours offer deep dives into showcased exhibits; afterward, the rooftop cafe is a great spot for a drink with spectacular downtown views. Don't miss its satellite – the **Holiday Theater** extends the museum's programming into the nearby LoHi neighborhood with concerts, film screenings, artist talks and more.

Confluence Park Activities

OUTDOOR PLAY

Named for the meeting of the South Platte River and Cherry Creek, **Confluence Park** was once the winter home of the Arapahoe people. But the 1858 discovery of gold in the rivers

 WHERE TO STAY IN DOWNTOWN & LOHI

Hostel Fish
Swanky hostel with plush dorms and cozy common areas. On-site restaurant-bar brings a party vibe. **$**

Lumber Baron Inn & Gardens
An 1890 bed-and-breakfast with five suites decked out in period furnishings and ceiling murals. **$$**

Kimpton Hotel Monaco
Art deco meets urban cowboy at this upscale hotel. Complimentary happy hour and bikes. Pets welcome! **$$**

sparked a stampede of white settlers to the area, pushing out the Arapahoe and leading to the founding of Denver. Today Confluence Park is a pocket of outdoorsy activity in downtown Denver. Come here to picnic on its terraced lawns, jog along the waterfront or even just to sun or splash on the park's small sandy beach. In the summer, you also can rent inner tubes and kayaks to take on a fun human-made stretch of white water. (Rentals available at **Confluence Kayaks**.) **Cherry Creek Trail**, a popular cycling route, starts here too, meandering 40 miles through urban landscapes and green spaces, including past the swanky **Cherry Creek shopping district**.

Nightlife in LoDo

JAZZ, COMEDY AND BURLESQUE

For live jazz, **Dazzle** is the downtown go-to. Located in the historic Baur's building, the confectioner-turned-club features mostly Colorado-based musicians. Come for the early show to take advantage of the great happy-hour deals (hello, $4 martinis).

If comedy is more your pace, head instead to nearby **Larimer Square**, home to **Comedy Works Downtown**. Though it's in a somewhat cramped basement-level theater, the club routinely brings in top comics from around the country. Consider stopping by on New Talent Night – tickets are discounted, and renowned headliners sometimes crash the event.

For a total change of pace in LoDo, the bawdy, sometimes naughty **Clocktower Cabaret** is the ticket. A table near the front will get you in the heart of the action, from drag queen theater and burlesque shows to aerialist performances. The theater is inside the historic D&F Tower on 16th Street Mall, once the tallest building between the Mississippi River and California. On holidays or for special events (say, a Rockies game), the tower is lit up.

The Anschutz Collection

TOUR THE OLD WEST

It's easy to walk past the **American Museum of Western Art**, thanks to the basement-level entrance and discreet signage, but make a point to visit. Set in the historic Navarre Building, the museum holds over 600 masterpieces from the Anschutz Corporation's private collection. Together, the work tells the story of the western expansion of the US as seen by artists from the early 19th century to the present day. Take a guided tour (offered twice daily) or pick up a wand with a narrated self-guided tour. Children over eight years old only.

LARIMER SQUARE

Larimer St, between 14th and 15th Sts, is where Denver was born.

Named after the city's founder, it was Denver's first city block, first commercial district, and home to its first bank, first bookstore and even the original City Hall.

By the 1940s, Denver was expanding, the old City Hall was torn down, and Larimer fell into disrepair. But a handful of the original structures were rescued by a conservation-minded developer, who gave the block its current name, and in 1971 Larimer Square (which is not a square at all) became Denver's first Historic District.

Today it's known for its boutique shops and fine dining, many with lovely outdoor seating beneath lights strung across the street.

Crawford Hotel	Oxford Hotel	Brown Palace Hotel
Luxurious and artful rooms inside Union Station, its restaurants, bars and light rail just steps away. $$$	Historic hotel with a prized art collection. Luxe, modern rooms are decked out in antiques. $$$	Denver's most famous hotel, hosting presidents and rock stars. Elegant rooms vary from modern to Victorian. $$$

BEST EATS IN LOHI

Tamales by La Casita
Hands down, the best tamales in town. Choose between green chile or red pork. $

Uncle
Simple decor belies big flavors at this ramen place; the spicy chicken is a fave. $$

El Five
Mediterranean-style tapas and floor-to-ceiling city views. Summer nights brings patio seating. $$

Wildflower
Creative Italian dishes integrating local flavors and influences; the art-deco dining room transports you. $$$

Little Man Ice Cream
Handcrafted ice cream – even vegan flavors – served from an iconic 28ft-high dairy jug. $

Paths through Commons Park

STROLL BETWEEN NEIGHBORHOODS

Located next to **Confluence Park** (p58), **Commons Park** is a perfect place for a walk, with hilly paths and a waterfront trail, and modern art installations dotting the landscape. It's also a nexus of sorts: to the east, **Millennium Bridge**, with its towering 200ft mast-like cable structure, connects the park to the **16th Street Mall** (p60); and to the west, **Highland Cable Bridge**, leads over the river into LoHi and its trendy restaurants and bars. If you're a skater, don't miss **Denver Skate Park** to the north, a 60,000-sq-ft concrete gathering place for some of the best skateboarders in town.

Downtown Denver Rink

ICE SKATE AMONG SKYSCRAPERS

From Thanksgiving to Valentine's Day, you can spin for free at **Southwest Rink at Skyline Park** the ice-skating rink in downtown Denver. The rink is at the base of the D&F Tower, skyscrapers all around. On certain days, DJs spin tunes, adding a dance party-like vibe. Skate rentals are available and hot cocoa is a must (sold at the concession stand).

High Tea at the Brown Palace

TASTE VICTORIAN-ERA DENVER

Join in a Denver tradition by taking high tea at the **Brown Palace Hotel**, Denver's most famous historic hotel. Guests are seated in the luxurious central atrium, with a sky-high stained-glass ceiling above and towers of finger sandwiches and scones served alongside fragrant pots of tea. Live music – piano or harp – harkens back to the Victorian era. Prepare your pinkies.

Iconic Downtown Spots

HISTORIC THEATER AND SCULPTURE

You'll find lots of red velvet and Aztec figures at the art-deco **Paramount Theatre**, one of the premier midsized theaters in the West. Listed on the National Register of Historic Places, it opened as a movie theater in the 1930s and still has the original Wurlitzer organ that accompanied silent movies. Today, the stage hosts a wide range of acts: author readings and bilingual variety shows, dance performances and concerts showcasing its old-timey train whistles and horse hooves.

 WHERE TO EAT IN DOWNTOWN

Denver Milk Market (Dairy Block)
Bustling and artsy food hall with options from ice cream to sushi. $

Snooze
Denver's hottest breakfast ticket, serving classic dishes and drinks with whimsical twists. Join the waitlist online. $$

Snooze
Denver's hottest breakfast ticket, serving classic dishes and drinks with whimsical twists. Join the waitlist online. $$

Ice skating at Southwest Rink at Skyline Park

PUBLIC ART FUND

Almost everywhere you turn, public art and cultural outlets are woven into Denver. The reason? State law directs a portion of sales taxes to cultural organizations large and small, resulting in an annual distribution of $60 million; additionally, a city ordinance requires that any public works project over $1 million dedicates 1% of its funding to the arts.

Over 400 public artworks have been funded through these means, including the giant *Dancers* at the Denver Arts Complex (p57), *National Velvet,* a modern red obelisk at Millennium Bridge, and gorgeous murals and installations in unexpected corners.

Even Denver's airport is widely known for its art collection, including the iconic *Blue Mustang,* known as Blucifer because of its glowing red eyes.

After the show, take selfies with the nearby *I See What You Mean,* Denver's beloved **40ft-tall blue bear**, which stands peering into the Convention Center. Commissioned by the city to create something for the site, the artist, Lawrence Argent, found himself inspired by a local newspaper photo of a bear peering into a Coloradan home – a surprising but not unfamiliar image in the state. Today, the giant bear epitomizes the friendly, playful and ever-curious spirit of the city.

Great Divide Brewing Company Tour

VISIT THE OG BREWERY

Geek out over craft beer with a tour of **Great Divide Brewing Company**. One of the country's most decorated breweries, Great Divide's exquisitely bold and balanced brews have won 18 Great American Beer Festival medals since its founding in 1994. Tours of its downtown brewhouse give you a behind-the-scenes peek at how its magic sauces are made, from brewing to packaging. Reservations recommended (16 and over only).

Biker Jim's Gourmet Dogs
Not your usual dogs; try off-beat meats like boar, reindeer and even rattlesnake wrapped in a bun. $

Mercantile
Half upscale market, half fancy favorite with elevated comfort food, served family style. $$$

A5 Steakhouse
Hipster steakhouse specializing in lesser-known cuts and tiki-style drinks. Save room for the sides. $$$

I LIVE HERE

Meghan Howes, a Brand Ambassador at Laws Whiskey House and longtime Denverite, shares a few of her favorite marijuana dispensaries in Denver.

Den Rec Downtown
A top LoDo spot with friendly, knowledge-able budtenders. It carries a great selection of high-tier flower at fair prices.

Simply Pure
A Black-owned dispensary in LoHi selling premium cannabis flower at a fair price. It focuses on sourcing cannabis that's organic.

Good Chemistry
A mid-level dispensary in Capitol Hill offering a wide selection of cannabis and lots of good deals. It grows much of its flower in-house too.

Wherever you go, don't forget to tip your budtender – remember, they're providing a service!

Downtown Aquarium

Fun for the Little Ones

ENGAGE YOUNG MINDS

Geared to kids eight and younger, you'll find there's something for just about every little one at **Children's Museum of Denver**: cooking classes and maker spaces, bubble play and rocket experiments. Dress-up and imaginative play are woven throughout with a firehouse, vet office, grocery store and more. And there are loads of physical activities too: a three-story climbing structure (helmets provided) and an outdoor aerial course are favorites. There's even a specially designed area for infants and toddlers. Come midweek for less of a crowd. Reservations required.

If you want to make a day of it, walk next door to the **Downtown Aquarium**. You'll see creatures from mountain rivers, coral reefs and rainforests in tanks totaling over a million gallons. (Randomly, there's also a desert exhibit and tiger den.) Kids especially like the 'mermaid' shows, featuring free divers decked out in sparkly tails and seashell bras, swimming alongside nurse sharks, sea turtles and barracuda. Admission is a little pricey (skip the add-ons) but a visit here is a nice change of scenery.

 WHERE TO DRINK IN DOWNTOWN, LOHI & PLATTE RIVER VALLEY —————

My Brother's Bar
An institution; come here for a no-frills pint (and maybe a burger) after a game.

Cruise Room
One of Denver's swankiest cocktail lounges, this art-deco gem opened the day after Prohibition.

Raíces Brewing Co
Latinx-owned brewery offering a range of craft beers, weekly cultural events and Latinx food trucks.

Elitch Gardens Amusement Park

HIGH OCTANE FUN STRAPLINE

If you're looking to shake things up (or your teens are driving you a little crazy), head to this impossible-to-miss **amusement park** along the riverfront. There are towering roller coasters and kiddie rides, water slides, tubing and a wave pool, plus live entertainment. Meow Wolf (p55) even has a ride here. Go online to save on admission. Open April to October.

Empower Field at Mile High

WATCH FOOTBALL OR A SHOW

The Denver Broncos play at **Empower Field at Mile High**, a 76,000-seat behemoth just west of Downtown. It's a special place on game day, bathed in Colorado sunshine and pulsing with orange-clad fans. The Broncos have experienced glorious highs and heartbreaking lows – it's like the Colorado weather, you just never know (so always bring a jacket). Arrive early to check out the **Colorado Sports Hall of Fame** (near Gate 1), which showcases Coloradan athletic prowess with special exhibits on its inductees. On off-days, come for a 90-minute behind-the-scenes tour of the stadium with stops at the visitors' locker room, the press booth and the stall of Thunder, the Bronco's live mascot. Or check-out the concert schedule – big-ticket performers often play here too.

Ball Arena Goings-On

WITNESS THE PROS

Denver loves its pro-sports teams, and fans turn out in force whether the team is winning or getting clobbered. And few venues are more electric than **Ball Arena** (previously known as the Pepsi Center, still the name many locals use). Come here to cheer on the champion Colorado Avalanche hockey team, the Denver Nuggets basketball team, whose mascot Rocky (pictured) is part of the show, or the Colorado Mammoth, the city's lacrosse team. The steep, tiered seating means there are no bad seats – even the nosebleeds have a good view and a great vibe.

When there's not a game on, come to Ball Arena for big-name concerts, from Brittany Spears to Bruce Springsteen.

Williams & Graham
Push past a wall of books to access artful cocktails and Old West luxe in this speakeasy.

Family Jones
Posh distillery serving creative cocktails and delicious nibbles. Reserve a cozy couch.

Jagged Mountain Craft Brewery
Laid-back brewery with an ever-changing selection of creative brews plus some go-to classics.

GOLDEN TRIANGLE, CAPITOL HILL & CHEESMAN PARK

MUSEUMS AND HISTORIC SIGHTS

Truly the heart of Denver, Capitol Hill, Golden Triangle and Cheesman Park are home to many of Denver's top attractions, and combined they embody the city's rich history and diversity. Where to start? Capitol Hill gets its name, of course, from the beautiful gold-domed state capitol; it was Denver's original Millionaire's Row, though most of the grand 19th-century mansions have been replaced by apartments and shops that lend the area its present-day energy and diversity. Golden Triangle and the nearby Art District on Santa Fe are home to art icons like the Denver Art Museum and Su Teatro, and were an important stage for Denver's historic Chicano Movement. Meanwhile Cheesman Park, and the adjoining Botanic Gardens, are sited on Denver's original city cemetery (book a ghost tour for all the spooky details) and are now lovely green spaces and a hub for Denver's vibrant LGBTIQ+ community. Altogether, this is a vital, fascinating and must-see part of town.

TOP TIP

Though some sights are free (here's looking at you Colorado State Capitol and US Mint) and many places offer reduced admission for kids, you can save some cash by using a City Pass (citypass.com/denver), a prepaid ticket package that bundles the cost of several sights around town.

Clyfford Still Museum
PERUSE A LIFETIME OF ART

Dedicated exclusively to the work and legacy of 20th-century American abstract expressionist **Clyfford Still**, this fascinating museum's collection includes more than 3000 of Still's bold and colorful pieces – some 93% of his lifetime production. In his will, Still insisted that his body of work be exhibited in a single space; Denver beat several cities for the prize of building a Still museum. The building, a beautifully stark structure, includes rooms of different heights and a unique waffled ceiling. Special events – talks and concerts, mostly – add a fascinating layer to a visit. A small maker's space helps keep kids busy; free admission for anyone under 17 is a welcome plus for families.

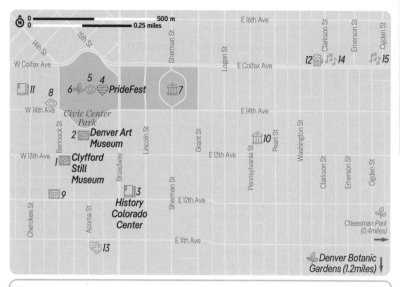

History Colorado Center

LEARN ABOUT THE STATE

Learn all about the Centennial State's people and places, from ancient to modern times, at **History Colorado Center**, a state-of-the-art museum in the Golden Triangle. Thoughtful and ever-changing exhibits present the spectrum of voices that make up the state; displays are high-tech and interactive to keep visitors engaged. Story times for young children and low-sensory mornings are occasionally offered too. If time permits, fold some of the museum's excellent programming into your visit – a city walking tour, archaeological dig, a lecture and more.

Denver Botanic Gardens

STROLL THROUGH URBAN GARDENS

A 24-acre oasis next to Cheesman Park (p69), **Denver Botanic Gardens** is a beautiful and soothing place to wander. Winding paths lead you through a spectacularly diverse collection of gardens with plants from around the world, water features and large-scale art by renowned artists like Calder and Chihuly. In summer, an outdoor concert series brings big-name acts to the gardens, with lawn seating surrounding the stage (buy tickets early and bring a picnic!). In winter, come for the holiday light extravaganza. Younger kiddos also will enjoy the **Mordecai Children's Garden**, where hands-on play, including splashing and wading in Pipsqueak Pond, is encouraged.

65

DENVER PRIDE FESTIVAL

Everyone is welcome at Denver's PrideFest, one of the nation's largest LGBTIQ+ events. And arrive they do, from near and far – over 500,000 people typically attend the two-day celebration in June.

Come for the kick-off Pride 5K (costumes encouraged) and stay for a weekend of free performances, drinks and eats, and general revelry in Civic Center Park (p68).

Don't miss the signature PrideFest Parade, with bedazzled floats and rainbow-clad revelers congregating in Cheesman Park (p69). Proceeds benefit The Center, the largest LGBTIQ+ community center in the Rockies.

Denver Art Museum

TAKE IN MASTERPIECES

The crown jewel of Denver's art scene, DAM houses an eclectic collection, from the works of the Old Master painters to the greats of modern contemporary art. It is also home to a stunningly rich collection of Native American art, one of the largest in the world. Special exhibitions keep the museum buzzing year-round and loads of interactive art stations and activities keep kids engaged. Choose a few exhibits to see and wander the rest of the time – it's a massive museum spread between two buildings: the titanium-paneled Frederic C. Hamilton Building, a work of modern angular art that creates uncanny natural-light tricks inside (and vertigo for some visitors, reportedly), and the newly renovated Martin Building, a glittering fortress-like structure with over a million reflective glass tiles on its outer walls. An expanded welcome center holds art studios and community exhibition space as well as a restaurant and cafe for mid-visit treats. Children under 18 are always free; adults enjoy free admission on select days almost every month – check the website for the current schedule.

Frederic C. Hamilton Building, Denver Art Museum

CHARLES STIRLING (TRAVEL)/ALAMY STOCK PHOTO ©

Golden dome, Colorado State Capitol

LGBTIQ+ TOP SPOTS

Blush & Bleu
Labyrinthine lesbian bar with theme nights like Latin Dance and Underground Poetry. Coin-operated pool table and loads of cozy seating areas too.

XBar
Two stories of madness with DJs, dancing and all types of drag shows. Especially popular with the younger LGBTIQ+ set.

Wild Corgi Pub
Inclusive neighborhood pub geared especially toward trans and nonbinary folks. Expect pub grub, darts, trivia nights and poker nights.

Hamburger Mary's
Drag-themed burger chain with variety shows, karaoke, bingo and more. Located in City Park West. Reservations recommended.

MORE IN GOLDEN TRIANGLE, CAPITOL HILL & CHEESMAN PARK

Colorado State Capitol Tour

EXPLORE AN ICONIC BUILDING

With a gleaming gold leaf dome, the impossible-to-miss **Colorado State Capitol** is a must for history and architecture buffs. It's home to the Governor's office as well as the Senate and House of Representatives, and a free 45-minute tour takes visitors through the behemoth structure, with guides sharing fun tidbits about its design and history, plus time to wander within the dome. Be sure to make a pit stop at the small **museum** on the 3rd floor for videos and building memorabilia too. Afterward, take selfies on the outer staircase, where the 13th step sits exactly 1 mile above sea level.

 WHERE TO EAT VEGETARIAN IN CAPITOL HILL

City O' City
Retro restaurant serving innovative vegan dishes running the gamut from kimchi to poutine. $

Corner Beet
Homey cafe with a smoothie menu as long as their food menu. Toast is their thing. $

Watercourse Foods
Longtime vegan favorite featuring comfort foods with Asian and Mexican influences. $

CITY TOURS

Denver is jam-packed with things to do and see. Several organizations offer a variety of tours to match the variety of visitors to the city.

Historic Walking Tours
Denver's preservation society offers 90-minute walking tours of the city's oldest neighborhoods. *historicdenver.org/tours-events/walking-tours/*

Denver Microbrewery Tours
Knowledgeable guides lead 2½-hour tours of award-winning breweries in LoDo and RiNo, tasting at least 10 different brews along the way. *denvermicrobrewtour.com*

Local Table Tours
Guided walking tours cover some of Denver's top locally owned restaurants, integrating drink pairings and neighborhood history. *localtabletours.com*

City Sessions
Cannabis industry veterans lead small and customized tours of grow operations and dispensaries, with a focus on cannabis production and trends. *citysessionsdenver.com*

Food trucks, Civic Center Eats

Civic Center Park Happenings

JOIN IN CITY LIFE

Stretching between Denver's **City Hall** and the **Colorado State Capitol** (p67), **Civic Center Park** was inspired by the 19th-century City Beautiful Movement with monuments and fountains, a library-turned-art gallery, and even a Greek-style amphitheater. Denver's largest cultural and civic events are typically held here, with every month bringing a different lineup, including the Marade (p78) and PrideFest (p66) events. A summertime favorite is **Civic Center Eats**, when food trucks roll into the park, live bands play and office workers picnic on the grass. Even if nothing is on deck, wander through the park, stopping to see iconic statues like *Bronco Buster* and On the War Trail, a cowboy and Native American warrior created in the 1920s by sculptor Alexander Phimister Proctor to pay homage to Colorado's Wild West roots.

Kirkland Museum of Fine & Decorative Art Collection

SEE BEAUTY IN FUNCTION

The **Kirkland Museum** showcases the beauty of decorative art – furnishings and decor – from every major design period from 1875 to the present. The art is displayed salon style, or as if you'd walked into someone's home, with groupings

 WHERE TO STAY IN GOLDEN TRIANGLE & CAPITOL HILL

Ember Hostel
Vintage chic hostel with upscale amenities and social atmosphere. The hot tub and fire pit are pluses. **$**

Hampton Inn & Suites Denver – Downtown
Dark and boxy chain hotel with indoor pool and DIY hot breakfast. The location is tops. **$**

Capitol Hill Mansion B&B
Historic mansion with elegant and unique rooms. The gourmet breakfast has a vegetarian bent. LGBTIQ+ welcoming. **$**

of furniture set alongside fine art and period pieces like phones and clocks; it allows you to appreciate the art in context, which is surprisingly rare. The museum also features paintings by Colorado artists, including the namesake artist, Vance Kirkland, whose studio is a centerpiece of the museum.

US Mint Tour

LEARN ALL ABOUT MONEY

The single largest producer of coins in the world – about 7.5 billion per year – the **US Mint** Denver offers free 45-minute guided tours of its facility (Monday through Thursday only). They're surprisingly interesting: you'll learn about the history of the mint and the manufacturing techniques behind the pennies in your pockets. Request your tickets by email. Note: No cameras or bags – not even purses or fanny packs – are allowed on the tour; carry what you need in your pockets.

Curious Theatre Performances

CATCH A SHOW WITH HEART

'No guts, no story' is the tagline of this award-winning theater company, set in a converted church. Plays pack a punch with thought-provoking stories that take on social justice issues. Stay for talk-backs at the end of each show, when actors engage with the audience about everything from the plot to the set. It's a small theater, so there's not a bad seat in the house.

Cheesman Park

SOAK IN CITY LIFE (AND DEATH)

Cheesman Park is a historic park located in its namesake neighborhood, one of the most LGBTIQ+ friendly in Denver. In June, join revelers here for the start of the PrideFest (p66), when a sea of rainbow flags fills the park. The rest of the year, Cheesman is popular for its jogging paths and wide grassy expanses, ideal for sunning, picnicking and epic volleyball games. Occupying what was once Denver's first cemetery, the park also is notorious for its paranormal activity – a botched effort in 1893 to relocate about 2000 bodies to another cemetery might be the cause. (Bones are still occasionally dug up while, say, repairing the sprinkler system.) Learn all the spooky details on an evening walkabout with **Denver Local Tours** (denverlikealocaltours.com), with guides sharing tidbits of history and stories of ghostly sightings and experiences.

I LIVE HERE: BEST COFFEE SHOPS IN DENVER

Emma Roberts, a long-time Denver barista, shares her go-to coffee shops.

Pablos Coffee
A welcoming Cap Hill coffee shop, this is a staple, serving good coffee drinks without being pretentious. Try the iced latte.

Hudson Hill
A cute multifunctional space in Capitol Hill serving coffee and cocktails. The seasonal drinks are especially good – go for the cardamom rose latte when it's offered.

Lula Rose General Store
Close to City Park, this retro coffee shop serves great drinks plus delicious breakfast sandwiches. Look for the giant 'Coffee Shop' sign on Colfax.

Crema Coffee House
A hipster coffeehouse in RiNo known for excellent beans that are sourced from 22 different roasters. Order a cortado.

Art Hotel
Plush, art-laden hotel next to the Denver Art Museum. Enjoy cocktails on the rooftop lounge. **$$**

Flora House Denver
Renovated 19th-century home with luxe, modern rooms. Self-serve continental breakfast and contactless check-in too. **$$$**

Patterson Inn
Victorian-era B&B with luxurious rooms, made-to-order breakfast and a reputation for being haunted. 21+ only. **$$$**

DENVER'S CHICANO MOVEMENT

Unbeknownst to many, Denver was a major hub of the Chicano Movement of the 1960s and 1970s.

'El Movimiento' fought racism, labor abuses and police violence against Latinos in Colorado and beyond. Rodolfo 'Corky' Gonzalez, a poet and boxer who later worked with Martin Luther King and Cesar Chavez, was born in Denver. The notorious West High School 'Blowout' – a three-day student walkout, violently broken up by police – also happened here.

Not surprisingly, Chicano roots run deep in Denver. La Alma/Lincoln Park, with its gorgeous murals, is a longtime gathering place for families and community organizers; in 2021 it was designated a Historic Cultural District. Nearby, the Santa Fe Arts District is home to more murals, plus terrific Latinx institutions.

Mile High 420 Festival

CELEBRATE CANNIBIS CULTURE

Denver's **420 Festival** is the world's largest cannabis celebration. Held every April 20 in Civic Center Park (p68), it draws over 50,000 attendees and features hip-hop artists and an omnipresent blue haze (despite it being illegal to smoke pot in public). Cannabis isn't sold – you gotta go to a dispensary for that – but expect lots of pot paraphernalia and food trucks too. (You know, munchies and all.) Security is tight, so expect long lines while bags are searched.

Concerts on Colfax

LISTEN TO LIVE MUSIC

Opened as a roller rink in 1906, the **Fillmore** has had many lives: a car manufacturing plant, a rec center, a nightclub and even a farmers market. Today, it's one of the most popular midsize music venues in town, its big open space hosting acts like Nelly Furtado and Sting. In a nod to its beginnings, you can even see the occasional roller derby match here too. If smaller venues are more your jam, head down the street to the **Ogden**, a one-time vaudeville stage with performers that still pack a punch (Lady Gaga, anyone?). If the house is jammed, make for the upstairs level, where the catwalk extends out into the wings with plenty of room to move. Wherever you end up, after the show, stop in the **1Up Arcade Bar** for dive bar drinks and throwback video games that still cost only a quarter a pop!

Molly Brown House Museum

TOUR A HISTORIC HOME

This beautifully restored house, designed by the noted architect William Lang, was built in 1889 and belonged to the most famous survivor of the Titanic disaster: the unsinkable **Molly Brown**. Guides take you on a 45-minute tour of the house, sharing the life and history of this Colorado legend, including her theater performances, her activity in progressive politics and women's organizations. Brown died in 1932, a woman ahead of her time. If the tour is sold out, you can still visit the house on your own – download the self-guided tour from the website.

KARA MATH/SHUTTERSTOCK ©

 WHERE TO EAT IN CAPITOL HILL & GOLDEN TRIANGLE

Pho-natic
Cheery cafe serving traditional pho and other Vietnamese faves. Window seats mean views of the Captiol. **$$**

Cuba Cuba Café & Bar
Cuban classics pair perfectly with the restaurant's island vibe in these adjoining turquoise houses with a palm tree. **$$**

Fruition Restaurant
Upscale neighborhood restaurant with contemporary farm-to-table American cuisine. Don't miss the craft cocktails. **$$$**

Just west of the Golden Triangle, the historically Chicano La Alma/Lincoln Park neighborhood is home to the Arts District on Santa Fe, a bohemian cultural district draped in murals and home to dozens of art galleries, studios and homegrown shops.

The heart of the district is four blocks long: start on the northern end of Santa Fe Dr, where **1 Armstrong Center for Dance**'s black-box theater showcases new works by Colorado Ballet (buy tix if there's a show on). From there head to the **2 Center for Visual Art**, the contemporary art gallery of Metro State University, known for bold exhibits by international artists. Afterward, walk a block south to **3 Museo de las Americas** and spend an hour taking in the ever-changing exhibits, which pay homage to the diversity of Latinx cultures. Keep heading south (generally), popping into galleries like **4 D'Art** or **5 RULE** or do some window-shopping

at artsy boutiques like **6 Art District Antiques** or **7 Green Lady Gardens**.

You'll soon run into **8 Denver Art Society**, a co-op with dozens of open studios where you can watch artists at work or wander through the cavernous gallery, admiring their finished work.

Hunger should be striking about now – hit up **9 El Taco de Mexico** at the southern end of the district. A no-frills, fluorescent-lit restaurant, it's known for its *chile relleno burrito,* a glorious disaster of stuffed peppers, refried beans and homemade salsa verde wrapped in a flour tortilla and smothered in cheese. Loosen your belt and cross the street to the mural-covered **10 Su Teatro Cultural and Performing Arts Center**. Born from the Civil Rights Movement, the company stages plays, concerts and films focused on the Chicano and Latinx experience. If there's a performance on, don't miss it!

THE GUIDE

DENVER

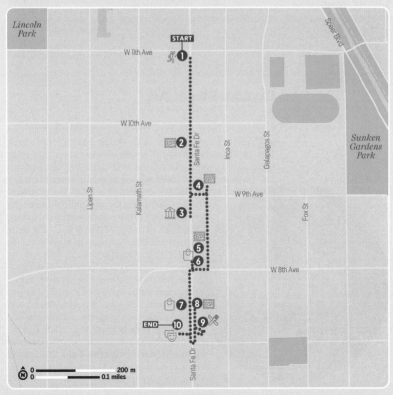

RINO &
FIVE POINTS

URBAN ART AND NIGHTLIFE

Comprising Denver's most dynamic region today, RiNo and Five Points have a long history. This was historically an African American enclave, the result of racial segregation and redlining, but became a thriving community all the same – its jazz clubs earned it the nickname 'Harlem of the West.' As redlining was curtailed in the 1960s, Black residents decamped for other neighborhoods, the sudden exodus leaving Five Points gutted, as empty as the old railyards and warehouses on its western edge. It wasn't until the 1990s that artists appeared and began converting those same warehouses into studio spaces and homes. Eventually the River North (or 'RiNo') Arts District was born, which is today home to galleries, bohemian cafes, breweries and lots and lots of murals. Five Points and RiNo are ever-evolving, with the influence of developers and interests of longtime residents often at odds. Nevertheless, it remains complex and supremely engaging, a place to visit with eyes wide open.

TOP TIP

RiNo Art District's website (rinoartdistrict.org) is a valuable resource for locals and visitors alike. It features detailed information about galleries, murals, monthly events and more. Interactive maps, organized by theme, make it especially easy to track down a favorite shop, restaurant or bar.

Explore Street Art

MURALS EVERYWHERE

Unexpected and totally fabulous, the trendy RiNo neighborhood is draped in hundreds of murals covering every sort of surface, from parking lot walls and alleyways to power boxes and garage doors. Bright, opinionated and ever-changing, the artwork stops you in your tracks, speaking volumes about Denver's diversity, history and musings of day-to-day life.

With over 200 murals and more added each month, it's easy to just wander the neighborhood and take them in. If you want a bit more structure, check out any number of online maps that pinpoint faves (RiNo's website is a good start: rinoartdistrict.org/art/murals). For an even deeper dive, take a guided tour; they're offered by various local companies and typically run around two hours, strolling past notable pieces and including details about the artists and the historical and social context of each. If in doubt, try **Denver Graffiti Tour** for its small groups and custom tours. Whichever way you see RiNo's murals, prepare to be wowed!

0 ——————— 500 m
0 ——————— 0.25 miles

♡ Denver March
  Powwow (1mile);
♡ National Western
🐎 Stock Show (1mile)

South Platte River

35th St
Wynkoop St
Wazee St
Walnut St

RIVER NORTH

37th Ave

Brighton Blvd

Lafayette St
Franklin St
Williams St

Bruce Randolph Ave

34th St
🖼4
🖼5
33rd St
Blake St
32nd St
🖼3
Walnut St
Larimer St
Lawrence St
30th St
31st St
7 🖼
🎵9
10
26th St
Curtis St
Champa St
2 🏛
Stout St
California St
Welton St
Downing St

Martin Luther King Blvd

E 31st Ave
E 30th Ave
Welton St

Broadway
Arapahoe St
27th St
26th St
Lafayette St

6 🚍
8 🎵 E 26th Ave

E 25th Ave

Blair-Caldwell
African
1 🏛 American E 24th Ave
Museum

E 24th Ave
E 23rd Ave
E 22nd Ave

Park Ave W
24th St

E 22nd Ave
E 20th Ave

Broadway
E 20th Ave
🏃11

HIGHLIGHTS

1 Blair-Caldwell African American Museum

SIGHTS

2 Black American West Museum & Heritage Center
3 Dateline
4 Dry Ice Factory
5 fooLPRoof contemporary art gallery
6 RedLine Contemporary Art Center
7 Visions West Contemporary

ENTERTAINMENT

8 Five Points Jazz Festival
9 Larimer Lounge
10 Nocturne Jazz & Supper Club
11 Shorter AME Church (Cleo Parker Robinson Dance Ensemble)

🏛

Blair-Caldwell African American Museum

LEARN NEIGHBORHOOD HISTORY

Tucked into the 3rd floor of its namesake library, this multimedia **museum** provides a thoughtful historical overview of African Americans in the region – from their arrival as pioneers in the pre-Civil War era to their achievements in the face of deep-rooted discrimination. Be sure to check out the exhibits on Wellington Webb, Denver's first African American mayor, and on the development of the Five Points neighborhood. The library itself houses archives and rare documents focusing on the rich cultural heritage of African Americans in the West.

73

BEST BREWERIES IN RINO & FIVE POINTS

**Odell Brewing
Five Points**
The OG of IPA, this two-story brewery dedicates half its taps to experimental releases brewed on-site.

Our Mutual Friend Brewing
Master of eclectic beers, artsy OMF makes award-winning brews from locally grown hops and barley.

Bierstadt Lagerhouse
Cheery warehouse serving slow pours of Denver's best lager. Yard games, live music, and even pro-wrestling are the norm.

Goed Zuu
Upscale brewery specializing in sour and wild ales; pair them with charcuterie or a butter flight (really).

ED ENDICOTT/ALAMY STOCK PHOTO ©

Five Points Jazz Festival

MORE IN RINO & FIVE POINTS

First Fridays in RiNo

ART WALK AND STREET PARTY

A long-standing tradition, First Friday is the day each month when Denverites head to the city's art districts to wander through art galleries, studios and co-ops that keep their doors open late. RiNo is among the liveliest of them all with show openings, live music and a general sense of revelry indoors and out. Start at the **Dry Ice Factory**, a collective of over 30 studios, and wander south from there. Favorite galleries include **fooLPRoof contemporary art gallery** for its range of mediums, **Dateline** for its emerging artists, and **Visions West Contemporary**, with art focused on the interplay of nature and society. Along the way, stop for drinks and nibbles – RiNo's streets, especially Larimer St, are lined with options. The event itself is always free.

 WHERE TO STAY IN RINO & FIVE POINTS

Queen Anne B&B
Victorian-era B&B with period antiques and artist-designed rooms, some with murals. Enjoy breakfast in the garden. **$$**

Source Hotel
Industrial chic hotel above its namesake food hall. Rooftop plunge pools become hot tubs in winter. **$$**

Ramble Hotel
Sophisticated, vintage-inspired boutique hotel with Death & Co, a luxe cocktail lounge, in the lobby. **$$$**

Live Music in RiNo

JAZZ AND INDIE ROCK

Art deco meets industrial chic in the heart of RiNo at **Nocturne Jazz & Supper Club**. Nationally touring musicians are regularly featured, but the real stars here are the artists in residence who take the stage for four- to eight-week runs to perform works by a musical icon or in a particular genre, or to explore their own compositions. Gussy up to fit in with the crowd. If hipster is more your style, head to the **Larimer Lounge** instead, a gritty proving ground for indie rock acts. With shows almost every night, it's a reliable bet for up-and-coming locals and touring bands. Escape to the patio when you need a break from the crowd.

RedLine Contemporary Art Center

ENGAGE WITH ART

RedLine is all about engagement between artists and their community. Come here to enjoy the huge gallery space, a year-round showcase of works by emerging Coloradan artists that's also used for art talks, performance art, even slam poetry nights. Whatever draws you in, be sure to peek into the studios lining the gallery walls; they're the workspaces of 15 artists-in-residence who welcome onlookers to their creative process.

Jazz in Five Points

MUSIC IN THE STREETS

If you're in Denver in early June, head to the two-day **Five Points Jazz Festival**, celebrating Five Points' African American roots and its past as one-time home to some of the best jazz clubs in the west. Over 50 bands perform on stages set up on Welton St, the heart of the neighborhood. If the kids are tagging along, bank on several kid-friendly activities too; everything from drum circles to face painting.

African American History in Colorado

COLORADO'S FIRST AFRICAN AMERICANS

At the **Black American West Museum & Heritage Center**, learn about the life of the earliest African Americans in the West: miners, soldiers, homesteaders and cowpokes. And don't miss the fascinating exhibit on Dearfield Colony, an exclusively African American settlement in northern Colorado (long since abandoned, but today listed on the National Register of Historic Places). The museum is in the former home of

WHY I LOVE RINO

Liza Prado, writer

'Walking RiNo's streets, I see possibility everywhere: the old warehouses turned brewpubs, once-forgotten alleys bursting with color, community-driven art centers where empty lots once stood.

It's my go-to for a night out – the vibrant restaurants and edgy bars offering, as if with extended hand, a great outing with friends.

I love that each time I go, RiNo is just a little different...a new mural here, a new menu there. RiNo is like being given the gift of discovery, the possibility of seeing something inspiring, of seeing something in a new light. Yes, change comes with its challenges, but like a person, RiNo feels alive, worth knowing and watching where it'll go next.'

THE GUIDE

DENVER

 WHERE TO EAT IN RINO & FIVE POINTS

Denver Central Market	Hop Alley	Safta
Warehouse turned gourmet marketplace, this food hall wows with its style and quality of options. **$**	Upscale Chinese restaurant with inventive dishes and cocktails. Housed in a former soy sauce plant. **$$**	Out-of-this-world Israeli comfort food – even wood-fired pita – served in a wel-coming industrial-chic dining room. **$$**

Dr Justina Ford, the first licensed African American female physician in Colorado who, barred from working in hospitals because of her race, set up a private practice in her home. The 19th-century home was originally located 12 blocks away; set to be demolished, it was moved to the current location and restored to house the museum.

A Colorado Tradition

SPORT YOUR STETSON

Saddle up for the **National Western Stock Show**, one of the country's biggest stock shows and a Denver tradition since 1906. Held every January in the National Western Complex on the northern edge of RiNo, the event includes 20+ rodeos, 15,000 farm animals, dancing horses and even dog shows.

Don't miss the iconic kick-off parade, when dozens of Longhorn cattle are herded down 17th St in downtown Denver, with high heels and power suits giving way to cowpoke hats, chaps and impressive belt buckles.

Denver March Powwow

CELEBRATE NATIVE AMERICAN CULTURES

Since 1984, Denver's Native American community has hosted an annual powwow in the **Denver Coliseum**. Over 100 tribes from across the US and Canada come together to celebrate their heritages through song, dance and storytelling. Held for three days every March, it's one of the largest powwows in the country. Join this impressive celebration, eat Native foods and buy Native art, all the while learning about the country's original inhabitants.

Cleo Parker Robinson Dance Ensemble Performances

WATCH MODERN DANCE

The **Cleo Parker Robinson Dance Ensemble** is one of the country's premier modern-dance companies. The namesake founder is a Denver native and still going strong in her 70s.

As the artistic director and choreographer, her work evokes the African American experience and often integrates African dance traditions – a window into and celebration of Black America.

If there's a show on when you're in town, don't miss it! The company performs around town, but opt for their home stage at the historic **Shorter A M E Church** in Five Points.

 WHERE TO DRINK IN RINO & FIVE POINTS

Finn's Manor
Tiny bar featuring Denver's top tap and spirits list. Food trucks on the patio are a hit.

Stem Ciders
A laid-back cidery with a country vibe. Come here for live bluegrass and trivia nights.

Infinite Monkey Theorem Winery
Mid-mod style lounge serving Colorado wines by the glass, can, slushy, and even Popsicle.

CITY PARK

OUTDOOR ACTIVITIES AND EVENTS

At the heart of City Park neighborhood is, of course, City Park itself – one of the oldest public spaces in Denver. Conceived shortly after Denver's founding, many of the park's current features – the winding paths, the lakes, the zoo and other buildings – have been established for well over a century. City Park neighborhood grew up around this mile-long park, many of its so-called Denver Squares (boxy brick houses) popping up after the 1893 silver bust, as they were cheaper to build than Victorians. Today, some of these same houses serve as cafes, bars and shops. Colfax Ave, running along the southern edge of the park, is still growing up. From its Wild West roots to today's mix of homegrown restaurants and hipster venues, it's a transitioning place, highlighting City Park's fascinating cross-section of people and places.

TOP TIP

Denver Museum of Nature & Science (p70) offers free days several times each year. Time your visit to save on admission; just arrive early to beat the crowds! Denver Zoo (p80) offers free days as well, but only by lottery – check the website for the deets.

City Park

ROSCHETZKY PHOTOGRAPHY/SHUTTERSTOCK ©

HIGHLIGHTS
1 City Park

SIGHTS
2 Denver Museum of
Nature & Science
3 Denver Zoo

EATING
4 Sprouts

ENTERTAINMENT
5 Sie Flim Center

SHOPPING
6 Tattered Cover
Book Store
7 Twist & Shout

CITY PARK

THE MARADE

Denver's Marade – part march, part parade – is a huge, joyous, serious, welcoming, historic and thoroughly Denver event. It's the largest Martin Luther King Jr Day celebration in the country, bringing together tens of thousands of Denverites to celebrate the life of Dr King and continue his fight for social justice.

It's a massive outpouring of local people – students, elders, politicians, artists, workers, families with strollers, and activists with bullhorns – joining and chanting to manifest a better world (even when it's snowing, which it often does in January). Marchers gather at the Dr King statue in City Park and march down Colfax Ave to Civic Center Park (p68) for rousing speeches.

City Park Goings-On

CORNUCOPIA OF ACTIVITY

City Park is the largest of Denver's open spaces, a 320-acre megapark located just east of downtown and modelled after NYC's Central Park. Come to stretch your legs on its leafy trails, to paddle-boat on its lakes or even to play a round of golf on its newly redesigned course (club rentals available). Or bring the kids to run wild on its sprawling playgrounds and splash pads or to check out the creatures at Denver Zoo (p80; its flamingos pictured below).

The Denver Museum of Nature & Science (p79) is another family fave, though adults will enjoy a quiet after-hours visit (including adult drinks) on most Friday nights. From spring to fall, a weekly farmers market brings a festival-like feel to the park too, with live music, food trucks and all manner of locally grown picnic fixings; and summer brings thousands of locals to free jazz concerts (p80) too. In winter, City Park is the starting point of the historic Marade in honor of Dr Martin Luther King, Jr. And oh, that view: Denver's skyscrapers with a snowcapped mountain background is the icing on City Park's multilayered cake.

RIGHT: KIT LEONG/SHUTTERSTOCK ©, BELOW LEFT: DIMARA/SHUTTERSTOCK ©

BEST SPOTS FOR BREAKFAST IN CITY PARK

Café Miriam
Charming French Moroccan cafe specializing in to-die-for crepes, tagines and breakfast croissant-wiches. $

Onefold
Shabby chic restaurant serving up organic fare with Mexican and Asian twists. Happy hour starts at 7am. $

Denver Biscuit Company
Big fluffy buttermilk biscuits star in every dish at this exposed brick diner, including French toast and biscuit bowls. $$

Syrup City Park
Homegrown pancake house serving up classic breakfast dishes along with handcrafted syrups and specialty butter. Monster bloody Marys too. $$

Dinosaur skeletons, Denver Museum of Nature & Science

MORE IN CITY PARK

Fill Up on Nature & Science

FUN WITH SCIENCE

Denver Museum of Nature & Science (DMNS) is a magnificent must-do, especially for kids. A massive three-story building, it's packed with exhibits that make science and the natural world interesting and fun. It takes on everything from dinosaurs to outer space, with loads of hands-on experiences, live shows and science demos (and a few old-school dioramas thrown in). Faves include Expedition Health, with state-of-the-art exhibits on the human body (on-site genetics lab anyone?), as well as a Discovery Zone for little ones with water play and even puppet shows. The IMAX theater and planetarium make for a welcome break. Don't miss the excellent temporary exhibits covering topics as varied as mythical creatures and the biomechanics of bugs. Timed tickets are required – save a bit by buying them online.

 WHERE TO EAT IN CITY PARK

SAME Café
Donation-based cafe serving an innovative and ever-changing menu to anyone who's hungry. Walk-in volunteers welcome. $

Tacos, Tequila, Whiskey (aka Pinche Tacos)
Mouthwatering street tacos served in a bricks-and-mortar restaurant. Order three to seal the deal. $

Ethiopian Restaurant
Longtime restaurant serving classic North African dishes plus injera bread to scoop it all up. $

City Park Jazz Concerts

LISTEN TO LIVE MUSIC

Every summer since 1986, City Park Jazz has produced concerts on **Ferril Lake** in City Park. Held on Sunday evenings, and always free of charge, well-known bands play everything from classic jazz and blues to R&B and salsa. The series typically attracts around 10,000 concert-goers each week – bring a picnic blanket, borrow a lawn chair or just join the dancing in front of the band stand. If hunger strikes, food trucks offer lots of options or BYO eats from **Sprouts**, a nearby natural food grocery store, with good made-to-order sandwiches, snacks and drinks. Come early to stake out a good spot!

Wildlife in Denver

SEE AND FEED WILD ANIMALS

Next to DMNS (p79), the **Denver Zoo** is a pleasant place to spend a morning, with expansive habitats and up-close views of over 3000 animals from around the world, even tigers and elephants passing on bridges overhead. Animal feedings are especially fun to watch, with staffers sharing interesting facts about the creatures and answering audience questions (signs are posted throughout the zoo with feeding schedules). For a nominal fee, you also can feed lorikeet parrots as you walk through their habitat or gentle cownose stingrays from the rim of their 15,000-gallon tank. If your budget can swing it, face-to-face encounters (up to six people) are possible with giraffes, sloths, rhinos and more, or get a behind-the-scenes tour of the zoo's animal hospital.

Sie Film Center Offerings

FILMS, BOOKS AND RECORDS

After a day in the park, chill out at the **Sie Film Center**, an arthouse theater screening independent and avant-garde films. Before the show, pop into the **Tattered Cover** next door, Denver's most beloved indie bookstore, or peruse the vinyl at **Twist & Shout**. The Sie also is home to the **Denver Film Festival**, the Rocky Mountain region's largest film festival, which brings over 200 films from across cultures, identities and countries to Denver every November. The fest includes Q&As, panel discussions and soirees with filmmakers and actors. Opening night is typically held at the beloved Ellie Caulkins Opera House (p57).

 WHERE TO DRINK IN CITY PARK

Thin Man
Bathed in red lights and religious art, this is the place for infused vodka and a local's vibe.

PS Cocktail Lounge
Sixties-style dive doling out free shots and red roses just for coming in. Cash only.

Cerebral Brewing
Award-winning brewery serving up everything from IPAs to sours. Flights come in beakers.

RED ROCKS PARK & AMPHITHEATER

WORLD-CLASS CONCERT VENUE

Renowned for its natural acoustics and stunning beauty, Red Rocks may well be the world's most iconic outdoor concert venue. Built between towering 300ft-high red sandstone fins, it was once a sacred gathering place of the Ute people, and was later used as a makeshift performance space until the city of Denver purchased the land and built a formal stage and seating. It wasn't until 1964, though, that Red Rocks debuted as a rock venue. And it did so in style, featuring The Beatles on their first US tour. Red Rocks has since become synonymous with big-name rock concerts, and bands like U2 and the Grateful Dead have even recorded live albums here. Even if you can't make a concert (some sell out in minutes), the venue and its surrounding 816 acres are free to visit during the day and host various non-music events, all of it well worth the 15-mile trek from Denver to explore.

TOP TIP

On Location (rrxshuttles. com) offers round-trip shuttle service from Union Station (p56) and the Capitol Hill neighborhood to Red Rocks on show nights. You'll avoid the hassle of negotiating parking lot traffic and won't have to worry about having a designated driver. The service costs about the same as a ride-share before surge pricing.

Red Rocks Amphitheater

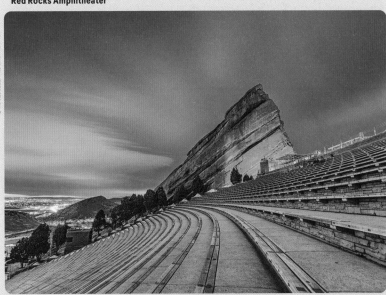

RED ROCKS PARK & AMPHITHEATER

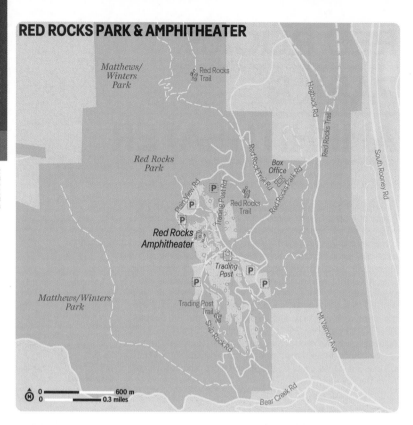

Matthews/ Winters Park

Red Rocks Trail

Red Rocks Park

Hogback Rd

Red Rocks Trail

South Rooney Rd

Plain View Rd

Trading Post Rd

Red Rock Trail Rd

Box Office

Red Rocks Park Rd

Red Rocks Trail

Red Rocks Amphitheater

Trading Post

Matthews/Winters Park

Trading Post Trail

Ship Rock Rd

Mt Vernon Ave

Bear Creek Rd

N   0 ———— 600 m
    0 ———— 0.3 miles

Red Rocks Concerts

LISTEN TO WORLD-CLASS MUSICIANS

There's something almost primal about attending a concert at **Red Rocks** – the sounds of instruments and song, the sight of people dancing, an umbrella of dark sky above, and the iconic 300ft-high red sandstone monoliths standing guard on either side. For many, it's reason enough for a trip to Colorado. Definitely try to score tickets – big-name musicians, symphony orchestras and solo artists perform all summer long. Most concerts start at sunset, with the rocks aglow and the twinkling city lights beyond.

Exercise class

MORE IN RED ROCKS PARK & AMPHITHEATER

Red Rocks Alternatives

MOVIES, YOGA, HIKING AND MORE

If a concert isn't in the cards, come for **Films on the Rocks**, when classic and cult faves are screened before packed audiences; arrive early to catch the pre-show performances by up-and-coming comedians and bands. Or come really early – like 7am early – to downward dog with fellow yogis at **Yoga on the Rocks**, a weekend class led by some of Denver's top instructors (BYO mat). Both cost around the same as they would in town.

During the day, you also can wander through the amphitheater for free, snapping photos and checking out the panoramic views. Or lose the crowds on two trails that wind through the hilly landscape, signature red-rock formations dotting the way. The shorter trail (1.4-mile loop) starts at the **Trading Post**, home to the **Colorado Music Hall of Fame**. Pop in before a hike to learn about the inductees, local music legends like Glenn Miller, John Denver, and Earth, Wind and Fire.

IF YOU ARE GOING TO A RED ROCKS CONCERT...

- Arrive early. You'll avoid bumper-to-bumper traffic and can tailgate with locals.
- Prepare to walk uphill. Red Rocks' parking lots are on a steep hillside below the amphitheater. When inside, your seat may be up a couple of hundred stairs.
- Bring layers. Temperatures can drop quickly after sunset!
- Stay hydrated. At 6450ft, Red Rocks' elevation is no joke. Bring empty water bottles to fill there or factory sealed non-alcoholic drinks. Non-glass containers only.
- Carry cash. Buy refreshments from ambulant vendors instead of standing in long lines.
- Smoke at your own risk. It's illegal to smoke weed in public, though you'll see plenty of people lighting up. If you're caught, you could face a fine and/or jail time.

WHERE TO EAT NEAR RED ROCKS

Red Rocks Beer Garden
Leafy patio pub, serving thin-crust pizza and a dozen Colorado beers on tap. $

Morrison Farmhouse
Charming country cafe with gourmet salads, sandwiches and charcuterie boards. Well-crafted cocktails and wines. $$

The Fort
Recreated adobe fort specializing in wild-game dishes and Rocky Mountain oysters. A Colorado institution. $ $ $

BOULDER

Where quirky meets alfresco

Welcome to the 'Boulder bubble,' a one-of-a-kind outdoorsy town.

Boulder
Denver

They call it the 'Boulder bubble' for a reason: the city of Boulder is like nowhere else on earth.

You'll sense the invisible 'bubble' that sets this destination apart in many ways. Socially, in Boulder's ultra-liberal politics. Spiritually, by the avid Buddhist and yoga scene. Mentally, with how the University of Colorado campus coexists with Naropa University, an alternative college founded in the 1970s by a Tibetan Buddhist monk. And quite literally, by a 45,000-acre open space buffer that walls the town.

This university town seems to live in perfect contradiction. It's simultaneously the most relaxed, 'hippie' town in Colorado (with one of the highest concentrations of marijuana shops in the country) but also incredibly well-off (as one of the most expensive cities in Colorado, with an average home price of more than $1 million).

Boulder has been named one of America's most creative cities and one of the nation's best art towns, but it's also full of scientists and has produced multiple Nobel Prize winners, National Medal of Science winners, and more

than a dozen astronauts. It's home to the National Center for Atmospheric Research and the National Institute of Standards of Technology. Yes, the Atomic Clock – which sets the pace for the rest of the country – ticks in this town.

Boulder has yielded three US Supreme Court justices, but is equally known for its Olympians and extreme athletes, drawn to the high altitude and rugged terrain for training, the same reason so many ski bums and rock climbers make it their home. Here, residents work as hard as they play. And that all comes together to make it a super fun place to visit.

Boulder is an outdoor-lover's paradise, backed up to the foothills and punctuated by the Flatiron rock formations. It's home to multiple lakes, including the popular 700-acre Flatiron Reservoir, more trails than you could possibly hike in one trip, and as many as 300 days of sunshine a year.

It's no wonder Boulder has been named the best place to live in the US and in Colorado. But even if you don't have a mill to drop on a home, Boulder has also been named one of the best places in the state to visit.

SHANE MOLENDA/SHUTTERSTOCK ©

THE MAIN AREAS

DOWNTOWN BOULDER
The heart of Boulder.
p90

CU CAMPUS & UNIVERSITY HILL
Live music and campus life.
p95

KIT LEONG/SHUTTERSTOCK ©

Hiking the Flatirons (p104)

NORTH BOULDER
The hub of the arts scene.
p100

SOUTH BOULDER
Family and outdoorsy fun.
p104

EAST BOULDER
Breweries and hidden gems.
p108

Find Your Way

Boulder's location is an ideal home base for travelers. It's 40 minutes to Denver; just over an hour to Rocky Mountain National Park; and a half-hour to the closest ski town, Eldora. It also has easy access to other ski resorts off I-70. You can get around Boulder without a car, unless you want to explore the mountains.

FROM THE AIRPORT

The Denver International Airport is about 45 minutes from Boulder, if traffic is light and you take toll roads. The AB bus and RTD's SkyRide are both cheap ways to get to the airport. A shuttle or taxi is quicker, but costs more than three times as much.

BIKE

Boulder has been repeatedly named the country's most bike-friendly city, and for good reason: bikes are the easiest way to get around, with so many one-way streets and limited free parking in downtown. It's easy to rent a bike at the many bike shops or bike-sharing stations.

Boulder Creek

Boulder Creek

Boulder Falls

Boulder Canyon Dr

Indian Peaks Wilderness Area

Flagstaff Rd

BUS

Boulder has better public transportation than many Colorado cities. Its easy and inexpensive bus system (once crowned the country's Best Public Transportation), RTD, can take you to the airport, all throughout town and to many nearby cities.

WALK

The downtown and campus areas of Boulder are incredibly pedestrian-friendly, which is only expected in the No 2 Most Walkable City in the state, according to Walkscore. Take a guided walking tour, follow the Boulder Creek Path through town, or enjoy the many hiking trails west of town.

Greenbriar Inn (3.4miles)

North Boulder
p100

36

Upslope Brewing Co

Gateway Fun Park Center

NoBo Art District

BookCliff Vineyards

Boulder Reservoir

Avery Brewing Co

Asher Brewing Co

119

East Boulder
p108

Upslope Brewing Co

Downtown Boulder
p90

Shambhala Center

Dairy Arts Center

Pearl Street Mall

Boulder Theater

Dushanbe Teahouse

Macky Auditorium Concert Hall

Fairy Rippon Outdoor Theatre

CU Campus

Fox Theatre

Fiske Planetarium

CU Museum of Natural History

Colorado Chautauqua

Sommers-Bausch Observatory

CU Campus & University Hill
p95

National Institute of Standards & Technology

National Oceanic and Atmospheric Administration

93

South Boulder
p104

National Center for Atmospheric Research

36

0 2 km
0 1 miles

Plan Your Days

Go on a picnic above the city, watch fire-eaters on the mall and stay in a Victorian landmark. And that's just in one day. You'll want to stay much longer.

Chautauqua Park (p106)

Day 1

Morning

Start with Boulder's heart: the **Pearl Street Mall** (p92). Go shopping (don't miss bootmaker John Allen Woodward), grab a chai at the **Dushanbe Teahouse** (p93), and enjoy the street performers – fire-eaters, contortionists and sometimes a guy who plays the piano upside down hanging from a tree.

Afternoon

Enjoy live entertainment and farm-fresh food at the popular **Boulder County Farmers Market** (p94). Grab a burger to go from **The Sink** (p96) and take it for a hike up nearby **Boulder Creek Trail** (p90). Have a picnic overlooking the city.

Evening

Stay at the **Hotel Boulderado** (p94), the city's oldest hotel, dating back to the early 1900s. Grab dinner and a glass of wine at **Frasca** (p94), one of Boulder's finest restaurants.

You'll also want To...

Be sure to visit the Boulder Museum of Contemporary Art, which features local and international artists, as well as performances, tours, workshops and other events.

SIGN THE CEILING

Grab a burger at **The Sink** (p96), a quirky Boulder institution whose walls are covered in paintings and words.

VISIT THE DAIRY

The **Dairy Arts Center** (p91)is Boulder's biggest multidisciplinary art center, with visual arts, theater, film, dance and music offerings.

CLIMB HIGH

Rock climbers from around the world flock to Boulder for its walls, both outside (nature) and inside (gyms).

PAGE LIGHT STUDIOS/SHUTTERSTOCK ©

FROM LEFT: MARAZE/SHUTTERSTOCK ©, MMD CREATIVE/SHUTTERSTOCK ©, GALEN A/SHUTTERSTOCK ©

Day 2

Morning
Start with elegant brunch at the **Greenbriar Inn** (p100), at the base of the foothills. After oysters and mimosas, explore the canyon and scenery. You might see deer and other wildlife.

Afternoon
See why Boulder's a biking paradise and rent a bike at a local bike shop or bike-share station. Pedal through the region's 150-plus miles of trails and/or head to North Boulder and explore the **art district** (p102).

Evening
See a show at the iconic **Boulder Theater** (p90) in downtown; there's always something exciting (and quality) happening here.

Day 3

Morning
This day's for hiking – year-round. A must-see is **Chautauqua Park** (p106), with trails of all levels. Feeling tough? Try the **Royal Arch Trail** (p107). Refuel at the **Chautauqua Dining Hall** (p106).

Afternoon
Visit **Boulder Falls** (p93), a 70ft waterfall. It's a short, simple hike with a big payoff. Head back to the **St Julien Hotel and Spa** (p94) to get ready for a real treat of an evening.

Evening
Drive up Flagstaff Mountain for jaw-dropping views and the best dinner in town: at the **Flagstaff House Restaurant** (p107). This family-run, landmark restaurant serves food that's just as impressive as the views. Finish with a nighttime hike; many trails are open for stargazing.

SEE A SHOW
The **Boulder Theater** (p90), **Fox Theatre** (p98) and **Chautauqua Amphitheater** (p106), attract big-name performers, but the smaller venues – like the **BDT Stage** (p111) –are fun too.

TASTE THE CULTURE
The **Dushanbe Teahouse** (p93) is a colorful, ornate restaurant designed by Boulder's sister city, Tajikistan. Enjoy full tea service on the Boulder Creek.

EXPERIENCE HISTORY
The **Colorado Chautauqua** (p106), an entertainment and education center dating back to 1898, is the only remaining Chautauqua in the nation that still runs year-round.

YOGA IN THE DOME
The **Fiske Planetarium** (p97) with one of the world's biggest and most sophisticated projection systems, offers yoga classes in its 360-degree dome.

DOWNTOWN BOULDER

THE HEART OF BOULDER

Downtown Boulder centers on the Pearl Street Mall, a pedestrian mall filled with local (and chain) shopping, over 100 different places to eat and drink, historic buildings and people-watching. Boulder's buskers – from contortionists to drummers – bring lively entertainment.

Downtown is home to some of Boulder's best restaurants – indeed, some of the best in the nation. Also head here for art galleries, festivals, live music, luxury hotels and the farmers market. Year-round, the mall is decorated, from lights in the winter to more than 15,000 tulips in the spring. It's no wonder this is the most popular destination in Boulder for visitors.

It butts up to the foothills, too, so if you keep walking past the shops, you'll find yourself on the Mt Sanitas trail that will lead you above the city. Boulder does a seamless job of blending business with nature.

There's so much to do downtown, you could make an entire vacation out of this neighborhood.

TOP TIP

The Pearl Street Mall feels like a fairy tale, with redbrick streets, turn-of-the-century buildings and the ever-present scent of garlic (thanks, Pasta Jay's). If you must pick one destination in Boulder, make it this. But don't stop when the walking mall ends. The mall extends further both east and west, and the full length is worth exploring.

Boulder Theater

AN ART-DECO ICON

You can see the Boulder Theater's neon sign glowing from blocks away. This 110-plus-year-old Colorado icon has hosted a variety of impressive performers over the decades, from musician Bonnie Raitt to stand-up comedians and film festivals. It's ideally located right in downtown, so you can grab food or drinks on the mall, walk to a show and make a whole night out of it. It's a Colorado Historic Landmark too – originally it was a silent-movie house. In the 1930s, it got the art-deco face lift that distinguishes it today.

Boulder Creek

A TOP URBAN BIKE PATH

Boulder Creek cuts through downtown. It's a short walk from Pearl St and runs right past the Dushanbe Teahouse (p93), ball fields and other trails.

Walk or bike along the shaded, paved **Boulder Creek Path**, named one of the top urban bike paths in the country.

In the summer, if the run-off isn't too fast, you can rent inner tubes and float down the water. Or dip your toes in the shallower sections.

If you'd rather relax, stretch out under the Colorado sunshine on the grassy banks of Central Park. Don't miss the **Eben G Fine Park** on the south side of the creek, with a playground and plenty of picnic space.

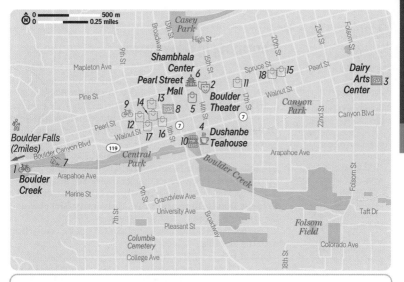

HIGHLIGHTS

1 Boulder Creek
2 Boulder Theater
3 Dairy Arts Center
4 Dushanbe Teahouse
5 Pearl Street Mall
6 Shambhala Center

SIGHTS

7 Eben G Fine Park

8 SmithKlein Gallery

ACTIVITIES

9 University Bicycles

EATING

10 Boulder County Farmers Market

SHOPPING

11 Bliss
see 8 Boulder Book Store

12 Classic Facets
13 Helping Hands
14 John Atencio
15 Jones + Company
   Modern Mercantile
16 Max
17 The Ritz
18 Todd Reed
see 12 Trident Bookseller and Cafe

Dairy Arts Center

BOULDER'S BIGGEST ART CENTER

Although Boulder is an artistic paradise, the 42,000-sq-ft **Dairy Arts Center** stands out for being the city's biggest multidisciplinary art center. There's always something going on here. No, really. It offers about 250,000 art experiences a year.

The Dairy (formerly a cow dairy, hence the name) houses 12 art organizations, four galleries, multiple stages, a movie theater, classrooms and a pretty hoppin' lobby and bar. See unique films, watch a ballet or aerial dance performance, catch stand-up comedy and even take art workshops here. In fact, the Dairy serves about 2000 music and dance students per year.

The art galleries feature an ever-changing lineup of local and international artists, and admission to see them is always free.

91

It's one part hidden gem, one part bucket list. Visit the downtown studio and shop of John Allen Woodward, one of the last remaining American bootmakers.

Woodward makes his boots, belts, wallets, handbags and exotic leather accessories all custom and by hand. He and his staff also make the silver accents and cut the gemstones themselves.

Watch them working through the windows, stop in and ask questions and (if you can splurge) order a custom pair of cowboy boots – an unbeatable souvenir of Colorado's Wild West.

Shopping in Downtown

LOCAL BUSINESSES GALORE

Pick up a memento of your time in Colorado and connect with locals in downtown, the best place to shop in Boulder. The heart of it all is the **Pearl Street Mall** from 11th to 15th streets, where you'll find the **Boulder Book Store** and **SmithKlein Gallery**. But there's more to downtown shopping than these four blocks.

West of 11th you'll find high-end options, like jeweler **John Atencio** and **Classic Facets**, an antique jewelry shop that has carried famous pieces, like a diamond necklace that belonged to actress May West. These coexist next to casual shops like **Trident Booksellers and Cafe**, **University Bicycles** and the **Helping Hands** cannabis dispensary. The 'West End,' as it's called, fades into a residential stretch before connecting with the foothills.

East of 15th is longer and less distinct, with a wider street and fewer pedestrians. It's home to trendy boutiques including **Jones + Company Modern Mercantile** and **Bliss**. Check out fine jewelry at **Todd Reed**. Make sure you venture onto the side streets too. Here, you'll find gems like the high-end clothing store **Max**, and Boulder's best costume shop, **The Ritz**.

Downtown features more than 150 retailers, and more than 80% of those are locally owned and operated. Take your time, window-shop and walk the whole stretch – from west to east, dipping north and south – to get the most out of downtown's shopping.

TRAVELVIEW/SHUTTERSTOCK ©

Pearl Street Mall

Shambhala Center

TAKE TIME TO BREATHE

Boulder has a strong Buddhist community, which you can experience at the **Boulder Shambhala Center**, founded by Tibetan Buddhist monk Chogyam Trungpa Rinpoche. Boulder's Shambhala Center is part of Shambhala, an international group of hundreds of meditation centers, all also founded by Rinpoche. The center offers the frequent, free, public, drop-in programs, such as meditation practice and educational talks. If you need a space to meditate, the Main Shrine Room is open to the public every day except Saturday.

RIGHT: FAINA GUREVICH/SHUTTERSTOCK ©, ABOVE RIGHT: JENLO8/SHUTTERSTOCK ©

Boulder Falls

A HIKE WITH A VIEW

A quick, 10-minute drive west of Boulder on Boulder Canyon Dr will bring you to an easy hike with a huge reward at the end: a waterfall. The hike itself is accessible to people of all ages and abilities, including dogs on leash.

The trail is short – you can make it to the top in about 10 minutes – and it was recently repaired and widened to make it even more welcoming. At the end of the 100yd hike, a 70ft waterfall tumbles down a narrow, tree-lined canyon. Make it a memory by packing a picnic to enjoy on the rocks.

Dushanbe Teahouse

WHERE ART MEETS FLAVOR

It's hard to miss, with its colorful, ornate exterior across from Central Park. The **Dushanbe Teahouse** is one of the most impressive places in town for its architecture, menu and history.

Even if you don't drink tea, this restaurant is worth a visit. The Dushanbe Teahouse was designed by more than 40 Central Asian artists in Boulder's sister city, Dushanbe, Tajikistan. They built it by hand with ancient techniques, then disassembled it and shipped it to Colorado to be put back together. The building symbolizes peace and connection.

The menu includes farm-to-table fare, Asian food, weekend brunch, desserts and a long list of teas. Drink a chai outside in the garden on Boulder Creek or enjoy full tea service inside by the copper fountain.

BEST RESTAURANTS IN DOWNTOWN

Frasca
This high-end Pearl Street Mall restaurant serves Northern Italian food paired with wine. $$$

Avanti Food and Beverage
Enjoy food, drinks and panoramic views in this multi-level, modern 'food court' featuring seven different restaurants. $

Sherpa's
Former Mt Everest sherpas serve up authentic Nepali food in this relaxed, hidden gem. $

Black Cat
The chef uses food from his own farm and other local farms to create innovative dishes at this intimate American bistro. $$$

SHERIE CROFT/SHUTTERSTOCK ©

Boulder County Farmers Market

MORE IN DOWNTOWN BOULDER

Boulder County Farmers Market

FANTASTIC FOOD, LOCAL GIFTS AND A BUZZING CROWD

This is more than a market. This is one of the most popular community events in Boulder when the weather warms up.

The nonprofit **Boulder County Farmers Market** has been named one of the best markets in the country multiple times, and it's easy to see why. More than 150 vendors line 13th St in downtown, between Canyon and Arapahoe St, next to Central Park. All vendors must grow or make their own food to sell it here. That means nothing is resold or bought wholesale; everything's local and made by the very people selling it. Plus, most of the farmers sell organic, non-GMO produce.

The produce and locally raised meat, in and of itself, makes it worth the crowds, but there's much more going on too. The market features free, live music and pre-made meals you can take to the nearby park or Boulder Creek for a picnic. You may find gyros, dumplings, kettle corn, gourmet cheese, hot sauce and freshly baked pastries, and the offerings are always changing. Also look for soap, wreaths, flowers and home decor. In true Boulder style, all waste from the farmers market is recycled or composted.

It feels like the whole city comes out to socialize at the Saturday morning market. The Wednesday evening market tends to be a little less busy, but it's still the place to be midweek.

 WHERE TO STAY IN DOWNTOWN

Hotel Boulderado
This elegant hotel (the first in Boulder) features Victorian-style rooms, as well as modern lodging, and a bar in the basement. $$$

St Julien Hotel and Spa
The St Julien is a luxurious, modern stay with Flatiron views and a full-service spa. $$$

Bradley Boulder Inn
For an intimate bed-and-breakfast in a charming, historic house, the Bradley feels like home. $$

CU CAMPUS & UNIVERSITY HILL

LIVE MUSIC AND CAMPUS LIFE

Boulder is a college town, which means it's ever changing, well traveled and has an upbeat energy. It also means that, even in one of Colorado's most expensive cities, you can find inexpensive food and entertainment that caters to students. Enter: University Hill.

'The Hill' is south of downtown and an extension of the University of Colorado campus – although it's fun for all ages. You'll find some of Boulder's best nightlife at the Fox Theatre and quick bites, like street tacos, burritos and burgers.

Across Broadway is where campus begins. In addition to the lecture halls, CU is home to museums, galleries, performance halls, a planetarium, an athletic field and an observatory.

For lunch, grab a taco from Taco Junky and Tequila Bar and take it to the nearby Norlin Quadrangle to enjoy underneath the shade of trees. You'll see why Boulder has been named the best college town in America multiple times.

TOP TIP

You're now entering Buffalo territory. The CU Buffs' home is Folsom Field, an impressive stadium that seats more than 50,000 fans, named after a former coach. If you want to watch the Buffs in style, score a seat in the Touchdown Club or pre-game on the Rooftop Terrace, with sweeping views of the foothills and Continental Divide.

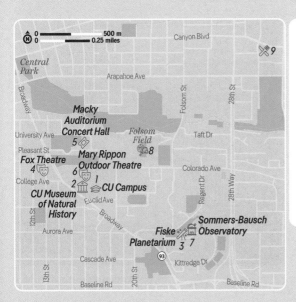

HIGHLIGHTS
1 CU Campus
2 CU Museum of Natural History
3 Fiske Planetarium
4 Fox Theatre
5 Macky Auditorium Concert Hall
6 Mary Rippon Outdoor Theatre
7 Sommers-Bausch Observatory

SIGHTS
8 Folsom Field

EATING
9 Buff Restaurant

CU Campus

NOT JUST FOR STUDENTS

You don't have to be a college student to enjoy the **CU campus**. Here, you'll find some of Boulder's oldest trees (part of about 5000 trees, spanning more than 100 different species), exciting football and sports games, Boulder's best 4th of July show, many free museums and galleries, inexpensive food in the student center, a relaxing library, high-caliber stage performances, tons of special events open to the public – the list goes on.

One annual event not to miss is the free **Conference on World Affairs**, which presents panels of interesting leaders and experts who discuss a variety of topics, from gender dynamics to technology developments.

The college itself is ranked in the top 3% of all world universities. It's one of the 35 US institutions in the Association of American Universities, considered the nation's leading research universities. CU's research centers on aerospace and space sciences; bio/health sciences; and climate, energy and sustainability. Overall, CU offers more than 4300 different courses across 150 fields of study.

You can feel the impact of the university beyond CU's grounds, too, in the many late-night restaurants, lots of cheap or free entertainment and food, great nightlife and breweries, and an invigorating, fresh, young energy.

Boulder is a highly educated city, with nearly three-quarters of the population holding a bachelor's degree or higher.

RED HERRING/SHUTTERSTOCK ©

Conference on World Affairs

Sommers-Bausch Observatory

BOULDER BY DARK

CU's **Sommers-Bausch Observatory** holds free, public stargazing every Friday night (weather permitting) when school's in session. After the sun sets, you can head up to the observation deck and have full use of various small and large telescopes, binoculars, and even the world's largest starwheel to look at the stars. Talk to local astronomers, professors and students about constellations and planets. Enjoy Boulder's often clear skies and an educational yet entertaining night under the open sky. This is offered through the Department of Astrophysical and Planetary Science.

LEFT: MECU/WIKIPEDIA CC BY-SA 3.0 © BELOW LEFT: RJ SANGOSTI/THE DENVER POST VIA GETTY IMAGES ©

Fiske Planetarium

IMMERSIVE ENTERTAINMENT

The **Fiske Planetarium** is a magical (and educational) destination on campus that features shows about science, nature, stars, art, music and more. Sit back in under the massive, 65ft-diameter dome (one of the nation's biggest) and watch laser shows and movies in the immersive theater. One of the world's most sophisticated projection systems brings the films to life all around you. A star machine projects 20 million stars.

For something different, try Yoga in the Dome on Sunday mornings (restorative yoga classes surrounded by a 360-degree movie of Colorado nature) or a Pink Floyd laser show in the evenings.

CU Museum of Natural History

THE LARGEST NATURAL HISTORY COLLECTION

See the largest natural history collection in the region at the **CU Museum of Natural History**. This free, public museum brings you up close with the cultural and natural history of Boulder, Colorado and beyond. It features nearly five million artifacts organized into five categories:

anthropology, botany, entomology, paleontology and zoology.

The museum is great for families too; check out its Discovery Corner, a hands-on exhibit room filled with art stations, books, discovery kits and other family-friendly exhibits. Identify fossils, solve

puzzles and put on a puppet show.

The museum also offers workshops, lectures, a gift shop and guided tours – including the free Spring Color Tree Walks in the springtime. An arborist walks you through campus to teach about the different trees and their history. **97**

Macky Auditorium Concert Hall

CU'S GOTHIC HALL

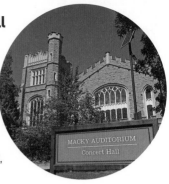

The **Macky Auditorium Concert Hall** on the CU campus is a 2000-plus-seat venue that frequently hosts local, national and international concerts, ballet performances, opera, guest speakers and more. The Gothic-style auditorium is the home base for CU's opera, jazz, orchestra and band programs. Catch a TEDx talk here if you can.

Over the years, Macky's stage has seen a long list of famous faces, including Eleanor Roosevelt, Conan O'Brien, Neil deGrasse Tyson, Bill Nye, the Dalai Lama, Jane Goodall, Robin Williams and more.

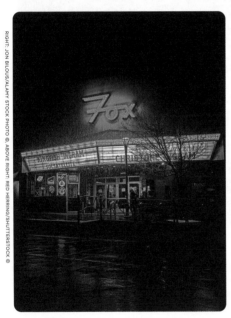

RIGHT: JON BILOUS/ALAMY STOCK PHOTO ©. ABOVE RIGHT: RED HERRING/SHUTTERSTOCK ©

Fox Theatre

A LEGENDARY STAGE

The **Fox Theatre** was named one of the best music venues in the country, and for good reason.

This concert venue, located on University Hill, is known for bringing high-caliber performers to an intimate venue (with a maximum capacity of 625). This is where the Dave Matthews Band filmed its music video for the song that broke the band. Rose Hill Drive recorded a live album here. Leftover Salmon grew a fan base at the Fox during its early years.

But the Fox also supports local favorites and up-and-coming artists. So you can bet whoever's on the ticket, the Fox curates some of Colorado's greatest entertainment.

Mary Rippon Outdoor Theater

ENTERTAINMENT UNDER THE OPEN SKY

Sit under the open, night, summer sky while watching a Shakespeare play.

That's one of the best things to do in Boulder every summer, when the Mary Rippon Outdoor Theater holds the annual Colorado Shakespeare Festival.

The Rippon Theater is an open-air, outdoor theater on the CU campus named after CU's first female professor and the first woman in the nation to teach at a state university. The first play presented here was a Shakespeare show in 1944.

That tradition continues today with one the oldest Shakespeare festivals in the nation, second only to Oregon's. Today, the Colorado Shakespeare Festival is one of the most respected Shakespeare fests in the country. Shows are performed here rain or shine.

Entrance to Folsom Field

MORE IN CU CAMPUS & UNIVERSITY HILL

Boulder like a Buffalo

THE ULTIMATE GAME DAY PLAN

Game day is a huge day in Boulder, and not just for the students. If you're in Boulder early September through late November and lucky enough to be in town for a home football game, here's how to party like a Buffalo.

Start the day with breakfast at the **Buff Restaurant**, nice and close to **Folsom Field**. This family-owned joint has been feeding students since 1995. Look for menu items, like Boulder Granola and 'Buffaquiles' (chili con carne, eggs, tortilla chips).

If you don't have any CU swag, head to **BoCo Life** or **Where the Buffalo Roam** on the Pearl Street Mall (p92). Here, you can get the hookup for all things Buff: shirts, hats, hoodies and stickers. Tip: you can also find a solid selection of gear in the **CU Bookstore** on campus.

Now that you look Buff, head to the **Rooftop Terrace Club**, in Folsom Field. Pre-game like a pro here with food and bevvies on the outdoor terrace. Note: you need to secure a pass for the club in advance, but it's worth it. Or instead, snag a Stampede gold lager – a brew made just for CU fans – at **Avery Brewing Company**.

And make sure you book the CU Buff room at the **Embassy Suites by Hilton**. The hotel is just a half mile from the CU campus, so you can walk or bike to the field and not have to worry about parking and traffic (you'll thank us later). The black and gold room comes complete with CU headboards, framed jerseys, signed photos and other CU art throughout.

WHY I LOVE BOULDER

Aimee Heckel, writer

'When I first began working in Boulder two decades ago, I joked I was infiltrating the 'enemy lines' from within; I went to the rival college. But even for rivals, Boulder's impossible not to love.

It's an unusual blend of beat poets, hippies, tech gurus, Olympians, astronauts and entrepreneurs, and it's often misunderstood for its ordinances (dogs have 'guardians,' not 'owners'). But it's that different way of thinking that also brings creativity, innovation, open-mindedness and inspiration.

It's easy to list the best attractions to visit in any given city. But it's really the people who shape a destination, and your experience. You can't paint Boulderites into a box. And that's exactly what makes them – and this city – so special.'

 WHERE TO STAY NEAR UNIVERSITY HILL

Basecamp Boulder Hotel	**Embassy Suites by Hilton Boulder**	**Hilton Garden Inn, Boulder**
This outdoor-centric hotel has a rock-climbing wall in the lobby. $$$	The Buff Room has CU headboards and decor in a black and gold room. $$$	Ideal for business travelers, the rooms here are decorated with local artwork on the walls. $$$

NORTH BOULDER

THE HUB OF THE ARTS SCENE

North Boulder (NoBo) is the gateway to the foothills, Lefthand Canyon and the town of Lyons. You'll drive through NoBo on your way to Estes Park and the Rocky Mountain National Park too – although this part of town deserves more than just a passing glance.

NoBo is best known for its arts scene. It's home to a long list of galleries, the NoBo Arts District, the NoBo Art Center, public art displays and regular art events. The First Friday Artwalks are popular, and NoBo artists are always a fixture at the annual Boulder Arts Week.

North Boulder is largely newer and a hidden gem for travelers, with restaurants that are just as delicious but less busy than downtown. There's easy trail access and parks with mountain views. The North Boulder Park has tables, a playground, a baseball field, a basketball court, slacklining and a 'tot track' for little cyclists. When it snows, you can go cross-country skiing here.

TOP TIP

The Museum of Boulder, which preserves Boulder's history and more, is on the cusp of downtown on the way to NoBo. It features rotating exhibits, as well as the ongoing, interactive, historical Boulder Experience Gallery; the fun Playzeum for kids; and the Google Garage, where kids can create and experiment with technology.

Gateway Fun Park Center

TIME FOR AN ADRENALINE RUSH

Check this one off your Colorado bucket list: **Gateway Fun Park** claims to have the state's longest go-kart track. Jump in a go-kart (both single and double seaters) and race along the 2100ft-long track, before hitting up the other entertainment at this family-friendly indoor and outdoor amusement park. Play mini-golf and arcade games. Or hit balls in Boulder's only batting cages and Boulder's only free-standing driving range. You'll find lots of novelty here.

Greenbriar Inn

BRUNCH WITH A VIEW

The very thing that makes the **Greenbriar** unknown to visitors is what makes it so special: its remote location.

This locally run restaurant is north of NoBo at the base of Lefthand Canyon. It's on nearly 20 acres of land, complete with a garden, trout pond, waterfall, hundreds of trees and a historic cabin. The Greenbriar has been a staple for more than 50 years.

The American-European restaurant is elegant, with white tablecloths and upscale service. Don't miss Sunday brunch, with oysters, lamb sliders, mussels, butter-poached crab and an eggs Benedict with farm-fresh eggs. It wouldn't be brunch without bevvies, and this restaurant's got it all, from a Chandon garden spritz to a Harvest Mimosa with natural apple cider.

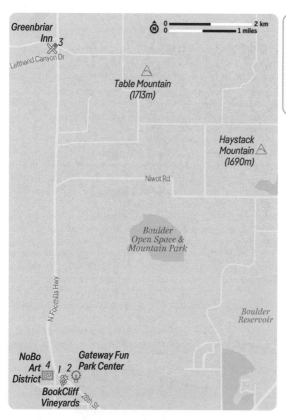

Greenbriar
Inn 3
Lefthand Canyon Dr

2 km
1 miles

Table Mountain
(1713m)

Haystack
Mountain
(1690m)

Niwot Rd

Boulder
Open Space &
Mountain Park

N Foothills Hwy

Boulder
Reservoir

NoBo
Art 4 1 2 Gateway Fun
District Park Center

BookCliff
Vineyards 28th St

HIGHLIGHTS
1 BookCliff Vineyards
2 Gateway Fun Park Center
3 Greenbriar Inn
4 NoBo Art District

DRINKING & NIGHTLIFE
see 1 BOCO Cider

BookCliff Vineyards

BOULDER'S WINE-TASTING ROOM

Try Colorado wine at **BookCliff Vineyards'** Boulder Winery and Tasting Room. BookCliff's wines are made from Colorado grapes grown in a vineyard in Palisade, where the family-run winery has a second tasting room.

BookCliff grows and uses its own grapes to assure consistency and quality, and you can learn all about its story during a wine-tasting and tour at the Boulder tasting room. Sign up for a behind-the-scenes guided tour, complete with wine samples paired with cheese and chocolate and a virtual tour of the Palisade vineyards.

BookCliff makes a variety of wines, spanning reds to whites to dessert bottles.

NoBo Art District

AN ART-LOVER'S PARADISE

The **NoBo Art District** is the heart of North Boulder and
Boulder's art scene. It started in 2009 with just a few local
artists and businesses. They decided to put together a map of
Boulder's First Friday open studio art shows to help promote
them and support local artists.

This small, grassroots effort grew into a robust group of
more than 200 professional artists and creative businesses,
and a well-developed art district located along Broadway and
in the nearby neighborhoods. Here, you'll find artist-friendly
warehouses, many art galleries and studios, and innovative
and inclusive community projects.

The NoBo Art District holds meetings, organizes art
installations, sponsors the First Friday events and spearheads
various art projects, such as NoBo Little Libraries (mini
'libraries' scattered throughout the area with books anyone
can borrow for free) and impressive sidewalk paintings.
Hundreds of local and guest artists have now participated in
the free, fun First Friday events, transforming NoBo into the
place to be in Boulder for art-lovers and travelers on a budget.

Boulder Arts & Crafts Gallery, Pearl St

DANIEL JOHN/SHUTTERSTOCK ©

RON ROYTAR PHOTOGRAPHY/ALAMY STOCK PHOTO ©

NoBo Art District neighborhood event

MORE ART EXPERIENCES IN NOBO

The Gallery @ Bus Stop Apartments
This hidden gem gallery (there aren't clear signs) features ever-rotating installations behind five glass garage doors.

Bohemia
Make art at Bohemia, a relaxing space for art workshops, private parties and more.

The Crowd Collective
This warehouse, with a gallery in front, is the workspace for 14 high-caliber artists.

MORE IN NORTH BOULDER

First Fridays

LOCAL ARTISTS OPEN THEIR DOORS

Follow the map through the streets and through doors to spaces you might never otherwise enter. Some are up staircases or tucked above a garage. Some aren't labeled at all. It's adventurous – and inspiring. It's Boulder's **First Friday Art Walk**.

At this regular, free event, creative businesses and Boulder artists open the doors of their studios to the public. Meet painters, photographers and sculptors face-to-face and see the space where they do their magic. Ask questions about their work (and buy some goodies to take home, if your budget allows). Some artists make art live and do demos for the occasion. It's not every day that you can watch a painting get created in live time while asking the artist about their inspiration – and then take that creation home with you.

First Fridays are self-guided, so go at your own pace. Download a map from the **NoBo Art District** website or view it on your phone, and follow your curiosity to the different studios. Trail the bright flags throughout North Boulder to the next artsy surprise. Not sure where to start? Pop by the information tent for recommendations.

You can also expect to find revolving themed exhibits, food trucks, live music, performances, and local libations from breweries, wineries and a cidery. Yes, Boulder has its own cidery, **BOCO Cider**, and the taproom is also set in North Boulder; it hosts live music, stand-up comedy and community events. Several times a night at the First Friday Art Walk, you will find guided tours of select studios too. It's easy to make a full, educational, inexpensive and entertaining night out of this event.

 BEST RESTAURANTS IN NOBO

Dagabi Cucina
Head to this hip, Spanish restaurant for tapas, pasta, pizza and wine. **$$**

Wapos
Fill up on traditional Mexican food (and margs!) for a reasonable price. **$**

Bacco
If you like specialty cheese and fun small plates, Bacco is the spot. **$$**

SOUTH BOULDER

FAMILY AND OUTDOORSY FUN

South Boulder – approximately south of Baseline Rd – is where you'll find local hangouts, family fun and outdoorsy adventures. Toward the southwest, you can find landmarks like the Colorado Chautauqua and the Flatirons.

Boulder's Flatirons are the slanted rock slabs that are the quintessential Boulder postcard. The Chautauqua is a historic entertainment and educational hub at the base of the Flatirons. Find mountain views, concerts, yoga, cottages to rent and a restaurant here. Around this area, you can experience hiking trails of all levels. This is also where you find access to climb the Flatirons.

Head further south to the Table Mesa area, where you'll find more locals than tourists, and find places to shop and eat without the Pearl St wait. This part of town is also home to a handful of ethnic restaurants that appeal to the widely traveled residents. South Boulder also has a number of science-based destinations.

TOP TIP

As soon as you pull into Boulder, you see them: slanted rocks perched above the city. The Flatirons, running along the eastern side of Green Mountain, are Boulder's biggest landmark. Hike these 300-million-year-old formations on the Flatiron Loop or Royal Arch Trail; climb the First or Third Flatiron; or go on a guided e-bike tour around them.

National Center for Atmospheric Research

HANDS-ON FUN FOR KIDS

Yes, one of Boulder's best attractions is a scientific research facility. The **National Center for Atmospheric Research (NCAR)** is seriously one of the coolest things to do in town, especially for kids.

NCAR is open to the public with hands-on exhibits, games, state-of-the-art exhibits and other ways to learn about the weather, climate and how the sun affects the earth. Kids can 'look' at the sun, touch a tornado simulation and pretend to steer a hurricane. Also, check out the educational theater and the art galleries.

You can sign up for a guided tour or take a self-guided tour of the facility following the app.

When you're done, NCAR is near great hiking trails that tend to not be too busy.

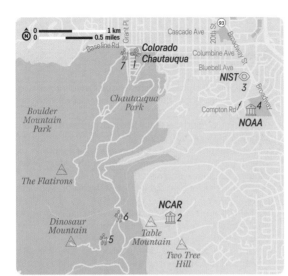

HIGHLIGHTS

1 Colorado Chautauqua
2 National Center for Atmospheric Research (NCAR)
3 National Institute of Standards & Technology (NIST)
4 National Oceanic and Atmospheric Administration (NOAA)

ACTIVITIES

5 Mallory Cave Trail
6 Mesa Trail
7 Royal Arch Trail

National Institute of Standards and Technology

SEE THE ATOMIC CLOCK

See what sets the pace for the rest of the US – literally – at the **National Institute of Standards and Technology (NIST)**.

This Boulder building is home to the NIST-F1 Cesium Fountain Atomic Clock (pictured left). This highly accurate clock determines the time for the country. It's so precise that it won't gain or lose one second in 80 million years. NIST is no longer open for walk-ins by the general public (it used to be), but you can reach out to request a private tour.

National Oceanic and Atmospheric Administration

DIVE INTO COLORADO'S WEIRD WEATHER

Science-lovers and families will enjoy the **National Oceanic and Atmospheric Administration (NOAA)**. This is where scientists study weather, the atmosphere, the climate and air.

NOAA offers free, public tours at 1pm every Tuesday, which are interactive and educational, so they make popular field trips. On the tour, you'll see the working lab and check out the national weather forecast (Colorado always makes for interesting and unexpected weather predictions). Don't miss the Science on a Sphere animated globe.

After the tour, head out back behind the building and follow the trails for impressive views. You'll see the environment around you through a totally different lens.

CHAUTAUQUA PARK & TRAILS

Chautauqua Park is always ranked one of the top things to do outdoors in Boulder.

The park itself stretches across 14 acres, and it provides access to about 48 miles of trails. Options include a self-guided history hike following the Chautauqua Historic Loop (a moderate to easy, 3.5-mile loop); the Enchanted Mesa Trail (medium to difficult, but only about 45 minutes long); Mesa Trail (a flat continuation of Enchanted Mesa that spans nearly 7 miles); and Chautauqua Trail (short but tough – only a half-mile long).

Colorado Chautauqua

ONE-OF-A-KIND HISTORY

Even without the history, **Chautauqua Park** is a must-see in Colorado and one of the most popular places to hang out in Boulder.

Chautauquas date back to the late 19th and 20th centuries, originally built as entertainment and education centers in rural communities. Think of them as gathering places for farmers and ranchers. They offered entertainment, speakers, teachers, art, music and more.

Even though a lot has changed since the 1800s, Boulder's Chautauqua still runs under that original premise. It feels like its own mini town, with cottages you can stay at; an **amphitheater** that hosts big-name musicians, comedians, speakers and other events; a dining hall with Flatirons views; a park where you can do yoga and have a picnic; a ranger station to give you hiking advice; and a system of trails to explore. You could plan an entire vacation in Boulder's Chautauqua and never need to leave the grounds.

You can still see and feel the history in the Chautauqua cottages, which retain many historical details. The still-functioning dining hall was one of the first buildings on-site.

Today, the Colorado Chautauqua is a National Historic Landmark, one of only 25 in Colorado. It remains the only Chautauqua west of the Mississippi and one of four left that haven't stopped running since they opened. Even more, it is the only remaining Chautauqua in the country that still operates year-round.

Cottages, Chautauqua Park

BRENT GOODWIN/SHUTTERSTOCK ©

Royal Arch Trail

Hiking in South Boulder

HIKE YOUR WAY THROUGH BOULDER

Boulder is a hiker's paradise, with 155 miles of trails and more than 60 parks. And while you can find dirt to kick up in any of the city's neighborhoods, some of the most memorable trails hide out in South Boulder.

Good things don't come easily, and that's true for the **Royal Arch Trail**. This hike is considered difficult. It's a 3.5-mile round trip – with an incredible payoff at the end. Per the name, this trail leads to a breathtaking rock archway. It's not as dramatic as Utah's famous arches, but the view will stick with you for life. That is, if you can handle the elevation gain and rocky terrain.

If you want a challenge – but for only a super short push – check out the Bat Cave, aka the **Mallory Cave Trail**. This path is less than a mile long and conveniently starts from the National Center for Atmospheric Research parking lot. Follow the route until you reach the iron gate. Peek through the cracks to see a cave where a rare species of bats live. Scramble up a rock notch if you want to get right up to the mouth of the cave. You can't crawl inside. But, um, did you really want to?

For an easier (but still moderately challenging) hike, take **Mesa Trail** to Woods Quarry, an abandoned rock quarry. Here, you'll see piles of sandstone remnants that hikers have arranged into makeshift couches, chairs and tables. Take a break on a rock couch before completing the 2.5-mile loop.

FLAGSTAFF HOUSE

If you eat at one place in Boulder (and you have the budget), make it the Flagstaff House. This landmark dishes up dinner with the best views in town. The Flagstaff House sits at 6000ft altitude on top of Flagstaff Mountain, with over-sized windows that look out over Boulder. In warmer weather, you can tip back a cocktail on the balcony.

The French-American food keeps pace with the views too. This restaurant has earned more dining and travel awards than any other restaurant on Colorado's Front Range. It's known for its wine program, surpassing 16,000 bottles. The best way to experience the Flagstaff House is via the chef's tasting menu with wine pairings.

 WHERE TO STAY IN SOUTH BOULDER

Chautauqua Cottages
Stay in a historic cottage at the base of the Flatirons. $$$

Foot of the Mountain Motel
This cabin-like motel is at the foot of Flagstaff Mountain and has tons of outdoor activities. $$$

Boulder Adventure Lodge
This A-Lodge, west of town in Fourmile Canyon, provides easy mountain and trail access. $$$

EAST
BOULDER

BREWERIES AND HIDDEN GEMS

East Boulder used to be forgotten, but it has filled out. Highlights include breweries, distilleries, art spaces, gyms, bars and restaurants. You'll also find East Boulder's Flatirons Golf Course, Boulder Country Club and the Frequent Flyers studio, which holds one of the most revered aerial dance festivals in the world.

East Boulder has long been home to less-busy trails, farmland (like the 63rd Street Farm) and Boulder's main bodies of water: Boulder Reservoir, Sixmile Reservoir, Valmont Reservoir, Baseline Reservoir, the Walden Ponds Wildlife Habitat and smaller ponds. So while it may not have the mountains, you can take full advantage of the open space.

Beyond the natural attractions, breweries are a huge pull. The city boasts more than a dozen, most of which are east of Broadway. Many have kitchens and entertainment, such as live music, book clubs and even beer running clubs. With so much brewski, it's no surprise that Boulder hosts multiple beer festivals.

TOP TIP

The Rayback is Boulder's dog-friendly food truck park, complete with a full bar, coffee shop, tap house, stage for live music, fire pit and outdoor games – all with mountain views. By day, it's a coffee shop where people work indoors. By night, it's a relaxed, indoor-outdoor gathering space with live entertainment and a rotating list of food trucks.

HIGHLIGHTS
1 Asher Brewing Co
2 Avery Brewing Co
3 Boulder Reservoir
4 Upslope Brewing Co
5 Upslope Brewing Co

SIGHTS
6 Celestial Seasonings

Avery Brewing Co

A LEADER IN CRAFT BREW

Avery Brewing Co is one of the OG craft breweries. It dates way back to 1993 as one of Colorado's first craft breweries.

Now decades later, nationally acclaimed Avery has led the way for the local brewery scene in Colorado and beyond. Its large taproom features more than 30 taps, including rotating rarities. Enjoy them with a seasonal, locally sourced menu (look for the fried chicken). As for the beers, Avery makes a ton, from its award-winning White Rascal Belgian-Style White Ale to fun seasonal flavors, like a chai-pumpkin beer aged in rum barrels.

Swing by the tasting room for a tour and a flight of the different flavors, which you can enjoy on the dog-friendly patio.

RIGHT: ED ENDICOTT/ALAMY STOCK PHOTO ©. ABOVE RIGHT: PHOTO BY KASHA BROUSSALIAN/ DIGITAL FIRST MEDIA/BOULDER DAILY CAMERA VIA GETTY IMAGE ©

Upslope Brewing Co

AWARD-WINNING CRAFT BEER

Upslope Brewing Co has a long list of awards for its beer, including multiple golds. This brewery has two locations in town, one in East Boulder and one in North Boulder.

This craft brewery embodies Boulder with its outdoor adventure emphasis; Upslope donates a percentage of its craft lager can sales to Trout Unlimited to protect and restore fisheries and watersheds.

In true Boulder style, sustain-ability is also a huge priority. All beer is packaged in 100% recyclable cans. All Upslope events produce zero waste, and it diverts 98% of its solid waste from the main production facility. Upslope was founded in 2008.

Asher Brewing Co

ORGANIC BEER IN BOULDER

Asher Brewing Co, founded in 2009, was the first all-organic brewery in Colorado. The beer is made from high-quality ingredients, with a close eye on environmentally sustainable and socially responsible practices.

At the taproom, you can try the flagship ales or a seasonal brew on tap while relaxing on the patio. The taproom is packed with plenty to do, including corn hole, darts and pool. Call ahead to book a free, guided tour through the small brewery next door.

East Boulder's flat, spacious land is home to a handful of working farms, including 40-acre Munson Farms, a peaceful escape at the edge of town. In warmer weather, you can buy fresh produce here, and in the fall, visit the charming, pick-your-own pumpkin (and squash) patch. Families love the inexpensive hayride and free corn maze.

Fun fact: Munson Farms was founded in the 1960s by an engineer at Ball Aerospace Corporation who started its antenna division and held more than 30 patents.

Boulder Reservoir

TAKE A DIP

A beach in land-locked Boulder? Yup, and it's one of northeast Boulder's top attractions. You can build sandcastles and go swimming at **Boulder Reservoir**, where you'll find one of the state's biggest, sandy swim beaches. Boulder Res spans 700 acres of mirror-like water with stunning mountain views. Take a dip in the lifeguarded swim beach (there's even a special area for young kiddos), or rent stand-up paddleboards or a canoe to explore the waters further.

Kids can enjoy the nearby playground or sign up for sailing or windsurfing summer camps through the city. You can also go water skiing, fishing and boating on the water. Pack a picnic for the shore or grill your lunch, play volleyball, kick back in the picnic area and watch for wildlife. Athletes also enjoy walking, running and cycling around the lake.

The Boulder Res isn't a natural lake. It was built in the 1950s to store drinking and irrigation water. Today, it supplies about 20% of the city's drinking water.

STEVE KRULL TRIATHLON IMAGES/ALAMY STOCK PHOTO ©

Boulder Peak Triathlon, Boulder Reservoir

KRISTOFFER TRIPPLAAR/ALAMY STOCK PHOTO ©

BEST BARS AND RESTAURANTS IN EAST BOULDER

Blackbelly
Blackbelly's chef won season five of Bravo's *Top Chef* show; the restaurant has an on-site butcher shop and raises its own animals and produce. $$$

BDT Stage
This is Boulder's long-standing theater restaurant, where you can enjoy Broadway-style shows alongside dinner. $$

Dark Horse
This casual bar is adorned with movie props, antiques and oddities, and, to add to the quirkiness, it serves Rocky Mountain oysters. $

MORE IN EAST BOULDER

Celestial Seasonings

THE TALE OF THE TOP HERBAL TEA

If you drink tea (and even if you don't), you probably know Celestial Seasonings, a major tea maker that moves millions of pounds of tea every year. Celestial Seasonings is the No 1 herbal specialty tea in the nation. And it's based right here in Boulder.

Its story is just as warming as its tea. Celestial Seasonings was founded by a group of local hikers in 1969 who ran across some naturally growing herbs and botanicals. They picked the herbs, dried them out and hand-packed them into tea bags to give to friends. That small start grew into the company it is today, a leader in the natural foods industry.

For years, Celestial Seasonings has offered tours of the factory and sold tea in an on-site shop and cafe. Here, you can find rare teas, teapots and cups, and other gifts and mementos. Browse the art on the walls – the same images that grace the tea boxes in the stores.

Note: the tours temporarily closed down due to Covid-19 restrictions. When in town, check to see the status and how you can take a free tour. It's fascinating to witness the process – and a jolt to walk into the mint room, where the air is so minty-fresh it might make your eyes tear up a little. When tours are running, you can taste different tea flavors and enjoy a tasty lunch in the indoor-outdoor cafeteria space.

Celestial Seasonings is perched on the eastern edge of town, so it's easy to miss if you don't know it's there, but it's definitely worth the drive.

WHERE TO GET ACTIVE IN EAST BOULDER

Streetside Dance
This dance studio offers classes in hip-hop, break-dance, African and more.

East Boulder Community Center
This is no ordinary rec center; it even has a climbing wall.

The Corner Boxing Club
Train with world-class coaches at this nonprofit boxing gym.

ROCKY MOUNTAIN NATIONAL PARK & NORTHERN COLORADO

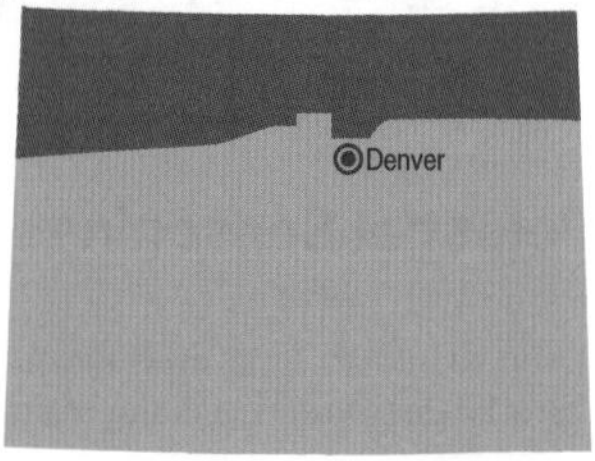

ACROSS THE GREAT DIVIDE

The wind whips wild and free through the northern reaches of Colorado.

⊙ Denver

With one foot on either side of the Continental Divide, Rocky Mountain National Park's vast expanse of wilderness leaves even repeat visitors in awe. It's here that you'll find the headwaters of the Colorado River – the principal architect of the Grand Canyon and the much-contested life-line of seven western states – as well as a handful of shrinking glaciers clinging high in the peaks, all that remains of the last ice age.

More recent history takes in the span of human habitation, from pre-historic mammoth hunters to the Ute and Arapaho, followed by the ever-surging waves of fur trappers, homesteaders, ranchers and other settlers from the 1800s on. The country's nascent conservation movement grew out of the increasing extraction, and destruction, of its natural resources, eventually leading to the creation of the national park system. Rocky Mountain was the 10th such park to be created, and was signed into existence in 1915.

At times, the park may seem like a victim of its own popularity, but all you need is a few days in the rest of northern Colorado to realize that there are still vast tracts of wilderness here that few people ever step foot in. Keep driving west and you'll come to one of the state's most down-to-earth ski resorts, Steamboat Springs (pictured), nestled in a pristine landscape that invites adventure by foot, mountain bike, horse and kayak.

HEIDI BESEN/SHUTTERSTOCK ©

THE MAIN AREAS

ROCKY MOUNTAIN NATIONAL PARK
Bugling elk, majestic peaks and gasp-worthy views.
p118

STEAMBOAT SPRINGS
Ski. Soak. Repeat.
p132

FORT COLLINS
Bikes and beer.
p140

Hiking a frozen Chasm Lake (p122)

Find Your Way

Stretching all the way to the border with Wyoming, northern Colorado is a massive and little-visited region. Outside of the national park, this is a place where off-the-beaten-path experiences reward the intrepid.

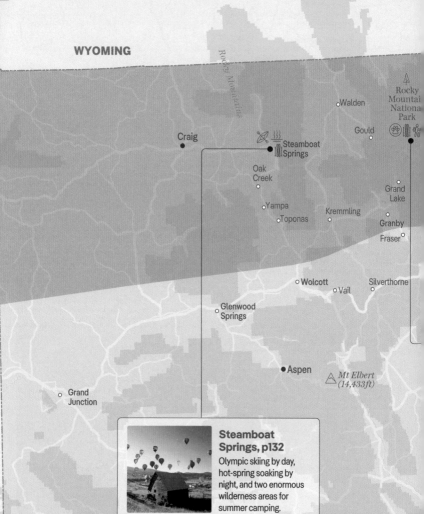

WYOMING

Rocky Mountains

Rocky Mountain National Park

Walden

Gould

Craig

Steamboat Springs

Oak Creek

Yampa

Toponas

Kremmling

Grand Lake

Granby

Fraser

Wolcott

Vail

Silverthorne

Glenwood Springs

Aspen

Mt Elbert (14,433ft)

Grand Junction

Steamboat Springs, p132

Olympic skiing by day, hot-spring soaking by night, and two enormous wilderness areas for summer camping.

CAR

You definitely need your own wheels. In some areas, gas stations are few and far between; always fill up before setting out. Trail Ridge Rd in RMNP is generally closed from late October through late May.

PARK SHUTTLE

In summer and fall, hiker shuttles run to RMNP's Bear Lake corridor (but nowhere else). The park encourages visitors to take these shuttles when possible, as this helps reduce traffic and parking woes. Reservations must be made in advance.

BUS & AIRPORT SHUTTLE

The Estes Park Shuttle runs between Denver International Airport and Estes Park, the gateway town to RMNP. Greyhound runs buses between downtown Denver and Fort Collins.

Wellington

Fort Collins

en Haven

Drake • Loveland

ites rk

Lyons

• Longmont

• Boulder

ederland

◎ Denver

• Conifer

• Colorado Springs

Fort Collins, p140

A low-key university town that's home to over 20 breweries, Fort Collins has earned its place as the craft beer capital of the state.

Rocky Mountain National Park, p118

A world of wildlife, the continent's highest continuous paved road and miles of aspen-laced hiking trails await at one of America's most popular national parks.

Plan Your Time

Most travelers will spend all their time in Rocky Mountain National Park (RMNP), which is massive enough that you can spend several days here – but don't forget to reserve your entry well in advance.

Ouzel Falls (p120)

Pressed for Time

Get up with the sun and hop on the shuttle or drive to the **Bear Lake trailhead** (p127), one of the most stunning – and popular – hiking areas. Yes, there will be crowds here, but there are so many trails, neck-craning Rocky Mountain panoramas and thundering waterfalls that you can't go wrong. Don't forget to bring plenty of food and water.

If you've managed to secure a vehicle permit, spend the rest of the day driving up to the high country along **Trail Ridge Rd** (p121). Stop by the **Beaver Meadows Visitor Center** (p121) on the way back to **Estes Park** (p129).

Seasonal Highlights

July through mid-October is the peak season in RMNP: the high country is (relatively) snow-free and the wildlife is active. In winter and early spring, hit the slopes in Steamboat.

FEBRUARY
Ski conditions are near their peak: powder at **Steamboat Springs** (p132) is deep; day trips into RMNP are absolute magic.

MAY
Spring runoff – when snow turns into mud – is in full force. By late May, **Trail Ridge Rd** (p121) should be open.

JUNE
Wildflowers are blooming at lower elevations; the high country is still covered in snow.

FROM LEFT: MARGARET.WIKTOR/SHUTTERSTOCK ©, MATT KILROY/SHUTTERSTOCK ©, DANIMARIE/SHUTTERSTOCK ©

Two Days to Explore

With two days, you can explore the lesser-known **Wild Basin** or **Lumpy Ridge trailheads** (p120). If you're acclimatized and in great shape, hike up to Chasm Lake (11,823ft).

If you've managed to snag a campsite at the **Boulder Field** (p122), try to summit Longs Peak (14,259ft) in a two-day trip. Mt Ida (12,874ft) is a gentler but no less stunning ascent along the **Continental Divide** (p122). **Outfitters** (p135) in Estes Park, meanwhile, can arrange fly-fishing excursions, via ferrata climbs and a host of other activities.

Too much heart-pounding action for you? In that case, drive south along the **Peak-to-Peak Hwy** (p130) to return to Boulder.

If You Have More Time

If you have at least three days, then we recommend trying to snag a coveted wilderness camping permit so that you experience the park the way it's meant to be experienced – on a **backpacking trip** far from the crowds (p122).

Alternatively, consider a road trip that follows Old Fall River Rd or Trail Ridge Rd over the **Continental Divide** (p122) and down into **Grand Lake** (p129).

From here, continue on to **Steamboat Springs** (p132) where you can saddle up for a horseback ride, go white-water rafting or hike the **Flat Tops** (p138). Afterward, circle back to the Front Range via Hwy 9 and I-70.

AUGUST

Rocky Mountain National Park (p118) is as busy as it gets; cooler temperatures at back-country campsites make for a great escape from summer heat.

SEPTEMBER

One of the best months: **aspens** shimmer gold, temperatures are cool but not cold, and bugling elk are in action.

OCTOBER

Last chance to visit before the snow arrives. **Trail Ridge Rd** (p121) closes for the season.

DECEMBER

The **ski season** kicks off in earnest with the holiday rush at Steamboat.

ROCKY MOUNTAIN NATIONAL PARK

Rocky Mountain
National Park

Denver

Lace up those boots and step into the untrammeled wilderness of Rocky Mountain National Park (RMNP), Colorado's crown jewel. A trip through the park will take you from riparian meadows, favored by herds of grazing elk and deer, up through the forests of ponderosa and spruce, before topping out on the windswept tundra. Here, where the earth meets the sky, the landscape contains galaxies of ephemeral summer wildflowers, and the silhouettes of sculpted peaks serve as a dramatic reminder of the last ice age.

Ford icy streams, huff up snow-dusted mountainsides and pass beneath groves of quaking aspen, fringed with gold beneath the sun. Like many national parks, it can be a zoo in the height of the summer season. But leave the main trailheads behind and you'll quickly find your own patch of solitude, so long as you're willing to share it with the wildlife that calls this place home.

TOP TIP

You must reserve your entry between late May and early October. Reservations should be made on recreation.gov on the first day of the month prior to your entry (thus May 1 for a June visit). A smaller number of last-minute reservations go on sale at 5pm for the following day.

Elk, Rocky Mountain National Park

LEFT: JONATAS NEIVA/SHUTTERSTOCK ©; RIGHT: PETER BOWMAN/SHUTTERSTOCK ©

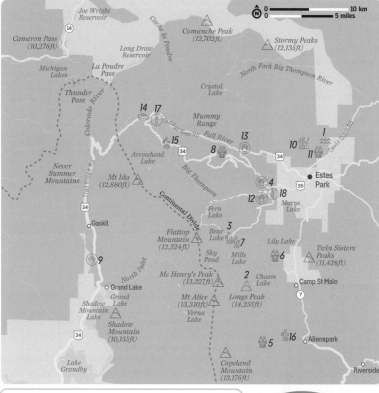

SIGHTS
1 Gem Lake
2 Longs Peak

ACTIVITIES & TOURS
3 Bear Lake
4 Beaver Meadows
5 Calypso Cascades
6 Eugenia Mine
7 Glacier Gorge Trailhead
8 Hidden Valley
9 Kawuneeche Valley
10 Lumpy Ridge

11 MacGregor Ranch
12 Moraine Park
13 Sheep Lakes
14 Trail Ridge Rd
15 Tundra Communities Trail
16 Wild Basin Trailhead

INFORMATION
17 Alpine Visitor Center
18 Moraine Park Discovery Center

Gem Lake, Lumpy Ridge (p120)

 WHERE TO CAMP INSIDE THE PARK

Glacier Basin
Ideally located in the Bear Lake corridor and surrounded by evergreens; 73 sites. **$**

Aspenglen
With only 54 sites, this is the smallest and quietest option in the park. **$**

Moraine Park
The biggest of the park's campgrounds near the Beaver Meadows Visitor Center; 244 sites. **$**

BEAR LAKE ALTERNATIVES

Couldn't score a coveted Bear Lake permit? Fret not, here are five great destinations that are accessible with the regular entry permit.

Trail Ridge Rd & Old Fall River Rd
High-altitude drives.

Lumpy Ridge trailhead
Inspiring rambles among giant boulders; Gem Lake is a favorite.

Wild Basin trailhead
Southern corner of the park; don't miss Ouzel Falls.

Longs Peak trailhead
Variety of hikes from child-friendly to the lung-busting peak itself.

Kawuneeche Valley
Little-visited area on the west side of the park.

HAVESEEN/SHUTTERSTOCK ©

Bear Lake

Day Hikes at Bear Lake

WATERFALLS AND GLACIAL LAKES

The **Bear Lake** and **Glacier Gorge** trailheads are the most popular destinations in the park – and for good reason. From here you'll have a front-row vantage point of the dramatic glacial valleys and hulking granite summits that make Rocky Mountain such a singular landscape.

Hikes range from easy jaunts to **Alberta Falls** (1.6 miles) or **Dream** (2.2 miles) and **Emerald Lakes** (3.6 miles) to more challenging excursions that follow the glacial valleys up to their origins. **Mills Lake** (5.6 miles) is a good choice, as is the **Loch** (6.2 miles), which can be extended to the exquisite **Lake of Glass** and **Sky Pond** (9.8 miles). And while **Flattop Mountain** (12,324ft, 8.8 miles) may not be the park's best summit, there's no denying its magnetic pull from down below.

The catch? The Bear Lake Corridor requires a special entry reservation between 5am and 6pm, and these sell out faster than cronuts. However, there are a few workarounds. One possibility is to catch a shuttle from Estes Park to the Bear Lake Park and Ride (reservations required) and then transfer to a free in-park shuttle. Another possibility is to reserve a campsite at Glacier Basin or Moraine Park. Finally, if you have a backcountry camping permit in the Bear Lake area, this will also grant you access. Remember: most high-country trails are snowbound through June.

 WHERE TO CAMP OUTSIDE THE PARK

Hermit's Hollow
Gorgeous spot in open space, minutes from the park. $

Olive Ridge Campground
One mile south of Wild Basin, this is convenient, but there's no water and it's close to the road. $

Camp Dick
Twelve miles south of Wild Basin in a glacial valley, Camp Dick is a good Plan B. $

Driving Trail Ridge Rd

DRIVE TO THE SKY

The highest continuous paved highway in North America, **Trail Ridge Rd** is a remarkable 4000ft climb, offering visitors the chance to experience the Rockies' high alpine tundra, complete with bighorn sheep, whistling marmots and eye-squinting panoramas in all directions. You can start in the east or west entrances of the park, make it a through trip or an out-and-back adventure, use it as a springboard for high-altitude hikes, or simply content yourself with a dozen superlative-worthy vista points.

Eleven miles of the road are above the tree line (the elevation above which trees can no longer survive) and you should be prepared for chilly temperatures (as much as 30°F cooler), intense sun, sudden thunderstorms and possible altitude sickness. Our number-one recommendation is to stay hydrated (water, not beer).

Time your visit for July, and you'll be in the tundra for the 40-day growing season, when the hardy meadows and lichen-covered boulders briefly light up with a rainbow of wildflowers. Among the can't-miss sights are the **Alpine Visitor Center** (11,796ft), which looks out over a hazy expanse of 400 sq miles, and the info-packed **Tundra Communities Trail**. Further west is the Continental Divide.

Trail Ridge Rd is only open from June through mid-October, and, as one of the Park's premier destinations, sees a lot of traffic. Expect to spend a half-day exploring.

Wildlife Watching

HERE AN ELK, THERE AN ELK

Spend any amount of time in Rocky Mountain and you'll experience it: two dozen cars pulled over on the side of the road, the passenger doors flung open and one herd of people crowding into a meadow to snap pictures of another herd of elk or deer. At which point you might wonder, who's watching who?

The park is home to some 800 elk, 350 bighorn sheep, 60 moose, 20 to 30 bears, an unknown number of mountain lions and countless mule deer – and those are just the big guys. Smaller critters include beavers, marmots, pikas, porcupines, otters, fox, coyotes and some 270 species of birds. While you probably won't spot the more elusive animals, if you pay attention, you'll likely see or hear traces of their passage.

Good places to look for wildlife include **Moraine Park** (start with the excellent Discovery Center), **Beaver Meadows**,

UTE TRAIL

Trail Ridge Rd was not the first passage across this stretch of the Rockies. Before it opened in 1932, Fall River Rd was already in operation (opened 1920, and still drivable today as an 11-mile dirt road).

However, both of these roads were, of course, based on far older routes: the original trails that the Ute and Arapaho used to cross the mountains when traveling between their summer and winter hunting grounds.

As you drive up Trail Ridge Rd, you'll intersect the Park's Ute Trail – which follows the original path – in four spots: at Deer Ridge Junction, at an unmarked trailhead about 2 miles past Rainbow Curve, at Fall River Pass, and at Milner Pass along the Continental Divide.

🏕 **WHERE TO CAMP NEAR GRAND LAKE**

Green Ridge
Quiet, clean and well situated for exploration on and around Shadow Mountain Lake. $

Sunset Point
Lovely views and a peaceful locale by Lake Granby. First-come, first-served. $

Stillwater
Gorgeous views over the lake, though the roadside location can be noisy. $

BEST PEAKS IN RMNP

**Lily Mountain
(4 miles; 9786ft)**
A great choice for your first Colorado summit.

**Mt Ida
(10 miles; 12,880ft)**
Awesome views on the Continental Divide; easily accessed from Trail Ridge Rd.

**Flattop and Hallett Peaks
(8.8 miles; 12,324ft)**
Going up Flattop? Tack on an extra mile and bag Hallett too.

**Chapin-Chiquita-Ypsilon
(9 miles; 13,514ft)**
Invigorating three-peak traverse in the Mummy Range.

**Continental Divide Ultimate Linkup
(35 miles)**
Tommy Caldwell and Alex Honnold's insane mountaineering circuit: 17 peaks, 65 technical pitches and 20,000ft of elevation gain.

Sheep Lakes, Trail Ridge Rd, and the marshy areas in the **Kawuneeche Valley**.

Note, however, that accidents involving animals are more common than you might think, and almost always involve an overeager human encroaching on an animal's space. Don't want a 1000lb bull with a massive rack of antlers trampling you? Follow the rangers' guidelines and stay at least 75ft away from elk and sheep, and 120ft away from moose and bears. And please, don't feed anything, no matter how cute it seems.

Bagging Longs Peak

KING OF THE FRONT RANGE

Iconic in every way, **Longs Peak** (14,259ft) is the pinnacle of Rocky Mountain National Park and one of Colorado's classic climbs. Longs is most often scaled via the exhilarating and exhausting Keyhole Route (15 miles round-trip), which features on many visitors' to-do lists. The top of this route is the crux, consisting of narrow traverses, vertiginous cliff faces and heart-pounding scrambling up polished slabs of rock. Not only should you acclimatize before taking this on, it's imperative to keep an eye on the weather at all times. Statistically, this is the deadliest hike in the park, and the average profile for fatalities is a 32-year-old male.

The golden rule is to be off the summit by noon lest you be struck by lightning. For Longs this can be accomplished in two ways: either start the climb by 2am or 3am, or secure a wilderness permit to camp at the Boulder Field, just below the Keyhole.

The good news is that you don't actually have to reach the summit to experience Longs. **Chasm Lake**, located at the foot of the Diamond – the legendary east face where rock climbers rope up to scale the 1000ft wall – is one of the park's best hikes (11,760ft; 8.4 miles round-trip), and features all the spectacular scenery of the peak without the risk and arduous ascent.

Camping & Backpacking

COUNT THE SHOOTING STARS

Let's be honest, you didn't really come to one of the country's most beautiful wilderness areas to sleep in a hotel room, right? Under the big Colorado sky, camping opens up a world of possibilities.

The park's five drive-to campgrounds stage popular campfire programs and are reasonably comfy, with flush toilets, running water, picnic tables, fire rings and bear boxes for food storage

 WHERE TO EAT IN ESTES PARK

Smokin' Dave's
Kick back and dig into buffalo ribs and chili verde at this northern Colorado institution. **$**

Bird & Jim
From 1960s hamburger stand to a foodie-driven kitchen serving tantalizing local fare. **$$**

Claire's on the Park
Emphasizing locally sourced ingredients in dishes like wild-game meat loaf and grilled lamb chops. **$$**

CAVAN IMAGES/ALAMY STOCK PHOTO ©

The Keyhole, Longs Peak

BEST BACK-COUNTRY CAMPSITES

Ypsilon Creek
Lawn Lake trailhead, 2.5 miles. Easy access makes this a good family choice.

Andrews Creek
Glacier Gorge trailhead, 3.6 miles. Great side trips to Andrews Glacier and Sky Pond.

Sandbeach Lake
Sandbeach Lake trailhead, 4.2 miles. Fantastic backcountry beach and lake.

Thunder Lake
Wild Basin trailhead, 6.8 miles. Base camp for summiting the remote Mt Alice (13,310ft).

Pine Martin
North Inlet trailhead, 7.8 miles. Springboard for multiday trips on the west side.

(no showers or cell service, though). It is imperative that you make reservations six months in advance. Longs Peak is the outlier here: it does not take reservations, nor does it have drinking water. Moraine Park is the only campground to remain open from October through May.

Want to pitch your tent far from the crowds? We hear you. Feast your eyes on the map of the Park's 120 backcountry campgrounds, which are located in some spectacularly remote locations, from the **Never Summer Range** to jewel-like alpine lakes in the heart of **Wild Basin**. Distances from trailheads range from 1.2 to 10 miles, ensuring that everyone from the littlest toddler to seasoned climbers can find a site to suit their tastes.

In addition to the usual array of backpacking gear, all backcountry campers must have a wilderness permit (reserve online at recreation.gov; collect in person) and a bear canister. Reservations open in early March, and many dates sell out immediately.

Ed's Catina
Kick back on the outdoor patio with a margarita and bison tacos. **$$**

Seasoned Bistro
Eclectic, seasonally driven menu that borrows from culinary influences from across the Americas. **$$$**

Rock Inn Mt Tavern
1937 landmark serving steaks, bison meatballs and a side of live bluegrass on stage. **$$$**

BEST HISTORIC SITES

MacGregor Ranch Museum
Living museum featuring original housing and working quarters. Located near Lumpy Ridge trailhead.

Holzwarth Historic Site
This homestead on the west side hosts historical reenactments and ranger-led programs.

Enos Mills Cabin
Naturalist Enos Mills (1870–1922) led the charge to establish Rocky Mountain National Park; his story is documented in his tiny cabin near the Longs Peak trailhead.

Camp Saint Malo
You can't miss this century-old stone chapel on the drive down to Wild Basin.

MARGARET.WIKTOR/SHUTTERSTOCK ©

Dream Lake

Rocky Mountain for Kids

BUST OUT THE S'MORES

The park is an incredibly fun place for families to explore, though it may take some trial and error to find everyone's happy place. Budget time for special activities – horseback riding, a ropes course, ranger activities – to break up the monotony of driving around and posing for photos. Camping is a great way to keep the kids engaged with the outdoors: what could be more fun than setting up a tent or hammock? The added downtime in camp gives kids the unstructured space needed to chase after bugs, scramble over boulders and lead the way on their own mini adventures.

Junior ranger activity booklets are a sure-fire hit, with the promise of a special badge after completing the various nature checklists, games, puzzles and questions. Don't miss the **Junior Ranger Headquarters** in **Hidden Valley**, which runs kids-themed programs throughout the day. It's located

WHERE TO EAT IN GRAND LAKE

Blue Water Bakery
Casual cafe with water views from its sidewalk tables. $

One Love Rum Kitchen
Colorful Caribbean joint: curried sandwiches, fish tacos and plenty of cocktails. $$

Sagebrush BBQ & Grill
Bric-a-brac covers the walls of this BBQ joint, which also serves steak and game dishes. $$

near the beginning of **Trail Ridge Rd**. Evening campfire and stargazing programs, often staged at campgrounds, are also a good bet.

A few family-friendly destinations in or around the park include: **Nymph Lake** and **Dream Lake** (Bear Lake trailhead), **Gem Lake** (Lumpy Ridge trailhead), **MacGregor Ranch** (adjacent to Lumpy Ridge), **Eugenia Mine** (Longs Peak trailhead), **Calypso Cascades** (Wild Basin trailhead), the **Moraine Park Discovery Center** (Bear Lake Rd), the **Alpine Visitor Center** (Trail Ridge Rd), and **Lily Lake and Mountain** (Hwy 7).

Rock Climbing

FROM LUMPY WITH LOVE

Climbing in the park is nothing short of amazing, but it's not for beginners – or even casual gym climbers. Still, we dare you to cast an eye on the granite protrusions of Lumpy Ridge and not feel the call of the wild stirring in the depths of your soul. So what to do?

The best advice is to sign up for a guided trip with **Colorado Mountain School** in Estes Park. Simply put, there's no better resource for climbers in Colorado – this outfit is the largest climbing operator in the region, has expert guides, and is the only organization allowed to operate within Rocky Mountain National Park.

Another possibility is the via ferrata in Estes Park. More accessible than a full-on multipitch climb, a via ferrata can be a good way to experience the thrill of alpine exposure without needing to master all the technical know-how. Check out the routes at **Kent Mountain Adventure**.

Horseback Riding

SADDLE UP, PARDNER

Horses are synonymous with the American West, and a trail ride through the park can be a great way to relive that bygone era when they were an integral part of life. There are a handful of stables in the area, and tours generally range from two hours to a full day. Pony rides for younger kids are also available.

If you're intrigued by the idea of a multiday pack trip through the backcountry, consider llamas. Sure-footed and accustomed to high elevations, llamas are considered to be lower impact than horses and mules. Several area outfitters run llama trips, including **Kirks Flyshop** in Estes Park.

NATIONAL PARK CYCLING

Cycling has continued to gain popularity despite the park's heavy traffic. It's a splendid way to travel, though it's restricted to paved roads and to one dirt road, Fall River Rd.

Climbing the paved Trail Ridge Rd has one big advantage over Fall River Rd (a 9-mile one-way climb of more than 3000ft): you can turn around should problems arise.

Less-daunting climbs and climes are available on the park's lower paved roads. A popular 16-mile circuit is the Horseshoe Park/ Estes Park Loop. For a bit more of a climbing challenge you can continue to Bear Lake Rd, an 8-mile-long route that rises 1500ft to the high mountain basin with a decent shoulder.

🏔 **WHERE TO RENT GEAR** ────────────────────────────

| **Estes Park Mountain Shop** | **Outdoor World** | **Never Summer** |
| One-stop outdoor shop and gear rental, carrying everything from clothing to snowshoes. | Tents, backpacks, sleeping bags, strollers, bear canisters and more; in Estes Park. | **Mountain Products** Super-friendly shop in Grand Lake, renting bear canisters and cross-country skis and snowshoes. |

PINE BEETLES

While mountain pine beetles have been around for a long time (there are 17 species native to the park), their impact on forests, particularly ponderosa and lodgepole pine, has reached unprecedented heights over the past two decades.

Drive up Trail Ridge Rd and you'll see lifeless stands of beetle-killed trees everywhere. Hotter, drier summers combined with warmer winters are at the root of the current epidemic. In addition to providing fuel for wildfires, the dead trees present another hazard: eventually, they fall over. If you're camping, pay close attention to where you pitch your tent.

Fishing
CAST FOR CUTTHROAT

While you certainly can't hunt in Rocky Mountain, you can fish, and casting for trout (crown, brook, rainbow and the native cutthroat) in lakes and streams is a popular activity. All you need is a current state license and your own rod, and you'll be good to go. Make sure you familiarize yourself with the regulations, and know when you are in catch-and-release waters.

The full-service **Kirks Flyshop** in Estes Park offers a number of guided packages in the park and around. It also rents out equipment, guides overnight hikes and offers float fishing and group excursions. Get your feet wet with the introductory two-hour evening hatch.

Snowshoe Safari
WINTER WONDERLAND

A silence so profound that it's deafening: if you've ever explored the Rockies on a winter day, you'll know the feeling. Whether you're wearing skis, snowshoes or just plain old snow boots, there's something particularly inspiring about fresh snowfall, transforming forest trails and jagged peaks into a picturesque tableau. The best part about visiting this time of year? Unlike Colorado's crowded ski resorts, you'll have Rocky Mountain's wilderness practically to yourself – during the winter, visitation drops by nearly 90%.

One of the easiest ways to get out into the snowy landscape is to strap on a pair of **snowshoes**. Snowshoes can get you across most trails in the national park, and the learning curve is practically nil – if you can walk, you can snowshoe. Look out for tours: national park rangers often lead walks on winter weekends.

Another popular winter activity is **cross-country skiing**. Its distinctive 'kick-glide' motion is harder to master, but once you've got it down, you can move faster than on snowshoes.

And if adventure is your calling, there's even more fun to be had. Learn how to use ice axes and crampons when you sign up for an ice-climbing class or a guided trip through the **Colorado Mountain School**. Climbing the park's dozens of dramatic ice curtains and pillars will be sure to keep your blood pumping even on the coldest of days.

 WHERE TO DRINK IN ESTES PARK

Avant Garde Aleworks
Good choice for local brew, with a pleasant vibe off the main strip.

Wheel Bar
Estes Park's favorite dive bar offers a rip-roaring good time and plenty of foot-long beards.

Bull Pin
A bowling alley, pool tables, air hockey and sports bar for those who enjoy a bit of action.

Sky Pond

Bear Lake to Fern Lake

HIKE AN ALPINE WONDERLAND

This day hike (9.2 miles) is a ranger favorite and is known for its diverse scenery. You'll climb up to the tree line and an alpine lake before dropping back down through fields of scree into a forested valley. Here you'll pass more lakes, waterfalls, aspen groves and elk-inhabited meadows. You can't miss **Lake Helene**, which sits serenely beneath the imposing, rough-cut cliffs of Notchtop and Flattop mountains.

Thanks to the park shuttle system, this is a one-way trip that requires no backtracking – and it's mostly downhill. Take the shuttle or park at the Bear Lake trailhead; when you arrive at Fern Lake, catch the shuttle back to the Park and Ride.

WHY I LOVE ROCKY MOUNTAIN NATIONAL PARK

Christopher Pitts, writer

'I've had plenty of climbing adventures in the park, but the one that sticks out the most was the time my 20-year-old friends and I foolishly decided to climb the Petit Grepon in April.

After snowshoeing in, we discovered we were ridiculously unprepared for the spring conditions and had to bail.

In the end, though, our failed summit attempt didn't really matter. Sky Pond had just started to thaw, and, at the end of the day, we were treated to the unearthly sound of a hundred ice shards chiming against one another every time the wind gusted through the snow-covered cirque. Absolute magic.'

GETTING AROUND

Rocky Mountain National Park is roughly one hour from Boulder and 90 minutes from Denver on Hwy 36. Alternatively, Hwy 7 also runs here from Nederland, passing the park's southern entrances on the way. Hwy 34 runs here from Fort Collins and I-25, continuing through the Park and on to Grand Lake, which serves as the western entrance. A shuttle runs from Estes to the Bear Lake corridor, but it's best if you have your own car.

Beyond Rocky Mountain National Park

Rocky Mountain National Park

Estes Park

Grand Lake

Denver

From the Indian Peaks to the far-flung gateway town of Grand Lake, RMNP's outskirts cover a lot of territory.

All roads lead to Estes Park: whether they're driving up Hwys 36, 34 or 7, over 90% of visitors to Rocky Mountain National Park will pass through this crowded gateway town. And if you don't know a WhisperLite from a Jetboil, the chances are you'll be spending the night here too – or, at the very least, stopping for dinner.

To the south of the Park lie the gorgeous Indian Peaks – essentially an extension of RMNP, but with fewer people. Meanwhile, those who make the trip to the little-visited western entrance at Grand Lake will be rewarded with a charming historic district and the deep, blue namesake lake, the largest in Colorado.

TOP TIP

Estes Park can be confusing: Hwy 36 leads to the Park's main Beaver Meadows entrance, while Hwy 34 leads to the Fall River entrance.

Grand Lake

LEFT: MARKEL ECHABURU BILBAO/SHUTTERSTOCK ©, RIGHT: GLENN TAYLOR/SHUTTERSTOCK ©

Estes Park

GATEWAY TO ADVENTURE

Estes Park is a hodgepodge of T-shirt shops and ice-cream parlors, its sidewalks crowded with tourists and streets jammed with RVs. But when the sun reflects just right off Lake Estes, or you spend an afternoon with a lazy coffee on the riverwalk, you might just find a little piece of zen.

Although the strip malls and low-rise motels can be unsightly, Estes promises every convenience to travelers: gear rental, guided tours, upscale hotels, fine dining and even an adventure park and via ferrata routes. There's also the **Estes Park Museum**, which has a commendable rotation of exhibits on local culture and history, as well as **Frozen Dead Guy Days**, which celebrates Grandpa Bredo Morstoel, a Norwegian transplant who is cryogenically frozen and held locally in dry ice awaiting reanimation.

In the grand scheme of things, however, you probably won't be spending much time here, outside of eating breakfast and dinner and catching some z's.

Grand Lake

COLORADO'S LARGEST NATURAL LAKE

As the western gateway to Rocky Mountain National Park, Grand Lake is a foil to the bustling hub of Estes Park. The historic district has a number of friendly local cafes and art galleries. The namesake lake – with a yacht club founded in 1901 – is blue and glorious, and offers a different suite of recreational thrills in the summer: think stand-up paddleboarding, speedboats and other flavors of water-powered fun. An amble along the boardwalk lining Grand Ave is pleasant, with a hodgepodge of corny souvenir shops, decent restaurants, T-shirt shops and a few character-filled bars.

A fun hike from the southern end of Granby Lake (accessed from Hwy 6 on the road between Granby and Grand Lakes) takes you up to Monarch Lake, where you can loop around a scenic alpine lake for a 4.1-mile round-trip.

THE STANLEY HOTEL

The white Georgian Colonial Revival hotel in Estes Park stands in brilliant contrast to the towering peaks of Rocky Mountain National Park that frame the skyline.

A favorite local retreat, this best-in-class hotel served as the inspiration for Stephen King's 1977 cult novel *The Shining*, in which recovering alcoholic and struggling writer Jack Torrance takes a job as the winter caretaker of the haunted Overlook Hotel, where things don't go *quite* according to plan...

If it's ghosts you're after, you should book room 401 to increase your chances of ghost-spotting – staff consider it the 'most haunted.' The hotel also offers evening spirited tours, which nonguests can join to learn all about the spooky history.

 WHERE TO STAY IN ESTES PARK

YMCA of the Rockies
If you're on a family getaway, it's hard to beat the incredible array of activities at the Y. $

The Landing
Cabins, villas and suites, all with gas fireplaces and handcrafted furnishings. $$

StoneBrook Resort
Romantic retreats at these adults-only cabins, which look out over Fall River. $$$

The Peak to Peak Highway

When you're driving up to Rocky Mountain National Park from Boulder or Denver, consider this scenic alternative either on the way there or when returning home. Colorado's first scenic byway (1918), the Peak to Peak Hwy (Hwys 72 and 7) is only 59 miles from Boulder to Estes, and gives you extra face time with the gorgeous Indian Peaks Wilderness and the southern expanse of RMNP.

1 Boulder Falls

Boulder Canyon is a devastatingly beautiful drive, but knowing where to stop can be a real head-scratcher. Don't miss the short but steep walk to these falls, which are halfway up the canyon.

The Drive: Continue up the canyon for another 7.5 miles. At the roundabout at the town's entrance, take the first exit (Hwy 72) to head north toward the park or the second exit to go into town.

2 Nederland

The delightfully ramshackle burg of Nederland is a magnet town for hippies looking to get off the grid. Nearby is local ski hill Eldora and a number of trails into the Indian Peaks. From the Hessie trailhead, you can easily reach Lost Lake (3 miles).

The Drive: Follow Hwy 72 north for 12 miles; the entrance to Brainard Lake is on the left.

ERICKPHOTOPRO/SHUTTERSTOCK ©

Brainard Lake

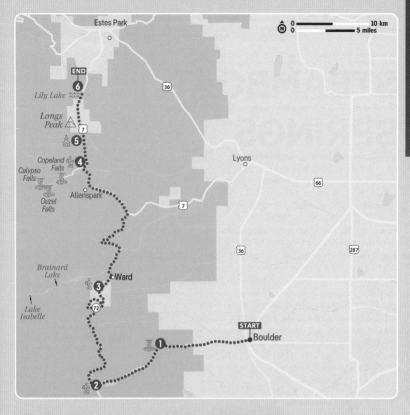

3 Brainard Lake

The best place to access the Indian Peaks is this fabulous recreation area (advance reservations required in summer), known for its moose and over two dozen hiking and cross-country ski trails. Highlights include the beautiful Lake Isabelle (4.9 miles) and the stunning Pawnee Pass (9.1 miles).

The Drive: Continue north on Hwy 72/Hwy 7 for 16 miles. The turn for the Wild Basin trailhead will be on the left.

4 Wild Basin

You made it! Wild Basin is the breathtaking southeastern corner of the park. If you can find parking at the trailhead, consider a quick jaunt to Copeland Falls (0.3 miles) or, even better, Calyspo Falls (1.8 miles) or Ouzel Falls (2.7 miles).

The Drive: It's a short 2 miles up Hwy 7 to the church on the left.

5 Camp St Malo

This gorgeous stone chapel, built upon a rocky outcrop and set against the magnificent backdrop of Mt Meeker (Longs Peak is just behind), might cause some drivers to wonder if they're seeing some sort of heavenly vision. Nope, it's a real church, dating back to 1935, and was even blessed by Pope John Paul II in 1993.

The Drive: Continue along Hwy 7 for 4.5 miles to Lily Lake.

6 Lily Lake

This highly photogenic spot is a great place to end the tour. This will be your first unimpeded view of the king of the park, Longs Peak, which rises magnificently to the southwest with its twin, Mt Meeker. A relaxing trail (0.8 miles) loops around the small lake.

STEAMBOAT SPRINGS

Steamboat Springs is America's original ski town, with a history that dates back to 1915, when the modest Howelsen Hill – named after the Flying Norseman, Carl Howelsen – first opened to the public. And indeed, the jumps at Howelsen have sent more athletes to the Winter Olympics than anywhere else in the country.

Today's resort is considerably larger than the trailblazing ski hill (still in operation), and the combination of abundant winter storms, a down-to-earth, old-timey rancher's charm, and one of the prettiest natural hot springs in the state keeps the regulars returning to this out-of-the-way corner. Shop for cowboy boots and Stetson hats in between powder-fueled days on the slopes, cozy up with a cup of coffee at the bookstore while planning an expedition into the little-known Flattops and Zirkel wilderness areas, or mellow out with a day fishing or floating on the Yampa River.

TOP TIP

Steamboat Springs consists of two major areas: the relatively regular grid of central Old Town, which straddles Lincoln Ave (US 40), and the newer warren of winding streets at Steamboat Village, centered on the Steamboat Mountain Resort ski area on Mt Werner southeast of town.

ACTIVITIES
1 Del's Triangle 3 Ranch
2 Old Town Hot Springs
3 Steamboat Springs Mountain Resort
4 Strawberry Park Natural Hot Springs
5 Yampa River

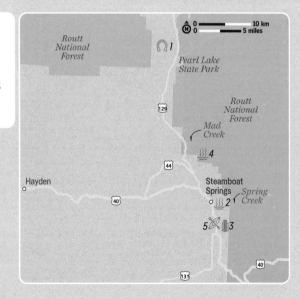

Chute 1, Steamboat

Skiing Steamboat

RIDE WITH THE OLYMPIANS

The 'Boat' is known for two things: glades and snow. Yes, you're thinking, all the resorts in the Rockies have snow. But Steamboat's famously light and fluffy powder, with storms blowing in from Wyoming and Utah, means the soft turns are virtually guaranteed. Throw in the cowboy-style charm and back-of-beyond location, and you have all the makings for a winter wonderland.

The stats speak for themselves: in total it's got 169 marked runs, 3668ft of vertical and nearly 3000 acres of terrain. While the summit only tops out at 10,568ft, Steamboat makes up for its dearth of high-altitude steeps with super-fun tree-slaloming runs: the gentle slopes and widely spaced aspens and spruce enable confident intermediate skiers to score first tracks in the glades with a touch less terror and a bit more grace than is generally possible.

HOWELSEN HILL SKI AREA

The continent's oldest ski area still in use and on the Colorado State Register of Historic Places, Howelsen is worth a gander simply to check out the aspiring Olympians vaulting off the jumps. And if you're a newbie skiier on a budget, this is a great place to practice: not only are lift tickets affordable, but they're even free on Sundays! Although there are only 14 runs, you can't beat the price.

There's also an indoor ice-skating facility, the Howelsen Ice Arena, which operates from October until April, in addition to 13 miles of cross-country trails.

In summer, check out the Howler Alpine Slide, an adrenaline-pumped rip down a 2400ft track.

 WHERE TO STAY IN STEAMBOAT

Rabbit Ears Motel
A diabolically chipper, pink-neon bunny welcomes guests at this simple roadside motel. $

Hotel Bristol
Small but sophisticated Western digs, with a ski shuttle, six-person indoor hot tub and downtown locale. $$

Vista Verde Guest Ranch
The most luxurious of Colorado's top-end guest ranches. If you have the means, this is it. $$$

BEST RESTAURANTS IN STEAMBOAT

Skull Creek Greek
From sheepherding to skiing: clever gyros and specialty pitas for hungry diners on a budget. $

Yampa Sandwich Company
This local sandwich chain is magic, and it opens early to sell boxed lunches. $

Rex's American Bar & Grill
Elk sausage, bison burgers and other carnivorous delights. $$

Laundry
Small plates, craft cocktails and pickled everything – arguably the best choice in town. $$$

Table 79
Great happy-hour specials, from buffalo cauliflower and tuna poke to portobello fries. $$$

LEFT: DAVID A LITMAN/SHUTTERSTOCK ©, BELOW RIGHT: VICKI L MILLER/SHUTTERSTOCK ©

Strawberry Park Hot Springs

Serious skiers will also dig a number of mogul runs on the hill, and although these runs are a virtual factory of Olympic skiers and snowboarders, you don't have to be world class to enjoy them. Wide, well-groomed runs are ideal cruising for intermediate skiers, making this mountain among Colorado's best all-rounders, particularly for families.

Want to nail some untracked lines? **Steamboat Powdercats**, a tried-and-true cat-skiing operator, offers guided backcountry tours on Buffalo Pass.

The **Ski Touring Center**, near the base of the resort, has excellent cross-country trails as well as home-cooked soups, chili and bread.

Healing Waters

STEAMBOAT'S HOT SPRINGS

Steamboat gets its name from the 150 natural springs in the area: one in particular was said to sound like a steamboat chugging up the Yampa River (civilization-starved French trappers clearly had fanciful imaginations). You can visit some

 WHERE TO SHOP IN STEAMBOAT SPRINGS

FM Light & Sons
This cowboy shop has been hawking Stetsons and boots since 1905.

Off the Beaten Path
Browse for books amid the fragrance of roasted coffee beans.

Ski Haus
Rent top-quality brands, buy used demo skis, and browse for camping gear.

of these mineral springs, collectively known to the Yampatika Ute as medicine waters, on a walk around town, but we recommend going straight to the good stuff: **Strawberry Park Hot Springs**.

Located 7 miles north of town, this is as idyllic as hot springs get, with a handful of natural outdoor pools set beside a rushing mountain stream and nothing but acres of wilderness surrounding you. Evening visits are particularly magical: whether you're treated to a meteor shower overhead or the molten silver of a full moon rising through the pines, soaking in the steaming pools – with the occasional plunge into the cool river – is a marvelously restorative experience. Note that after dark, it's adults only. In winter, you'll need AWD and snow tires to get here; if your vehicle isn't equipped, or it's a busy weekend, take the shuttle instead. Alternatively, consider staying the night in the rustic lodging. Entry reservations are required.

If you're with kids or prefer a less rustic environment, the **Old Town Hot Springs** is another option. Smack dab in the center of town, there's a 230ft waterslide, a climbing wall and even a lap pool.

Summer Adventures

HIT THE TRAILS

Come summertime, **Steamboat Mountain Resort** turns the mountain into a theme park, but the real highlight is the 50 miles of bermed-out mountain-bike trails. Rent a bike at the bottom, pay for a gondola ride and lay waste from the top. Even if you're a first-timer, this is really, really fun. Otherwise, **Spring Creek** and **Mad Creek** are just two of the singletrack highlights that flow through the stands of aspens around town; bike rentals are easy to find.

The **Yampa River** (pictured right) is another popular summer draw. **Bucking Rainbow Outfitters** runs a variety of half- and full-day raft trips, from Class II to Class IV, and also has the **Blue Sky West** tube shack right on the water if you're after a more mellow day. **Steamboat Flyfisher** is the area's best fly shop, and organizes guided fishing trips.

If you're interested in saddling up and experiencing the local cowboy culture, Del's Triangle 3 Ranch has both trail rides and pack trips in the **Routt National Forest**. They're located about 20 miles north of town.

THE TREAD OF PIONEERS MUSEUM

First opened in the Zimmerman House in 1959, this museum has a long history dedicated to the peoples and cultures of the Routt County.

Over the years, it has continued to expand, and is now situated in two turn-of-the-century Victorian homes (one relocated here in 1988).

With an intriguing mix of permanent and temporary exhibits, expect even-handed displays on Native American weavings, pottery and basketry, the evolution of skiing, an introduction to Steamboat and Western heritage, and a hands-on exhibit for kids.

Visitors can also take guided tours of the period-furnished ranch house. The museum is closed on Sundays and Mondays.

GETTING AROUND

Most people get into town by car from Denver via Rabbit Ears Pass on Hwy 40, though you can fly into Yampa Valley Regional Airport.

Steamboat Springs Transit runs a free bus service along Lincoln Ave, connecting to the ski resort.

Beyond Steamboat Springs

With wide-open skies and hills dappled with the shadows of passing clouds, Steamboat's surrounds are a slice of yesteryear Colorado.

Dotted with willow scrub and stands of bone-white aspens, their leaves blazing orange-gold in the fall, this untouched region of northern Colorado invites exploration. To the north lies the far-flung alpine charms of the Mt Zirkel Wilderness, part of the Routt National Forest that extends south from Wyoming. To the southwest is the often-overlooked Flat Tops Wilderness: a massive area of high volcanic plateaus, glacier-carved cirques, and grazing elk and sheep. If you want to get off the grid, this is an excellent choice.

Keep driving west along Hwy 40 and you'll eventually wind up in the hardscrabble Utah desert, where a rich trove of fossils awaits at National Dinosaur Monument.

TOP TIP

Many roads in this area are of the dirt and gravel variety, but still passable by 2WD cars. However, check first.

Devil's Causeway (p139)

MATT GRIMALDI/SHUTTERSTOCK ©

CALL POWELL/SHUTTERSTOCK ©

Gilpin Lake, Mt Zirkel Wilderness

Mt Zirkel Wilderness

BOBCATS, BEARS AND BALD EAGLES

One of the five original wilderness areas in Colorado, **Mt Zirkel Wilderness** is an untamed, roadless expanse dotted with icy glacial lakes and granite faces, and is rife with opportunities for isolated backcountry hiking and camping. It's intersected by the Continental Divide and two major rivers, the Elk and the Encampment. Locals swear by the **Zirkel Circle** hike, which connects Gilpin and Gold Creek Lakes in a glorious alpine trek over roughly 10 miles. It starts at the Slavonia Trailhead, about 30 miles (one hour) north of Steamboat.

Boldly rising from the center of the area is the 12,180ft **Mt Zirkel**, named by mountaineer Clarence King to honor the German geologist with whom he reconnoitered the country in 1874. Zirkel is a fantastic summit but a long excursion: at 18 miles with 4000ft of elevation gain, this is best done as a two-day trip.

THE MEEKER INCIDENT

Like much of the West, the Flat Tops has seen its share of bitter conflicts over resources.

The most infamous moment took place in 1879, when Indian agent Nathan Meeker attempted to convert the White River Utes to Christianity. When Meeker plowed up pasture lands used for grazing and horse racing, it was the last straw: the Utes retaliated and killed Meeker and 23 men, and took a number of women and children as hostages.

The consequences were devastating: political pressure from miners and other settlers had already been mounting to expel the Utes from Colorado, and following this incident, earlier treaties were rescinded and the majority of Natives were forcibly relocated to Utah.

 BEST CAMPSITES NEAR STEAMBOAT

Cold Springs Campground
Gorgeous spot in the Flat Tops. The larger Bear Lake and Horseshoe campgrounds are nearby. $

Seedhouse Campground
Twenty-four reservable sites in the Mt Zirkel Wilderness. It's 25 miles north of Steamboat. Water available. $

Summit Lake Campground
Cheap and only 13 miles from Steamboat, but the road is rough. No water. $

HAHNS PEAK

Twenty-seven miles north of Steamboat Springs is this quasi-ghost town.

Built on the windswept plain at the base of a 10,774ft extinct volcano, it was originally a gold camp (the German founder Joseph Hahn was predictably betrayed by one of his partners, who absconded with all the gold – be right back with more supplies! – and left him to starve to death during the first winter), and later the terminus of the Wyoming railroad.

In 1898, two famous outlaws from the Wild Bunch were jailed here in the 'Bear Cage,' which was not as fearsome as it sounds. They easily escaped, were just as easily recaptured, and then proceeded to escape again using a whittled gun covered with tinfoil.

Trappers Lake

Top hikes accessed easily from Steamboat include the **Mad Creek** (9 miles round-trip) and **Red Dirt** trails (12.7 miles round-trip); follow Elk River Rd north from Steamboat to the Mad Creek trailhead (7.5 miles) and Red Dirt trailhead (8.5 miles).

Detailed maps and information on hiking, mountain biking, fishing and other activities in this beautiful area are available at the **USFS Hahns Peak Ranger Office** off Hwy 40 in Steamboat.

The Flat Tops Wilderness

A GEOLOGICAL TOUR DE FORCE

Ready to check out a forgotten corner of Colorado? Drive 30 miles south from Steamboat through the historic ranching and railroad towns of Oak Creek and Yampa, and then take a hard right. Those mighty mesas looming ahead are the **Flat Tops**, the remnants of 52-million-year-old volcanic uplift and glacial erosion.

Today, a drive down the unpaved 83-mile scenic byway between Yampa and Meeker leads to trout-filled lakes,

 STATE PARKS NEAR STEAMBOAT

Pearl Lake State Park
This small alpine lake is a glorious spot for camping and canoeing; 26 miles north of Steamboat.

Steamboat Lake State Park
Boating, fishing and bird-watching near Pearl Lake State Park. Campsites and cabins.

Stagecoach State Park
On the edge of a large reservoir, 16 miles south of Steamboat. Convenient location.

LEFT: MIGHTYPIX/SHUTTERSTOCK ©. BELOW RIGHT: ZACK FRANK/SHUTTERSTOCK ©

backcountry campgrounds and herds of elk and sheep. Expect to spend a good three hours back here – more if you take the recommended detour to the otherworldly **Trappers Lake**, an excellent spot to pitch a tent and clamber up onto the surrounding plateaus. A popular backpacking trip that begins near Trappers is the **Chinese Wall** (#1803), which is often combined with other trails to form a 22.5-mile loop.

A slightly easier day out is via Stillwater Reservoir, only 16 unpaved miles southwest of Yampa. Just past the Cold Water Springs campground is the start of the spine-tingling **Devil's Causeway** hike (#1119), which climbs to a razor's edge ridge. As you inch your way across the rocky outcrop, you'll be treated to stupendous views of the cirques on either side, with sheer 600ft drop-offs in both directions. Although it's only 6 miles round-trip, at nearly 12,000ft, it'll feel like a lot more. Expect to spend the day.

Dinosaur National Monument

LONELY BONES

At the end of desolate stretches of blacktop in the sparsely populated northwest corner of the state, **Dinosaur National Monument** (pictured below right) is arguably Colorado's most remote destination, but for travelers fascinated by prehistoric life on earth it is worth every lonely mile. It's one of the few places on earth where you can reach out and touch a dinosaur skeleton, snarling in its final pose, petrified eternally in rock and stone.

The indoor highlight of the national monument, the **Dinosaur Quarry Wall**, shows off some 1500 dinosaur bones – you can see everything from allosaurus to diplodocus and stegosaurus. The Jurassic strata containing the fossils gives a glimpse of how paleontologists transform solid rock into the beautiful skeletons seen in museums, and how they develop scientifically reliable interpretations of life in the remote past. Follow this up with the **Fossil Discovery Trail** (wear sunscreen!) to the **Morrison Formation**, one of the most spectacular open-air collections of dinosaur bones in the world.

These two sights are both on the Utah side of the park, near Vernal. It's a solid 2½-hour drive from Grand Junction, and a touch longer from Steamboat.

GREEN RIVER RAFTING

The other main attraction in the area is the only source of water for miles around: the Green River, which eventually flows into the Colorado River in Canyonlands National Park, hundreds of miles south.

Head out into the riverine wilderness with Adrift Dinosaur on one-day rafting trips down Split Mountain Gorge; four-day expeditions to the Gates of Lodore; or five days down the Yampa Canyon. In Dinosaur National Monument itself, campgrounds shaded by groves of cottonwood trees bring welcome relief for sunblasted travelers.

If you're exploring this part of the world, it's worth considering the 60-mile trip north to the Flaming Gorge Reservoir, a popular recreation area in Utah that attracts boaters, fishers and campers.

GETTING AROUND

The Flat Tops are best accessed from Yampa, 30 miles south of town on Hwy 131. Mt Zirkel lies to the north along County Rd 129. For Dinosaur National Monument, it's a straight shot west along Hwy 40.

FORT COLLINS

Fort Collins will never be the brightest star in the Colorado firmament – in a state that stretches from the granite-packed superlatives of Rocky Mountain National Park to the whispers of the past in the piñon scrub of Mesa Verde, there are simply too many other destinations vying for a visitor's attention. But 'overlooked' suits this university town just fine: this is a place that feels as unpretentious and honest as you can get.

For travelers, Fort Collins is most likely to wind up on the itinerary if you're headed north or south on I-25. The exception, of course, is if you're a serious beer drinker. If that's the case, you'll already know that the town is home to more breweries than anywhere else in the state.

Outdoor adventures await at the Horsetooth Reservoir, Lory State Park, and along the undammed Cache la Poudre River.

TOP TIP

New Belgium, the town's most famous brewery, runs two styles of tours: the free 45-minute version (first-come, first-served) and the longer 90-minute tour, available for a fee. Make reservations well in advance if you're interested in the latter.

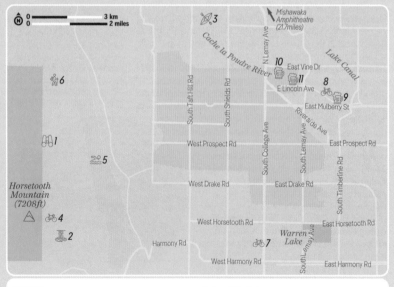

SIGHTS
1 Arthur's Rock
2 Horsetooth Waterfall

ACTIVITIES
3 Cache la Poudre River
4 Horsetooth Mountain Open Space
5 Horsetooth Reservoir
6 Lory State Park
7 Recycled Cycles – Pedago

DRINKING & NIGHTLIFE
8 Beer & Bike
9 Funkwerks
10 New Belgium Brewery
11 Odell Brewing Co

Cyclist, Tour de Fat

Beers & Bikes

TWO-WHEELED, HOP-POWERED FUN

In 1988, a Fort Collins engineer named Jeff Lebesch lugged a mountain bike and a beer-lover's pocket guide over to Belgium, cycled across the lowlands, jotted down some local beer-making tips and piqued Flemish curiosity with his bike's 'fat tires.' Three years later, Jeff and Kim Jordan co-founded the **New Belgium brewery** in their basement (first brews: Dubbel Abbey and Fat Tire), and the rest, as they say, is history.

In the decades since, Fort Collins has gone on to become a craft beer powerhouse, today accounting for over 20 breweries and 70% of the beer produced in Colorado.

Luckily for you, you don't have to get behind the wheel on your own personal Tour de Fat. Some 285 miles of bike lanes means that the town, and its outskirts, is a good spot for cyclists. Rent a cruiser at a bike shop like **Recycled Cycles – Pedago** has e-bikes – or try a brew cruise with **Beer & Bike**, and pedal your way from one vat of hops to the next.

East Lincoln Dr stretches from **Odell**, Fort Collin's first craft start-up (1989), to the saisons and wild sours of **Funkwerks**. College Ave, linking the delightful Old Town and university areas, packs in its own share of stops, from Equinox to Prost.

BEST BREWERIES IN FORT COLLINS

Odell
Twenty-one beers on tap, from classics to local faves and pilot projects.

New Belgium
Everyone knows Fat Tire, but don't miss the limited edition Belgian Reserves.

Horse and Dragon
Out-of-the-way favorite with convivial tasting room and patio.

Gilded Goat
Two locations to sample the Goat's taster trays and special releases.

Funkwerks
If you're a fan of farmhouse saisons and funky sours, this is the spot.

 WHERE TO STAY IN FORT COLLINS ─────────────

Fernweh Inn and Hostel
As charming as a B&B, with the perks of a hostel: kitchen, laundry and loaner bikes. **$**

Armstrong
Unique rooms in an elegantly renovated boutique hotel in the heart of Old Town. **$$**

Elizabeth Hotel
Quirky luxury option, with in-room record players and an instrument lending library. **$$$**

Easy Outdoor Escapes

WATER, ROCKS AND TRAILS

Located 4 miles west of Fort Collins is **Horsetooth Reservoir**, created in 1949 to provide a reliable water source for the region's farms. You can't actually see the 6.5-mile-long reservoir from town, as it's hidden by a high ridge on its east side, which was plugged with four massive dams.

Horsetooth is now the city's favorite recreation area, welcoming over 550,000 visitors annually. Swimming, motorboating, stand-up paddleboarding, kayaking, camping and fishing are all popular at designated beaches and coves along the shores. Rock climbing and bouldering sites can also be found along both the eastern and western banks of the reservoir.

On the southwest side of the reservoir is the **Horsetooth Mountain Open Space**, crisscrossed with 29 miles of hiking and biking trails. Popular destinations include **Horsetooth Falls** (2.5 miles round-trip) and the rocky outcrop of **Horsetooth Mountain** itself, which, according to legend, is the remains of a giant whose heart was cut twice by the Arapaho chief Maunamoku. The hike up to Horsetooth Mountain climbs 1300ft over 2.1 miles (one way).

At the northwestern side is **Lory State Park**, which has another 26 miles of trails. The most popular destination here is **Arthur's Rock** (3.4 miles round-trip), a prominent feature of the landscape with superb views over the reservoir. Backcountry camping is possible in Lory if you're looking for an easy getaway.

Cache la Poudre River

WET AND WILD

Colorado's only nationally designated wild and scenic river, the **Poudre** (rhymes with neuter) allegedly gets its name from a band of French trappers who, caught in a raging blizzard in the early 1800s on their way to Wyoming, lightened their wagons by burying a cache of gunpowder near the mouth of the river canyon.

White-water rafting is an awesome way to experience the intense beauty of the Poudre, and outfitters in town arrange for half-day trips on the lower section (Class 3, ages seven and up) and all-day trips starting in the more technical **Mishawaka Falls** section (Class 4, ages 13 and up).

 WHERE TO EAT IN FORT COLLINS

Ginger and Baker
A winning trifecta: rooftop wine bar, streetside cafe, and bakery and market. **$$**

Farmhouse at Jessup Farm
Local seasonal fare is the emphasis here, from pumpkin risotto to shepherd's pie. **$$**

Restaurant 415
Old Town hot spot serving salads, pizzas and more. Vegan and gluten-free options. **$$**

Poudre River

ARAPAHO NATIONAL WILDLIFE REFUGE

For birdwatchers, this is one of the best destinations in Colorado.

Nearly 200 species of bird frequent the summer sagebrush and wetlands of the Arapaho National Wildlife Refuge, 105 (long, if lovely) miles west of Fort Collins on Hwy 14, on the Cache la Poudre–North Park Scenic Byway.

The star of the show is the sage grouse and its spring mating ritual – the lek – an elaborate, territorial display of spiked tail feathers, puffy chests and nearly comical braggadocio. But you may also spot pronghorn antelope, coyote, moose and elk.

If you're visiting the refuge or its surrounding back-country, the dusty hamlet of Walden is the nearest place for a hot shower and decent shelter.

Hwy 14 through the river canyon also qualifies as a scenic byway, and driving upstream reveals one bend after another filled with wild sights, from rock climbers ascending the cliffsides to bighorn sheep doing the same thing – but without ropes.

In addition to a handful of trailheads and superb campsites, the canyon also holds an awesome human-made attraction, the **Mishawaka Amphitheatre**, roughly 24 miles from town. Walter Thompson first built his incredible venue in 1916, and the spirit of the place – restaurant, bar and music hall – remains over a century later.

 GETTING AROUND

Fort Collins is 65 miles north of Denver, off I-25. It's 46 miles from Boulder, and 41 miles from Estes Park.

Fort Collins is a very bike-friendly city, but short-term bike rentals are limited. Try Recycled Cycles or Pedago for e-bikes. Outside of the downtown area, however, it's best to have your own car, even for nearby excursions to the reservoir.

VAIL, ASPEN & CENTRAL COLORADO

LIFE AT 110%

Brave the white-knuckle drive through a raging winter storm and you'll be blessed the morning after with a snow-kissed trip to heaven.

Denver

Spend enough time here, and eventually you'll hear it: that wild, uninhibited shriek of pure joy as someone, somewhere, launches themselves off the top of something insanely steep and into the void. They might be on a snowboard or a mountain bike, strapped into a paraglider or attached to a rope. But whatever it is that they're doing, you can be sure that that primal scream – that momentary release from all of life's weight upon their shoulders – is the same cry that echoes in dozens of valleys across the Rockies. Ski bum or millionaire, Olympic athlete or unknown kid, moments like these are ones that we all can share. Indeed, moments like these are the reason that so many people come here and, in some cases, never leave.

But there's more to it than supercharged fun. Back in camp, as evening falls and the fire flickers beneath the vastness of the night sky – when the sudden snap of a branch beyond the circle of light catches our full attention – these, too, are moments when we feel uniquely alive. It's in the ragged Elk Mountains outside Aspen (pictured left) and the mesmerizing swirl of the Arkansas River near Salida. The silence of falling snow atop Vail Mountain and a stranger's smile in Carbondale. If you're lucky enough to catch sight of it, don't forget to smile back.

Welcome to the Colorado Rockies.

TETRA IMAGES/ALAMY STOCK PHOTO ©

THE MAIN AREAS

IDAHO SPRINGS
Denver day trips.
p150

WINTER PARK
Ski like a local.
p156

BRECKENRIDGE & SUMMIT COUNTY
Four unique resorts.
p160

JOHN P KELLY/GETTY IMAGES ©

Breckenridge (p160)

VAIL	**ASPEN**	**SALIDA & THE ARKANSAS RIVER VALLEY**
Big powder, big fun.	Beautiful landscapes, beautiful people.	River-running, bike-pedaling adventure.
p172	**p183**	**p197**

Find Your Way

I-70 is Colorado's aorta, running straight through the center of the mountains. Unless you fly to Aspen or Vail, you can't avoid it – expect lots of traffic, especially on the weekends.

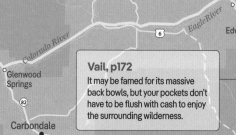

Vail, p172

It may be famed for its massive back bowls, but your pockets don't have to be flush with cash to enjoy the surrounding wilderness.

SHUTTLE

Private shuttles, like the Epic Mountain Express and Home James Transportation, run directly between Denver International Airport and most ski resorts.

BUS

The public Bustang runs from Denver's Union Station to Frisco, Vail and Glenwood Springs. Excellent bus networks (usually free) serve all the communities in the mountain counties, allowing you to get between the slopes, town and your accommodations with minimum hassle.

CAR

If you're only here to ski, a car will be more hassle than it's worth. If you've got other plans, however – hiking, biking, ghost towns – an AWD vehicle is best. Parking, bad weather and traffic can be a headache.

Aspen, p183

From Independence Pass to the Maroon Bells to the Hotel Jerome, this is Colorado at its most sublime and glamorous.

Glenwood Springs

Carbondale

Basalt

Redstone

Snowmass Village

Aspen

Maroon Bells-Snowmass Wilderness

Maroon Lake

Buckskin Pass

Marble

Maroon Bells (14,163ft)

Crystal

Ashcroft

Raggeds Wilderness

Gunnison National Forest

Kebler Pass (9,9980ft)

Crested Butte

Colorado River

Eagle River

Wolcott

Edwa

Gunnison

0   20 km
0   10 miles

THE GUIDE

VAIL, ASPEN & CENTRAL COLORADO

Winter Park, p156
Mountain fun that's easily accessed from Denver or the west side of Rocky Mountain National Park.

Idaho Springs, p150
Tour a gold mine, drive up a fourteener or hike to a glacier – and be back in Denver in time for dinner.

Breckenridge & Summit County, p160
Home to four ski resorts and historic Breckenridge, the aptly named Summit County is packed with sky-scraping alpine adventure year-round.

Salida & the Arkansas River, p197
The snow-capped Collegiate Peaks form the backdrop to one of the most popular stretches of white water in the country.

Map labels:
Fraser, Nederland, Indian Peaks Wilderness Area, Winter Park, James Peak (13,294ft), Central City, Vasquez Peak Wilderness, St Mary's Glacier, Clear Creek, Idaho Springs, Jones Pass, Berthoud Pass (11,315ft), Empire, Georgetown, Eagles Nest Wilderness, Ptarmigan Peak Wilderness, Mt Goliath Natural Area, Vail, Loveland Pass, Mt Evans (Mt Blue Sky), Summit Lake, Silverthorne, Dillon, Eagle-Vail, Vail Mountain, Shrine Pass, Dillon Reservoir, Keystone, Guanella Pass, Mt Bierstadt (14,060ft), Minturn, Frisco, Copper Mountain, Holy Cross Wilderness, Red Cliff, Vail Pass, Breckenridge, Mt Evans Wilderness, Mt of the Holy Cross (14,005ft), Quandary Peak (14,265ft), Boreas Pass (11,481ft), Grant, Bailey, Tennessee Pass, Fremont Pass, Hoosier Pass (11,541ft), Alma, Leadville, Fairplay, Mt Massive (14,421ft), Mt Elbert (14,433ft), Twin Lakes, Independence Pass (12,095ft), Twin Lakes Reservoir, Buffalo Peaks Wilderness, Antero Reservoir, Continental Divide, Collegiate Peaks, Collegiate Peaks Wilderness, Cottonwood Pass (12,126ft), Buena Vista, Mt Princeton (14,197ft), Nathrop, St Elmo, San Isabel National Forest, Monarch Pass (11,312ft), Monarch Crest Trail, Poncha Springs, Salida, Colorado Trail, Arkansas River

147

Plan Your Time

How you plan your time will largely depend on whether you're here in summer or winter. Regardless, leave yourself at least a day to get acclimatized – most towns are a minimum 8000ft above sea level.

Summertime, Vail (p175)

If You Only Do One Thing

Skiing made Colorado the destination it is today, and if we had to pick how to spend one perfect blue-sky day, it would be on the slopes. While each resort has its own distinct personality, when push comes to shove, they all deliver the goods – that is, fresh powder and spectacular scenery. There's no need to complicate your life: eat a big breakfast, grab your skis or board, and hop on the nearest chairlift. Ride until you run out of steam. Then cruise down to town for dinner, margaritas and a soak in the hot tub.

Seasonal Highlights

In winter and early spring, it's all about the snow. Summer in the high country comes later (late June–August), but cooler temperatures make this an ideal time to visit.

JANUARY
The **International Snow Sculpture Championship** brings temporal art to Breckenridge. Winter storms are dumping powder across the Rockies.

APRIL
The ski season is coming to a close, and festivals like **Winter Park's Spring Bash and Splash** herald outdoor concerts and wacky competitions.

JUNE
The rivers are raging and paddling season is underway, celebrated with **FIBArk** in Salida, the nation's oldest white-water festival.

FROM LEFT: FAINA GUREVICH/SHUTTERSTOCK ©, BELOZOROVA ELENA/SHUTTERSTOCK ©, ARTUR DIDYK/SHUTTERSTOCK ©

Three Days to Travel

In summer, there's more reason to explore. Start with a day in **Breckenridge** (p160) hiking, biking or panning for gold, or head up to **A-Basin** (p170) to scramble up the continent's highest via ferrata (13,000ft).

The next day, cross **Vail Pass** (p168) on the way to historic Leadville, via Minturn, Camp Hale National Monument and **Tennessee Pass** (p181).

In **Leadville** (p181), rent a bike and pedal the **Mineral Belt loop** (p181) – or some wicked fast singletrack – while your body adjusts to life at 10,000ft.

The following day, tackle **Mt Elbert** (p187), the state's highest peak, cross **Independence Pass** (p179) to **Aspen** (p183) or enjoy white-water thrills in **Salida** (p197).

Three Days in Aspen

Day One

Tour the historic downtown in the morning, followed by a hike beneath the Maroon Bells and a log-cabin dinner in **Ashcroft** (p185).

Day Two

Spend an hour or two in one of the town's museums, then take a down-valley bike ride on the **Rio Grande Trail** (p192) or adrenaline-piqued mountain biking at **Snowmass** (p185).

Day Three

Drive to historic **Redstone** (p195) and the ghost town of **Crystal** (p196), capped off with a hot springs soak at **Avalanche Ranch** (p195) or **Glenwood Springs** (p191). Finish with a drive up **Independence Pass** (p179), stopping to hike at the **Grottos** or **Lost Man trails** (p195), and then on to Vail (north) or Salida (south).

JULY

The high country is snow-free, wildflowers are blooming and the **Aspen Music Festival** (p187) kicks off the peak summer season.

AUGUST

Hundred-mile high-altitude ultramarathons and 24-hour mountain-bike-till-you-drop races in **Leadville** (p181)? Now that's a vacation.

OCTOBER

Aspens blaze gold across the state; it's a fabulous time for one last road trip before the snow begins.

DECEMBER

Ullr Fest in Breck celebrates the god of snow while **Snow Days** brings live music to Vail. Ski season has begun!

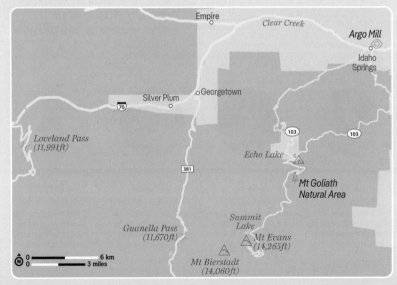

IDAHO SPRINGS

If you're only in Denver for a limited time, you can barrel up the road to Idaho Springs for a quick taste of Colorado's rough-and-tumble gold-rush history. The rowdy gaggle of prospectors, gunslingers and rapscallions who dashed here to get rich in 1859 – all part of the larger Pike's Peak Gold Rush – have been (mostly) replaced by a notably more genteel crowd of day-tripping skiers, hikers and bikers on blindingly chromed-up Harleys, but the historic buildings along Miner St retain the creaking floors and antique character of the city's colorful past.

To the south of town rises Mt Evans (in the process of being renamed), one of the dominant landmarks of the Front Range and visible from Denver. Evans, together with Pikes Peak, is just one of two fourteeners you can drive up and is the highest paved road in North America.

TOP TIP

I-70's mountain stretch – particularly during ski season – often resembles more of a parking lot than a highway. On weekends, we strongly recommend avoiding peak times (6am to 9am westbound; 2pm to 6pm eastbound), but always check traffic conditions before setting out. Snow can be treacherous; make sure your vehicle is equipped for bad weather.

SERENETHOS/SHUTTERSTOCK ©

Argo Mill

INDIAN SPRINGS

When gold was first discovered in Idaho Springs, it was thanks to these hot springs, which must have seemed heaven-sent on a frigid winter day. Today, these mineral waters are the closest soak to Denver, and while they can't compare with other Colorado locales, few will argue with their convenience.

Some 60,000 gallons of hot water emerge here daily, enough for the resort to have a variety of different soaking experiences. The main area is a family-style heated swimming pool that sits beneath a translucent dome and is surrounded by tropical plants.

More serious hot springs aficionados may prefer the clothing-optional geothermal pools, which are located in underground steam caves.

Gold Rush Legacy

IDAHO SPRINGS OR BUST

The year 1859 marked the beginning of the Pike's Peak Gold Rush, and while many early prospectors congregated along the South Platte River, the territory's first big find was made in **Idaho Springs**. On a cold January day, steam rising from nearby hot springs attracted one George Jackson, who proceeded to stumble upon placer gold in Clear Creek. Like many a miner, he hoped to keep his find a secret, but it wasn't long before the word was out and claims were filling the valley.

With the dozens of mines that sprung up in the area came the **Argo Mill** – that's the huge red building on the hill above town. Tours of the Argo explain how mills separate precious ore from waste rock, in addition to taking visitors inside the

 WHERE TO EAT IN IDAHO SPRINGS

Smokin' Yards BBQ
Texas-style brisket and Carolina pulled pork ensure the parking lot here is perpetually full. **$**

Main Street Restaurant
Dependable diner, with breakfast burritos, omelets, massive pancakes, burgers and BLTs. **$**

Clear Creek Cidery
Cider flights and Sonoran-style grub, from chimi-changas to Oh-My-Gawd green chili. **$$**

ST MARY'S GLACIER

Wildflowers and wind-swept trails, boulders and snowfields – these are the disproportionately big rewards for the easy hike up to St Mary's Glacier. The modest elevation gains, short distance (half-mile) and summer snow make it ideal even for the littlest hikers. Although the area gets fairly busy on summer weekends, the views are remarkable, and a scramble around the lake will bring you to the 'glacier' itself.

If you want to make a day of it, the trail to James Peak (13,294ft) continues up another 3 miles past the base of the snowfield to the summit. It was named after the botanist Edwin James, who made the first recorded summit of Pikes Peak in 1820.

incredible 4.2-mile transport and drainage tunnel that connected to Central City. If you've ever wondered why the US Mint has a branch in Denver, the amount of ore that once came out of mills like the Argo is your answer.

Other sights in the area include the Phoenix Mine, whose tour gets you underground for 45 minutes, followed by a gold-panning session.

Mt Evans Scenic Byway

MT BLUE SKY

Less than an hour west of Denver's skyscrapers is **Mt Evans** (14,265ft). From Idaho Springs to the summit, the road ascends roughly 6600ft in altitude over 28 miles, passing through montane, subalpine and tundra ecosystems. One stop you don't want to miss is the **Mt Goliath Natural Area** (11,540ft; park at the Dos Chappell Nature Center), where you can check out some of the oldest living organisms on the planet: the gnarled, wind-sculpted bristlecone pine. The trees here range from 900 to 2000 years old.

Continuing on the road past **Summit Lake**, which freezes solid in winter, you're likely to encounter Rocky Mountain goats and bighorn sheep. From the parking lot (pictured below) it's then a short but lung-busting scramble to the summit's transcendent views.

The highway is only open from June to September; reserve your entrance tickets one month in advance. There's a campground at **Echo Lake**, just before the fee station.

Mt Evans was originally named after the Colorado Territory's second governor, John Evans, who played a key role in the 1864 **Sand Creek Massacre**, during which an estimated 150 Arapaho and Cheyenne – mostly women and children – were killed by the US Cavalry. A proposal to rename the peak Mt Blue Sky, in honor of Colorado's Indigenous population, was underway at the time of writing.

GETTING AROUND

Almost halfway between Denver and several big ski resorts along I-70, Idaho Springs makes for a good pit stop. Take exit 240 for the main downtown area and Mt Evans. St Mary's Glacier is just west of town at exit 238 (Fall River Rd).

Beyond Idaho Springs

Before you motor on through this stretch of I-70, consider a stop in Georgetown or Loveland Pass.

Day-trippers who are yearning for a quality mountain adventure, but have limited time in the Mile High City, will want to consider these easy escapes in the Front Range. Both Guanella Pass (accessed from Georgetown) and Loveland Pass slingshot drivers into the high country, and in summer make for remarkably convenient trailheads for high-altitude hikes.

Guanella Pass in particular packs in everything you could want from a scenic byway: wildlife, mellow walks, campgrounds and one of the Front Range's most popular fourteeners, Mt Bierstadt. While accomplished mountaineers will find this particular summit crowded, the gentle grade and festive atmosphere make this a great choice for first-timers.

TOP TIP

If you plan on hiking near Guanella Pass, arrive at dawn in order to secure a parking spot.

Loveland Pass (p155)

GEORGETOWN LOOP RAILROAD

For the full silver-mining experience, hop on the Georgetown Loop Railroad, once part of a system that snaked through Clear Creek Canyon to connect Denver with rich mines in Silver Plume.

Chugging along this loop is an entertaining way to leave the I-70 corridor and enjoy expansive views over Clear Creek Valley. The ride is short – only 15 minutes each way, with a pause to tour a mine in between – but the scenery from one of the open passenger cars can make for a breathtaking, if chilly, afternoon.

Themed events, seasonal packages and add-ons such as tours of the Lebanon Silver Mine also feature. Plan on spending about half a day. Book ahead.

Georgetown Loop Railroad

Historic Homes in Georgetown

A SILVER MINER'S DREAMS

Smaller and more soulful than Idaho Springs, historic **Georgetown** has a mix of Victorian architecture, second-hand bookstores and cafes that make it a pleasant stopover on the way up or down I-70. At the end of 6th St (the main drag) is the 1875 **Hotel de Paris**, opened by the mysterious Frenchman Louis Dupuy. Tours take visitors through 23 furnished rooms, filled with luxury furnishings. The 1867 **Hamill House** also offers tours of the one-time private residence of a silver-mine owner, providing a glimpse of upscale tastes in 19th-century Colorado. The most distinctive landmark in Georgetown (not open to the public) is the all-important 1875 **Alpine Hose No. 2 Firehouse**, with a white clapboard facade and distinctive square belltower, where hoses were once dried.

 WHERE TO EAT IN GEORGETOWN

Georgetown Coffee and Tea
For a pastry and a pick-me-up. $

Cabin Creek Brewing
Lakeside views, small-batch beers and the usual run of pub grub. $$

Coopers on the Creek
From elk tartare to duck poutine, this is the most stylish choice for famished hikers and skiers. $$

Driving Loveland Pass

ROCKY MOUNTAIN HIGH

The alpine scenery in the Front Range is breathtaking enough, but it's not until you make it to **Loveland Pass** (11,990ft) that you really begin to feel that Rocky Mountain magic. The gateway to Summit County, the pass is flanked by a ski resort on either side – Loveland and Arapahoe Basin – and offers easy access to high-altitude hiking in the summer months.

The opening of the Eisenhower Tunnel in 1973 made the pass more of a scenic detour than a necessity, but if you're not in a rush, the hairpin turns bring inspiring views. It remains open year-round, though it can be treacherous in winter and will close in bad weather.

Accessible from the Loveland Pass parking lot, the steep, 2-mile jaunt to **Mt Sniktau** (13,234ft) is a convenient way to experience the thrill of alpine hiking. If you barely broke a sweat on the way up, extend your day by following the ridge in the other direction to **Grizzly Peak** (13,427ft).

Guanella Pass Scenic Byway

FOURTEENERS AND ALPINE LAKES

Built atop an old wagon road that once connected the silver-mining towns of Georgetown and Grant, this 22-mile drive (11 miles to the pass) climbs up to 11,669ft, and is an excellent staging point for fishing excursions and several alpine hikes. Sightings of bighorn sheep and mountain goats are not uncommon.

From the pass, you can ascend **Mt Bierstadt** (14,060ft; 7 miles round-trip), one of the most popular and accessible fourteeners along the Front Range. A shorter and less-crowded option is **Silver Dollar Lake** (3 miles round-trip; pictured right): this inspiring trail is mostly above the tree line and graced with thousands of tiny wildflowers in summer. The trailhead is located just past **Guanella Pass Campground**, at 11,000ft. The pass itself closes in winter, though the road is usually plowed past the Silver Dollar Lake trailhead.

GETTING AROUND

Georgetown and Guanella Pass are 45 miles west of Denver, off I-70. The exit for the Loveland Ski Resort and Pass is located just before the Eisenhower Tunnel.

155

WINTER PARK

Winter Park   ◉ Denver

When everyone else is stuck in traffic on I-70, those in the know will veer off the interstate for Hwy 40, making the climb over Berthoud Pass and down into Winter Park. Located less than two hours from Denver, this unpretentious resort is a favorite with Front Rangers, who drive here to ski fresh tracks each weekend. Beginners can frolic on miles of heavily trafficked groomers, while experts test their skills on Mary Jane's SUV-sized bumps. For skiers with disabilities, the resort also offers one of the best adaptive skiing programs in the US.

The congenial oh-so-slightly 1970s town is a wonderful base for year-round romping. Most services are found either in the ski village, which is a mile south of Winter Park proper, or strung along US 40 (the main drag). Follow Hwy 40 and you'll get to Fraser, Tabernash and the back side of Rocky Mountain National Park.

TOP TIP

Winter Park gets kudos for being one of the few big ski resorts to offer free parking near the base of the mountain. Coveted spots near Mary Jane fill up fast, so be sure to arrive early. The Vintage Lot is the main paid parking area.

Ski lift, Winter Park

ELLEN BARONE/ALAMY STOCK PHOTO ©

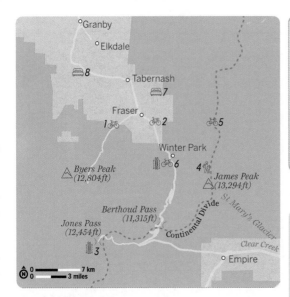

ACTIVITIES
1 Creekside/Flume Loop Trail
2 Fraser River Trail
3 Powder Addiction
4 Rodgers Pass
5 Rollins Pass
6 Winter Park Resort/ Trestle Bike Park

SLEEPING
7 Devil's Thumb Ranch
8 Snow Mountain Ranch

Ski the Bumps

WHEN IT HURTS SO GOOD

Winter Park encompasses seven main territories and has a maximum vertical drop of more than 3000ft. It's most famous for the leg-crushing moguls on **Mary Jane**, though there's plenty more here to explore. Intermediate skiers can get above the tree line in the **Parsenn Bowl** (12,060ft), while experts will drop over the other side of the ridge to the glades of **Eagle Wind** or the off-piste chutes and cliffs in the **Vasquez Cirque**. Roughly one-third of the main Winter Park mountain is groomed for greenies – and the addition of red wagons in which to tote the kids' skis is a nice touch as well.

Slopestyle fans will enjoy the seven terrain parks: you can learn to ride rails and pipes at **Starter**, kick it up a notch at **Ash Cat**, or catch big air in the **Rail Yard**. Other winter activities include a tubing hill, a small skating rink, ski bikes, snowshoeing and sunset s'mores snowcat tours.

On the other side of Berthoud Pass and only 45 minutes from Denver, **Powder Addiction** provides snowcat-accessed backcountry skiing off Jones Pass. Avalanche gear, skis/boards, lunch and beer are included.

BERTHOUD PASS

The site of one of Colorado's first ski resorts (1937–2002), Berthoud Pass (11,307ft) remains a popular spot for backcountry skiers and snowshoers, with over 50 lines and 25 miles of descent, spread evenly over blue and black runs. There is significant avalanche danger here, however, so don't even think about going out unless you have the proper gear and training. Friends of Berthoud Pass offers free avalanche courses in winter.

The pass is also a great place to get on the Continental Divide Trail in summer. Stanley Mountain (12,521ft) is a 7-mile round-trip hike; from the parking lot, cross the highway to access the trail.

 WHERE TO STAY IN WINTER PARK

Snow Mountain Ranch	Trailhead Inn	Devil's Thumb Ranch
The YMCA has the best family digs around, from yurts to cabins and hotel rooms. **$**	Excellent midrange option, with reclaimed-timber decor and wildlife watercolors on the walls. **$$**	The cowboy-chic lodge is a must for a romantic weekend escape. **$$$**

THE SKI TRAIN

The Rockies may have better snow than the Alps, but they definitely can't compete with the romance of throwing your snowboard on a TGV in Paris and waking up a few hours later in snow-covered Bourg-St-Maurice. Voilà – no traffic-clogged highways necessary.

The sole exception to this is Winter Park, Colorado's only ski resort served by train. The Winter Park Express runs from Denver's Union Station direct to the slopes, passing through 31 tunnels on the way. The service operates Friday to Sunday, January through April. And if you're flying into DIA, the A-Line to Union Station guarantees a seamless rails-to-resort experience.

LEFT: CHRIS SELBY/ALAMY STOCK PHOTO ©. BELOW RIGHT: EXCELLENTALS/SHUTTERSTOCK ©

Mountain biking

ROCKY MOUNTAIN NATIONAL PARK

Winter Park is the perfect base from which to explore Grand Lake and the little-visited western entrance to **Rocky Mountain National Park** (p118), a mere 35 miles north.

Summer Sports

TWO-WHEELED THRILLS

When the temperature begins to rise, hiking and biking rule. The paved 5.5-mile **Fraser River Trail** runs through the valley, from the ski resort to Fraser, connecting to 600 miles of mountain bike trails.

If you don't want to sweat the uphills, head to the **Trestle Bike Park**, the ski resort's summer incarnation, which features three lifts and over 40 miles of free-ride trails for all levels. For something slightly more tame, try out the **Creekside/Flume Loop**, a 5-mile trail that mixes easy green and blue singletrack, with minimal climbing.

On the other hand, if you *do* want a workout, then give **Rollins Pass** a go. This popular though rugged 14-mile 4WD road leads almost to the top of the 11,660ft pass (now closed), which is famous for its railroad history. In the mid-1860s, JA Rollins established a toll wagon-road over the pass from Nederland and Rollinsville; early

 WHERE TO CAMP IN WINTER PARK

Idlewild Campground
Not the most secluded spot, but it's an awesome location for mountain bikers. $

Robber's Roost
Five miles outside of town on the road up to Berthoud Pass, with 11 sites. No water. $

Broome Hut
The first cabin in the Grand Huts backcountry system linking to Grand Lake. Reserve. $

in the 20th century David H Moffat's Denver, Northwestern & Pacific Railway crossed the Continental Divide here.

First known as Boulder Pass, then Rollins Pass, it also earned the appellation 'Corona' because railroad workers considered it the crown at the 'top of the world.' Remnants of the original line (a tunnel and trestle) make it of particular interest to railroad buffs. Bikepackers refer to this route as the Indian Peaks Traverse (take it all the way into Nederland or Boulder), but there's plenty of hiking to do up here too. The traverse to **Rodgers Pass** (5 miles round-trip) from the trestle is both mellow and beautiful. From here, you can easily summit the west side of **James Peak** (13,294ft).

The turnoff for Rollins Pass is located between the Winter Park resort and town; the road is extremely rocky and you definitely need AWD and high clearance. When you reach an intersection on the way up, keep going straight. Bear in mind that the last couple of miles probably won't open until July at the earliest because of snowpack.

Ranch Life

RIDE THE RANGE

For an all-inclusive getaway, consider spending the night at one of the valley's ranches. **Devil's Thumb Ranch**, the classiest digs in the Winter Park area, offers an abundance of outdoor adventure, all of which is open to the public. In winter Nordic fiends descend for a scenic 65-mile network of groomed cross-country trails. Lessons and rentals are available, and they offer ice skating and fat biking too. In the summer it's all about the horseback riding and mountain biking on 5000 acres of Colorado high country. Youngsters will enjoy the 1600ft zip line and hatchet throwing, while anglers are practically guaranteed a catch on a guided tour.

The nearby **Snow Mountain Ranch**, run by the YMCA, is the slightly cheaper version: 60 miles of cross-country trails in winter (rental equipment available), plus tubing, fat biking and even dog sledding. In summer, activities morph into horseback riding, mountain biking and climbing and challenge courses. Sleeping options range from yurts and campsites to fully furnished cabins and hotel rooms.

BEST RESTAURANTS IN WINTER PARK

Pepe Osaka's Fish Taco
You like sushi. You like fish tacos. And as it turns out, you love sushi tacos, because...why not? $$

Randi's Irish Grill and Pub
Field-to-fork ethos meets all your pub favorites. Oh yeah, there's beer too. $$

Idlewild Spirits
Excellent cocktails made from their own spirits, plus small plates to munch on. $$

Fontenot's Seafood & Grill
Bringin' New Orleans' tasty brand of seafood love to the mountains. $$

Tabernash Tavern
Fresh local ingredients and a creative kitchen makes the Tavern tops. $$$

Devil's Thumb

GETTING AROUND

Winter Park is 70 miles west of Denver; turn on to Hwy 40 at the little town of Empire. Home James Transportation runs a shuttle from DIA. Winter Park's free shuttle system, the Lift (wpgov.com), runs from the ski resort through town to Fraser; buses come every 10 to 15 minutes from 7:30am to 2am (hours vary with the season).

BRECKENRIDGE & SUMMIT COUNTY

Denver

Breckenridge

When it comes to ski towns with a soul, Breckenridge is near the top of the list. The colorful Victorian architecture recalls its origins as a rough-and-tumble mining outpost, and reminders of 19th-century fortune-seekers are still scattered throughout the area. But while summer visitors may be eager to try out panning for gold, there's really no debating it: wintertime rules.

That's when you'll see the real crowds: from ski bums to young families clomping down Main St, all eyes cast on the hulking Tenmile Range. And that's Breck for you – with a four-chairlift combo and a snap of your fingers, you'll be all the way at the top of Peak 8, where the turns are silky smooth and the views go on forever. And when the distant horizon fades from pink to blue to black, it's time to retreat to the hot tub and contemplate the Milky Way, arcing silently overhead.

TOP TIP

Breck is not big, and you can easily walk to everything on Main St and the parallel Ridge St (even in ski boots). Parking is limited, however, and traffic can be hellacious in winter, so leave the car at your accommodations or in one of the skier lots.

Breckenridge

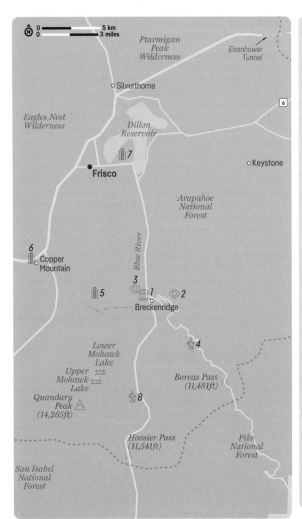

WHAT'S IN A NAME?

George Spencer officially founded the town of Breckenridge in November 1859 as a base camp for miners.

Allegedly, he originally named the town 'Breckinridge' after the USA's sitting vice president, John C. Breckinridge of Kentucky. It was sheer flattery, of course. Spencer wanted a post office and, politicians being politicians, he was rewarded with the first post office between the Continental Divide and Salt Lake City, Utah.

But when the Civil War broke out in 1861, and the vice president became a brigadier general in the Confederate army, the decidedly pro-Union citizens of Breckinridge decided to change the town's name. the 'i' became an 'e,' and has been Breckenridge ever since.

SIGHTS
1 Barney Ford Museum
2 Country Boy Mine
3 Lomax Placer Mine

ACTIVITIES
4 Baker's Tank
5 Breckenridge Ski Resort
6 Copper Mountain
7 Frisco Nordic Center
8 McCullough Gulch

**Old wagon,
Country Boy Mine (p163)**

EPIC DISCOVERY

Breck's eco-minded summer fun park combines learning about the local ecosystems with a laundry list of made-for-thrills activities: big-air bungee trampoline, climbing walls, ropes course, a zip-line tour, three alpine slides and the 2500ft forest coaster.

Mountain bikers can haul their bikes up the Colorado Super Chair from the base of Peak 8 to the 11,000ft Vista Haus summit and cruise (or fly, depending on the run) down one of 11 designated trails, two of which wander over to Peak 9. You can rent bikes at the base of Peak 8 or in town; rental shops will be able to suggest plenty of other rides, as there are over 200 miles of mountain-bike trails in the area.

History Tour

COLORFUL CHARACTERS

Breckenridge has come a long way since its days as a makeshift 1860s mining camp, but you can still get a sense of some of the characters who once lived here. When touring the town, the first stop should be the **visitor center** on Main St, which has a small but excellent free museum.

From here, head over to the **Barney Ford Museum**. Ford was an escaped slave who became a prominent entrepreneur and Colorado civil-rights pioneer, and made two stops in Breckenridge, where he ran a 24-hour chopstand serving delicacies such as oysters. He also owned a restaurant and hotel in Denver. The museum is set in his old home, where he lived from 1882 to 1890.

Next is the **Edwin Carter Discovery Center**, which introduces the life of a Pike's Peak Gold Rush prospector who first arrived in Breck in 1860. An original environmentalist, Carter noticed the impact of mining on wildlife early on, documenting genetic deformities that he suspected were linked to leaching toxins. He eventually became a taxidermist to preserve the wildlife he encountered in the area, and his collection grew to some 3300 pieces, which were displayed in his house (now the museum). After he died, the majority of his collection became the original foundation of the **Denver Museum of Nature & Science** (p79).

Skiing from Breck

NO FRIENDS ON POWDER DAYS

When Main St is at 9600ft and the peaks are so plentiful that the founders went with numbers over names, you know the skiing is going to be good. The resort spans Peaks 6 to 10, and thanks to the long and relatively flat green runs down low, Breck has always been known as a great family mountain. Beginners won't want to miss runs like Silverthorne and Red Rover. But if you're ready to step it up a notch, don't fret – there are plenty of thrilling diversions higher up.

A favorite intermediate or 'blue' run is Cashier on Peak 9. Another great intermediate run on **Peak 7** is Wire Patch, featuring a series of 'rollers' – mini-hills, not moguls. **Peak 6** offers access to two intermediate bowls above the tree line. Brave the gusting wind and take the creaking T-bar from Peak 7 or Peak 8, which pulls skiers to the single-black terrain of the **North Bowl** and the double-black bumps in the **Horseshoe Bowl**. And once you've got your snow legs under you, don't

 WHERE TO STAY IN BRECKENRIDGE

Bivvi Hostel
A modern hostel with a log-cabin vibe, the Bivvi wins points for style, friendliness and affordability. $

Fireside Inn
This long-running hostel and B&B has cozy private rooms and dorms, plus the requisite hot tub. $

Lodge at Breckenridge
High above town off Boreas Pass Rd, this hotel's draw is the breathtaking panoramas. $$$

Peak 8

BACKCOUNTRY HUT TRIPS

For some, back-country skiing is what it's all about: pristine snow, all-pervading quiet and the magic of waking up in the wilderness on a winter's day.

If you're keen, look into the Summit Huts Association, which operates five huts, which are accessible in winter by ski and snowshoe, and usually sleep around 20 people. All have amenities such as wood-burning stoves, full kitchens and solar-powered lights; in addition, three have wood-burning saunas.

The most popular hut is Francie's Cabin, a great choice for first-timers (though all groups should have at least one experienced, avalanche-trained member). Note that you will need to enter a lottery in March to book a hut for the following year.

miss the highest chairlift in North America, the **Imperial Express** (12,840ft). This drops you off just below the summit of **Peak 8**, where you can traverse north along the ridge to Whale's Tail and Peak 7 Bowl, or steel yourself for the short, steep and lung-crushing hike up to the true summit (don't drop your gear!), where the views and terrain are simply spectacular. From here you can drop into the Imperial Bowl or the extreme Lake Chutes.

From here you can cruise all the way down to Main St, picking up the 4 O'Clock Trail on the way: a descent of 3400ft in elevation, over nearly 4 miles in length.

Access the mountain from the free **BreckConnect Gondola**, which runs from downtown Breckenridge Station (Watson Ave) and serves the Nordic Center, Peak 7 and Peak 8; a shuttle serves Peaks 9 and 10 at the southern end of town.

Panning for Gold

STRIKE IT RICH

Just how much work was it to pan for gold? Short answer: a lot. Don't believe us? Give it a try at one of two Breckenridge sites: the **Country Boy Mine** or the **Lomax Placer Mine**. The

 WHERE TO EAT IN BRECKENRIDGE

Downstairs at Eric's
Locals flock to this game-room-style basement joint for the brews, burgers and mashed potatoes. **$**

Sancho Tacos & Tequila
Patio chillin' and street tacos that run the gamut from Baja fish to duck confit. Family-style orders too. **$**

The Canteen
Why reinvent the wheel? All the ski-town staples are here, from burgers and flatbreads to Korean BBQ tacos. **$$**

Country Boy Mine puts together a full package of activities, from an actual tour of the mine and panning for gold to a treasure hunt and extreme sledding in winter. To get here, take the Purple Shuttle.

The Lomax Mine was a surface (placer) mine, so its operations were a bit different. In addition to panning for gold, you'll also learn how mining-town chemists assayed the valuable claims and check out the actual sluices and flumes used in such mines. This site, which was active in the 1860s, also gives visitors the chance to sniff around a miner's cabin, complete with wood-burning stove, musical instruments, snowshoes, pack saddles and other sundry items needed for survival. On Ski Hill Rd, you can walk here from town. And yes, if you find a gold nugget, it's yours to keep.

Summer Hikes

QUAD-BUSTING FUN

Summer in Breck brings invigorating hikes to high alpine lakes, waterfalls and nearby fourteeners. The sweat factor is up to you, but one thing's for sure: you won't run out of options. For a gentle introduction, try out **Boreas Pass**. Although you can drive all the way to the top of the pass, we recommend parking at the lot halfway and walking to **Baker's Tank** (6 miles round-trip). This is an equally beautiful winter snowshoe excursion.

Deep-green **Lower Mohawk Lake** is tucked onto a tundra shelf with the ruins of a miner's cabin just below. Upper Lake views are an even more spectacular moonscape: marbled rocks, stunted trees and inky lake views. That clear buzz is the quiet roar of the cosmos. It's 7 miles round-trip.

The 2.8-mile round-trip hike to **McCullough Gulch** is short enough for families, though huffing up the 1000ft of elevation gain will require some perseverance. Luckily you'll have plenty of scenery along the way: the meandering streams that you follow from the trailhead eventually turn into thundering falls and, after that, a glacial lake.

Quandary Peak (14,265ft; pictured left) is one of Colorado's easiest fourteeners. Though you'll see plenty of dogs and children, 'easiest' may be misleading – the summit remains 3 grueling miles from the trailhead. Note: for both Quandary and McCullough Gulch, you must reserve a parking spot or a shuttle seat in advance.

GETTING AROUND

Breck's most convenient parking lots are located at the base of the gondola, but fill up quickly. A free lot on Airport Rd is a good alternative for day-trippers. Free Ride buses serve the town and ski area and depart from next to the gondola.

Beyond Breckenridge

Welcome to Summit County and South Park: home to three more ski resorts, the Dillon Reservoir and the country's highest post office.

The aptly named Summit County is close enough to Denver for a day trip but far enough away to feel like you've truly escaped the Front Range sprawl. In summer, cyclists enjoy the endless miles of paved bike paths that connect the major towns, while hikers scale the peaks in high country. Winter, of course, is all about the snow. Copper, A-Basin and Keystone each have their unique personalities, and an awesome free shuttle system connects them all with Breckenridge. On the other side of Hoosier Pass is the high-altitude prairie of South Park, tucked between the Mosquito Range, Kenosha Pass and the Arkansas River Valley.

TOP TIP

Summit County's handy free bus service links Frisco, Dillon, Breckenridge, Keystone, A-Basin and Copper Mountain.

Cycling the Boreas Pass (p164)

RIGHT: SPRING IMAGES/ALAMY STOCK PHOTO ©, LEFT: ROSEMARY WOLLER/SHUTTERSTOCK ©

OUTLETS AT SILVERTHORNE

Located just off I-70 at exit 205 are three shopping outlets of designer-brand stores with discount prices. Brands include Calvin Klein, Levi's, Gap, Le Creuset and dozens of others.

Not only is there a shuttle that runs between the villages (free), there are also shuttles here from Vail (Summit Express), Copper Mountain and Breckenridge (Summit Stage). The Blue River runs right next to the outlets, so if your group is of a divided mind when it comes to shopping, note that fly-fishing is always a possibility.

And if you left some essential piece of outdoor gear at home, REI is right on the other side of the interstate.

Dillon Reservoir

Summit County Sailing

DILLON RESERVOIR

In 1961, Denver finally made good on its turn-of-the-century plans to create a mountain reservoir for the city. The old townsite of **Dillon** disappeared beneath the rising waters, and a new Summit County playground came into being. Driving down I-70, you can't miss it: a glittering expanse of blue backed by snowy peaks, with 27 miles of largely undeveloped shoreline.

In summer, anyone with a hankering to get out on the water can rent a stand-up paddleboard (SUP), kayak, sailboat or pontoon from one of two marinas: the main one in Dillon (30 minutes from Breck), or the smaller one in Frisco (15 minutes from Breck). An outdoor amphitheater is the setting for big-name concerts in the evenings, and a gorgeous paved bike path circles the water for superb Summit County views.

And if you're looking to pitch a tent? There are several campgrounds tucked between the forest and the shoreline, all connected to a network of hiking and mountain bike trails. Winter brings ice fishing and cross-country skiing. The **Frisco**

 WHERE TO STAY IN DILLON

The Pad
There's a variety of rooms at this hip hostel, from dorms to private shipping containers with kitchenette. $

Prospector Campground
Dillon's main USFS campground (107 sites) is located on the south side of Dillon Reservoir. $

Homewood Suites
Near the Dillon Marina, all rooms come with kitchens, while the hotel has EV charging and an indoor pool. $$

Nordic Center has 25 miles of cross-country ski trails on the Dillon Reservoir peninsula, on the south side of the reservoir. A tubing hill is also located here and is a good diversion for kids.

Note that swimming is prohibited – the water is too cold.

Geek Out on Cabin Construction

FRISCO HISTORIC PARK

Unusual for Summit County, the turn-of-the-century mining town of **Frisco** stands alone, with nary a ski run in sight. It makes for a great base, however, and the six-block stretch of historic Main St is where you'll find almost everything you could need. There are plenty of cute cafes and good restaurants, and it dead-ends at the scenic **Dillon Reservoir**, where you'll find a small marina.

Frisco's top billing goes to the **Historic Park**. Set on the site of the original town saloon in 1889, and later converted into the town's second school in 1901, this museum features a number of historical displays, including one on the Ute nation, a diorama of the original Ten Mile Canyon railroad that fed and connected the mining camps of Leadville and Frisco, and a historic map of Colorado (c 1873).

The main attractions, however, are the half-dozen old mining cabins scattered out back. Aficionados of log-construction techniques will appreciate the double-dovetail joints at the **Dills Ranch House** (c 1890) and the **Bailey House** (c 1895). Inside the **Trappers Cabin**, visitors will find the kind of pelts that once sustained the area's meager economy prior to mining. Other prize specimens include the Frisco jail and the town chapel, which now screens a 15-minute documentary video.

Cycling Summit County

HIGH-ALTITUDE CRUISING

Frisco is Summit County's hub for fabulous paved bike paths. From the Frisco Marina you can wrap most of the way around the reservoir to Dillon (7.5 miles), a great family trip with minimal elevation gain, and then on to Keystone (13.5 miles, 1200ft elevation gain) – or pedal around the other side and back to Breckenridge (9.5 miles, 500ft elevation gain).

PEAK ONE

A trail runs straight out of Frisco, taking you right up to the beginning of the Tenmile Range. You can make this as short or long as you like, but either way get ready to sweat. It's 1.5 miles up to the ridge, where the trail forks; head right (north) to Mt Royal (10,052ft) for the easy summit.

Otherwise, opt for the tougher workout and turn left (south) to continue up the ridge to Peak One (12,805ft), which is 3.7 miles from the trailhead located at the west end of 2nd Ave. Tenmile Peak (12,933ft) is another 0.6 miles from here, but be prepared for some continuous class 3 scrambling along the ridge.

WHERE TO EAT IN DILLON

Dillon Dam Brewery
One of Summit County's best, with dishes like pan-seared honey-sriracha salmon. $$

Sauce on the Blue
Sophisticated Italian backing onto the Blue River and fashioned with industrially chic decor. $$

Arapahoe Cafe & Pub
This 1940s roadside cafe and motel is still the grooviest place to eat in town. $$

BEST RESTAURANTS IN FRISCO

Butterhorn Bakery & Cafe
A bright pastel-brushed diner, always packed for breakfast and lunch. Vegan options. $

Lost Cajun
A festive Louisiana soundtrack and jambalaya greet hungry diners here. $

Prost
It's bottoms up at Frisco's welcoming Bavarian beer hall, serving elk and bison bratwurst and pretzels. $

Pure Kitchen
Eclectic global offerings, from cauliflower hummus and zoodles to banh mi sandwiches and flatbreads. $$

Bird Craft
Thai-ish fried chicken, poke bowls and papaya salad from the folks at Outer Range Brewing. $$

Alternatively, you can head off in the other direction to climb **Vail Pass** (12 miles, 1550ft elevation gain) and roll all the way down to Vail. If you rent a bike from **Pioneer Sports** in Frisco, they'll throw in a complimentary shuttle to the top of Vail Pass.

Remember that you can take bikes on Summit Stage buses if you run out of steam or only want to go one way.

Copper Mountain

THE LOCALS' PICK

The base village may be a bit too planned for some, but even the staunchest critics wouldn't thumb their noses at the mountain itself. Rising 2738ft up to the 12,441ft summit, **Copper** has 2507 acres of terrain, carved with over 140 trails equally divided for beginner, intermediate, advanced and expert skiers. No chichi Vail attitude here – Copper takes you back to skiing's play-hard roots, and indeed, perks like free parking make it a favorite with locals.

It's an easy mountain to navigate – all levels have their own slice of paradise served by separate lifts, meaning beginners are unlikely to be run over by experts at the bottom of the mountain (and vice versa). Shredders won't want to miss the famous **Woodward** terrain parks: there are 10 in all, running from beginner to the pro-level **Central Park**. Several of the parks were developed in partnership with Olympic gold medalists.

There are plenty of other activities here as well, including 15 miles of free cross-country and snowshoe trails, a tubing hill, and, in summer, a bike park, golf course and adventure zone. Copper is a half-hour drive from Breckenridge.

Keystone Resort

SUMMIT COUNTY'S BEST FAMILY RESORT

Keystone is known as a kid-friendly destination: it's got plenty of groomed greenies and blues, plus an enormous snow fort, ice rink and off-slope cookie decorating. Because, let's admit it: most kids don't want to ski all day, every day. When they are on the slopes, however, be sure to hit **Schoolmarm**, an awesome 3-mile cruise that drops 2339ft, but keeps it wide open so there's plenty of space to practice those turns.

If you're not a newbie, don't be fooled into thinking that all the terrain here is tame – with 3149 skiable acres and a

 WHERE TO STAY IN FRISCO

Peak One Campground
Frisco's main campground (80 sites) is located on the southwest shore of the reservoir. $

Inn on Galena
Friendly B&B with serene atmosphere and 15 wonderfully comfortable rooms. $$

Frisco Lodge
Receiving guests since it first opened as a stagecoach stop in 1885. $$

ARINA P HABICH/SHUTTERSTOCK ©

Keystone

THE BARN

Freestylers who want to learn their way around a terrain park should head straight to this way-cool 19,400-sq-ft playground: it's a year-round snowboard, ski, skate and BMX training camp complete with trampolines, skate parks, jumps and, thankfully, foam pits.

It serves all levels of athlete, from beginners to the young and sponsored. The mandatory intro class grants you access to drop-in sessions.

During summer the Barn offers week-long day and overnight training camps, while on the mountain are two terrain parks made with leftover snow.

When you've picked up the basics, you'll be ready for winter at Copper: unique terrain parks include the family cross zone, the intro-level half pipe and the super pipe.

3128ft vertical drop, it's unlikely you'll get bored, regardless of your ability. There are three main mountains: **Dercum** (frontside), the **Outpost** and the **Outback**; it's also the only Summit County resort to offer night skiing. A new lift-served alpine area, the **Bergman Bowl**, was scheduled to open in 2023. In the meantime, snowcats serve the Outback Ridge. Or go all in with a full-day tour – lunch in a backcountry yurt and fat skis included. It's a half-hour drive from Breck.

 WHERE TO EAT IN KEYSTONE

Inxpot
Hippie-run, rock 'n' roll coffeehouse does righteous breakfast sandwiches and jet-fueled coffee. $

Montezuma Roadhouse
By the gondola in River Run, drop by for power bowls, soups, salads and sandwiches. $$

Ski Tip Lodge
This veritable piece of Rocky Mountain history welcomes diners with a roaring fire and delectable cuisine. $$$

IKON VERSUS EPIC

Sticker shock is a big part of the Colorado ski experience, and it's not just limited to Vail and Aspen. The initial slack-jawed disbelief soon changes to stubborn denial, and that's where those season passes, known as either Epic or Ikon, come in.

Depending on where you plan to ski, you can buy anything from two-day blocks to discount base passes to the whole hog at 62 resorts across multiple continents.

In Colorado, the resorts break down like this: Epic includes Vail, Breckenridge, Keystone, Beaver Creek, Crested Butte and Telluride. Ikon includes Winter Park, Copper, Steamboat, Eldora, A-Basin and Aspen. Consider all the options, and buy months ahead for the best deals.

LEFT: DAN LEETH/ALAMY STOCK PHOTO ©. BELOW RIGHT: KIT LEONG/SHUTTERSTOCK ©

Lift to Montezuma

Arapahoe Basin

COSTUME-CLAD EXTREME SKIING

You won't catch any Texans in 10-gallon hats or fur-clad ladies from the Upper West Side at **A-Basin**. Offering up some of North America's highest (13,050ft) and most extreme in-bounds terrain, this is a resort (we use the term loosely) that caters to hard-core riders only. Chutes, cliffs and heart-in-your-throat steeps are the draw, but A-Basin is also beloved for its goofy, no-frills vibe. Want to ski dressed up like a giant banana? Want to ski naked? This is your spot.

The back bowl, known as **Montezuma**, is where you'll find two dozen or so hair-raising intermediate-to-expert runs. The Jump is the biggest, baddest run on Montezuma, beginning with a 10ft drop off the mountain's ledge onto a steep 35-degree slope. The **East Wall** (summit 13,050ft),

 WHERE TO STAY IN KEYSTONE

Ski Tip Lodge
Historic 1800s stagecoach stop with an authentic log-cabin ambience and 10 country-style rooms. **$$$**

Summit County Mountain Retreats
Manages a good selection of condos, homes and ski-in, ski-out lodging. **$$$**

Keystone Lodge & Spa
Hotel-style accommodations at Lakeside Village, with comfortable rooms, pool and spa. **$$$**

which includes the hike-to Shit for Brains, is A-Basin's other legendary backcountry-style area. Or just keep it simple and do laps on one of Colorado's most famous lifts, the **Pallavicini** (or Pali), which accesses some of the steepest in-bounds terrain in the state.

Superlative chasers lunch at **Il Rifugio** – located at 12,456ft, this is the highest restaurant in North America. When temps warm up enough, large tailgate cookouts and parties take over the Beach (the front-row of the parking lot). It's the last resort standing in spring, often staying open into June.

A new via ferrata offers in-shape hikers the chance to experience alpine exposure once the snow melts. Alternatively, give the high-altitude disc golf course a whirl. It's a half-hour drive from Breck and 15 minutes from Dillon.

Day Trip to South Park

HOME OF KYLE AND CARTMAN

Follow Hwy 9 south from Breck and after 11 miles of steady climbing, you'll come to Hoosier Pass (11,539ft) and the Continental Divide. From here you'll be looking out over the **South Park basin**, a high-altitude prairie where the bison once roamed. On the other side of the pass is funky **Alma**, the highest incorporated town in the US, standing at an elevation of 10,578ft. It's surrounded by four fourteeners, thousand-year-old stands of bristlecone pine and scores of old mining claims. If you want to explore, follow the unpaved Buckskin Rd (Co Rd 8) 6 miles west toward Kite Lake – high-clearance AWD is recommended for the last mile.

Otherwise, continue 5.5 miles down Hwy 9 until you reach **Fairplay**. South Park's main settlement was originally a mining site and supply town for Leadville (pack burros briefly clopped back and forth over the 13,000ft Mosquito Pass to the west), and you can stop here to visit **South Park City**, a recreated 19th-century Colorado boomtown. Get a taste of life back in the good-old, bad-old days of the gold rush through the 40 restored buildings on display, which range from the general store and saloon to a dentist's office and morgue. And yes, *South Park* fans, Fairplay does bear more than a passing resemblance to the hometown of Kyle, Cartman and the boys.

ACCLIMATIZATION

Denver may be a mile high, but Summit County is nearly 2 miles high. Even if you're not coming from sea level, let that sink in for a second. No matter how good a skier, or hiker or cyclist you are, and no matter how much you work out, nothing really prepares your body for the shock of oxygen-thin air.

There are a few things you can do to minimize the impact, however. Drink plenty of water so that your body adapts to Colorado's low humidity. Give yourself time to acclimatize before hiking a fourteener or launching yourself down a double-black run. Finally, remember that the ultraviolet rays are much stronger up here: bring sunscreen, sunglasses and brimmed hat.

SOUTH PARK CITY

GETTING AROUND

The Summit Stage, Summit County's handy free bus service, links Frisco, Dillon, Breckenridge, Keystone and Copper Mountain year-round. In winter, buses (Swan Mountain Flyer) run from Breckenridge to A-Basin via Keystone.

VAIL

Standing on the edge of the Sun Up Bowl on a brisk February morning, the sun glinting off icy peaks in the distance and miles of untracked powder spread out beneath you – and knowing that it goes on and on and on, all the way to Outer Mongolia – is the stuff that Colorado dreams are made of. Long easy groomers, kids' adventure playgrounds, glades, cliffs, chutes, terrain parks, wide-open bowls and backcountry-esque delights – whatever type of riding you do, you're bound to find it here.

Factor in Vail's gourmet offerings, well-coiffed clientele and powder-fueled staff and you have an adrenaline-addled yuppie utopia. Indeed, stress does not cling to the bones long here... until you get the bill. And, even then, you'll have had such a good time that the memories will last far longer than that icy splash of buyer's remorse.

TOP TIP

With 31 lifts in operation it can be tough to find your way around, so spend some time studying the trail map. The two high-speed gondolas will get you out of the base areas: Gondola One (heated and wi-fi–enabled) serves Vail Village; Eagle Bahn serves Lionshead.

Vail

MARGARET.WIKTOR/SHUTTERSTOCK ©

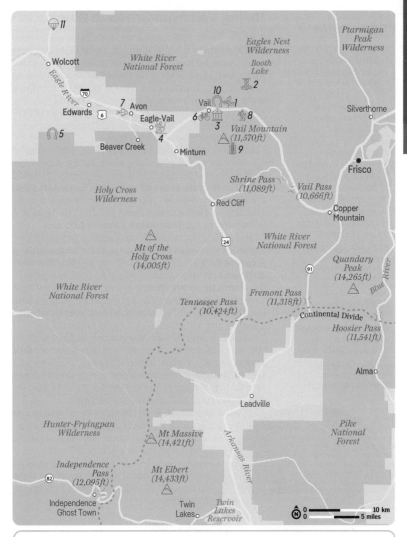

SIGHTS

1 Betty Ford Alpine Gardens
2 Booth Falls
3 Colorado Snowsports Museum

ACTIVITIES & COURSES

4 Apex Mountain School
5 Bearcat Stables
6 Bike Valet
7 Gore Creek Fly Fisherman

8 Nature Center
9 Vail Mountain
10 Vail Stables
11 Zip Adventures

 WHERE TO DRINK IN VAIL

Yeti's Grind
Vail's best coffee comes from this indie cafe on the ground floor of the Solaris.

Root & Flower
Celebrate in style with wines by the glass or cocktails, paired with cheese and salumi plates.

Vail Brewing
Small-batch local brews and a sunny terrace are a reason to celebrate at the local taproom.

Skiing Vail from Green to Black

BLUE SKY BLISS

Tenth Mountain Division veteran Peter Seibert and his friend Earl Eaton climbed Vail Mountain in the winter of 1957. After one long look at those luscious back bowls, the pair knew they'd struck gold.

At the time, the mountain was owned by the forest service and local ranchers. Seibert and Eaton recruited a series of investors and lawyers, eventually got a permit from the forest service and convinced nearly all of the local ranchers to sell. Much of the construction budget was raised by convincing investors to chip in $10,000 for a condo unit and a lifetime season pass.

Finally, on December 15, 1962, the dream came alive. The cost of a lift ticket? $5 for nine runs.

Vail Mountain is hands-down one of the best ski resorts in the world, with 5317 skiable acres, 195 'trails,' two terrain parks, and, ahem, some of the highest lift-ticket prices on the continent. You can subdivide the mountain into three main zones: the front side, the back bowls and Blue Sky Basin. Distances are vast, and you will spend a lot of time getting from one place to another, so if you have a specific destination in mind, plan carefully.

Beginners should stick to the front side, where most of the runs are groomed and the north-facing slopes offer good snow cover (particularly up top), even on sunny spring days. The **Gopher Hill Lift** and **Little Eagle Lift** areas are best for first-timers. Other good green runs include Lost Boy in **Game Creek Bowl** and the Tin Pants and Sourdough in the **Sourdough Express Lift** area.

Intermediate skiers have plenty of options, including Slifer Express, Cappuccino and Christmas in the **Mountaintop Express Lift** area; Northwoods in the **Northwoods Express Lift** area; Avanti, Lodgepole and Columbine in the **Avanti Express Lift** area; and Dealer's Choice in Game Creek Bowl. But if you're itching to experience the massive back bowls, try out Poppyfields in the **China Bowl** – it's groomed and will get you down to the bottom safely.

For experts, meanwhile, there is simply no limit to where you can go back here. The seven legendary bowls are **Sun Down**, **Sun Up**, **China**, **Siberia**, **Teacup**, and *Inner* and **Outer Mongolia**. The wide-open, spruce-dotted slopes here include favorites like Over Yonder (Sun Up), Forever (Sun Down) and Bolshoi Ballroom (Siberia).

Blue Sky Basin is the furthest-flung destination – this is an all-day trip (pack a lunch). Although there are a few blue runs here, because of the distance and the lack of amenities, this is an area best saved for the experts. In bad weather and flat light, skiing the back bowls can verge on impossible – stick to the tree runs on the front side.

For Free

SAVE A BUCK

Vail will always be an expensive destination, but you don't *have* to max out your credit card. The **Nature Center** offers guided tours all summer

ARINA P HABICH/SHUTTERSTOCK ©

WHERE TO STAY IN VAIL

Gore Creek Campground
Nineteen tent sites nestled in the woods by Gore Creek, 6 miles east of Vail village. $

Vail Mountain Lodge
With only 20 rooms and seven condos, this plush choice is as boutique as Vail gets. $$$

Arrabelle
A massive, chalet-style resort with top-shelf service and a variety of accommodations. $$$

long, from full-day backcountry hikes to more family-oriented activities. Free creekside nature tours run on Sundays; other popular kids activities include wildflower walks and evening trips to the beaver pond or stargazing with s'mores. There are also four short interpretive trails open to the public.

Another hiking option is the 2-mile walk to the 60ft **Booth Falls**, which follows USFS Trail 1885 into the Eagles Nest Wilderness Area. Continue beyond the falls to encounter meadows filled with wildflowers and views of the Gore Range. If you've got the energy, keep going to **Booth Lake**, 4.1 miles from the trailhead, with an elevation gain of about 3000ft.

Betty Ford Alpine Gardens is the highest botanical gardens in the US. Stop by for a soothing stroll past rock gardens, native alpine plants and collected species from as far as the Himalayas. Look out for activities, like yoga, butterfly launches and plant sales.

Humble but informative, the **Colorado Snowsports Museum** takes you from the invention of skiing to the trials of the 10th Mountain Division (p179), a decorated WWII alpine unit that trained in these mountains. There are also hilarious fashions from the past, as well as the fledgling Colorado Ski & Snowboard Hall of Fame.

Summer Adventures

CLIMB TO THE EAGLE'S NEST

All the usual suspects set up shop in the summer, including cycling, horseback riding, climbing and zip-lining.

Bearcat Stables and **Vail Stables** run one- to three-hour rides, as well as longer trips like a four-day ride to Aspen.

Gore Creek Fly Fisherman will set you up with new and used gear for rent or purchase. Don't miss the free casting clinics at 10:30am daily in summer.

Zip Adventures runs six zip-line tours over Alkali Canyon, with plenty of time to work on your primal scream. Easy and exhilarating, the two-hour romp is worth the splurge. **Apex Mountain School** and **Paragon Guides** run guided climbing and mountaineering trips in both summer and winter, while **Bike Valet** rents cycles and runs a shuttle up to Vail Pass for the easy, scenic cruise back down.

Vail's summer amusement park (Epic Discovery) gets so-so reviews, though the gondola ride into the high country will always be impressive. But better still is a tandem flight with **Vail Valley Paragliding**.

BEST RESTAURANTS IN VAIL

Little Diner
The most popular place for a made-from-scratch breakfast is in Lionshead; no reservations. $

Sweet Basil
Vail's most celebrated restaurant: the seasonal, eclectic new American fare is consistently excellent. $$$

La Nonna
Chef Simone Reatti brings the Italian Alps to Colorado, from house-made gnocchi to roasted lamb. $$$

Up the Creek
Unpretentious creek-side patio with great lunchtime deals and divine farm-to-plate dinners. $$$

Mountain Standard
Casual spin-off of Sweet Basil: raw bar, salads, and mains from the grill or rotisserie. $$$

GETTING AROUND

If you're driving here, note that the base areas are traffic-free; drivers must park at the Vail Village or Lionshead parking garages.

The Eagle County Regional Airport is 35 miles west of Vail. Shuttles run from Denver International Airport and Summit County resorts.

Vail Transit loops through all the Vail resort areas. Most buses have bike and ski racks and all are free.

Beyond Vail

Backcountry ski runs, 19th-century railroad towns, CIA training grounds and Colorado's highest summits await in the mountains outside Vail.

It's refreshing how many quirky little mountain towns surround a resort that does its best to cater to the 1%. Follow the Top of the Rockies Scenic Byway south along Hwy 24 and you'll pass Minturn and Red Cliff, the gateways to the Holy Cross Wilderness Area, where you'll find some of the most spectacular hiking in the area.

Further along is Leadville, a creaky old mining town known for adventure in the surrounding hills. You can climb the two tallest peaks in Colorado, run a 100-mile race, mountain bike for 24 hours straight, cross-country ski to a gourmet meal or simply continue driving on to Aspen. Well, what are you waiting for?

TOP TIP

Save some cash by spending the night in Minturn, Red Cliff or Leadville instead of at Vail's mega resorts.

Holy Cross Wilderness Area

CAVAN-IMAGES/SHUTTERSTOCK ©

Shrine Pass

Backcountry Fun, All Year Round

MULTIUSE SHRINE PASS

Halfway between Copper Mountain and Vail is **Shrine Pass** (11,178ft), accessed via an 11.5-mile dirt road/ski trail that links up with the town of **Red Cliff**. In summer, this is a very popular multiuse trail: you can drive it, bike it (three to four hours), use an ATV and, of course, go hiking – **Shrine Mountain Trail** is 4.2 miles round-trip; the trailhead is 2.25 miles up the road. From Julia's Deck (Mile 3.75) you have good views of Mount of the Holy Cross. Biking is the most interesting option because once you hump the pass (2.5 miles in), it's all downhill to Red Cliff. If you have two cars you can set up a shuttle; otherwise sign up for a bike tour with Bike Valet in Vail.

In winter this area is known as the **Vail Pass Recreation Area**. It's used by both snowmobilers and backcountry skiers and boarders (often teaming together for the uphills), but with 55,000 acres of wilderness you should be able to find some

AVALANCHE

For serious skiers and snowboarders, the lure of fresh powder and untracked backcountry terrain is a powerful temptation, a chance to experience that heady rush of feel-good dopamine that momentarily overrides the rest of the brain's circuitry.

Unfortunately, the risks associated with backcountry skiing are hardly inconsequential – if you get caught in an avalanche, the odds are you won't survive.

While it's convenient to believe that most avalanche victims are naive and unprepared, Colorado's unstable snowpack does not discriminate: experts are just as likely to be swept under. If you're going out of bounds, you need to know how to minimize risk: get trained, carry the necessary equipment and check the daily avalanche forecasts from the Colorado Avalanche Information Center.

 WHERE TO EAT AROUND BEAVER CREEK

Craftsman Brew Co
Down the road in Edwards are gourmet sandwiches, small plates and, of course, beer. $$

Vin 48
Share a round of small plates, like braised venison cheeks, at this Avon-based wine bar. $$$

Beano's Cabin
This destination restaurant involves a 20-minute open-air sleigh ride to a glowing cabin on the slopes. $$$

INDEPENDENCE PASS

Aspen's jaw-dropping back door, **Independence Pass** (p179) is one of the most popular drives in the state and has loads of scenic overlooks, campgrounds and hiking trails.

seclusion. The forest service grooms 50 miles of trails back here, allowing you to get between Shrine Pass, Red Cliff and Camp Hale. Additionally, there are four huts in the area (Shrine Mountain, Fowler, Jackal and Janet's Cabin) for overnight trips. Avalanche gear and training are a must. If you've got the cash, **Vail Powder Guides** run a full day of snowcat skiing.

To get here, take the Vail Pass exit (190) off I-70. The **Minturn ranger office** has maps and trail descriptions for the area – you must pick up a map before you go, as it's quite likely you'll get lost without one.

MOUNT OF THE HOLY CROSS

Mount of the Holy Cross first caught the nation's attention in 1873, when William Henry Jackson photographed the mountain on the Hayden Expedition.

His photography, along with Thomas Moran's paintings of the mystical 'snow cross,' symbolized the Colorado wilderness for millions of 19th-century Americans.

Pilgrimages to view the cross led to the construction of a shelter at the summit of Notch Mountain in 1924. You can still climb to the shelter – it's a strenuous 10.2-mile out-and-back hike, and affords sublime views of the Bowl of Tears and the snow cross (through mid-July) to the west. Begin hiking at the Fall Creek Trailhead, off the unpaved Tigiwon access road, 3 miles south of Minturn.

Beaver Creek

SKI WITH THE VIPS

Breach the regal gates in Avon and you'll emerge onto a private mountain road skirting a picturesque golf course as it climbs to the foot of a truly spectacular ski mountain. **Beaver Creek** feels like one of those delicious secrets shared among the rich kids, and it is indeed a privilege to ski here.

Today, the perfectly maintained grounds and neo-Tyrolean buildings lend a certain looming grandeur, as do names like the Park Hyatt, set in the main village, and Ritz Carlton, in nearby **Bachelor Gulch**. Beaver Creek is a mellower, more conservative place than Vail and typically an older scene. It's the kind of destination where grandparents bring the whole family to enjoy a slew of all-natural adventures.

It's no secret: winter rules. The mountain boasts a 4040ft vertical rise serviced by 16 lifts, with 150 trails through aspen forest and a wide variety of ski terrain.

Beginners like it in Beaver Creek because the mountain's easy runs are at the top, so they can enjoy the same spectacular views as the more advanced folks. Intermediate skiers have less choice, but the **Coyote Glades** and blue-cruiser **Arrowhead Mountain** are both good choices, as are **Redtail** and **Harrier** on the main mountain.

Experts should head to the double black diamonds at **Royal Elk Glades** and Bald Eagle off the **Grouse Mountain Express** lift – the runs are every bit as challenging as anything at Vail. **Golden Eagle** – the site of the Birds of Prey Men's World Cup Downhill course – gives you the chance to try out a competition-class downhill run, while the **Stone Creek Chutes** spike the adrenaline.

The posh reputation keeps away some – but that just means more powder for you.

 WHERE TO EAT IN MINTURN

Kirby Cosmos
Casual Carolina BBQ, with stalwarts like pulled-pork sandwiches, jalapeño poppers and short ribs. $

Mango's
Hidden in off-the-grid Red Cliff, a three-story mountain pub famous for its fish tacos. $$

Minturn Saloon
Sit by the crackling fireplace and savor bowls of green chili at this historic après-ski hangout. $$

HEAVYT PHOTOGRAPHY/SHUTTERSTOCK ©

Red Cliff Bridge

Top of the Rockies Scenic Byway

FROM VAIL TO ASPEN

Linking the two most famous ski resorts in the state is this gorgeous high-alpine drive. You'll cross two mountain passes, with Colorado's two tallest peaks dominating the horizon as you go. This is a 2½-hour drive without stops – if you take your time, expect to spend all day. Better yet, spend the night in Leadville or Twin Lakes.

From I-70, follow Hwy 24 south through **Minturn**, a charming 1887 railroad town with a handful of cafes and saloons. Passing the Holy Cross Wilderness Area to the west, you'll soon reach the Insta-worthy **Red Cliff Bridge**, arching magnificently over the Eagle River. Pay homage to the 10th Mountain Division at **Camp Hale**, before crossing **Tennessee Pass** (p181), after which **Mt Massive** looms supreme as you drive toward Leadville, former silver queen.

Further south, **Mt Elbert** dominates the horizon. Hang a right on Hwy 82 and head over to **Twin Lakes** (p182), a historic mining town on the shores of the largest glacial lakes in the state. Climb up over **Independence Pass** (p179; summer and early fall only) and cruise down into Aspen, stopping at the **Independence Ghost Town**, 4 miles from the top of the pass.

CAMP HALE NATIONAL MONUMENT

Established in 1942, Camp Hale was created specifically for the purpose of training the 10th Mountain Division, the Army's only battalion on skis. At its height during WWII, there were over 1000 buildings and some 14,000 soldiers housed in the meadow here.

After the war Camp Hale was decommissioned, only to be brought back to life again in 1958, this time by the CIA. Over the next six years, CIA agents trained foreign freedom fighters in guerrilla warfare.

In 1965 Camp Hale was officially dismantled, and the land returned to the US Forest Service. Today, it's a popular spot for mountain biking, hiking and cross-country skiing.

🛏 **WHERE TO STAY IN MINTURN** ————————————————————————

The Bunkhouse
The Ikea-chic Bunkhouse features 30 custom-built pods in the cheapest digs near Vail. **$**

Minturn Inn
Set in a 1915 log-hewn building, this cozy B&B turns on the mountain charm for affordable rates. **$$**

Green Bridge Inn
In rustic Red Cliff (no cell service), this vintage inn has 14 deluxe rooms for a character-filled stay. **$$**

MELANZANA

This unique outdoor clothing brand began in Leadville as Eggplant Mountain Gear in 1994 and never looked back. Patagonia may be more famous, and Black Diamond may have revolutionized the gear, but only Melanzana can claim to be 100% made in the US. Using only Polartec fabric (made in Tennessee), every single item in this store is produced behind the counter, using solar power to boot.

With only 20 people sewing, this is definitely not fast fashion: shopping for Melanzana's iconic hoodies is a personalized experience, and requires a pre-booked appointment. On average, the store is booked out one month in advance, but same-day appointments do open up in the event you didn't plan ahead.

SANDRA FOYT/SHUTTERSTOCK ©

Remnants of the mining industry, Leadville

Riding the Minturn Mile

DON'T GET LOST

If you're itching to head off-piste, consider the **Minturn Mile**. One of the most famous out-of-bounds ski runs in the US, it's accessible from the top of Chairs 3 or 7 on Vail Mountain.

At the top of the turn on **Lost Boy**, stay left and hike about 15 minutes up to **Ptarmigan Ridge**. Here you can take the access gate and begin a descent of 3 miles (roughly one hour) to the town of Minturn. Advanced skills are a must as you'll encounter a wide range of terrain, from deep powder to ice, slush, dirt, logs and rocks. At about the midway point you'll find the **Beaver Ponds**, which may require removing your skis or board, before hitting the **Luge**, a twisty old fire road that races the rest of the way down.

 WHERE TO STAY IN LEADVILLE

Inn the Clouds Hostel	**Tennessee Pass Sleep Yurts**	**Delaware Hotel**
Guests get the run of this hostel, which includes two common areas, games room and a large kitchen. $	Sleeping in the backcountry has never been so luxurious, with room service and even luggage delivery. $	Antique-strewn Victorian hotel that dates back to 1886, with high ceilings and lace curtains. $

Remember that you'll be skiing beyond the resort boundaries – it is *not* patrolled. If you get lost or injured, you'll be on your own, and if you require rescue it will come at considerable expense. It's imperative that you ski with someone who has prior knowledge of the terrain and route, and be sure to have proper gear, equipment and an updated report on conditions. It is, by all accounts, a magnificent experience and requires a toast at the Minturn Saloon upon arrival.

Nordic Skiing & Winter Glamping

TENNESSEE PASS

Tennessee is just one pass among many in central Colorado, and while it may not be as glamorous as its brethren, it actually has loads more to do. You'll know you've arrived when you spot the entrance to the ski areas: the downhill resort is the small but affordable **Ski Cooper**, which is a great place to learn the basics. If you've got more experience, they also run snowcat tours on **Chicago Ridge**.

The **Nordic Center**, meanwhile, has 15 miles of groomed trails that leave from the base of Ski Cooper, and which are open to cross-country skiers and snowshoers. The highlight is the 1-mile haul to everyone's favorite gourmet yurt: the **Tennessee Pass Cookhouse**.

And if you've always dreamt of nestling up in a snowy wonderland, check out the **Tennessee Pass Sleep Yurts**. With a woodburning stove, kitchenette and even luggage delivery and room service, this is a great way to enjoy all the magic of a quiet winter night without having to wake up in a snow cave with frostbitten toes.

Leadville Mining Tour

QUIRKY MOUNTAIN VIBES

Originally known as Cloud City, **Leadville** was once Colorado's second-largest city (population 40,000) and a quintessential Wild West town, where fortunes were made and lost overnight, swindlers ruled the roost and Doc Holliday got into a shootout with the law and won.

It was silver, not gold, that brought riches to the lucky few in Leadville, but after the bottom dropped out of the silver market in 1893, the city took a serious nosedive. You'll find the remnants of the past all over town: start with the surprisingly good **National Mining Hall of Fame**, before sauntering over to the **Healy House** and **Dexter Cabin**, two of the oldest homes in Leadville. The **Tabor Opera House** was once one of the premier entertainment venues in all of Colorado, if

LEADVILLE 100

The Leadville 100, held in August, is one of the most famous and longest mountain-bike races in the world: 100 miles of lung-crushing, adrenaline-fueled riding on the old silver-mining roads that go from 9200ft to 12,424ft and back again.

Not ready to sign up? Try the Mineral Belt instead: this paved 12-mile trail is a great place to start exploring Leadville on bike or foot, looping around town past historic points of interest and beautiful scenery. It's also open to cross-country skiers in winter. Cycles of Life has everything you need to hit the trail in all seasons, including fat tires and cross-country skis in winter.

WHERE TO EAT IN LEADVILLE

High Mountain Pies
Ultra-popular pizza joint with great toppings, though seating is limited. $

Treeline Kitchen
Welcoming family-owned restaurant focusing on simple but delightful mains and salads. $$

Tennessee Pass Cookhouse
Diners hike, snowshoe or cross-country ski 1 mile to an elegant four-course meal in a yurt. $$$

MT ELBERT

Colorado's tallest peak and the second-highest in the continental US, Mt Elbert (14,433ft) is a relatively gentle giant.

There are three established routes to the top, none of which are technical. The most common approach is via the northeast ridge; it's a 9-mile round-trip hike with 4700ft of elevation gain, so expect to spend most of the day. The turnoff for the main trailhead is just south of Leadville on Rte 300.

Just next door and dominating the western horizon is Mt Massive, the state's second-tallest peak (14,421ft), with more total area above 14,000ft than any other peak in the state. The classic summit route (13.6 miles) is a real bruiser, however.

CAMPSMOKE/SHUTTERSTOCK ©

Mt Elbert

not the West, and hosted the likes of Houdini, Oscar Wilde and Anna Held.

Final stop is the **Matchless Mine** (tours available), where silver magnate and Colorado senator Horace Tabor made and then lost millions in the 1880s, and where his glamorous and sensational wife, Baby Doe, eventually froze to death after spending the last three decades of her life in poverty.

Twin Lakes History Tour

DOUBLE THE FUN

Set on the shores of the largest glacial lakes in Colorado, at the base of Independence Pass, **Twin Lakes** was once a convenient rest stop on the Aspen–Leadville stagecoach line. First called Dayton during the 1860s gold rush, it was renamed Twin Lakes in 1879 when the silver rush revived the village.

Several historic structures still stand on the north lake shore, including the **Red Rooster Tavern** (aka the town brothel), now the visitor center. Canoe and SUP rentals are available in town; boat tours also run daily.

On the south shore of the main lake is **Interlaken**, the vestiges of what was once an exclusive resort, built in 1879. The ruins are a lovely 5-mile hike (round-trip) along the lake; this is as easy as walking gets at 9400ft. There's good signage and you can even go inside millionaire James Dexter's 'cabin.' The turnoff for the Interlaken trailhead is 0.6 miles after you turn onto Hwy 82.

GETTING AROUND

Hwy 24 runs 37 miles south from Vail to Leadville. From Leadville it's another 15 miles south to Hwy 82 and Independence Pass. Eagle County Regional Transportation

Authority offers affordable transport to Eagle County Airport, Beaver Creek, Minturn and even Leadville. Buses depart from the Vail Transportation Center.

Denver
Aspen

ASPEN

What if the world was full of beautiful people, who were all kind, environmentally minded and well-intentioned? Well, that's Aspen for you: when you drive into town, it's like entering the alternate John Denver dimension. But don't run off screaming just yet.

Aspen is unique in that it attracts intellectuals and world leaders, artists and activists, Hollywood celebs on the down-low and eccentric ski bums. This particular mix wasn't an accident: the mind-body-spirit ethos goes back to the 1940s, with the founding of the town's triumvirate: the Aspen Institute, a think tank that brings together top scientists, economists and artists; the Aspen Music Festival; and, of course, the Aspen Skiing Company.

Aspen may be wealthier than ever, but the unparalleled natural beauty and collision of ideas that brought all these people here is still freely accessible – as long as you know where to look.

TOP TIP

If your hotel doesn't have parking or you're just visiting for the day, save yourself the hassle and head straight for the town parking garage on Rio Grande Pl, which has the best daily rates around. Free RFTA buses connect Aspen with the Highlands (Maroon Bells), Snowmass and Buttermilk.

Aspen

OSCITY/SHUTTERSTOCK ©

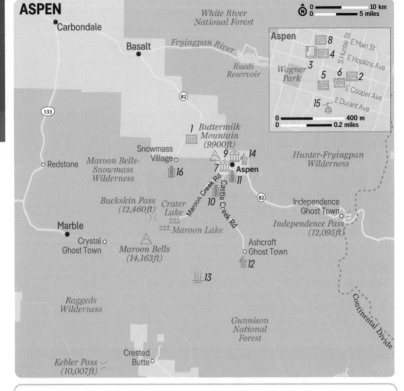

ASPEN

SIGHTS

1 Anderson Ranch Arts Center
2 Aspen Art Museum
3 Aspen Historical Society
4 Baldwin Gallery
5 Christopher Martin Gallery
6 Galerie Maximillian
7 Holden Marolt Mining & Ranching Museum
8 LIK Fine Art Aspen
9 Wheeler/Stallard Museum

ACTIVITIES

10 Aspen Highlands
11 Aspen Mountain
12 Cathedral Lake Trail
13 Conundrum Hot Springs
14 Hunter Creek Trail
15 Silver Queen Gondola
16 Snowmass

🛏 WHERE TO STAY IN ASPEN

Difficult Campground
The largest campground near
Aspen and one of four sites
at the foot of Independence
Pass. $

St Moritz Lodge
Come ski season, this
European-style lodge is one
of the cheapest deals in town.
$$$

Tyrolean Lodge
Spacious personalized rooms,
some with kitchenettes and
fireplaces. Another affordable
choice. $$$

Silver Queen Gondola

Skiing the Four Mountains

IN POWDER WE TRUST

Aspen, for all its money, taste and eccentricity, owes its current status to the surrounding slopes. Above all, this is a ski town and one of the best in America, with four mountains accessible from a single lift ticket – each offering a different adventurous twist.

Aspen Mountain offers more than 3000ft of steep vertical right from the front door of the Little Nell. There's no beginner terrain here, just 675 acres of bumps, trees and World Cup–worthy runs served by the **Silver Queen Gondola** (in 1946 it was the single-seat Lift 1, the longest chairlift in the world).

Intermediate skiers and riders will dig **Ruthie's**, a wide-open groomed run with sweeping views. Local tip: stay skier's right at the top of Ruthie's and you'll head into the **Jerry Garcia Shrine**, accessed from the FIS and Ruthie's lifts.

Snowmass is the biggest of the four, with over 3300 acres of ridable terrain and 150 miles of trails – this is the best all-around choice. **Sneaky's** is a wide-open cruiser and the perfect blue groomer, with sweeping views of the Roaring Fork Valley, while those looking for a challenge can ski into powder and trees on either side of the run. Any run in the **Cirque** or the **Hanging Valley Headwall** will suit the adrenaline set. At some point make your way to the **Elk Camp** chairlift, which has awesome views of the Maroon Bells from the top.

NORDIC BLISS

Local outdoor outfitter Ute Mountaineer has operated the Aspen Cross-Country Center, set on Aspen's public golf course, for nearly three decades. Located near the Aspen-Snowmass Nordic Trail System (a 60-mile web of village-to-village trails linking Aspen with Snowmass, Ashcroft and Basalt), the center is a convenient spot to rent gear, take a lesson or head out on a guided tour.

Ashcroft Ski Touring, meanwhile, serves 20 miles of groomed trails through 600 acres of backcountry – it's a bit more wild than your typical Nordic center. The mountain backdrop is spectacular, and the nearby ghost town of Ashcroft is equally eerie. They also rent classic cross-country ski equipment and snowshoes and run guided tours.

Annabelle Inn
Personable and unpretentious, rooms at the quirky Annabelle are cozy without being overly cute. $$$

Limelight Hotel
Sleek and trendy, the Limelight's brick-and-glass modernism reflects Aspen's new school. $$$

Hotel Jerome
Superb service and relaced elegance are the trademarks of this historic landmark. $$$

THE MAROON BELLS SHUTTLE

The most important thing to know when visiting the Maroon Bells is that you can't just drive there and park wherever you want – this area sees some 300,000 visitors each summer, so access is strictly controlled. Most visitors will need to park at the Aspen Highlands – it's very pricey, so we recommend taking the free RFTA bus from Rubey Park in Aspen – and then take a half-hour shuttle ride (late May through October).

You must reserve shuttle tickets in advance. Alternatively, if you're planning a backpacking trip, you can reserve a parking spot at the trailhead (5pm to 8am only).

The access road is not plowed in winter, when you can cross-country ski to Maroon Bells Lake.

Maroon Bells

Buttermilk has lots of beginner-friendly cruisers and great instructors, but it also has some gnarly terrain parks: this is where you can ride the same hits and 22ft superpipe as Chloe Kim, Shaun White and all your favorite X Games athletes.

Last but not least is **Aspen Highlands**. You know all those amazing promo shots of beautiful people joyfully hiking atop an exposed snow-covered ridge with skis flung over a shoulder? That's here. Although there are some beginner and intermediate runs here, the Highlands is all about extreme skiing in the stunning hike-to **Highland Bowl**: expect chutes, vertiginous drop-offs, glades and super steep lines that plunge 3600 vertical feet.

The Maroon Bells

EXPLORING THE ELKS

If you have but one day to enjoy a slice of pristine wilderness, spend it in the shadow of Colorado's most iconic mountains: the pyramid-shaped twins of **North Maroon Peak** (14,014ft) and **South Maroon Peak** (14,156ft). Eleven miles southwest of Aspen, it all starts on the shores of **Maroon Lake**, an absolutely stunning spot backed by the towering, striated summits. The surrounding wilderness area contains nine passes over 12,000ft and six fourteeners. Some jut into jagged granite towers, while others are of a more generous slope and curve, nurturing a series of meadows that seem to gleam from the slopes.

 WHERE TO EAT IN ASPEN

Big Wrap
These creative, vaguely healthy and definitely affordable wraps have won over legions of fans. $

White House Tavern
As American as a crispy chicken sandwich and kale salad, this is Aspen's premier lunch stop. $$

Meat & Cheese
While the produce at this farm-to-table market may be local, the culinary expertise spans the globe. $$

You can spend an hour up here or several days: the choice is yours. **Crater Lake** is only 1.8 miles one way, making for a nice day hike. If you're hungry for a little bit more altitude, we suggest pressing on to **Buckskin Pass** (12,462ft; 4.8 miles one way) – from the narrow ledge you can see mountains erupt in all directions. This is the start of one of the most popular hikes in Aspen: the **Four Pass Loop** (28 miles), a stunning multiday backpacking trip that crosses three other 12,000ft passes.

Another popular hike goes to **Crested Butte**, roughly 11 miles away (but 100 miles by car). From Crater Lake continue to West Maroon Pass (12,480ft), then descend to the Schofield Pass Trailhead on the Crested Butte side, where you'll need to arrange for a shuttle to take you the additional 14 miles into town. **Maroon Bells Shuttles** will actually drive your car to either trailhead so that it's waiting for you upon arrival. The minimum hiking time is six hours, but plan on 10.

Ghost Towns

FROM BOOM TO BUST

The first thing that anyone on an Aspen history tour should do is to check out the **Aspen Historical Society**, which runs a variety of tours, from the famous 1889 Jerome Hotel and Wheeler Opera House to 90-minute downtown city walks. They also manage two specialist museums: the **Wheeler/Stallard Museum**, set in an 1888 Victorian house, and the **Holden Marolt Mining & Ranching Museum**, which includes visits to a mining mill and historic homestead.

Further out on Castle Creek Rd but absolutely worth visiting is the **Ashcroft Ghost Town**, a silver-mining town founded in 1880. What remains are mostly miners' cottages (log cabins with tin roofs), a couple of broken-down wagons stranded in the waist-high grass, a post office and a saloon. At its height in 1893 about 2500 people worked here, but the silver veins were quickly exhausted and by 1895 the town's population had plummeted to 100 residents.

At the foot of Independence Pass is another boomtown gone bust, **Independence**. This one-time tent camp exploded in the summer of 1879, when a lucky miner struck gold on the 4th of July. The site offers the chance to see the remains of the old livery, the general store and a miner's cabin or three. After its population peaked at 1500 residents, the town fell away during the harsh winter of 1899, when supply routes were severed.

BEST ENTERTAINMENT IN ASPEN

Aspen Music Festival
Every summer, the best classical musicians from around the world come to Aspen to perform and teach.

Belly Up
The top nightspot in town, showcasing performers from John Legend to Modest Mouse in intimate surrounds.

Wheeler Opera House
A working theater since 1887, the Wheeler still stages opera, films, concerts and musicals.

Theatre Aspen
Nonprofit theater that stages award-winning musicals and plays from its gorgeous complex in Rio Grande Park.

Mawa's Kitchen
Beloved French- and African-inspired cuisine, plus a fun crepe shack in Snowmass. **$$$**

Matsuhisa
This converted house is the original Colorado link in Matsuhisa Nobu's global sushi empire. **$$$**

Pine Creek Cookhouse
This log-cabin restaurant, located 1.5 miles past Ashcroft's ghost town, has the best setting around. **$$$**

CYCLING & MOUNTAIN BIKING

There's no shortage of two-wheeled fun in the Aspen area. Road cyclists can pedal the easy Rio Grande Trail (42 miles to Glenwood Springs), the harder Maroon Bells Rd (11 miles) or the masochistic Independence Pass.

If you're eager for blistering downhill and jumps, head for the Snowmass Bike Park, though there are also plenty of free singletrack classics to choose from: the 10.5-mile Rim Trail is a top Snowmass ride that leaves from the Rodeo Lot.

Linking Snowmass with Aspen is the much loved Sky Mountain Park, with a variety of terrain, while in Aspen itself you can head straight out into the open space on the Smuggler-Hunter Creek Loop – extending it all the way to Sunnyside if you're up for a challenge.

Art Tour

CULTURE VULTURE

Aspen, like most towns in the Rocky Mountains, is less about seeing and more about experiencing. But with a handful of outstanding art venues, this is the most culturally happening spot west of Denver. Start with **Aspen Art Museum**, with three floors of gallery space enveloped in a lattice-like exterior designed by Pritzker Prize–winner Shigeru Ban. The rotating contemporary exhibits are always free. The museum collaborates regularly with the **Anderson Ranch Arts Center** in Snowmass, an artists' residency that hosts regular workshops and master classes, in addition to displaying works in its own gallery.

Smaller galleries in Aspen include two on nearby Cooper St: **Galerie Maximillian** and the **Christopher Martin Gallery**. Peek in through the windows of Maximillian and you'll see any number of famous 20th-century names, from Chagall to Lichtenstein, mixed in with works from contemporary American and British artists. Martin, meanwhile, specializes in reverse glass painting, a technique that dates back to the Middle Ages, which he uses to tease out dynamic swirls of color on acrylic disks and rectangles.

The two-floor **Baldwin Gallery** on Galena St is one of the oldest in Aspen and specializes in contemporary American art. Around the corner on Hopkins Ave is the work of self-taught Aussie photographer **Peter Lik**, who focuses on vibrant panoramic landscapes that sometimes appear to be in 3D.

Hiking in Aspen

LACE UP YOUR BOOTS

The Maroon Bells trailhead is the starting point for some of Aspen's most famous hikes (the Four Pass Loop, Crested Butte), but if you want to avoid the crowds and shuttle logistics, there are plenty of other trails to explore.

The **Hunter Creek Trail** leaves right from town (N Mill St to Lone Pine Rd), following the creek northeast for about 4 miles, after which it links up with a plethora of other trails, including the popular network at nearby **Smuggler Mountain** (10,700ft).

Castle Creek Valley is also a great spot to explore. Here you'll find the steaming **Conundrum Hot Springs**, west of Castle Peak (14,265ft), which are the reward for 8.5 miles and over 3000ft of climbing on the Conundrum Creek Trail (USFS Trail 1981). The pools here have outrageous alpine views, including glimpses of steep avalanche chutes and waterfalls. It's hugely popular, and you must make reservations on recreation.gov in advance in order to stay at one of the campsites here. Bear canisters are also required.

 WHERE TO DRINK IN ASPEN

Aspen Brewing
With seven signature beers and a sun-soaked balcony, this is the place to unwind.

Woody Creek Tavern
Enjoying a margarita at Hunter S Thompson's favorite watering hole is well worth the 8-mile drive.

Hooch
Fun speakeasy mixing signature cocktails like the Wolf of Wall Street and the Notorious F.I.G.

Hunter Creek

Further up the valley is **Cathedral Lake Trail**, which is particularly stunning in fall when the aspens shimmer gold. With 2000ft of elevation gain over 3 miles, however, it's definitely no walk in the park. The trailhead is located near the Ashcroft ghost town; if you don't have AWD, park at the lot near the road.

Hut-to-Hut Ski Trips

SAY GOODBYE TO LIFT LINES

Imagine the thrill of gliding through the backcountry on skis: just you, your friends and quiet snowfall blanketing the mountainside. Well, thanks to the **10th Mountain Division Hut Association**, which manages a system of over 30 huts (some with wood-burning saunas), it can be done – without having to spend the night in a snow cave.

The huts are connected by a 350-mile trail network ideal for cross-country skiing and snowshoeing in winter, and mountain biking and hiking in the summer. You'll be out in the wilderness, so at least one person in your group should be an experienced backcountry skier familiar with avalanche safety. Better yet, go with a guide like **Aspen Expeditions**.

So how do you sign up for all this winter fun? The catch, of course, is securing reservations: these huts are incredibly popular and space is limited. Winter reservations for the following year begin with a member-only lottery on March 1. Call-in reservations for nonmembers open up on June 1. In other words, you have to plan your trip six to 12 months in advance and be somewhat flexible with your dates (avoiding weekends is key).

ACES

The Aspen Center for Environmental Studies manages the 25-acre Hallam Lake wildlife sanctuary that hugs the Roaring Fork River and miles of hiking trails in the Hunter Creek Valley.

With a mission to advance environmental conservation, the center's naturalists provide free guided hikes and snowshoe tours, raptor demonstrations (eagles and owls are among the residents) and special programs for families.

Popular guided tours include the Ice Age walk in Snowmass, hikes to Crater Lake in the Maroon Bells and year-round birding excursions.

There are two other locations in the region: Rock Bottom Ranch near Basalt, which offers farm tours, and the Catto Center at Toklat, across from the Ashcroft ghost town and where you'll find an artist in residence.

GETTING AROUND

Aspen is 41 miles south of Glenwood Springs on Hwy 82, and roughly four hours from Denver. The road to Aspen via Independence Pass is only open from late May to early November. The Aspen-Pitkin County Airport has flights from Denver and several other US cities.

Aspen's downtown is best navigated on foot, while free RFTA buses run to the surrounding towns and ski areas.

Beyond Aspen

Aspen's allure isn't the town but its surrounds: a snowball's throw in any direction and you're sure to hit Elk Mountain bliss.

Dominated by the magnificent, twin-peaked Mt Sopris (12,965ft), the rural Roaring Fork Valley is the gateway to Aspen. While you may be tempted to zip on through, we'd advise that you take the time to make a few detours and soak in some hot springs. At Carbondale is the junction for the romantic Crystal River valley, which cuts through a vivid and often-overlooked tract of wilderness beneath Chair Mountain. Near Basalt, Fryingpan River and Ruedi Reservoir make up the breadcrumb trail that leads to another stretch of pristine landscapes and forested campsites. And exiting through Aspen's back door takes you to the top-of-the-world wonderland of Independence Pass.

TOP TIP

Glenwood Springs, Carbondale, Basalt and campsites along Independence Pass all offer affordable alternatives to staying in Aspen.

Mt Sopris

HAVESEEN/SHUTTERSTOCK ©

Glenwood Hot Springs

Soaking in Glenwood's Hot Springs

SPA DAY

Let's start with the fun stuff. Doc Holliday – gunfighter, gambler, Wild West legend and, uh, dentist – died in Glenwood Springs. Why he came here is the first clue to the town's long-standing appeal: thermal hot springs. In Holliday's day they were thought to have restorative powers; he hoped they'd ease his chronic respiratory ailments.

Today, the main **Glenwood Hot Springs Resort** pumps out 3.5 million gallons of mineral water a day, flowing through two main pools: the 400ft-long big pool at 90°F and the 100ft-long therapy pool at 104°F. Kids have access to a splash zone, while adults can rejuvenate at the hotel and spa.

If you want a more intimate soak, **Iron Mountain Hot Springs** offers a relaxing setting with 16 small pools. The **Yampah Spa**, meanwhile, is something else entirely: at 110°F, entering these caves feels like descending into one of Dante's layers of hell. First developed by the Ute hundreds of years earlier for therapeutic purposes, the steam-filled natural caves have been a commercial facility since the 1880s.

Glenwood is one hour from Aspen, off I-70.

WHY I LOVE GLENWOOD SPRINGS

Christopher Pitts, writer

'Everyone oohs and ahhs over Aspen, but let's take a moment to spread some love to Glenwood too. While I never pictured my ideal hot springs experience as a gargantuan swimming pool, there's something about the location that keeps me coming back. Usually, I'm on the way home from some dust-covered fun in the Utah desert, muscles sore and in need of a break after hours of driving. Glenwood Springs lies at the perfect spot on I-70, and an hour or two spent floating in the warm mineral waters, amid all the playing kids, chilling parents and day-tripping tourists, is the perfect way to re-enter civilization after a week in the wilderness.'

🛏 WHERE TO STAY IN GLENWOOD SPRINGS

Glenwood Hot Springs Lodge
if you're coming here specifically for the hot springs, the on-site hotel is the top pick. Pool access included. **$$**

Hotel Denver
Convenient downtown location and charming interior makes this historic property a solid choice. **$$**

Hotel Colorado
Although it's on the National Register of Historic Places, the rooms are in need of a refresh. **$$**

DOC HOLLIDAY

It's appropriate that the hike to Doc Holliday's memorial at Linwood Cemetery in Glenwood Springs might leave you breathless: the life of the legendary man was shaped by labored breathing.

Seeking relief for tuberculosis, John Henry Holliday (1851–87) moved west from his native Georgia. He set up a dental practice in Texas, but the wheezing scared away patients.

Turning to gambling and hanging out in saloons, Holliday met Wyatt Earp, with whom he participated in the most famous shootout of Western lore at the OK Corral.

Despite the memorial, Holliday's exact place of burial is unknown: the records were lost when the cemetery was moved from an earlier location down the hill.

Getting Activein Glenwood Canyon

BIKE, HIKE OR RAFT

Gorgeous Glenwood Canyon offers all sorts of diversions. Cycling over the smoothly paved **Glenwood Canyon Trail**, under the canyon walls, makes an excellent afternoon for riders of all abilities. The path follows the Colorado River upstream below the cantilevered I-70, and the river often drowns out the roar of traffic. It's about 18 miles from the Yampah Vapor Caves to Dotsero at the other end of the canyon; a good midway destination is Hanging Lake, roughly 10 miles up the canyon.

The 1.2-mile **Hanging Lake Trail** leads to a waterfall-fed pond perched in a rock bowl on the canyon wall. It's a strenuous 1½- to three-hour round-trip with a 1020ft elevation gain, but well worth the huffing and puffing. A huge visitor increase in recent years, however, has led to problems such as vandalism and illegal parking, and you must now reserve a permit in advance. The 3.5-mile **Grizzly Creek Trail** is another popular hike that gets out of the main canyon, though it's a tougher workout.

Beginning in May, the roaring **Colorado River** holds everything from beginner float trips to extreme white-water rafting. Most trips depart from east of town, on the stretch below the Shoshone Dam. Also look out for trips down the smaller Roaring Fork River.

Glenwood Canyon's Adventure Park

SCREAAAAAMMMMM

This family-oriented destination lumps together several attractions at once: the **Fairy Caves** (once billed as the eighth wonder of the world), a full-on amusement park, and a tram ride 1300 ft up to the top of Iron Mountain. The regular cave tour is the main attraction here: this is the largest cave in Colorado open to the public. The Wild Tour of the caves, meanwhile, is a heart-racing experience for would-be spelunkers, allowing guests to crawl through narrow passages, though we like the **Giant Canyon Swing**, which sends folks squealing 1300ft in the air above the Colorado River at 50mph.

Exploring the Roaring Fork Valley

SMALL-TOWN CHARM

The **Roaring Fork Valley** runs from Glenwood Springs (down valley) to Aspen (up valley), connected by Hwy 82 and the paved Rio Grande bike trail. In the shadow of twin-peaked

 WHERE TO EAT IN GLENWOOD SPRINGS

Slope & Hatch
Cajun andouille fries along-side mouthwatering taco selection (margarita-grilled shrimp!). Yum. $

Sweet Coloradough
Great indie bakery south of town, with cronuts, eclairs, doughnuts and bagel sandwiches. $

Taqueria El Nopal
Tasty variety of tacos and pupusas (stuffed tortillas) that go well beyond the usual Col-Mex fare. $

Rainbow trout, Fryingpan River

BEST RESTAURANTS IN CARBONDALE

Village Smithy
Adored by locals; the best breakfast in town. $

SILO
It's the ingredients, not the menu, that matters here. Never complicated, but always delicious. $

Phat Thai
It may not look like the markets of Chiang Mai, but you won't find any naysayers here. $$

Goat Kitchen
Good selection of pitas, salads, burgers and pasta dishes at this Mediterranean-themed restaurant. $$

Carbondale Beer Works
As they say, 'make beer, not war,' and the local brewery is doing a fine job of that. Pub grub too. $$

Mt Sopris (12,965ft), artsy **Carbondale** – 13 miles from Glenwood – is one of the most charismatic spots to cool your engine and grab a bite to eat when traveling up or down valley. Check out **Steve's Guitars**, an unassuming guitar shop that turns into an intimate one-room acoustic music venue on weekend nights. Shows at this community favorite start around 8:30pm on Friday and/or Saturday nights, but it's best to turn up earlier if you want a seat. The cover charge varies, so bring cash. The small gallery at **Carbondale Arts** also merits a detour.

A further 10 miles up valley is **Basalt**, Aspen's humble neighbor and down-to-earth little sibling. Set at the confluence of the Fryingpan and Roaring Fork Rivers, it's framed by gold-medal trout waters, making this cute but humble town something of a fly-fishing paradise. **Taylor Creek Fly Shop** rents rods and runs guided tours. Also on the river is

The Pullman
Glenwood Spring's hippest hangout, where the open kitchen whips up modern American dishes. $$

Glenwood Canyon Brewing Co
In the Hotel Denver, where the beers are hoppy and the night scene lively. $$

Co. Ranch House
Sustainably raised local ranch ethos, with an emphasis on grilled steaks and pan-fried trout. $$$

REDSTONE INN

Tucked away behind massive red cliffs, this hotel occupies a little slice of Rocky Mountain heaven.

Opened in 1902 as bachelor housing for miners, the historic inn occupies 22 acres of pristine, secluded land surrounded by national forest.

Paying homage to the American arts-and-crafts movement, the red-roofed lodge features more than 60 pieces of authentic Gustav Stickley furniture.

Also look out for locally quarried and hand-cut marble, and gorgeous, hand-crafted wrought-iron light fixtures in the rooms and lobby. It can feel dated, but if you're here for historical charm and natural beauty rather than state-of-the-art luxury, you'll leave smiling. Note that wi-fi is limited and there is no cell service.

Independence Pass

a white-water park for kayakers and stand-up paddlers to play in. The tiny town has a historic main street strip, where you'll find plenty of dining options and cute boutiques. It's only 20 minutes to Aspen's ski slopes; stock up on groceries and outdoor gear at the newer **Willits Town Center**, 4 miles northwest on Hwy 82. Basalt is also the gateway to little-visited **Hunter-Fryingpan Wilderness Area**.

Climbing Independence Pass

TOP OF THE ROCKIES

Looming at 12,095ft, **Independence Pass** is one of the most high-profile mountain passes along the Continental Divide. Perhaps it's the proximity to Aspen (just 20 miles away on Hwy 82), or maybe it's the celeb quotient (Kevin Costner has a ranch on the western slope). But we think it's the drive itself.

Views range from pretty to stunning to downright cinematic, and by the time you glimpse swaths of snow on the ridges below, you'll be living in your own IMAX film. Late season you'll see everyone from guys dressed in full camo to – no kidding – unicyclists attempting the unthinkable.

 WHERE TO STAY IN THE ROARING FORK VALLEY

Chapman Campground
One of six campgrounds along the Fryingpan River, 29 miles east of Basalt. $

Cedar Ridge Ranch
Ah-mazing farmstay north of Carbondale, where guests sleep in either safari tents or a yurt. $$

Basalt Mountain Inn
One of the most affordable places to stay in the Aspen area; only 20 minutes from Snowmass. $$

Along the way you'll pass hiking trails, fourteeners, serene campgrounds and even a ghost town (Independence, on the western slope; p187). For a short hike, check out the family-friendly **Grottos Trail**, which leads to a series of thundering waterfalls (also on the western slope).

If you're after bigger fish, consider climbing 14,336ft **La Plata Peak**, the state's 5th highest. The trail leaves from South Fork Lake Trailhead on the eastern side of the pass. There are two routes to the top: the mellower Northwest Ridge and the more challenging Class III Ellingwood Ridge. Both routes are roughly 9.5 miles round-trip with over 4000ft of elevation gain. Start early and remember: it's not a climb for beginners.

The pass is only open from late May to late October.

TWIN LAKES

On the east side of Independence Pass are the **Twin Lakes** (p179) and Hwy 24, which connects Leadville with Salida.

History & Hot Springs

YOU LOAD 16 TONS...

Seventeen miles south of Carbondale on Hwy 133, **Redstone** was a true company town, quite unlike the 'every man for himself' spirit of the gold rush era. Founded in 1890 by John C. Osgood, a multimillionaire and head of the Colorado Fuel & Iron Company, Redstone was one of the early experiments in welfare capitalism, where workers were provided with higher standards of living but discouraged from forming unions. The town was created to carbonize coal from Coalbasin Mine, and the first thing you'll see as you drive up the highway is the remains of some 50 beehive coke ovens, lined up across from the town entrance. When the mine closed in 1909, the town was virtually abandoned overnight, though new residents have since moved in over the past few decades.

Several of the original buildings are still standing, including the original chalet-style workers' cottages and Osgood's personal residence, the 42-room **Redstone Castle**. Located 1 mile south of town on a private road, it was thoroughly renovated in 2017 and is open for tours in summer. You can even stay at the imposing neo-Tudor **Redstone Inn**, built in 1902 as a dormitory to house miners.

However, the best lodging in the area is **Avalanche Ranch**, along Avalanche Creek. In addition to the 15 cabins and five covered wagons are lovely geothermal pools to soak in – open to nonguests if you reserve.

HIKING TRAILS ON THE PASS

One of the most popular summer playgrounds in Aspen and a great family hike, the Grottos area is accessed via a complex web of short trails (most about half a mile) that sprout from old Weller Station on the original Independence Pass wagon road, leading to cascades and the unique water-carved slots known as the Ice Caves. Other trails here include Lost Man, a classic high alpine excursion past peaks and lakes. There are two trailheads; start at the upper one (past mile marker 59, last switchback before the pass), and you'll already be at 11,500ft. From here, hiking to Lost Man Lake is 4.7 miles round-trip, with only 1100ft of elevation gain.

WHERE TO EAT IN BASALT

Wienerstube
You just can't lose with sausages, schnitzel, sauerkraut and beer at this Austrian-themed restaurant. **$$**

Free Range Kitchen & Wine Bar
Steve and Robin Humble work uniquely with local farmers and ranchers; worth the trip from Aspen. **$$$**

Cafe Bernard
Owned by a French chef, this is a good spot to indulge in escargots and other delicacies; breakfast too. **$$$**

DOWN-VALLEY SKIING

Serious skiers head up-valley to Aspen or east on I-70 to Vail. But Sunlight Mountain Resort, 12 miles south of Glenwood Springs on Garfield County Rd 117, survives by offering good deals to families and intermediate skiers.

The downhill area has 72 runs over 730 acres, with 2000ft of vertical. The cross-country ski area features 18 miles of groomed track and snow-skating trails, plus snowshoeing and ice-skating areas. Equipment and rentals are available at the mountain or in town at Sunlight Ski & Bike Shop.

In the summer, check out the horse-back riding and cycling activities. A shuttle serves Glenwood Springs; call for the latest schedule.

Crystal Mill

Crystal Ghost Town

100 YEARS OF SOLITUDE

One of Colorado's most famous ghost towns, **Crystal** is also one of the most photogenic, though it is smack in the middle of nowhere – which is certainly a good thing, as long as you're up for the detour.

The first mining in the area took place in the 1860s, but access was so poor it wasn't until the 1880s that it really picked up. By 1893 there were a half-dozen mines producing silver, lead and zinc, and the population spiked at several hundred. Despite having been virtually abandoned by 1915, there are several fairly intact structures still standing, including the iconic **Crystal Mill**, a turn-of-the-century power generator.

To get here, you'll need to pass through tiny **Marble**, whose quarry (still in operation) has supplied stone to some of the most famous statuary in the US, including the Lincoln Memorial and Tomb of the Unknown Soldier. **Out West Guides** runs a variety of horseback-riding and fishing trips from town.

Marble is located 28 miles south of Carbondale, about 6 miles up County Rd 3. After Marble the dirt road to Crystal is another 6 miles, but you'll need a high-clearance AWD vehicle to make the trip; it is accessible only from June to November. If your car isn't up to the task, contact **Crystal River Jeep Tours**. Budget three or four hours for a visit to Crystal.

GETTING AROUND

The Roaring Fork Valley is served by RFTA buses, with stops in Glenwood Springs, Carbondale, Basalt and Snowmass. Hwy 82 runs 41 miles (one hour) from Glenwood to Aspen, continuing up over Independence Pass and down into Twin Lakes. Hwy 133 begins in Carbondale, heading south to Paonia.

Denver

Salida & the
Arkansas River

SALIDA & THE ARKANSAS RIVER

When a town of 5500 people has three microbreweries and just as many mountain bike shops, you know something's up. A former railroad hub turned ranching community turned outdoor mecca, this is quintessential Colorado: where mud-spattered pickup trucks cruise the streets alongside battered Subarus adorned with rooftop kayaks, and mighty peaks form distant postcard panoramas everywhere you look.

Blessed with a historic redbrick downtown and backed by the massive Collegiate range, Salida is not only an inviting spot to explore but also has an unbeatable location along the Arkansas River and Browns Canyon National Monument, one of the most popular stretches of white water in the US.

The plan of attack is to raft, bike or hike during the day, then come back to town to refuel with grilled buffalo ribs and a cold IPA at night.

And did we mention that the sun always shines?

TOP TIP

The town of Buena Vista, just 25 miles north, is an equally alluring location in which to base yourself. Alternatively, campgrounds along the river are picturesque, but not all have running water or shade. Go to cpwshop.com and search for 'Arkansas Headwaters Recreation Area' to make a reservation.

Salida

JACOB BOOMSMA/SHUTTERSTOCK ©

MONARCH PASS

Monarch Pass (11,312ft), 23 miles west of Salida, has a vintage tramway that hauls visitors an additional 1000ft to the top of the Continental Divide, where a gift shop and cafe warms the hands and hearts of the skimpily dressed. For those who are adequately prepared, however, the pass is a good launch pad for hikes (the Continental Divide and Colorado Trails) and bike rides (Monarch Crest).

Just downhill from the pass is Monarch Mountain, the local ski resort that has plenty of powder without the attitude. Although the 800-acre resort is on the small side, you'll still find excellent varied terrain and, most importantly, affordable lift tickets. For a real treat, sign up for their backcountry snowcat ski tours.

SALIDA

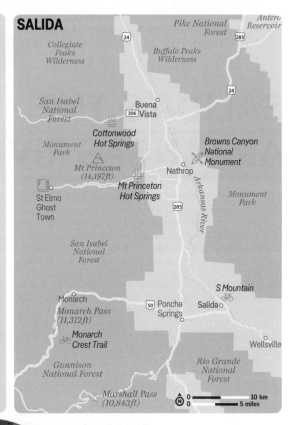

Rafting the Arkansas

READY, SET...PADDLE!

DAN LEETH / ALAMY STOCK PHOTO ©

The headwaters of the **Arkansas River** are Colorado's best-known stretch of white water, with everything from extreme rapids to mellow ripples. Although most rafting companies cover the river from Leadville to the Royal Gorge, the most popular trips descend through **Browns Canyon National Monument**, a 16-mile stretch that includes Class III to IV rapids, running between Buena Vista and Salida.

 **WHERE TO STAY IN SALIDA**

Simple Lodge & Hostel
It may be simple, but it's got a full kitchen and a comfy communal area that feels just like home. $

Amigo Motor Lodge
This cool motel is not only Southwestern stylilsh, but it also has five retro Airstream trailers to sleep in. $

Palace Hotel
The atmospheric three-story Palace is a 1909 landmark with 14 personalized vintage suites. $$

If you're with young kids or just looking for something more low key, **Bighorn Sheep Canyon** is a good bet. Those after more of an adrenaline rush can head upstream to the **Numbers** or downstream to the Royal Gorge (p274), both of which are class IV to V. If you'd like to go solo, most outfitters also rent duckies (inflatable kayaks).

Water flow varies by season, so time your visit for late May or early June for a wilder ride – by the time August rolls around, the water level is pretty low. If you're rafting with kids, note that they need to be at least six (sometimes older, depending on the trip/outfitter) and weigh a minimum of 50 pounds.

Most companies are based just south of **Buena Vista**, close to where Hwys 24 and 285 diverge, and typically also offer full-day packages that include zip-line tours or horseback riding. To get here, drive north from Salida for roughly half an hour.

Biking S Mountain

NO PAIN, NO GAIN

First impressions of mountain biking may leave you wondering what sort of sick masochist came up with this sport. You spend an hour gasping for breath as you climb up a steep hill, pedaling over skull-sized boulders on a way-too-narrow path. If you fall, you'll tumble back down the hill, roll over a carpet of prickly pears, and break multiple bones. How is this enjoyable? But trust us, when you reach the summit and start slaloming through the pines and zipping around banked turns, you will definitely be having fun. So much fun that you might decide you want to pedal up that damn hill a second time.

Salida's excellent trail system starts just across the river beneath the giant S: rent a bike from **Sub-Culture Cyclery**, pedal down F St and across the bridge (stopping to check out the old caboose) and start exploring. We recommend sticking to the green trails at first, especially if you're coming from sea level.

If you've done this before, then you know: the **Monarch Crest Trail** awaits. One of the most famous rides in Colorado, this is an extreme 35-mile adventure, with fabulous high-altitude views. It starts off at **Monarch Pass** (11,312ft), follows the exposed ridge 12 miles to **Marshall Pass** and then either cuts down to **Poncha Springs** on an old railroad grade or hooks onto the Rainbow Trail. Cycle shops in town run shuttles to both **Monarch Pass** and **Methodist Mountain** (Little Rainbow Trail).

WHITE WATER ALTERNATIVE

—

The **Royal Gorge** (p274) near Cañon City is another popular stretch of white water on the Arkansas River.

BEST RESTAURANTS IN SALIDA

Sweetie's
Uber-popular and superfriendly, with an incredible selection of over 60 sandwiches. $

Amicas
Thin-crust wood-fired pizzas, panini, veggie lasagne and microbrews on tap. $$

The Fritz
This fun park-side joint whips up clever American-style tapas, from elk sausage to fried green tomatoes. $$

The Biker and the Baker
The only place in Salida that combines the winning combo of brunch, wine and dessert. $$

Boathouse Cantina
Snag a table by the river and watch the kayakers float by. The buffalo chili and fish tacos ain't bad either. $$

GETTING AROUND

Located at the 'exit' of the Arkansas River Valley, Salida occupies a prime location at the crossroads of Hwys 285 and 50. The downtown stretch, centered on F St, is small and easily navigated on foot.

Beyond Salida

The mighty Collegiate Peaks beckon with snow-kissed hot springs, scenic drives, ghost towns, campgrounds and alpine hikes.

Salida isn't the only rafting town along the Arkansas – be sure to check out Buena Vista (that's pronounced 'byoona vista,' pardner; p198) to the north, which makes for an excellent pre- or post-trip pit stop to your river or mountain adventure. Stroll down Main St, grab a coffee or ice cream, and check out the funky rock formations east of the river.

All of the experiences outside of Salida can be done in a day, but if you're planning on bagging a peak, make sure you get an early start so that you don't get caught in an afternoon storm. Expect to drive anywhere from 30 minutes to an hour one way.

Denver

Collegiate Peaks
Cottonwood Hot Springs
St Elmo
Ghost
Town
Mt Princeton Hot Springs
Salida

TOP TIP

In need of a spa getaway? Consider a luxury stay and soak at the Mt Princeton Hot Springs.

Buena Vista Main Street

H. MARK WEIDMAN PHOTOGRAPHY/ALAMY STOCK PHOTO ©

Mt Princeton Hot Springs

COTTONWOOD PASS

Ever wonder what it's like to drive to the moon? Then wind your way 19 gorgeous miles on County Rd 302 to Cottonwood Pass (12,126ft).

After passing Cottonwood Hot Springs, you'll reach the Avalanche Trailhead on the north side of the road, with Mt Yale's summit flickering in and out of the trees (9.5 miles round-trip). Further uphill you'll come to Denny Creek Trail (4.6 miles round-trip to Hartenstein Lake), then Ptarmigan Lake Trailhead (6.8 miles round-trip).

The drive to the pass goes from moderately sinuous to downright jagged as you approach the edge of the timber-line, the Collegiate Peaks spread out before you against the big blue sky.

For high-altitude hikers, the Continental Divide couldn't be easier to access. The pass is open June through October.

Collegiate Hot Springs

UNWIND IN STYLE

It doesn't have to be 10 below with thick snowflakes falling from the sky to enjoy a soak in an outdoor hot spring, but hey – it doesn't hurt. There are two springs within an easy drive of both Salida and Buena Vista, and whether you're relaxing the muscles after a hard day's play or warming the cockles of your frozen swimsuit on a winter night, they both deliver.

Mt Princeton Hot Springs is a sprawling, four-star hot-springs resort, which is popular with families and spa-goers. There are 30 natural pools on the property that differ in size and atmosphere, including soaking pools, an expansive swimming pool and a 400ft water slide. Don't let that last feature scare you off: the full-service spa will ensure you bliss out in peace. Many guests stay the night. It's located in the shadow of Mt Princeton, off County Rd 321.

Cottonwood Hot Springs is the New Agey option, but we mean that in the best possible way. It's more intimate,

---

🛏 **WHERE TO STAY IN BUENA VISTA**

Cottonwood Lake Campground
A gorgeous pine-dappled bowl and lake makes this one of the most picturesque spots in the area. $

Chalk Lake Campground
One of three campgrounds between the Mt Princeton Hot Springs and St Elmo ghost town. $

Collegiate Peaks Campground
Nice site on the way up to Cottonwood Pass at 9800ft and a good base camp for climbing nearby peaks. $

ABROWNE/SHUTTERSTOCK ©

BUENA VISTA HERITAGE MUSEUM

Before Salida was named county seat in 1933, the honor belonged to Buena Vista, as evidenced by the 1882 Chafee County Courthouse on Main St.

However, in true Wild West fashion, the court records didn't come to Buena Vista willingly. No sir, it required a posse of local men, who rode a locomotive 17 miles north to the rival town of Granite in the dark of night. They held the sleep-addled sheriff at gunpoint and loaded all the Chafee County records and court furniture onto the train's flatbed car, then returned home to stash their haul until the new courthouse was built three years later.

Today the building holds the Buena Vista Heritage Museum, whose exhibits introduce different aspects of regional history.

St Elmo Ghost Town

and the leafy grounds, gushing fountains and wind chimes evoke a more contemplative atmosphere. While it's a cheaper soak, it's in need of a renovation and the lodging options are just OK. Both springs are about 15 minutes from Buena Vista and 30 minutes from Salida.

St Elmo Ghost Town

A PROSPECTOR'S FADED DREAMS

An old gold-mining ghost town tucked amid the Collegiate Peaks, **St Elmo** makes for a fun excursion. The drive is the best part: the road wends its way past stands of redolent ponderosa pine, a wildlife-viewing meadow and jagged peaks before petering out at what is Colorado's best-preserved ghost town.

Of course, it wasn't about the scenery back in the good ol' days – there was gold in this here creek! Most buildings were built in or around 1881: the schoolhouse, an old mercantile building and a miners exchange are among the best kept of the bunch.

The only catch to this spectacular setting is that St Elmo is also a staging point for ATV and snowmobile enthusiasts, who follow the forest service road up to **Tincup Pass**. The revving of not-too-distant engines can take away some of the charm, so try to avoid weekends.

 WHERE TO STAY IN BUENA VISTA ───────────

Railroad Bridge Campground
Six miles north of town, past a series of blasted tunnels, is this basic site by the Arkansas. No water. **$**

Ruby Mountain Campground
A popular put-in for Browns Canyon rafting trips and trailhead for hikes into the national monument. **$**

Surf Chateau
Split-level lofts are in English-style row houses; more traditional rooms have patios overlooking the river. **$$**

If you've got the time and energy, you can continue on 5 miles to **Hancock**; the turnoff is just before St Elmo. From here it's a 3-mile hike up to the **Alpine Tunnel** – a failed attempt to get a railroad through the mountain – and amazing views from the Continental Divide.

If you want to have the place to yourself, stay the night: the **Ghost Town Guest House** is a local B&B (really!) and there are three popular USFS campgrounds on the way up. They're all nice, but **Chalk Lake** has a choice location with views of Mt Princeton. Reservations are essential. Just before the turnoff to the campground is a parking lot for the **Agnes Vaille Falls Trail** (on your right), a short half-mile hike up to a waterfall. It's the perfect spot to stretch your legs.

St Elmo is on County Road 162, 11.5 miles past Mt Princeton Hot Springs. The road turns to dirt about halfway up. In summer it's not a problem, but in winter or muddy conditions you'll want an AWD.

Hiking the Collegiates

STANDARDIZED TESTS NOT REQUIRED

Who said the Ivy Leagues had to be stuck-up and stressed out? Laced with 105 miles of trails, the Collegiate Peaks has the highest average elevation of any wilderness area in the US: eight peaks exceed 14,000ft, including the state's 3rd- and 5th-highest summits, **Mt Harvard** and **La Plata Peak**. (Princeton, Yale, Oxford and Columbia rank 20th, 21st, 26th and 35th respectively.)

Huron Peak (14,012ft; pictured below), meanwhile, doesn't have the name recognition of its neighbors, but it is arguably the top climb. But the best hikes here don't necessarily involve peak bagging. Easier day trips include **Ptarmigan Lake** (6.6 miles; 14 miles from Buena Vista on County Rd 306), **Kroenke Lake** (8 miles; access County Rd 365) and as much of the Colorado Trail (p45) as you want to do (access Avalanche Trailhead, 9 miles from Buena Vista on County Rd 306). You can also pick up the Continental Divide Trail (p45) atop both Monarch and Cottonwood Pass.

Remember that storms in the Collegiates can blow in fast, so don't hesitate to turn back if the weather gets dicey. For detailed descriptions and maps, stop by the ranger office in Salida.

BUENA VISTA'S BEST RESTAURANTS

Buena Vista Roastery
Hatch plans for the day over a cup of organic fair-trade coffee and a giant blueberry scone. $

Viking Food Truck
Evan and Anna grill 11 varieties of burger, five melts (we like Swiss cheese and rye) and fried chicken. $

Deerhammer
Single-malt whiskey and gin pair with smoked wings and fried cheese curds at Buena Vista's distillery. $

House Rock Kitchen
A fire pit, sofa, live band and horseshoes – dinner here is like hanging out at a backyard BBQ. $$

GETTING AROUND

The Collegiates are easily accessible from Salida; alternatively, Buena Vista is an even closer jumping-off point for many destinations. Hwy 285 runs north–south through the valley.

MESA VERDE & SOUTHWEST COLORADO

HISTORY AND OUTDOOR ADVENTURE

From red-rock desert to towering mountain peaks, the landscape is as diverse as the history of the region itself: welcome to Southwest Colorado.

●Denver

Southwest Colorado is the stuff of dreams. There's magnificence at every turn: rugged snowcapped mountains and other-worldly red-rock desert, sweeping alpine meadows and deep dark canyon bottoms. It was the home of the Ancestral Puebloans and, later, the Ute who lived on its mesa tops and hunted its mountain valleys. Gold and greed pushed the Utes out – an American storyline – to be replaced by soldiers, miners, farmers and ranchers, all looking for a new life in the Wild West. Modern times have added a new set of locals: people seeking outdoor adventure by boot, bike, ski and more.

The influence of the myriad people who have walked these lands is still visible today: the cliff dwellings in and around Mesa Verde National Park, the historic mining towns like Ouray and Silverton, the small-town wineries and hot spring spas, and, of course, the tony ski resorts of Crested Butte and Telluride.

And then there's the vast spaces in between, like Colorado National Monument and its miles of back-country trails, Black Canyon of the Gunnison, still untamable with vertigo-inducing drops, and Weminuche Wilderness with boundless DIY adventure to be had.

Southwest Colorado's real pull, however, might well be its independent spirit, which has drawn people to the area for millennia.

JOSEPH SOHM/SHUTTERSTOCK ©

THE MAIN AREAS

Painted Wall (p236), Black Canyon

Find Your Way

Southwest Colorado is a vast and varied region extending from Grand Junction's wine country to the high desert around Mesa Verde. The San Juan Mountains form a verdant, rugged spine.

CAR

To fully explore the region, bring or rent a car. It'll give you freedom to stop in small mountain towns, tour archaeological zones, access trailheads and pop into wineries, all at your own pace. For sites off the beaten path, consider a high-clearance 4WD vehicle.

BUS

Bus service is limited in the region. Bustang Outrider will get you to hubs like Grand Junction, Montrose and Durango as well as popular ski destinations like Telluride and Crested Butte.

PLANE

There are several small airports in the region: Grand Junction, Montrose, Gunnison-Crested Butte, Telluride, Cortez, Durango and Pagosa Springs. There are plenty of commercial flights to and from Denver, but few within the region itself.

Grand Junction, p244

A small town with old-school charm that serves as an optimal base for outdoor adventures in Colorado National Monument and nearby wine country.

Mesa Verde National Park, p210

A one-of-a-kind national park and Unesco World Heritage Site, Mesa Verde's cliff dwellings inspire awe and respect.

Fruita Loma

Palisa

Grand Junction

Dove
Creek

Cortez
Peak Poi
(8571ft)

Mesa Verde
National Park

Towaoc

Chapin Mesa
(8143ft)

Black Canyon of the Gunnison National Park, p234

A spectacular and little-visited national park with 2000ft walls and dramatic craggy spires. A winding road along the rim makes visiting easy.

○ Snowmass

● Aspen

○ Paonia

○ Crested Butte

● Delta

Gunnison River

Black Canyon of the Gunnison National Park

● Gunnison

Blue Mesa Reservoir

Morrow Point Reservoir

50

Ouray, p222

A historic mountain town located in a dramatic box canyon with hot springs, ice climbing, high-altitude hikes and more.

Ridgway State Park

Dallas Divide

Ridgway

Mt Sneffels (14,150ft)

Ouray

Tellurride

Ironton

Lake City

Red Mt Pass

Lizard Head Pass

Silverton

South Fork

Continental Divide

Wolf Creek Pass

San Juan National Forest

Mancos

○ Durango

Chimney Rock

○ Pagosa Springs

0
0
N
50 km
25 miles

Plan Your Time

Travel options vary immensely by season, and few top attractions are available year-round. Decide on the main thing you want to do – wine tasting, skiing, visiting archaeological sites – and base your trip around that.

Cliff Palace (p211), Mesa Verde National Park

TRAVELVOLO/SHUTTERSTOCK ©

If You Only Do One Thing

Head straight to **Mesa Verde National Park** (p210), a spectacular Native American archaeological site known for its elaborate and well-preserved cliff dwellings. Take a **ranger-led tour** (p211) to **Cliff Palace** or **Balcony House** (p212) and prepare to climb ladders, crawl through tunnels and descend ancient stone steps.

Spend the rest of the day **hiking to petroglyphs** (p212) and exploring other structures on the **Mesa Top Loop Rd** (p212). Stay after sunset for **tribal performances** (p212), celebrating the culture of the modern-day descendants of the people who once lived here.

Seasonal Highlights

Winter is ski and snow season, while spring is green, especially at lower elevations. Summer is best for hiking and fall brings autumn colors and cooler weather.

JANUARY

Ski season is in full gear and **Ouray Ice Festival** (p224) attracts ice climbers from near and far.

FEBRUARY

Quirky winter festivals like **Silverton Skijoring** (p231) and **Durango's Snowdown** (p218) showcase the creativity and fun-loving character of the region.

JUNE

Telluride Bluegrass Festival (p229) kicks off the summer festival season. The legendary San Juan Mountains fill with hikers, bikers and campers.

FROM LEFT: ARINA P HABICH/SHUTTERSTOCK ©, GARY GRAY/GETTY IMAGES ©, C FLANIGAN/FILMMAGIC/GETTY IMAGES ©

Three Days to Travel Around

When you've seen Mesa Verde National Park, drive to **Telluride** (p229), a magnificent mountain town tucked into a box canyon.

Spend the morning hiking to Colorado's tallest waterfall, **Bridal Veil Falls** (p229) or challenge your fear of heights (and upper body strength) on the spectacular **Via Ferrata** (p231). In the afternoon, kick around town, have a nice meal and take a sunset ride on the **Gondola** (p230).

On your last day, make a beeline to **Black Canyon of the Gunnison National Park** (p234) where you'll be rewarded with spectacular canyon vistas along the park's **South Rim Rd** (p236).

If You Have More Time

From Black Canyon, head to **Grand Junction** (p244), a good base for touring the red-rock landscape in **Colorado National Monument** (p247) or **winetasting in Palisade** (p250).

The next day, head back south, stopping at the excellent **Ute Indian Museum** (p241).Continue to historic **Ouray** (p222) and hike a portion of the **Perimeter Trail** (p223) before spending the rest of the day soaking in the **Ouray Hot Springs** (p225).

In the morning, head to Durango on the epic **Million Dollar Hwy** (p226). End your trip on the historic **Durango & Silverton Narrow Gauge Railroad** (p218), taking in the Southwest's majestic mountain views.

JULY

Mountain flowers are in full bloom just in time for Crested Butte's **Wildflower Festival** (p243) and the **Lavender Festival** in Palisade (p250).

SEPTEMBER

Cooler days begin and the crowds disperse at the national parks. September also means harvest season and **wine tasting**.

OCTOBER

Magnificent **aspen groves** paint the landscape in brilliant yellows and golds. Prepare to leaf peep!

DECEMBER

Powder hounds hit the slopes around the region, including **Telluride, Crested Butte** and **Wolf Creek**.

MESA VERDE NATIONAL PARK

Mesa Verde National Park is one of the largest Native American archaeological sites in the US and certainly the best preserved. Nestled into a stunning landscape of canyons and mesas, it holds over 5000 ancient structures and 600 elaborate cliff dwellings. The site was inhabited by the Ancestral Puebloans for over 750 years, before being abruptly abandoned in 1300 CE. No one knows exactly why.

Mesa Verde sat undisturbed until 1888 when it was 'discovered' by two white ranchers who were following a tip from a local Ute Indian. Their family, the Wetherills, proceeded to sell artifacts from the site and to serve as guides. In 1906, with increasing visitor numbers, it was designated a national park and eventually became an Unesco World Heritage Site. Today, Mesa Verde is an archaeological wonderland and a sacred site to the descendants of the Ancestral Puebloans. It is place to respect and to explore, to learn about and delve into the mysteries of ancient America.

TOP TIP

If you find an artifact – say, a fragment of pottery – leave it untouched. An artifact, once removed from its original context, is incredibly difficult for archaeologists to analyze. Instead, take a photo or create a drawing and alert a ranger to its location.

SIGHTS
1 Balcony House
2 Cliff Palace
3 Step House

ACTIVITIES
4 Mesa Top Loop Rd
5 Morefield Campground Amphitheater
6 Petroglyph Point Trail

SLEEPING
7 Far View Lodge

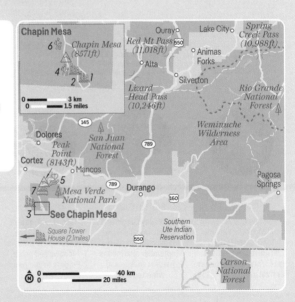

COLIN D. YOUNG/SHUTTERSTOCK ®

Square Tower House

PRACTICALITIES

Scan this QR code for prices, opening hours and other basic information.

Experiencing Mesa Verde

Mesa Verde National Park spans 81 sq miles over two broad mesas, each rife with Ancestral Puebloan dwellings. Some are on the mesa tops, but the most compelling are those built into high cliff walls. While you can see many from vista points, touring them means adventure at great heights, clambering up and down ladders, even crawling through tunnels...all to peer into the park's magnificent dwellings up close.

DON'T MISS

Cliff Palace

Balcony House

Step House

Petroglyph Point Trail

Mesa Top Loop

Square Tower House

Long House

Cultural performances

Ranger-Led Tours

Taking a ranger-led tour is one of the most rewarding ways to experience Mesa Verde. You'll deep dive into the history and lives of the Ancestral Puebloans and have access to otherwise restricted dwellings like Cliff Palace, Balcony House and Long House. But they're not for the faint of heart! Most involve walking along cliff edges, climbing up and down wooden pole ladders and crawling through tight spaces...but they're so worth it. Plan on taking two tours if you have the time.

Cliff Palace

Cliff Palace is the largest known cliff dwelling in the American southwest, a grand engineering achievement with 151 rooms and 23 kivas (ceremonial enclosures) that once housed 25 families. It's remarkable for its fine construction and efficient design. Check out Cliff Palace on an hour-long tour, retracing the same paths taken by the enclave's original inhabitants. In the summer, twilight tours are offered too.

Balcony House

Balcony House tour requires you to descend a 100ft staircase, climb a 32ft ladder and crawl through a 12ft tunnel...and that's just to get there. There are even more ladders and steps on the way out. But it's well worth the effort: the 38-room village is built in a cliffside alcove with a long arching roof and offers panoramic views of Soda Canyon, 600ft below.

Step House

Wetherill Mesa has the park's only self-guided cliff dwelling: Step House. A short but steep 0.8-mile trail leads to a two-in-one village, with 7th-century pit houses standing alongside 13th-century multistoried dwellings. Informational booklets are available at the entrance; a ranger is typically at the site to answer questions.

Top Loop Rd

A complement (or alternative) to scrambling through the park's cliff dwellings is a 6-mile driving tour along the Mesa Top Loop Rd. At various pull-offs, visitors can enjoy magnificent overlooks of Cliff Palace and other cliff dwellings or take short paths to a dozen different surface sites (no teetering ladders on this route). A free audio tour, played on any smartphone, leads the way.

Petroglyph Point Trail

This 2.4-mile loop trail follows a leafy footpath once used by the Ancestral Puebloan people. Dropping below the canyon rim, it's occasionally steep and rocky before it makes a short scramble back to the top of the mesa. Look for the petroglyphs at the 1.4-mile mark – a 35ft-wide wall with almost three dozen human and animal figures, spirals and handprints. A gate at the trailhead is locked in the evenings. If you arrive in the early morning, begin the trail in reverse.

Cultural Performances

In summer, the park hosts cultural performances and demonstrations by native peoples with ancestral connections to the park. Fascinating and educational, the demonstrations are a way to learn about Mesa Verde's ancient inhabitants and their modern-day descendants. Performances are in the Morefield Campground Amphitheater, typically in the evenings.

Overnight Stays

Stay overnight in the tasteful **Far View Lodge** (reservations recommended) or car camp at **Morefield Campground**, just steps from the park's general store and gas station.

GETTING AROUND

There is no public transportation in Mesa Verde. Plan on driving yourself and allot plenty of time to explore the park. The roads are steep, narrow and winding, so even a short distance can be slow going. Plan on an hour to drive from the highway turnoff to sites on either Chapin Mesa or Wetherill Mesa, and 45 minutes between the two. Watch for cyclists and wildlife!

TOP TIPS

- Visit May to October. Winter and spring bring closures to several park areas and amenities and tours are suspended.
- Fill your tank before you arrive – you'll be driving a lot. In a pinch, there's a gas station at Morefield Campground.
- Ranger-led tours only can be reserved online. Buy tickets 14 days in advance to assure a spot – they sell out fast!
- The museum is closed until 2025. Pick up informational booklets around the park to learn more about each site.
- Cellphone service is limited; download audio tours and maps ahead of time.
- Morefield Campground almost always has walk-up availability. On holiday weekends, expect a party zone.

Beyond Mesa Verde National Park

◉ Denver

Canyons of the Ancients National Monument
Purgatory Resort
Hovenweep National Monument
Cortez
Weminuche Wilderness Area
Mancos
Durango
Four Corners Monument
Mesa Verde National Park

Rich in archaeological sites and opportunities to get outdoors, Mesa Verde's surroundings beckon explorers of all stripes.

Brimming with archaeological sites and natural beauty, Mesa Verde's surroundings are an ideal place to explore and to learn about the ancient peoples who made this high desert home. Small towns pepper the landscape, offering traveler amenities as well as insights into the area's modern-day life and residents – the Native Americans, the ranchers, the artists and the big-city expats. Woven through it all, a treasure trove of trails leads hikers and bikers (and historic train riders) through high desert, red-rock canyons and the largest mountain wilderness in the state. Hot springs and homegrown ski areas are the cherries on top.

TOP TIP

The region's ruins are considered sacred by several tribal nations. Respect the signage and don't enter structures, climb on walls or touch petroglyphs.

Hovenweep National Monument (p216)

ZACK FRANK/SHUTTERSTOCK ©

213

I LIVE HERE: THE SUN DANCE

Ricky Hayes, Weeminuche Ute tribal member and a Ute Mountain Ute Tribal Park guide, shares his insight on a Ute ritual, which he has participated in several times.

'The Sun Dance is one of the most sacred ceremonies for my people, performed as a deep blessing for the tribe and the earth. It takes place the third week in June in a specially made lodge on Sleeping Ute Mountain. For four straight days, we pray, dance and fast – no food or water. The ceremony is sometimes called the 'Thirst Dance' because of this. The fasting is especially difficult, given the physical effort and the heat. Many people collapse but, eventually, rise and continue.'

2KAHNS PHOTO ARTS/SHUTTERSTOCK ©

Ute Mountain Ute Tribal Park

Ute Mountain Ute Tribal Park Ruins

BACKROAD ARCHAEOLOGICAL TOUR

Ute Mountain Ute Tribal Park is a dramatic landscape of towering mesas and buttes, and visiting there is a unique and unforgettable way to learn about Ancestral Pueblo communities. Ute tribal members guide visitors on half-day or full-day tours, following a network of rough dirt roads to reach several cliff dwellings and petroglyph sites, hiking along narrow cliffside trails and clambering up ladders to access them. Along the way, guides share in-depth interpretations of the ruins, relating them to their present-day culture. The 125,000-acre park belongs to the Weeminuche band of the Ute Nation of Indians, one of seven Ute bands that once inhabited the entire state (and beyond). It neighbors Mesa Verde National Park (p210). Tours offered April to October only.

 WHERE TO STAY IN CORTEZ

Retro Inn at Mesa Verde
Classic roadside motel decked out in 1950s splendor with modern amenities. Breakfast included. **$**

Kelly Place
Rare gem with ruins and desert trails on-site. Choose a tasteful adobe-lodge room, casita or campsite. **$$**

Canyon of the Ancients Guest Ranch
Western chic vacation rentals set on a historic ranch. The largest sleeps eight. **$$$**

Cortez Cultural Center Performances

LEARN ABOUT NATIVE CUSTOMS

Cortez' modest **cultural center** is well worth a stop, especially in the summer when Ute, Navajo, Lakota and Hopi tribal members give nightly dance performances and craft demonstrations to showcase and celebrate their cultures. Events are free and open to the public.

Four Corners Monument Selfie

FOUR PLACES AT ONCE

Don't be shy: everyone who visits **Four Corners** lies down on the marker so they're in four states at once. It makes for a good photo, even if not 100% accurate; government surveyors have long since admitted the marker is almost 2000ft east of where it should be, but it is still the legally recognized border point marking the intersection of Arizona, New Mexico, Utah and Colorado.

Canyons of the Ancients Sites

EXPLORE ANCESTRAL PUEBLOAN RUINS

Visually stunning and imbued with ineffable historical and spiritual energy, **Canyons of the Ancients National Monument** is home to the largest known concentration of archaeological sites in the country – over 6000 sites at last count. The sites, accessible off rough roads and remote trails, are spread over 170,000 acres of public land and span 12,000 years of human history. They range from singular hogans to entire ancient pueblos: a once-thriving population center that grew and persisted for thousands of years.

The **Anasazi Heritage Center** is an important first stop. A fascinating museum and research center, it doubles as the national monument's **visitors center** and has informative films and exhibits. Be sure to touch base with the rangers here; depending on your vehicle and timing, they can recommend specific sites and give you maps. In general, a high clearance vehicle is needed to access the trailheads for the national monument's sites; from there, hiking or biking is a must. The **Southwest Colorado Canyons Alliance** also leads recommended tours.

If you don't have a 4WD vehicle, the easiest ruin to visit is **Lowry Pueblo**. It's located about 25 miles northwest of the Visitors Center on (mostly) paved roads. Dating to 1060 CE, the site has several stone structures and nine kivas, including

WHY I LOVE CANYONS OF THE ANCIENTS

Liza Prado, writer

'Hiking through McElmo Canyon, the red earth dotted with yucca plants and sage brush, I can almost see them – the people who once called this red canyon home, carrying woven baskets filled with plants and berries, passing me on their way to their brick homes that (amazingly) still stand in the alcoves today.

I can almost smell the smoke from their cooking fires and hear the sounds of their everyday life carried through the canyon – the chatter, the chopping of wood, the children playing.

This place transports me, fills me with wonder and reminds me that, regardless of time or circumstance, we're all connected. For me, that's what travel is all about.'

✂ WHERE TO EAT IN CORTEZ

Silver Bean
Full lineup of caffeinated drinks and burritos, sold from an old-school Airstream trailer. **$**

Farm Bistro
Made-to-order comfort food prepared with (mostly) local ingredients. Plenty of vegan and gluten-free options too. **$$**

Stonefish Sushi
Standard sushi menu with Southwest touches like prickly-pear chili sauce and Colorado seared beef. **$$**

the 47ft **Grand Kiva**, which is believed to have been used for spiritual rites.

Alternatively, head to the southern entrance of the **Sand Canyon Trail**, a relatively flat 6.5-mile (one-way) trail that leads you through the breathtaking **McElmo Canyon**, with several cliff dwellings tucked into natural alcoves along the way. The largest, **Saddlehorn Pueblo**, is just 1 mile from the trailhead. For a post-hike treat, stop at the lovely **Sutcliffe Vineyards**, just down the road.

The Villages of Hovenweep National Monument

DIY RUIN-HOPPING

Hovenweep is a collection of five Ancestral Pueblo villages peppered across the red-rock canyons of Colorado, Utah and the Navajo Nation. Built between 1200 and 1300 CE, the archaeological sites are known for their impressive towers, most perched on canyon rims. The largest and easiest to access is the **Square Tower Community**, a clutch of well-preserved structures lining a beautiful sandstone canyon near the **Visitor Center** (Utah); a relatively flat loop trail (2mi) leads you through the site. The other ruins are located 4 to 9 miles away, most along unmaintained dirt roads. An adventure for sure, 4WD and high clearance vehicles are recommended, especially after heavy rains.

Crow Canyon Archaeological Center Programs

WORK ALONGSIDE ARCHAEOLOGISTS

If you're interested in archaeological digs, **Crow Canyon** is your place. A nonprofit research institute outside Cortez, it offers day- and week-long educational programs to nearby excavation sites; students work alongside experts, learning excavation and lab techniques while deepening their understanding of the Ancestral Puebloans.

Four Corners Mountain Biking

BACKCOUNTRY BIKING

The Four Corners area offers some epic mountain biking, with miles and miles of single track and dirt roads, climbing to high mesas, through rolling woodlands and over exposed slickrock. **Phil's World** is a favorite: a massive 32-mile trail system with one-way tracks for all levels through a beautiful pinon juniper

 WHERE TO STAY IN MANCOS

Mancos Inn & Hostel	Jersey Jim	Willowtail Springs
Homey spot with country-style rooms and a dorm. Common areas include a fully stocked guest kitchen. **$**	Historic fire-lookout tower with a kitchen, outhouse and epic forest views. But no water! Reserve early. **$**	Idyllic 60-acre wildlife sanctuary with country-chic cabins and lakeside home. Kitchens come stocked with goodies too. **$$$**

Absolute Bakery & Café

**BEST PLACES
FOR DRINKS
IN DURANGO**

Ska Brewing
Award-winning craft
beer served in a laid-
back tasting room.
Full menu and food
trucks too.

Bookcase & Barber
Modern speakeasy
hidden behind a
bookcase. Enter via
the barbershop and
bring the password!

Diamond Belle
Old-timey bar
with waitresses in
Victorian-era fishnets
and feathers. Live
ragtime packs the
house most evenings.

Starlight Lounge
LGBTIQ+ friendly
bar and lounge
with outdoor stage.
Weekly drag nights
and lip-synching
competitions.

**Durango Coffee
Company**
Western-themed
coffee house with
loads of nooks and
crannies to settle into.

forest. Other local favorites are **Boggy Draw**, located north of Dolores, and **Stoney Mesa Loop**, with gorgeous views and a technical rocky descent. Stop in Cortez' **Kokopelli Bike & Board** for trail talk and rentals.

An Afternoon in Mancos

ART, EATS AND DRINKS

Santa Fe eat your heart out. With a growing art scene, chilled-out vibe and cattle drives right through town, **Mancos** (MAN-cuss) has its own special brand of cowpoke quirk. Located just 7 miles west of Mesa Verde National Park (p210), it makes for an easy and worthwhile stop too. Park at the **Visitors Center** and walk west along the main drag, Grand Ave, ducking into galleries that feature local artists like **Artisans of Mancos** and **Raven House Gallery**. Continue to **Mancos Common Press**, another must: a restored historic letterpress that offers one-day classes and sells creative prints, cards and more. When hunger strikes, **Absolute Bakery & Café** is the go-to, specializing in farm-to-table meals and organic breads and pastries; you also can grab a big sandwich for the trail (and don't miss the lavender lemonade). Afterward, check out **Fenceline Cidery**, serving up hard ciders made from wild apples and live music on weekends; in the summer, nab a seat on its riverfront patio.

 WHERE TO STAY IN DURANGO

Adventure Inn
Simple, well-maintained motel on the trolley line. Rooms have extras like minifridges and docking stations. **$**

General Palmer Hotel
Elegant Victorian-era hotel decorated in period style. Cozy library and rooftop terrace are pluses. **$$**

Rochester Hotel
Boutique hotel with a Hollywood-meets-cowboy vibe. Enjoy the garden concert series in the summer. **$$$**

DURANGO ART BRIGADE

Walking through Durango, you'll see sculptures and art installations everywhere, from street corners to parking lots, and murals in unexpected places like dumpsters, planters and storage containers.

Many are thanks to the Durango Art Brigade, a public initiative launched in 2020 to promote economic recovery and resilience in the city's business districts. The initiative has continued and expanded in the years since, despite the Covid-19 pandemic, with art popping up throughout the city and showcasing Durango and the artists that call it home.

FLORIDASTOCK/SHUTTERSTOCK ©

Durango & Silverton Narrow Gauge Railroad

Snowdown Celebration in Durango

QUIRKY WINTER FUN

Dubbed the 'Cure for Cabin Fever,' Durango's **Snowdown Celebration** is a lighthearted weeklong event that coaxes thousands to its city streets. Held in early February, every year has a different theme – Intergalactic, Old West, Superhero, Shakespearian – that's translated into costumed festival-goers and a hundred different events, including a nighttime parade, beard growing contests, joke-offs, theater performances, cat yoga and even kickball in skis!

Durango & Silverton Narrow Gauge Railroad

BREATHTAKING MOUNTAIN TRAIN RIDE

Whether you're a train buff or not, don't miss riding the **Durango & Silverton Narrow Gauge Railroad**. A National Historic Landmark, it has hauled over $300 million in gold and silver on its tracks since 1882. Today, vintage locomotives carry passengers in Victorian-era carriages and open-air gondolas on a spectacular 45-mile route that follows the Animas River to Silverton (p233), offering one jaw-dropping mountain vista after another. The trip takes nine hours, including two hours in the tiny but interesting town of Silverton (to lop off 90 minutes, return by bus). Those looking to access the backcountry can

 WHERE TO EAT IN DURANGO

11th Street Station
Auto repair shop turned culinary collective serviced by food trucks, a bar and a coffee stand. **$**

James Ranch
Farmstand grill showcasing the ranch's own organic grass-fed beef, artisanal cheeses and fresh produce. **$$**

Steamworks Brewing Co.
Industrial meets ski lodge at this popular brewery featuring hearty pub grub with Cajun influences. **$$**

arrange to step off at the **Needleton** or **Elk Park** stops; to return, hikers must flag down passing trains. In winter, the route is shortened to 26 miles, with deep snow limiting the train's reach. Regardless of the season, reserve early.

Soaring Tree Top Adventures

ZIP-LINING THROUGH THE FOREST

If taking the train to Silverton (p233) doesn't pack enough of a punch, stop part way for this heart-stopping **zip-line course** – the longest zip-line course in the world, in fact. The 27 zip-lines range from 56ft to 1400ft long, running through the dense San Juan National Forest. The full course takes 5.5 hours to complete, including a gourmet lunch served high up in the trees. There's no access by road, but admission includes train travel in a deluxe car (helicopter rides extra).

Purgatory Resort Runs & Singletrack

ALL-LEVELS SKIING, RIDING AND BIKING

Offering some of the best value skiing and boarding – and one the best resort names anywhere! – **Purgatory Resort** has outstanding terrain, a friendly local vibe, and none of the lines and hassle at Front Range resorts. Lift tickets are under a hundred bucks, and kids under 12 ski for free; there are also great lodging deals if you're staying for a few days. The resort is evenly split between greens, blues and serious blacks, plus terrain parks and snowcat skiing. And Purgatory is blanketed by 260in per year of that famous San Juan deep stuff – pure heaven! If you're here in summer, rent a bike on-site and spend the day cruising the mountain resort's 20 trails, from mellow to technical. Or head into the backcountry, where 400 miles of singletrack awaits. Located 25 miles north of Durango.

Soaking in Durango's Hot Springs

ALL-AGES SOAKING

If you need a good soak after a day on the slopes or trails, this is the place: 26 hot spring pools (85°F to 107°F), all bubbling with healing minerals and infused with oxygen to maximize their benefits. Adults-only pools are set on a beautifully landscaped hillside, in tranquil spots with views of Durango's red sandstone mountains; live music on select evenings adds ambience. If you're traveling with children, come for the resort-style swimming pool, kid-friendly soaking pools and a rain tower that periodically drops steaming water on willing victims. Reservations required.

FORT LEWIS INDIAN SCHOOL

Overlooking Durango, Fort Lewis College is a well-respected school with a notable Native American student population – over 45%, representing 185 tribes.

The reason?

Native Americans attend tuition-free as part of the school's charter. The 1911 directive, perhaps, was an attempt at making things right.

Prior to becoming a college, Fort Lewis was an Indian boarding school, whose purpose was to eradicate student tribal identity and to force assimilation into mainstream culture.

Recent discoveries at other Indian boarding schools point to the assault and even murder of students. Today, state and tribal researchers are digging deeper into Fort Lewis' past; time will tell what Native American children actually endured here and what reparations will be made.

El Moro
Haunted gastropub serving innovative small plates and damned good cocktails. Ground zero for Durango hipsters. **$$$**

Ore House
Durango's best steakhouse serving free-range meats with mouthwatering sauces and sides. Casual and rustic environs. **$$$**

Cream Bean Berry
Artisanal ice-cream shop featuring inventive flavors, gluten-free waffle cones and vegan frozen treats. **$**

The Ruins at Chimney Rock

WANDER PAST ANCIENT RUINS

Chimney Rock is a fascinating archaeological site perched on a forested mesa, about 80 miles east of Mesa Verde, just outside Pagosa Springs. Built in the 11th century at the foot of two rocky pinnacles, it was a thriving commercial center and key lunar observatory of the Ancestral Puebloan people. Today, 200 structures remain, including many impressive examples of Chacoan architecture. Two trails lead you through the site: the lower one is an easy quarter-mile paved loop past pit houses and the **Great Kiva**; the upper one is a moderately strenuous hike along a narrow ridge to a 35-room **Great House**. For a deeper dive, book a tour with **Chimney Rock Interpretive Association** – Full Moon and Night Sky visits are especially rewarding. Don't miss the museum! Open May to September.

Pagosa Springs' Pools

SOAKING IN TOWN

Pagosa Springs, located about 90 miles east of Mesa Verde, is known for its hot springs. Its aptly named wellness resort, **The Springs**, has 25 artificial pools fed by the healing, mineral-rich waters of the **Mother Spring**, the deepest known geothermal spring in the world. Wander about its terraces, all overlooking downtown, dipping into pools of varying size and temperature (83°F to 111°F), a few even with direct access to the icy waters of the San Juan River – perfect for cooling off between soaks. If the admission fee is onerous, two smaller nearby spas are fed by the same hot spring but charge half the price: **Overlook Hot Springs Spa**,with rooftop tubs, and **Healing Waters Resort & Spa**, with a swimming pool and clothing-optional areas.

Wolf Creek Powder

EPIC POWDER SKIING AND RIDING

One of Colorado's best-kept secrets, **Wolf Creek Ski Area** has the deepest average annual snowfall in the state – a whopping 430in. Steep and deep, it's geared toward advanced skiers and boarders, and has terrific chutes and tree skiing, though there are some decent groomers and greens too. Come here after a big storm for waist-high powder and an incomparable white carpet ride. Almost best of all, Wolf Creek's distance from a big city and lack of on-site lodging (the nearest is in Pagosa Springs) has kept it happily isolated, meaning short lift lines and plenty of opportunities to lay first tracks. Don't expect

 BEST PLACES TO STAY IN PAGOSA SPRINGS

River Walk Inn
Inviting hotel rooms with direct access to Pagosa's riverside trail. Continental breakfast included. **$**

Fireside Inn Cabins
Cozy and well-appointed log cabins sitting along the San Juan River; perfect for families. **$$**

Springs Resort & Spa
Modern hotel rooms with 24/7 access to Pagosa's best hot springs and unlimited wellness activities. **$$$**

Weminuche Wilderness Area

MAJOR LUNAR STANDSTILL

Like many ancient peoples, Ancestral Puebloans were supremely attuned to celestial phenomena, including those that unfold over years, not merely weeks or months.

Moonrise, for example, shifts north and south in a cycle lasting 18.6 years. It includes two 'pauses,' when the moon rises in the same place for roughly three years (known today as the major and minor lunar standstills).

At Chimney Rock, the Great House was built such that, during the major lunar standstill, the full moon appears to rise exactly between the twin stone spires. Archaeologists point to this as evidence of just how skilled – in astronomy, engineering and more – the Ancestral Puebloans were.

anything fancy though – the lodge and lifts are definitely old school! Located about 120 miles east of Mesa Verde, it makes for a doable baut long day trip.

Waterfalls of Weminuche Wilderness Area

CAMERA-READY CASCADES

Weminuche Wilderness Area is the most extensive wilderness in Colorado. Named for a band of the Ute tribe and spanning 780 sq miles, it offers myriad opportunities for hiking and camping. Near Pagosa Springs, though, waterfalls take center stage. For a moderate hike, **Four Mile Falls** (6.2 miles round-trip) is a memorable double-cascade that ranges from wispy to thundering, depending on the season. Or look for the 100ft-high **Treasure Falls** – it's visible from the highway, but a short steep hike (1 mile round-trip) to the observation area is a worthwhile, mist-soaked pleasure and especially good if you have kids. (It's also stunning in the winter, frozen solid.) **Piedra Falls** (1 mile round-trip) is another beauty, reached via short hike following a scenic backroads drive.

GETTING AROUND

The Mesa Verde region has three small airports, which makes it easy to access the region: Cortez Municipal Airport, Durango-La Plata County Airport and Pagosa Springs' Archuleta County Airport. Once on the ground, the towns are small enough to navigate on foot, though Durango and Pagosa Springs have public buses to reach neighborhoods further afield. Between towns or to reach archaeological sites and trailheads, you'll need your own vehicle. Rentals are available at the regional airports.

OURAY

⦿ Denver

● Ouray

With gorgeous waterfalls draping the box canyon and soothing hot springs dotting the valley floor, Ouray (you-RAY) is a privileged spot, even by Colorado standards. It's a world-class ice-climbing destination, while for hikers and 4WD fans it's a playground of rugged terrain and stunning landscapes. Ouray sits on what was for centuries the summer hunting grounds of the Uncompahgre Utes. In the 1870s, the Utes were pushed out by the crush of miners who descended on the San Juan Mountains in search of silver and gold (and federal policies that favored them). Ouray soon became one of the fastest-growing towns in the region; at its height it had over 30 active mines and a population of over 2500 people. Today, it's a well-preserved mountain village with just 1000 full-time residents. Its only paved street, Main St, is registered as a National Historic District, and houses most of the town's gift shops, cafes and inns.

TOP TIP

Being situated at the bottom of a box canyon means that most of Ouray's hikes involve steep elevation gains. Consider carrying trekking poles – they'll help steady your footing on both the uphills and downhills!

Ouray Ice Park (p224)

DANITA DELIMONT/SHUTTERSTOCK ©

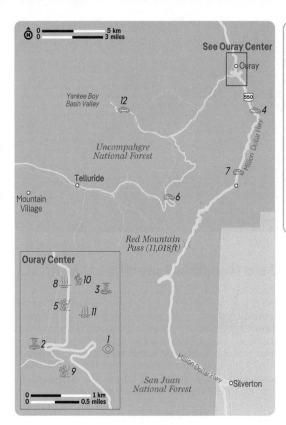

SIGHTS
1 Baby Bathtubs
2 Box Cañon Falls
3 Cascade Falls

ACTIVITIES
4 Alpine Loop (4WD route)
5 Basecamp Ouray
6 Imogen Pass (4WD route)
7 Million Dollar Hwy
8 Ouray Hot Springs
see 9 Ouray Ice Festival
9 Ouray Ice Park
see 9 Ouray Via Ferrata
10 Perimeter Trail
11 Wiesbaden Vapor Cave
12 Yankee Boy Basin (4WD route)

Ouray's Perimeter Trail Hike

HEART-PUMPING HIKE WITH VIEWS

Forming nearly a complete loop around Ouray, this 6-mile hiking circuit is one of the most scenic ways to experience the 'Switzerland of America.' Beginning across from the **visitors center** (there's free parking), the clockwise trail charts an up-and-down path through forests and aspen groves, across creeks and bridges, and even a one-time miners' potato patch turned alpine meadow.

Highlights include the spectacular **Cascade Falls**, **Baby Bathtubs**, a series of smooth tub-like rock divots, and the Ouray Via Ferrata/Ice Park (p224) where you can spy people clambering along sheer rock (or ice) faces.

The piece de resistance is **Box Cañon Falls**, a thundering 285ft waterfall that drops into a spectacular quartzite canyon. There's a modest fee to enter the canyon – a small park rich in birdlife – but you also can stay on the trail and admire the falls from a sky bridge. The full circuit takes four to five hours to complete; for a shorter hike, there are several entry points along the outskirts of town.

HOT SPRINGS 101

The steaming hot springs in and around Ouray are a geological byproduct of the San Juan Mountains.

The massive shifting, lifting and subducting of tectonic plates that created the mountains also created cracks deep in the earth's crust. As rain and other surface water seep down toward the earth's mantle, it becomes superheated; when it hits one of these fissures, it returns to the surface as a hot spring, its healing minerals collected en route, seemingly ready-made for soaking.

THE MAN BEHIND THE NAME

The town of Ouray is named after a 19th-century chief of the Uncompahgre band of the Ute tribe.

The US government named Ouray, a known peacekeeper who spoke several languages, 'Head Chief' of all Utes in Colorado, despite having no authority to do so.

Ouray represented the Utes in several treaty negotiations with the US, his more conciliatory positions often at odds with other Ute chiefs. All of this makes for a complicated legacy: Ouray's decisions are credited with saving his people from the death and destruction that befell so many other Native American tribes but at the cost of losing vast tracts of ancestral lands and, ultimately, the removal of the Utes to far-off reservations.

ARINA P HABICH/SHUTTERSTOCK ©

Ouray Hot Springs

Gold Mountain Expedition Via Ferrata

TRAVERSE AND SCALE MOUNTAINS

Ouray's newest via ferrata is located on **Gold Mountain Ranch**, a private property accessible only through the outfitter **Basecamp Ouray**. In addition to using steel rungs, cables and wobbly sky-high cable bridges to traverse the mountain, the route includes scaling about 1800 vertical feet, more closely mimicking natural rock climbing. The trip includes bonus peeks into an abandoned century-old mining operation – from the tunnel entrance to its blacksmith shop.

Ouray Ice Park Routes

CLIMB FROZEN WATERFALLS

Even if you're just mildly curious, don't miss the world's largest human-made public **ice park** – 2 miles of frozen cascade after frozen cascade in the **Uncompahgre Gorge**. The ice climbing is world class, but the spectacle alone is worth bundling up to see. With over 150 routes, there's a sublime (if chilly) experience for climbers all skill levels. The park is free, but newbies should get instruction through local outfitters like **Basecamp Ouray**; equipment rentals are available at local shops. In mid-January, the park hosts the **Ouray Ice Festival**, a popular three-day event with climbing competitions, clinics and nightly parties.

 WHERE TO STAY IN OURAY

Amphitheater Campground
High-altitude campground with bird's-eye views of the Uncompahgre Valley and several hiking trails nearby. **$**

Box Canyon Lodge & Hot Springs
Geothermically heated motel with modern pineboard rooms and 24/7 access to spring-fed barrel hot tubs. **$$**

Beaumont Hotel & Spa
Luxurious 19th-century hotel decked out in magnificent period furnishings. Ages 16 and over only. **$$$**

Ouray Via Ferrata Routes

PULL YOURSELF ACROSS MOUNTAINS

Traversing the same dizzying terrain as the Ice Park, the **Ouray Via Ferrata** is its summertime counterpart: the yin and yang of the Uncompahgre Gorge. Created for the adventurous and the vertigo-free, this series of steel cables, metal rungs and suspension ladders allows you to pull yourself up and across the steep mountain walls that line the Uncompahgre River. The reward: magnificent alpine views, the sound of the raging waters below and a feeling of serious badassness. The Via Ferrata's two routes are free, but definitely hire a guide like **San Juan Mountain Guides** unless you're an expert climber.

Ouray Hot Springs Waterpark

SOAK IN HISTORIC SPRINGS

For a healing soak or kiddish fun, try the **Ouray Hot Springs**. The hot springs were considered sacred by the Ute people who used them for hundreds of years before they were pushed from the region; later, miners soaked in the same waters to help heal their bodies. Today, the hot springs are a year-round waterpark surrounded by 13,000ft mountain peaks; come here for the eight-lane lap pool, waterslides, a climbing wall overhanging a splash pool and several adults-only soaking areas (78°F to 106°F). The geothermal water is crystal-clear and free of sulfur smells – a major plus. It's sourced near the Box Cañon Falls (p223) and the Weehawkin Spring, the latter providing Ouray's drinking water too.

Wiesbaden Vapor Cave

SOAK UNDERGROUND

A quaint hotel with public soaking facilities, **Wiesbaden** boasts Ouray's only 'natural' vapor cave. Carved into the mountain (and under the main lodge), two hot springs feed it – one seeping steaming water into a shallow soaking pool (107°F to 109°F); the other providing a cooling mineral-rich cascade (78°F). The dim lighting, rough cavern walls and sound of dripping water are more reminiscent of a mine shaft than a luxe spa, but it's still a treat. Outside there's a small spring-fed pool (included) and a private, clothing-optional soaking tub with a waterfall (reservation only).

SPOTTING THE BLACK SWIFT

Migrating over 4300 miles from north-western Brazil to the western US, the protected black swift is notoriously difficult to spot.

It could be the days it spends flying so high it's beyond the sight of the naked eye. Or its travel speeds, which can exceed 100mph. Or else its habit of nesting high on isolated waterfall ledges or deep inside coastal caves.

Committed ornithologists go to extremes to find black swifts, exploring deep into the wilderness to catch a glimpse.

The exception to this elusiveness? Ouray's Box Cañon Falls, a once-remote waterfall, now accessible by bridge, staircase and walkway, and where summertime visitors can spy these birds and their one-egg nests camouflaged against the dark canyon walls.

🍴 **WHERE TO EAT IN OURAY**

Maggie's Kitchen
Graffiti-bombed hole-in-the-wall serving deliciously sloppy burgers and fries. Nab a seat on the deck. **$**

Kami's Samis
Bright, modern spot with decadent breakfasts and gourmet sandwiches. Gluten- and dairy-free options too. **$$**

Bon Ton Restaurant
Historic restaurant in the St Elmo Hotel specializing in classic American and Italian fare. **$$$**

BEST WATERING HOLES IN OURAY

Ouray Brewing
Bustling brewery with chairlift bar stools and a sunny rooftop deck, perfect for people-watching.

Ouray Wine Garden
Casual garden seating at a historic home turned B&B. Local wines and hefty charcuterie boards served.

KJ Wood Distillers
Atmospheric tasting room serving award-winning gin and whiskey made with local barley and blue corn.

Full Tilt Saloon
Popular pub with two patios and free pool. Live music and happy-hour specials are serious draws.

JUDITH LIENERT/SHUTTERSTOCK ©

Red Mountain Pass

Jeeping in the San Juans

SEE THE BACKCOUNTRY

A vast network of old mining roads zigzagging through the spectacular San Juan Mountains makes Ouray ground zero for some of the best 4WD touring in the state. Routes take visitors on rugged backroad trails, through isolated alpine basins and past towering snowcapped peaks, with ghost towns and abandoned mines making for fascinating stops along the way. Popular routes include **Yankee Boy Basin** (18.8 miles), known for its waterfalls and wildflowers; **Imogene Pass** (17.5 miles), for its steep and rocky ride; and **Alpine Loop** (65 miles) for its variety of alpine passes, some pushing 13,000 ft. If you're comfortable driving rough mountain roads, rent a Jeep in town or, instead, book tour a tour with **San Juan Scenic Jeep Tours**. Hiking, hunting and fishing drop-offs are easily arranged too.

Million Dollar Hwy Views

EPIC MOUNTAIN DRIVE

The so-called **Million Dollar Hwy** is a truly mind-blowing section of Hwy 550 connecting Ouray and the tiny town of Silverton (p233). Some credit the moniker to a roadbed rich in valuable gold ore. Others say it cost $1 million to build. Whatever the reason, expect 25 miles of hairpin turns that cut through the forested Uncompahgre Gorge, its brooding mountains looming large and close, snow clinging to their lofty peaks. Drive with caution – the road is challenging, even in good weather, and the lack of guardrails doesn't help! Be sure to take advantage of pullouts; **Ironton** ghost town is popular with photographers and the **Red Mountain Pass** (11,018ft) is a favorite for its 360-degree views.

GETTING AROUND

A small, relatively flat town, Ouray is easily navigated on foot; most businesses are on or near the main drag. Having a 4WD vehicle makes it easy to explore the surrounding area (rentals available), though tour agencies easily fill in the gaps. For those arriving by car, there's plenty of free street parking.

Beyond Ouray

Ouray's surroundings offer awe-inspiring mountain-scapes and an appealing small-town vibe, with recreational opportunities at every turn.

Denver

Orvis Hot Springs
Ridgway State Park
Ouray
Telluride
Silverton Mountain Resort

In the heart of the spectacular San Juan Mountains, the towns surrounding Ouray are quintessential western Colorado: old-time mining outposts turned picture-perfect mountain towns offering countless opportunities to ski, bike, hike, fish...even just to bask in some high-altitude sunshine. You'll find high-end restaurants and rooftop bars, a thriving arts community and free-spirited festivals, and shops ranging from fine boutiques to kitschy gift shops. The area is imbued with history too: the lives of early miners and ranchers, and the Ute Indians before them, are the story of Colorado itself. Together, Ouray's surroundings paint a layered picture of the western slope. Visit Telluride for the high life, Ridgway for its nod to the Old West and Silverton for its no-holds-barred attitude.

TOP TIP

Before heading out to see the regional sights, make sure they're open. Many businesses close seasonally, typically mid-October to mid-May.

Silverton (p233)

RICHARD BROADWELL/ALAMY STOCK PHOTO ©

BEST ALT-ACCOMMODATIONS NEAR TELLURIDE

Bivvi Hostel Telluride
Chalet-style hostel with spacious bunk- and private rooms, each with en-suite bathroom and patio. Lockers, gear room and full breakfast included. $

CampV
Dotted with art installations, this high-desert escape has everything from tent sites and glamping to luxe Airstreams and cabins. Regular events include concerts, art workshops and yoga retreats. $$

Dunton Hot Springs
Ghost town turned exclusive log cabin resort offering all manner of mountain experiences. Hot springs pepper the property, indoor and out. $$$

LEFT: MICHAEL VI/SHUTTERSTOCK ©. BELOW RIGHT: JOSEPH SOHM/SHUTTERSTOCK ©

Gondola, Telluride

Telluride's History Museum & Tour

LEARN ABOUT TELLURIDE'S PAST

Designated a National Historic Landmark in 1964, Telluride is one of the country's most iconic Victorian-era towns, its streets lined with elegant buildings that once served as flophouses and saloons, schoolhouses and churches. Stop in the Smithsonian-affiliated **Telluride Historical Museum** to deep dive into the town's history, not only its mining past but also its beginning as Ute hunting grounds and transformation into a world-class ski town. Self-guided walking tours are available at the museum and online. Or take a **guided walking tour** with local Ashley Boling (📞970-728-6639), who has been giving engaging town tours for over 20 years.

Ride Telluride's Gondola

EPIC VIEWS

Linking the town of Telluride and the ski resort's Mountain Village, the free 12-minute ride on '**The G**' affords stunning box

 WHERE TO STAY IN TELLURIDE

Telluride Town Park Campground
Creekside campground in the heart of Telluride with showers, wi-fi, a pool...even tennis! $

Camel's Garden
Artful hotel at the base of the gondola. Hit the 25ft hot tub at sunset. $$$

Lumière
Ski-in, ski-out luxury lodge in Mountain Village, breathtaking views of the San Juans included. $$$

canyon panoramas as it transports you up and over 10,540-ft Coonskin Ridge. Get off midway at **Station San Sophia** for easy access to the slopes in the winter or hiking and biking trails in the summer. Or wander through the station to mountain chic restaurant-bar **Allreds** – a local hot spot for sunset drinks (don't miss the hand-cut truffle fries!).

Telluride Ski Resort Runs

SKIING AND BOARDING IN STYLE

Known for plunging runs and deep powder, and boasting gorgeous San Juan Mountain views and a certain high-society *je ne sais quoi*, **Telluride Ski Resort** is a truly special place. Decent sized in terms of lifts and acres – it has three distinct areas served by 19 lifts – Telluride has an outsized supply of advanced and expert terrain, from steeps and trees to wide open cirques, and even more if you are willing to hike for it, including iconic **Palmyra Peak**. And yet there are ample options for beginners and intermediate cruisers, including the playful 4.6-mile-long **Galloping Goose** run. Telluride's only Achilles heel is the snowpack: it takes an especially deep blanket of snow for the resort to open fully.

Telluride's Festivals

BANJOS, HULA HOOPS AND MORE

The **Telluride Bluegrass Festival** is the town's most famous fest, a summer solstice celebration of folk music and mountain life. It draws big-name bands and over 10,000 revelers each day – many donning hula hoops as dance partners. The main stage is set in the leafy **town park**, with stalls selling all sorts of food and local brews; late-night concerts and free workshops are held in smaller venues around town. Tickets sell out fast for the June event – buy early and consider a combo ticket-and-camping package for an all-in experience.

If you can't make the bluegrass fest, don't fret – Telluride hosts some two dozen other festivals throughout the year. Faves include: the groovy **Telluride Mushroom Festival** (pictured right); **Mountainfilm**, an environmental film festival; the internationally recognized **Telluride Film Festival**; and the season-ending **Blues & Brews Festival**.

TRANSFER WAREHOUSE

Dating from 1906, the Transfer Warehouse served as Telluride's transportation hub for everything from gold to groceries until its roof caved in under the weight of snow in 1979.

Left virtually untouched for 40 years, Telluride Arts purchased and transformed the historic site into an open-air cultural center, a place where art exhibits, concerts, dance parties and more are held throughout the year.

Plans to add indoor spaces, including a rooftop bar, are in the works. In the meantime, stop by to see what's on when you're in town.

🍸 **WHERE TO DRINK IN TELLURIDE**

There
Swanky social alcove serving creative cocktails and nibbles, with an East meets West bent.

Telluride Brewing Co.
Popular no-nonsense brewery with a Western warehouse vibe; don't miss the award-winning Facedown Brown.

Last Dollar Saloon
Shoot pool and spin stories at 'The Buck,' the locals' favorite late-night haunt.

MINING BUFFS' DRIVING TOUR

An active mining town for well over a century, Silverton's 'rich' history is well worth a day of exploring. Located just 25 miles south of Ouray (p222), it's also an easy day trip along gorgeous mountain roads.

Start 8 miles east of Silverton at the **1 One Hundred Gold Mine**, where you'll don a hard hat and ride a vintage mining tram a third of a mile into a once-active mining tunnel. Former miners lead the tours, sharing fascinating anecdotes about life underground and gold mining through the years; they often perform drilling demonstrations with old-school equipment. Panning for gold is included – a treat for little ones, especially (the sluice box is regularly 'salted' with gold dust and other goodies).

Afterward, head back toward town, stopping at **2 Mayflower Gold Mill**, the longest-running mill in the San Juans. Detailed signage leads you through the site, describing how gold, silver and other metals were extracted, using the imposing and still-intact machinery. The Aerial Tram House is a highlight, its tram buckets that once carried men and ore, still hanging on cables leading from the mill to now-closed mines. And don't miss the Guard Shack and its exhibits on the high-ticket (and creative) robberies the mill experienced.

End at the **3 Mining Heritage Center Museum**, a sprawling 14,000 sq-ft-complex with well-conceived exhibits, including a recreation of the Sunnyside Mine, an actual miners' boarding house and rare train memorabilia. The museum is attached to the meticulously restored 1902 county jail, which instantly transports you to Silverton's early days.

Save a bit by getting the **Heritage Pass** if you think you'll hit all three. Note: These three attractions are open from May to October only.

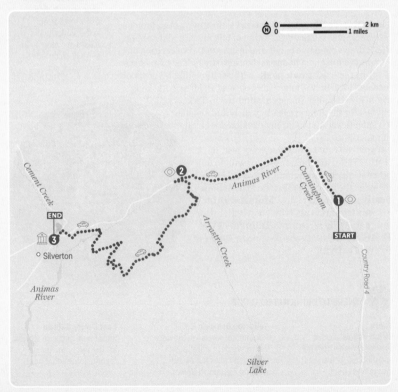

JEREMY JANUS/SHUTTERSTOCK ©

Bridal Veil Falls

Day Hikes from Telluride

WATERFALLS, LAKES AND PANORAMIC VIEWS

A network of nearly two dozen trails branches out like arteries from the heart of Telluride, a spectacular mountain town just a 50-mile drive from Ouray (or 10 miles as the crow flies over the craggy Sneffels Range). Hikes crisscross the town's box canyon, from easy strolls along the scenic **Telluride River Trail** (4.4 miles) to the strenuous wildflower-filled **Sneffels Highline Trail** (12.5 miles), an offshoot of the popular **Jud Weibe Trail** (3.1 miles). For something in between, hike to Colorado's tallest waterfall, the 365ft-tall **Bridal Veil Falls** (2.5 miles to the bottom; 3.4 miles to the top) along rocky switchbacks through a thick aspen forest, passing two smaller waterfalls along the way. From there, extend your hike by continuing up a narrow mining road, eventually passing through alpine meadows and forests to the otherworldly **Blue Lake** (5.7 miles, 12,400ft). Looking for more? A dozen more trails start at the **Mountain Village** at Telluride Ski Resort (p230).

NOTORIOUS BLAIR ST

It may be a quiet street today, but Notorious Blair St was once the epicenter of Silverton's vibrant vice trade, home to brothels, dance halls, variety theaters and saloons.

Miners from camps throughout the region came to Silverton for supplies, and to Notorious Blair St to blow off steam.

Every February, the rowdiness returns in the form of Silverton Skijoring, a popular two-day hybrid competition where skiers are pulled at top speeds behind galloping horses on courses with rings, jumps and gates. The winner gets a cash prize. It's not exactly lewd but certainly irreverent (and fun to watch)!

  WHERE TO EAT IN TELLURIDE

Butcher & Baker
Cute breakfast spot with generous to-go sandwiches and sides perfect for the trail. **$**

Siam
Cozy Thai restaurant in one-time family home. Patio seating and occasional live music too. **$$**

Chop House
Western fare prepared with panache, from savory elk steaks to bison ribeye. **$$$**

Telluride's Via Ferrata Course

SKY-HIGH ADRENALINE RUSH

Suspended 500ft in the air, pulling yourself across the eastern face of Telluride's box canyon on thick cables and iron rungs, you might wonder what you've gotten yourself into. But one glance says it all: bird's-eye views of the craggy San Juan peaks, a thick carpet of aspen and fir trees all around, the iconic **Bridal Veil Falls** on one end, and the oh-so-tiny-looking town grid on the other. It's high adventure in a harness. Go with a guide unless you're an expert climber. Try **Mountain Trip**. Note: climbers under 5ft will have to stretch to their limits (or create work arounds) to reach some rungs.

Orvis Hot Springs Pools

CLOTHING-OPTIONAL SOAKING

Even if baring it all makes you uncomfortable, the steaming rock pools and garden setting make the clothing-optional **Orvis Hot Springs** hard to resist. Yes, it does get its fair share of nudists, but the variety of soaking areas (90°F to 114°F) means you can scout out the perfect spot. On-site accommodations, even camping, include two days of unlimited soaking...a sweet deal! Located 9 miles from Ouray.

Ridgway State Park Waterplay

ONE-STOP FISHING, PADDLING AND SWIMMING

Fishing aficionados should head to **Ridgway State Park**, home of **Paco**, the Blue Ribbon–rated tailwater of the Uncompahgre River. Fourteen miles from Ouray, this gorgeous stretch of river is stocked with native trout, including browns, rainbows and cutthroat; catch and release only. Fishing not your thing? The park's turquoise **reservoir**, with its jaw-dropping views of the Sneffels Range, has a swim beach and is a popular for paddleboarding and kayaking. Rentals are available on-site and in nearby Ridgeway through **Rigs Fly Shop & Guide Service**.

San Juan Huts Base Camp

BACKCOUNTRY OVERNIGHT ADVENTURE

Spend your days exploring the mountains and your nights in the **San Juan Huts**, a series of basic huts owned and operated by its namesake outfitter, and extending 215 miles from Durango through Ridgeway, Ouray and Telluride to

 WHERE TO EAT IN RIDGWAY

Tacos del Gnar
Delicious fusion riff on street tacos in a fast-casual setting. Booze served too. $

Kate's Place
One of the best breakfast joints around, set in a cute and colorful spot. $

Eatery 66
Food truck turned hipster restaurant with an ever-changing menu of sandwiches, salads and treats. $$

Moab, Utah. You can base yourself in one hut, or travel hut-to-hut by foot, skis or bike, accessing trails rarely used by others, the great outdoors seemingly all yours. Rental includes basic supplies and amenities; mountain bike trips include food too.

Silverton Mountain Skiing

EXPERT SKIERS AND RIDERS ONLY

Silverton Mountain Resort is unlike any other Colorado resort, with a motto that says it all: No Frills All Thrills. There are no condos, no grooming, not even any proper runs and only one dinky lift. And yet that one lift puts you at the top of hundreds of acres of backcountry bowls, chutes, trees and steeps – and even more if you're up for hiking. It's North America's steepest and highest resort (the peak is over 13,000ft) with arguably the best powder lines and expert-only terrain anywhere. Add to that heli-skiing – available in single drops or six-drop passes – and it's no wonder Silverton is the stuff of legend.

There are guided and unguided options – check the website for details. Avalanche gear is required (and available for rent). Located just 23 miles south of Ouray.

Silverton Powdercats Trips

SNOW CAT SKIING AND RIDING

More accessible to families and intermediate skiers than big bad Silverton Mountain Resort, **Powdercats** is a friendly and professional operation running guided ski and snowboard trips on **Molas Pass** (pictured right), just outside of Silverton. A snow cat delivers your group to great drop-in points; most groups get about 10 runs in for the day. The guides know the best powder stashes, drop-offs, tree runs and more, all while keeping everyone safe and smiling. Avi beacon included. Reserve well ahead of time. Most trips depart from **Molas Lake Trail**, 1 mile north from the summit of Molas Pass.

BEST BEVVY SPOTS IN SILVERTON

Avalanche Brewing Company
Longtime local brewery that pulls a crowd; look for the skis inside and out. Pizza served too!

Columbine Roadhouse
Popular music venue with open-air bar and stage. Located on the edge of town, where the Million Dollar Hwy ends.

Coffee Bear Silverton
Modern coffeehouse with Western flair. Known for its square-shaped breakfast burritos and epic rooftop views.

GETTING AROUND

Telluride Regional Airport is the main airport in the Ouray region; Montrose Regional Airport is nearby and often has cheaper flights. There's no public transportation outside of Telluride – in town, there is a free town shuttle, gondola (p230) and a commuter bus – so having your own vehicle is the best way to get around. A range of vehicles can be rented at the airports and in Ouray and Telluride, including Jeeps and other 4WDs. From May to October, travelers also can ride from Silverton to Durango on the Durango & Silverton Narrow Gauge Railroad (p218).

BLACK CANYON OF THE GUNNISON NATIONAL PARK

⊙Denver

● Black Canyon of
the Gunnison
National Park

Steep, narrow and utterly spectacular, the Black Canyon of the Gunnison National Park is a massive 2700ft-deep gash in the earth, etched out over millions of years by the Gunnison River and volcanic uplift. Declared a national park in 1999, for visitors it offers breathtaking views, challenging hikes and myriad climbs; no matter how you experience it, you're sure to leave with a sense of awe (and a little vertigo).

Black Canyon has proven a formidable obstacle to humans trying to best it. Though early Utes had settlements along its rim, no people have lived within the chasm itself. Efforts to create a train route through it were limited (some say, doomed) and were eventually abandoned. Only its river has been tamed; a water diversion tunnel and a series of upriver dams keep the canyon's river at a predictable flow, while providing water and electricity to neighboring communities.

TOP TIP

The national park is split by the canyon into the South Rim and North Rim. No bridge connects the two sides even though, at their closest, they are just 1100ft apart. Allow at least two hours to drive between the two areas, about 80 miles on (mostly) paved roads.

Black Canyon of the Gunnison National Park

LEFT: KYOOTAEK CHOI/SHUTTERSTOCK ©. RIGHT: RUSLANKPHOTO/SHUTTERSTOCK ©

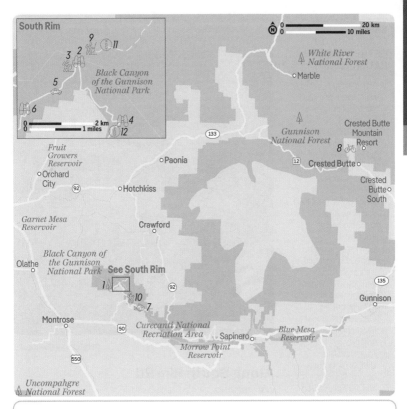

THE GUIDE

MESA VERDE & SOUTHWEST COLORADO

SIGHTS
1 Black Canyon of the Gunnison National Park
2 Chasm View
3 Painted Wall
4 Pulpit Rock Overlook
5 South Rim Rd
6 Sunset View

ACTIVITIES, COURSES & TOURS
7 Gunnison River
8 Lupine Loop

9 North Rim
10 Oak Flat Loop

INFORMATION
11 North Rim Ranger Station
12 South Rim Visitor Center

**Juniper tree,
Black Canyon of the Gunnison National Park**

235

SAFETY IN THE BLACK CANYON OF THE GUNNISON NATIONAL PARK

- There are few guard-rails, even near the steepest drops – keep small children close and watch your step, especially while taking selfies!
- Don't throw anything into the canyon. Even a small rock could prove fatal to someone hiking or climbing below.
- Paddling on the Gunnison River is highly discouraged – it's swift, rocky and cold. For water sports, head instead to neighboring Curecanti National Recreation Area (p240).
- To protect the wildlife, pets must be kept leashed, and are not allowed on hiking trails, in the Inner Canyon Wilderness, or on ranger-led walks. During the summer, dogs cannot be walked – or even carried – around the South Rim Campground due to potentially aggressive mule deer defending their fawns.

LEFT: TAMPA/SHUTTERSTOCK ©, BELOW RIGHT: GALYNA ANDRUSHKO/SHUTTERSTOCK ©

Pulpit Rock Overlook

Along South Rim Rd

EASY DRIVING, THRILLING VIEWS

With views of 2000ft canyon walls and colorful craggy spires, driving along the rim of the Black Canyon of the Gunnison is the most accessible and popular way to experience this national park. For 7 miles, the flat, winding **South Rim Rd** hugs the canyon's edge with a dozen pull-offs and overlooks offering heart-stopping vistas. Hit them all, or just select a few if you want to leave time for hiking. Good options include **Pulpit Rock Overlook**, a fingerlike outcropping with expansive river views; **Chasm View**, the narrowest point in the canyon, just 1100ft across; **Painted Wall**, Colorado's tallest vertical cliff (2250ft), named after its magnificent pink pegmatite stripes; and **Sunset View**, with dramatic vistas at the day's end.

 BEST PLACES TO STAY IN BLACK CANYON OF THE GUNNISON NP

South Rim Campground	**East Portal Campground**	**North Rim Campground**
Large campground (88 sites) in a scrub forest near the Visitor Center. Open year-round. $	Leafy riverside campground (15 sites) accessible by steep paved road. Tents only. First-come, first-served. $	Remote rim-side campground (11 sites) off a dirt road. First-come, first-served. $

Oak Flat Loop Trail

LEAFY WALK WITH VIEWS

If you're looking for a below-the-rim hike without hoofing it clear to the canyon bottom, **Oak Flat Loop** is a good option. Starting at the **South Rim Visitor Center**, it's a 2-mile loop through an aspen and Douglas-fir forest, with openings in the trees providing spectacular views of the canyon. A moderately strenuous hike, it features a 400ft drop before the trail meanders back to the surface.

North Rim Rock Climbing

SCALING SHEER WALLS

The **North Rim** is all about rock climbing. Much less traveled but reachable by dirt road, it's a full-on adventure area with 145 multi-pitch climbing routes rated between 5.9 and 5.13, including along the **North Chasm** and to the top of the **Painted Wall**. Unless you're an expert climber, a guide is a must. Try **Mountain Trip** or **IRIS**, an outdoors company catering to women, non-binary and trans people.

Inner Canyon Wilderness Routes

SCRAMBLING TO ROCK BOTTOM

Hiking to the bottom of the Black Canyon (and back up!) is a punishing but awe-inspiring way to spend a day.

There are six routes through the inner canyon – three from each rim, ranging from 1800 to 2700 vertical feet, and promising untrammeled wilderness, magnificent river-canyon views and solitude. All are primitive hiking experiences on unmarked and unmaintained trails, involving scrambling over boulders and loose rocks and navigating by natural landmarks. Hikers must have a **Wilderness Use Permit**, available for free at the **South Rim Visitor Center** or **North Rim Ranger Station** beginning at 3:30pm the day prior – only five to 20 permits per route are allotted each day, and they go fast, especially in the summer. Most routes end in riverside campsites – a treat to stay overnight if you're up for carrying the extra gear and supplies.

Whichever route you take, start early and be prepared! The Visitor Center has helpful binders listing recommended supplies as well as step-by-step photos of each route – peruse them before heading out.

INTERNATIONAL DARK SKY PARK

Black Canyon of the Gunnison is an outstanding place for stargazing, thanks to its clear dry weather and exceptionally dark skies.

In 2015 the park became one of Colorado's first official International Dark Sky Places (the state has 10 now), thanks not only to its dark skies but also the park's work to limit light pollution and to educate visitors on astronomy, nocturnal ecosystems and more.

Summer brings loads of free astronomy programming by park rangers and members of the Black Canyon Astronomical Society. In September, the park hosts Astro Fest, with nightly telescope viewings, guest lectures by astronomers, and info on the night sky.

BLACK CANYON TRAIN TRACKS

From 1882 to 1949, the Denver & Rio Grand (DRG) train traveled through the upper reaches of the Black Canyon, showcasing its sheer 2,000ft-high canyon walls and the raging Gunnison River.

Part of a Denver-Salt Lake City line, building the 15-mile track proved expensive and a dangerous endeavor, claiming numerous lives and costing an astounding $165,000 per mile.

When it was completed, the track was plagued by rock falls and avalanches, and it was eventually abandoned, with a safer route being built through Grand Junction.

Today, the train tracks are almost entirely gone, submerged beneath the waters of the Curecanti National Recreation Area. A railyard exhibit at the Cimarron Visitor Center is the only reminder of what was once here.

RYAN BONNEAU/ALAMY STOCK PHOTO ©

Fly fishing, Gunnison River

Fishing on the Gunnison River

CASTING ON GOLD MEDAL WATER

Driving down the incredibly steep and curvy **East Portal Road** to the canyon bottom, anglers will find some of the best fishing in Colorado. Designated as Gold Medal Water, the Black Canyon's section of the Gunnison River is a top spot for rainbow (catch and release) and brown trout (bag limit of four). Be sure to get a Colorado fishing license before your first cast; lures and flies only.

GETTING AROUND

Black Canyon of the Gunnison National Park is only accessible by private vehicle. There's plenty of parking at the South Rim Visitor Center as well as at pullouts along the South Rim and North Rim roads. In the winter (late

November to late April), the South Rim Road is only open to vehicles up to the Visitor Center; the remainder is open to cross-country skiers and snowshoers. The East Portal and North Rim roads are entirely closed in the winter.

Beyond Black Canyon of the Gunnison National Park

Denver ◉

Morrow Point Reservoir • • Crested Butte
• Montrose
Shavano •
Valley • **Black** • Blue Mesa
Canyon of Reservoir
the Gunnison
National Park

From museums to backcountry adventure, the Black Canyon surroundings provide historical context and outdoor fun year-round.

The region surrounding Black Canyon of the Gunnison National Park is as diverse as the canyon is deep. On the western edge, Montrose is a nondescript town whose main role is supplying goods to the surrounding communities. But it also happens to have some ancient sites and museums that are worth a stop. On the region's eastern edge, Crested Butte is a spectacularly beautiful mountain town with a rich mining history and quirky sensibility; it's all about the outdoors here, and maybe some naked skiing too. Between those polar opposites lies the stark beauty of Curecanti National Recreation Area – a huge reservoir system formed by the damming of the Gunnison River, and a popular place for water play.

TOP TIP

Gas up at the start of each day. Long stretches of empty roads mean gas stations are few and far between.

Crested Butte (p242)

JOHN DE BORD/SHUTTERSTOCK ©

DRY MESA DINOSAUR QUARRY

Uncompahgre National Forest is home to Dry Mesa Dinosaur Quarry, the site of the most diverse cache of Jurassic-period dinosaur specimens ever found. Over 4000 dinosaur bones were unearthed here, belonging to everything from colossal crocodiles and turtles to winged lizards and fierce carnivores, and even the 8ft shoulder blade of a 120ft-long herbivore dubbed Supersaurus. And yet an entire skeleton was never found: the bones were deposited haphazardly on top of each other, the likely result of periodic droughts and flash floods washing them to this spot from near and far, over thousands of years. Today, after three decades of excavation, the quarry is covered up, only a couple signposts remaining where an epic discovery was once made.

Curecanti National Recreation Area

Blue Mesa Reservoir Outings

ADVENTURE ON THE WATER

Impossible to miss from Hwy 50, **Blue Mesa Reservoir** is Colorado's largest body of water, with nearly 100 miles of shoreline, its sapphire waters edged by sweeping mesas, volcanic spires and secluded canyon walls. This is the heart of the **Curecanti National Recreation Area**, an otherworldly playground neighboring the Black Canyon of the Gunnison National Park (p234), created from a series of dams and reservoirs where the Gunnison River once flowed freely. Explore the waters by boat and be sure to bring fishing gear – it's the largest kokanee salmon and lake trout fishery in Colorado. Paddlers will especially enjoy the calm waters at the **Bay of Chickens**, but beware of strong afternoon winds! For rentals, gear and guides, head to the **Elk Creek** and **Lake Fork Marinas**. And if you'd rather stay on dry land, try **Dillon Pinnacles Trail** (4 miles round-trip), offering close-up views of the area's striking volcanic spires, with the reservoir always within view.

 BEST PLACES TO STAY IN MONTROSE

Cedar Creek Lodging & RV Park	**Canyon Creek B&B**	**Hampton Inn Montrose**
Well-equipped RV park with campsites, cabins, yurts and even tiny houses, many along a creek. **$**	Immaculately restored B&B with three cozy rooms. Happy hour and an outdoor hot tub are perks! **$$**	Comfortable chain hotel next to the Montrose Airport. Small pool, free shuttle and breakfast included. **$$**

Boating on Morrow Point Reservoir

RANGER-LED TOUR THROUGH BLACK CANYON

This popular **pontoon tour** takes you on a gentle 1½-hour ride on **Morrow Point Reservoir** in **Curecanti National Recreation Area**. Winding through the upper Black Canyon, park rangers provide insight on the stunning scenery, wildlife and history of the area. Expect waterfalls, towering peaks and volcanic spires, including the legendary **Curecanti Needle**. Boats leave from the dock near the end of **Pine Creek Trail**, a 2.5-mile round-trip hike including 232 steps – allow an hour for the moderate trek. Book early!

Ute Indian Museum Offerings

LEARN ABOUT THE UTES

One of the few American museums dedicated to a single tribe, the **Ute Indian Museum** in Montrose examines the many cultural and historical layers of Colorado's longest continuous residents. Artifacts, displays, videos and hands-on exhibits together paint a powerful portrait of the Ute people, past and present. There are regular speaker series and film screenings too. The museum sits on the homestead of legendary Ute Chief Ouray and his wife, Chipeta; she is buried in the adjoining **Ouray Memorial Park**. Located just 15 miles from Black Canyon of the Gunnison National Park (p234).

Shavano Valley Petroglyphs

PETROGLYPH TOUR

Just west of Montrose, **Shavano Valley** is home to a spectacular petroglyph site dating from 1000 BCE. Accessible by private tour only, the 26 well-preserved panels are set in red sandstone cliff faces and boulders, many depicting plants and animals, people and anthropomorphic figures, even representations of the still-celebrated Ute Bear Dance. The Ute Indian Museum offers docent-led tours of the site and provides referrals to private guides. Tours last two hours, along a short trail.

Museum of the Mountain West

MOSEY BACK IN TIME

For an authentic-as-it-gets Wild West museum, Montrose's **Museum of the Mountain West** doesn't disappoint. A recreated Old West town, the grounds here feature buildings

---

THE WORLD'S LARGEST ORGANISM

Crested Butte's **Kebler Pass** is (definitely? probably? maybe?) home to the world's largest organism: a grove of quaking aspen trees. For sheer biomass, whales and dinosaurs have got nothing on self-cloning plants like aspens, which can generate thousands of stems from a single root system. That's the case on Kebler Pass, where vast stands of towering aspen trees, so gorgeous when alight in fall colors, are actually single organisms. There are other contenders: a 'humungous fungus' in Oregon and massive sea grass forests in Australia, not to mention a rival aspen grove known as Pando in Utah. Scientists say that proving which one is biggest would be nearly impossible, but you can guess what Coloradans think!

✕ BEST PLACES TO EAT IN MONTROSE

Horsefly Brewing Company	**Colorado Boy**	**Camp Robber**
Popular brewhouse known for its Tabano Red and pub grub. Live music most weeks. **$**	Creative pizzas and craft beers in the historic center. Gluten-free crust and salads offered too. **$**	Fine dining meets strip mall. Serves Americana with contemporary New Mexican and Italian twists. **$$**

BEST PLACES FOR APRÈS IN CRESTED BUTTE

Uley's Cabin Ice Bar
Literally, an ice bar – snow-covered bar top included – at the bottom of the 'Peanut' run at Crested Butte ski resort.

Dogwood
Chichi cocktail lounge in a historic miner's cabin. Innovative drinks feature house-infused liquors and pair well with flavorful appetizers.

Montanya Rum
Artisanal rum distillery serving potent mixed drinks, sippers and flights in a midcentury modern tasting room. Reservations recommended.

Eldo Brewery
Low-key brewery serving pints and Himalayan eats. Live music most nights.

relocated from nearby settlements, including a saloon, clinic, jail, chapel, numerous storefronts, and even the original building where boxing champ Jack Dempsey trained. Each is overflowing with memorabilia, from prosthetic eyeballs to bank safes. For a few extra bucks, guides in period dress will lead you through the museum, adding interesting and wacky anecdotes.

Crested Butte Mountain Resort Offerings

BRAVE THE STEEPS

An expert's paradise, **Crested Butte's ski resort** has some the most stomach-lurching steeps in Colorado with infamous runs like **Rambo**, the steepest in-bounds run in the country, and **Teocalli 2 Bowl**, reachable by a 20-minute hike. The green and blue terrain are more limited, sure, but the resort's gorgeous vistas, powdery snow and hat-head charm make it appealing no matter your level. Acquired by Vail Resorts in 2018, the resort got some much-needed upgrades to its lifts and other facilities, but hasn't lost its irreverent and renegade spirit – locals are still known to take runs naked at the end of the season. The resort also has a terrific **Nordic Center**, and partners with the **Adaptive Sports Center** to promote mountain access for people of all abilities. It's located 2 miles north of town and 90 miles from Black Canyon of the Gunnison National Park (p234).

Lupine Loop Trail

MOUNTAIN BIKING AND WILDFLOWERS

With over 450 miles of singletrack trails, Crested Butte is one of the best and most diverse places to mountain bike in the state. A newish addition to its vast mountain biking network, the aptly named **Lupine Loop** takes riders alongside fields of lupines and other wildflowers and through dense aspen forests. The 13-mile intermediate-level ride has just enough climbing to keep you honest and a fun jaunty descent at the end. The ride starts right from town and has sections of both dirt road and singletrack. For any biking needs, local outfitters like **Alpineer** and **Big Al's Bicycle Heaven** offer rentals, retail, maps, clothing and more.

SEAN XU//SHUTTERSTOCK ©

WHERE TO EAT IN CRESTED BUTTE

Frank's Deli
Local fave serving hearty sandwiches and breakfast burritos perfect for the trail. Ask about specials! **$**

Secret Stash
Award-winning pizzeria with boho-vibe, teahouse seating and tapestries included. Creative cocktails pack a punch. **$$**

Sunflower
Inventive, locally sourced dishes served in a homey cabin-like setting. Menu changes with seasonal ingredients. **$$$**

Crested Butte Bike Week Events

ALL THINGS BIKING

The world's oldest bike festival, **Crested Butte Bike Week** is a celebration of all things bike-ish, from technical demos and curated rides to a wacky race known as **The Chainless**, where costumed riders, using bikes with the chains removed, coast crazily from Kebler Pass (p241) down to CB – whoever can stay off their brakes the most without crashing, wins! Held every June.

Crested Butte Mountain Heritage Museum

HISTORICAL SNAPSHOT

This small but impressive museum makes the case that CB is the true birthplace of mountain biking (suck it Marin County!) with original 'klunker' bikes and funny, informative exhibits. There are great displays on mining and skiing plus self-guided historical tour maps of town too.

Wildflower Festival Hike

THE SCIENCE OF BEAUTY

More than skiing, more than its mountain-chic ethos, even more than mountain biking (though some will quibble), Crested Butte is most famous for one thing: wildflowers.

From vast hillsides of mule's ears to riverside pockets of elephant heads and shooting stars, and practically everywhere between, Crested Butte is absolutely saturated in wildflowers. Not surprisingly, the city hosts a popular **Wildflower Festival**, typically in the second week of July. The programming is almost as varied as the flowers, from guided walks to painting and photography classes, and even how to make wildflower-infused cocktails.

One unique option is a wildflower tour with the **Rocky Mountain Biological Laboratory**, a research and educational institute in the one-time ghost town Gothic, just north of town. Scientists lead walks where you'll learn not just about flowers, but also the history, geology and meteorology that make this location so special.

FAT TIRE REVOLUTIONARY: NEIL MURDOCH

In April 1998, Neil Murdoch – local CB eccentric and the founder of mountain biking as the world knows it – slipped out town with just his clothes and a bike, hours before federal marshals closed in. Murdoch, aka Richard Barrister, had settled in little-known Crested Butte in 1974 after skipping bail on a cocaine smuggling charge in New Mexico. A consummate tinkerer, Murdoch began outfitting old Schwinn bikes to be ridden off-road, including adding low gears and wide knobby tires – thus the 'Fat Tire Revolution' was born. When he disappeared, Crested Butte rallied behind Murdoch in absentia, even establishing a fund for his legal defense. He was eventually caught in 2001, but is still revered as the godfather of mountain biking.

GETTING AROUND

Two regional airports service the Black Canyon region – Gunnison-Crested Butte Regional Airport and Montrose Regional Airport.

Once here, public transportation is extremely limited so the best way to explore the region is in your own vehicle (there are car-rental agencies at both airports); 4WD is especially useful in the winter or if you're planning to explore the backcountry.

The exception is Crested Butte, where Mountain Express provides free and frequent bus service between town, the resort and most condominium locations.

GRAND
JUNCTION

Named for its location at the confluence of the Colorado and Gunnison Rivers, Grand Junction is an agricultural hub and a right-of-center stronghold in an increasingly left-leaning state. As a travel destination, Grand Junction's backers quip the city's motto could be 'Gas and Gatorade' as many road trippers view the city as a convenient pit stop between the better-known destinations of Moab, Utah and the Colorado Rockies. Even Coloradans seem unaware of what Grand Junction has to offer. But anonymity has its advantages: Grand Junction not only has small-town charm but also has engaging places to visit, and you'll often have them to yourself. And with loads of traveler amenities, Grand Junction makes a convenient base camp for the myriad outdoors options surrounding it – from stunning vistas in Colorado National Monument to Colorado's very own wine country.

TOP TIP

Grand Junction has Western Colorado's largest airport and best selection of car rentals. Flying to Denver is certainly going to be cheaper but could require a long drive on busy I-70. Check for flight deals to Grand Junction; it may be a better hub for your Colorado adventures.

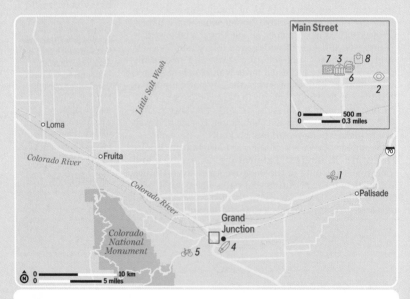

SIGHTS
1 Little Book Cliffs Wild Horse Area
2 Main St
3 Museum of Western Colorado

ACTIVITIES
4 Las Colonias Park
5 Lunch Loop Park

DRINKING
6 Ramblebine Brewing

ENTERTAINMENT
7 Art on the Corner

SHOPPING
8 A Robin's Nest of Antiques & Treasures

Stroll through Downtown

ART, ANTIQUES AND MORE

Soak in Grand Junction's small-town charm with an afternoon stroll. Start on **Main St**, between 3rd and 7th Streets, where colorful murals brighten large brick walls and the wide walkways host **Art on the Corner**, an outdoor exhibit of over 100 whimsical sculptures, large and small. Peruse the quirky boutique shops along the way – **A Robin's Nest of Antiques & Treasures**, the largest vintage shop on the western slope, is a sure hit. From there, stop at the **Museum of Western Colorado**, with impressive exhibits ranging from Ancestral Puebloan pottery to Wild West firearms. Wrap it up with a pint at **Ramblebine Brewing**, a warehouse-style taproom serving everything from IPAs to sours.

Paddling in Las Colonias Park

SUPING LESSSONS AND TOURS

Stand-up paddleboarding isn't terribly difficult, but a few pointers on proper balancing, paddling and steering can make a world of difference. GJ's artificial **Butterfly Lake**, in **Las Colonias Park**, is a great place to practice the basics before you graduate to an open-water paddle down the adjacent **Colorado River**. Rentals, lessons and tours are available on-site through **Grand Junction Adventures**.

Biking Lunch Loop Park

MOUNTAIN BIKING NEAR DOWNTOWN

Bikers of all levels will enjoy loop-de-loop fun at **Lunch Loop Bike Park**, while advanced riders can tackle the famous **Tabeguache/Lunch Loop Trail System**. The bike park, located at the beginning of trail system, has rollers, berms and singletracks of various sizes and pitches – a great place to hone your balance and gear management. Longer trails, including a 142-mile ride to Montrose, offer tough biking and spectacular views in equal measure.

BEST PLACES TO EAT IN GRAND JUNCTION

Pablo's Pizza
With sidewalk seating and small-town vibe, these creative thin-crust pies are easily the best in town. $

Dream Café
Modern diner with to-die-for breakfast, from eggs Benedict and quiche to chocolate hazelnut French toast. $

Copeka Coffee
Retro coffee shop specializing in vegan and vegetarian treats. $

Tacoparty
Hipster taco joint showcasing an ever-changing menu of locally sourced ingredients, from produce to proteins. $$

Devil's Kitchen
Rooftop restaurant and bar with elevated regional dishes and magnificent Grand Mesa views. $$$

 GETTING AROUND

Downtown Grand Junction is very walkable – there's little traffic and most businesses are located around a four-block section of Main St. Beyond downtown, driving your own car is the most convenient way to get around.

Rentals are available at the Grand Junction Regional Airport and street parking is prevalent. Alternatively, Grand Valley Transit provides limited bus service around town or you can rent a bike from a handful of shops.

Rattlesnake
Canyon

Fruita Grand Junction
● ●Palisade
Colorado
National   Paonia
Monument

Denver
◉

Beyond Grand Junction

The Grand Junction surrounds are brimming with outdoors options, from myriad trails and climbing routes to quiet vineyards and agritourism offerings.

The high-desert landscape surrounding Grand Junction is often overshadowed by flashier parts of the state. But, taking a moment to explore, visitors will find a place rich in beauty and outdoors activities. From wine tasting and picking your own lavender to dramatic red-rock hikes and some of the best singletrack biking in the west (plus dinosaur sites galore!), it is a surprisingly layered part of Colorado. Almost best of all, the region is conveniently compact, with most of its sights and activities located just a few miles apart, making it possible to have a full day's activities without spending half of it in your car.

TOP TIP

This is a high-desert playground, and staying hydrated is essential. On trails, carry at least 1 gallon of water per person per day.

Joe's Ridge

IAMSAMROGERS/SHUTTERSTOCK ©

DAN LEETH/ALAMY STOCK PHOTO ©

Colorado National Monument

JOHN OTTO'S VISION

We can all thank an eccentric trail-building hermit with burros named Foxy and Cookie for the formation of the Colorado National Monument. John Otto came to the Grand Junction in 1906 and was thunderstruck by the red cliffs and sandstone spires west of town – 'the heart of the world,' as he famously called them. Otto campaigned tirelessly for federal recognition of the canyonscape, giving tours, writing editorials and sending letters to politicians. Importantly, he also cut a network of trails, mostly by himself with a shovel and pickaxe, so when President Taft signed an order creating Colorado National Monument in 1911, it was ready for visitors.

Colorado National Monument Vistas

DRIVING AND HIKING PAST RED ROCKS

Don't let the rather mundane name fool you, nor your eagerness to reach more famous destinations east or west of here: **Colorado National Monument** is a stunning natural area and well worth a visit. A warren of ancient canyons crisscrosses the mesa just 16 miles west of Grand Junction, their sheer walls painted a gorgeous cedar red. Erosion by water and ice has left long rocky fins, dramatic sandstone spires and massive overhangs.

The most popular way to experience the park is via the 23-mile-long **Rim Rd**, which weaves along the cliff edges, with 19 pullouts offering stunning vertiginous vistas of the canyon walls and monoliths. There's outstanding hiking too, allowing you to appreciate the formations close-up: **Devil's Kitchen** (1.9 miles round-trip) is a popular short hike and scramble to a natural 'room' inside a large stone outcrop, or take the longer **Monument Canyon Trail** (11.6 miles round-trip), which passes many of the park's most interesting natural features, including the **Kissing Couple**, **Independence Monument** and the **Coke Ovens**.

 WHERE TO STAY IN GRAND JUNCTION

Castle Creek Manor
Suburban B&B with five tasteful rooms, each with hot tub and independent entrance. Adults only. **$**

Camp Eddy
Charming urban campground on the Colorado River. Fully equipped tiny homes and Airstreams lend a hipster vibe. **$$**

Hotel Maverick
Plush, modern rooms with spectacular views. Located on CMU's campus with students working the front desk. **$$**

Rattlesnake Arches

BACKCOUNTRY CAMPING IN COLORADO NATIONAL MONUMENT

Camping in Colorado National Monument is sublime, with dark starry skies and a nighttime orchestra of frogs, crickets and coyotes.

While there is one established campground – Saddlehorn Campground – backcountry campers can find a spot just about anywhere along the park's 46 miles of trails. Favorites include Monument Canyon for its rock sculptures, Black Ridge for its vistas and No Thoroughfare Canyon for its isolation.

Wherever you pitch your tent, a backcountry permit is required (free at the visitor center) and campers should set up at least 100ft off the trail and out of sight and hearing of other campers. Bring plenty of water, and note that fires, bikes, drones and pets are not allowed.

Rock Climbing in Colorado National Monument

CLIMBING SANDSTONE

Colorado National Monument is a sandstone dreamland for climbers. **Otto's Route** on **Independence Monument**, the park's iconic 450ft tower, has a very doable 5.9 rating, while **Sentinel Spire**, just across the valley, is another bucket-lister with beautiful crack routes. Meanwhile, giant slabs and long cliff lines throughout the park offer scenic bouldering, scrambling and top-roping for all levels. Head to **Summit Canyon Mountaineering** for gear, maps and recommendations.

Kokopelli & 18 Road Trails

HIGH-DESERT BIKING

Just 12 miles west of Grand Junction, **Fruita** is home to some of the best mountain biking in the west and has a fraction of the crowds found in nearby Moab, Utah. The riding here is incredibly scenic, with long open roadways along the mesa, and exhilarating and challenging singletrack through rocky

 WHERE TO STAY IN FRUITA

Saddlehorn Campground
Colorado National Monument's only drive-up campground with potable water and flush toilets. Open year-round. **$**

James M Robb Colorado River State Park
Lakeside campground with 60 sites, clean bathrooms and even a playground. Located near Dinosaur Journey. **$**

Balanced Rock Motel
Tidy and well maintained, this modern motel is an excellent value. Popular with mountain bikers. **$**

canyons and dense forest. The dry, mild high-desert climate also allows for a long riding season that stretches from late April to mid-November. **Kokopelli Trail** is Fruita's most famous; 142 miles of ruggedly beautiful advanced-level riding leading all the way to Moab. Staying closer to town, the **18 Road** area has trails and roadways for all levels. Check out **Over the Edge Sports** – a full-service bike shop and Fruita biking institution, which offers guided rides and advocates for responsible trail use.

Trail Through Time

PALEONTOLOGIST FOR A DAY

The best of four interpretive dinosaur trails around Fruita, **Trail Through Time** is a 1.5-mile loop in the high desert of **Rabbit Valley Research Natural Area**. You can learn loads about the prehistoric landscape from interpretive signs, touch in-situ bones and, in summer, check out the active **Mygatt-Moore Quarry**, where over 2000 dinosaur bones have been unearthed since the 1980s. Better still, join paleontologists on half- or full-day digs in the quarry, a program offered through **Museums of Western Colorado** Paleontology Division; children over five welcome.

Dinosaur Journey Museum Exhibits

LEARN ABOUT FRUITA'S DINOSAURS

Fruita is home and namesake to one of the world's smallest known dinosaurs – the one-pound *Fruitadens* – and is rich with paleontological finds. The small **Dinosaur Journey Museum** explains why, and has a fantastic collection of fossils and skeletons, interesting multimedia demos plus animatronic dinos that snort steam and jerk around. It can be a little bit corny at times, but it's still informative and definitely fun for the younger members of the party.

The Arches of Rattlesnake Canyon

HIKE A HIDDEN TREASURE

Twenty miles from Grand Junction in the stunning high desert of **McKinnis Canyons National Conservation Area**, **Rattlesnake Arches Trail** (12.4 miles round-trip) leads visitors past nearly three dozen natural arches – the most in the US outside Arches National Park. The trail begins on a scenic sagebrush mesa and splits: a lower trail gets you up close and personal with eight of the largest arches, including

MIKE THE HEADLESS CHICKEN FESTIVAL

In 1945, Fruita farmer Lloyd Olsen chose a bird named 'Mike' for dinner and, hoping to preserve as much of the tasty neck as possible, lopped off the chicken's head, but missed the all-important brain stem.

Mike the (newly) Headless Chicken did not fall over and die – to the contrary, he stayed alive for another 18 months, fed grain and water via eyedropper, and became the subject of news reports, magazine covers and actual scientific studies. (He even toured Atlantic City, with his owner and his severed head, preserved in alcohol.)

Naturally, the townspeople of Fruita created a festival in Mike's honor; celebrated every June, it includes chicken-themed runs and contests, live music, disc golf and more.

 WHERE TO EAT IN FRUITA

Hot Tomato Café
Bustling pizza joint and cyclist hangout. Good salads and selection of Colorado beers on tap. **$**

Aspen Street Coffee
Good spot for breakfast sandwiches and strong coffee. After hours, it pivots to a wine bar. **$**

Karma Kitchen
Family-run restaurant serving Indian and Nepali comfort food. On weekends, expect a wait. **$$**

Cedar Arch, measuring 76ft across, while an upper trail offers views from above and (if you dare) a walk across some of the sandstone arches. Be sure to take plenty of water and keep your eyes for peeled for wildlife like desert bighorn sheep and golden eagles. The trail's namesake, the midget faded rattler, is venomous but rarely seen. The access road is rough, especially the last 2 miles; visitors in 4WD or high-clearance vehicles can reach the main trailhead, while most park and walk once the road becomes impassable.

Wineries in Palisade

TASTE COLORADO WINES

Twelve miles east of Grand Junction, **Palisade's** warm, dry microclimate and volcanic soil isn't just great for growing peaches – it turns out it's ideal for grapes as well. The town has over 20 vineyards, mostly small-scale family farms along dirt roads. While it's no Napa Valley, their low-key ambience is part of the attraction. Most offer free tastings and some have extensive tours. Rent a bike or book **Palisade Pedicab** to tour the vineyards, following the **Fruit and Wine Byway**. Favorites include the award-winning **Colterris**, known for its *Vitis vinifera* wines and cave tastings; **Maison La Belle Vie**, a country casual winery specializing in small batch wines; and **Sauvage Spectrum**, a newcomer known for its sparkling wines.

Tour SunCrest Orchard Alpacas & Fiber Mill

LEARN ALL ABOUT ALPACAS

If cuteness were currency, the McDermott family would be sitting on a Palisade gold mine with their combination alpaca farm and fiber mill. Meet the fuzzy, inquisitive creatures (a smaller cousin of the llama) and then take a tour of the fiber-processing plant. Or turn up the cute and pair off with your own alpaca for a mini-trek through the peach orchard.

Sage Creations Organic Farm Visit

PICK YOUR OWN LAVENDER

Each summer, a sea of purple greets you at this organic lavender farm in Palisade. Take a **self-guided tour** to learn about lavender varietals and pick a basketful of your own from its gorgeous fields (basket and scissors provided). In late July, the farm also participates in the **Colorado Lavender Festival**, a multiday event including farm tours, cooking demos and loads of lavender goods.

 WHERE TO STAY IN PALISADE

Spoke and Vine Motel
Sleek and modern motel with nice details like breakfast delivered, bike storage and contactless check-in. **$$**

Wine Valley Inn Palisade
Victorian B&B with wraparound porch, clawfoot tubs and clothing-optional hot tub. Adults only and LGBTIQ+ friendly. **$$**

Wine Country Inn
Big cookie-cutter hotel with vineyards, buffet breakfast and a pool. Afternoon wine receptions are a hit. **$$**

Wild mustangs, Little Book Cliffs

Little Book Cliffs Wild Horse Area

HIKE PAST WILD MUSTANGS

Little Book Cliffs is home to one of the last protected bands of wild mustangs in the US – about 100 horses on some 36,000 acres of craggy canyons and plateaus. Several trails run through the reserve, making it possible to see different families of horses – either studs with a small harem of mares or bands of young stallions. The easiest access is via the **Main Canyon Trail** (8 miles round-trip), off I-70 (Cameo exit), 16 miles east of Grand Junction. The trail runs through a spring-fed canyon – its vegetation and fresh water a draw for the mustangs, especially in winter and spring. Alternatively, split off onto **Spring Creek Trail** (10 miles round-trip) with towering voodoos, flowering cacti and a gurgling creek. If you see horses, don't approach or pet them – they are wild after all – and give foals especially a wide berth.

Tour Paonia

SIP, EAT AND SHOP

Take a 70-mile drive from Grand Junction to **Paonia**, an artsy town surrounded by organic farms and vineyards, with views of towering mesas and snowy peaks. Start at **Stone Cottage Cellars**, a family-run vineyard known for its full-bodied syrahs. From there, enjoy a charcuterie board and a flight of wines on the veranda of the upscale **Azura Cellars** (peek into its art gallery too). Then beeline to **Delicious Orchards** for fruit picking, live music and hard-pressed ciders. Finish up with a stroll down historic **Grand Ave**, popping into Paonia's boutiques and thrift shops, with a late lunch at **Flying Fork Café**, a farm-to-table Italian restaurant.

HIGH-COUNTRY NEWS

At a time when local and regional reporting seems in inexorable decline, the *High County News* (HCN), published in quirky Paonia, Colorado, stands as a journalistic lodestar. Nonprofit and fiercely independent, HCN focuses on the American West, covering 12 states and scores of Indigenous communities.

Its stories are regularly picked up by national media and it's considered required reading for politicians, policymakers and activists. Although best known for its environmental coverage, HCN also has outstanding reporting on the arts, science, Native American affairs and more.

The magazine was founded in 1970 by rancher and conservationist Tom Bell; today it has over 30,000 subscribers and publishes a magazine, newsletter and website, plus regular special reports.

GETTING AROUND

The best way to access and explore the region is in your own vehicle; rentals are available at Grand Junction Regional Airport. Otherwise, Grand Valley Transit provides limited bus service to and around Grand Junction, Fruita and Palisade. Bicycle rentals also are readily available.

SOUTHEAST COLORADO & THE SAN LUIS VALLEY

PIKES PEAK OR BUST

Cast your eyes on the larger-than-life landmarks that once guided travelers across the Great Plains.

Denver ●

Colorado's arid southeast is a place of high deserts backed by craggy peaks and flat-topped mesas, where silvery sage and scraggly juniper morphs into the quaking aspens and hardy pines of the central mountains. Dotted with signature landmarks – Pikes Peak, the Great Sand Dunes, the Royal Gorge and the Garden of the Gods (pictured) – southern Colorado interweaves dramatic vistas with hard-scrabble history to great effect.

In this stripped-down setting, the bones of the earth are particularly evident: fossilized dinosaur footprints, massive petrified sequoia stumps and the volcanic vestiges of the Spanish Peaks serve as stark reminders of a geological timescale in which human life is no more than the blink of an eye.

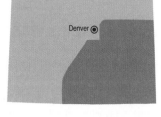

OLEG KOVTUN HYDROBIO/SHUTTERSTOCK ©

But a fascinating human element lingers here too. Come to discover a time when the area was part of Mexico and played host to the Santa Fe Trail, which brought together the intersecting lives of Native Americans, Hispanic settlers, French trappers, grizzled prospectors, and the covered wagon trains of hope-filled American homesteaders.

From the mysteries of the San Luis Valley to the craggy summits of the Sangre de Cristo range, from rafting the rapids of the Arkansas River to chugging along on a historic steam train, and from huffing to the top of Pikes Peak to driving the treacherous routes of old stagecoach roads, a magnificent journey through the parched wilds of southeast Colorado awaits.

THE MAIN AREAS

COLORADO SPRINGS
Museums meet the great outdoors.
p258

GREAT SAND DUNES & THE SAN LUIS VALLEY
Desert dunes and Hispanic heritage.
p265

CAÑON CITY & THE ROYAL GORGE
Sheer cliffs, river runs and a historic railroad.
p273

TRINIDAD & THE SANTA FE TRAIL
Old forts and tall grasses.
p277

Tower of Babel, Garden of the Gods (p259)

Find Your Way

The north–south interstate I-25 links Denver with Colorado Springs, Pueblo and Trinidad. East–west Hwy 50 links up with Cañon City, while Hwy 160 runs west to the massive San Luis Valley.

Lost Creek
Wilderness
Area

Pi
Nat
For

24

Floriss

Florissant Fossil
Beds National
Monument

Cri
C

9

Continental Divide

285

San Isabel
National
Forest

Salida

Poncha
Springs

Arkansas River

Gold Belt
Byway

Ca
C

50

Poncha Pass
(9010ft)

50

Texas
Creek

Coaldale

San Isabel
National Forest

Westcliffe

96

Sangre de Cristo
Wilderness Area

114

69

Great Sand Dunes & the San Luis Valley, p265

This massive dune field draws visitors to the San Luis Valley, bound by the jagged Sangre de Cristo and San Juan mountain ranges.

Cr Rd T

285

Crestone

Gunbarrel Rd

17

Cr Rd G

112

Hooper

Great Sand Dunes
National Park

Del Norte

160

San Luis
Lake

Wolf
Creek
Pass

Rio Grande
National
Forest

Alamosa

160

Fort Garland

Rio Grande

159

South San Juan
Wilderness Area

285

Conejos River

142

San Luis

Manassa

159

Antonito

17

Cumbres
Pass

CAR

With little public transportation in the area, there's no question that renting a car is the way to go. Several scenic byways have unpaved sections; depending on your level of interest, you may want to rent an AWD vehicle.

TRAIN

Amtrack's Southwest Chief, running from Chicago to LA, stops in Trinidad, CO, near the New Mexico border. A handful of historic steam trains are still in operation, but are not useful for getting around.

BUS

Bustang runs between Colorado Springs, Denver and Pueblo, with another route running west from Pueblo with stops in Cañon City, Salida and Alamosa. Greyhound runs along the I-25 corridor, with stops in Colorado Springs, Pueblo and Trinidad.

Colorado Springs, p258

Drive up a fourteener, scramble over red-rock formations and learn something new at the city's unique museums.

Cañon City & the Royal Gorge, p273

Get your thrills in the Royal Gorge adventure park or take a tour of the Old West past dinosaur quarries and former gold mines.

Trinidad & the Santa Fe Trail, p277

This little-visited corner of the state rubs up against the high mesas of New Mexico, and is chock-full of frontier history.

Woodland Park

Manitou Springs

Colorado Springs

nrose

Pueblo

Arkansas River

an Isabel ational rest

Walsenburg

La Veta

Spanish Peaks Wilderness

West Spanish Peak (13,626ft)

Cuchara

Trinidad

Fishers Peak State Park

Comanche National Grassland

Purgatoire River

0   50 km
0   25 miles

NEW MEXICO

Plan Your Time

Many visitors will get no further than Colorado Springs and Pikes Peak, though detours to the Royal Gorge, the San Luis Valley and Trinidad are easy and rewarding journeys.

PHIL BERRY/SHUTTERSTOCK ©

Royal Gorge (p274)

If You Do Only One Thing

Start the day in **Colorado Springs** (p258) with a trip to the **Garden of the Gods** (p259). Stroll through the park and admire the wafer-thin red-rock formations, but don't lose sight of the day's objective that looms in the background: **Pikes Peak** (p263).

Drive to **Manitou Springs** (p264), from where you can either take the cog railway straight up the mountainside or follow the 19-mile serpentine highway thousands of feet up to the wind-whipped summit.

All that elevation change will likely leave you exhausted, so enjoy a lazy afternoon strolling through Manitou, before returning to Colorado Springs to replenish your calories in style.

Seasonal Highlights

Late spring and early fall are the perfect times to explore low-elevation destinations, while the height of summer offers a window of opportunity to hike the high country.

JANUARY

Winter is less frigid than you might think – strip down to short sleeves for the **Great Fruitcake Toss** in Manitou Springs.

MAY

Spring is lovely in the Front Range. Celebrate with festivals like **MeadowGrass** and **Territory Days** in Colorado Springs.

JUNE

The legendary **Pikes Peak International Hill Climb** comes at the end of the month. The Sand Dunes, meanwhile, will soon be too hot.

A Few Days to Travel Around

From **Colorado Springs** (p258), drive southwest to **Cañon City** (p273) and the **Royal Gorge** (p274). Let loose in the adventure park up top or go off-road and enjoy the local mountain-biking trails and sport climbing at nearby **Shelf Rd** (p276).

The next day, follow the **Gold Belt Scenic Byway** (p276) to **Cripple Creek** (p276) and back; spend the rest of the day in historic **Salida** (p197), upstream on the Arkansas River. From here, it's a 90-minute drive through **San Luis Valley** (p269) to the **Great Sand Dunes** (p265), one of the more surprising national parks and also one of the most ecologically diverse.

Return to Colorado Springs via **La Veta** (p281) and the **Spanish Peaks** (p281).

If You're Road-Tripping across the State

Instead of zipping through the plains on I-70, why not follow the old **Santa Fe Trail** (p280) along Hwy 50 instead?

The first site is the Japanese internment camp at **Amache** (p281); a detour north will take you to the **Sand Creek Massacre memorial** (p281). Back on Hwy 50 in Las Animas are the **Boggsville homestead** and **Bent's Old Fort** (p280).

Bear left at the fork to follow Hwy 350 through the **Comanche National Grasslands** (p280), where a full-day detour brings you to the country's largest dinosaur track site and the ruins of an abandoned mission. From here it's another hour to **Trinidad** (p277) and the New Mexico border.

JULY

Warmer temperatures and smaller waves make the challenging **Royal Gorge** (p274) white-water experience more friendly for first-timers.

AUGUST

The mercury's soaring, but don't miss the fun at the **Colorado State Fair and Rodeo** in Pueblo.

SEPTEMBER

On your marks, get set... That's right it's time to start running – up **Pikes Peak** (p263). It's one-half trail race, one-half marathon.

OCTOBER

The aspens are turning gold and the **Emma Crawford Coffin Races** are back in Manitou Springs – just in time for Halloween.

COLORADO SPRINGS

Denver

Colorado Springs

One of the nation's first destination resorts, Colorado Springs is now the state's second-largest city and one of many faces. A strong military presence underpins the city's economy and population, with nearly 100,000 veterans and 45,000 active troops living in the area.

The Air Force Academy is the most well-known military institution here, followed closely by the controversial Space Command and NORAD (North American Aerospace Defense Command). The latter's 30-megaton-proof nuclear bunker, buried deep in Cheyenne Mountain – yes, *that* Cheyenne Mountain west of town – is the stuff of urban legend and has been fodder for Hollywood filmmakers for decades. Alas, the facility is not open to tour groups.

Most visitors, however, aren't here for the army bases but the natural landscape: the Garden of the Gods and the anthem-inspiring Pikes Peak combine to draw over 23 million people to Colorado Springs annually.

TOP TIP

Colorado Springs can be divided into two distinct neighborhoods, bisected by I-25 and connected by the east–west Colorado Ave and Hwy 24. The downtown area lies to the east, while Old Colorado City, the original 1860s settlement, is to the west.

Garden of the Gods

LEFT: JOHN HOFFMAN/SHUTTERSTOCK ©. RIGHT: INFINIUMGUY/SHUTTERSTOCK ©

RED ROCK CANYON OPEN SPACE

A former quarry and part of the sandstone formation that runs through the Garden of the Gods, this 787-acre park was nearly developed into a golf course and townhouses. Thanks to committed residents who fought the good fight, however, it's now a fabulous local park, where you can hike, mountain bike and rock climb, without all the tourist hoopla.

Plenty of trails, such as Sand Canyon, Mesa and Contemplative, loop through the park, and can be combined for walks of 2 to 6 miles. Rock climbers have access to over 90 bolted routes. Sign up with Front Range Climbing or the Pikes Peak Alpine School for a guided day out.

SIGHTS
1 Cheyenne Mountain Zoo
2 Colorado Springs Fine Arts Center
3 Garden of the Gods
4 National Museum of World War II Aviation
5 Olympic and Paralympic Training Centers
6 Pioneers Museum
7 Rock Ledge Ranch
8 US Olympic & Paralympic Museum
9 Will Rogers Shrine of the Sun

ACTIVITIES
10 Overdrive Raceway

SLEEPING
11 Great Wolf Lodge

Garden of the Gods

RED-ROCK CATHEDRALS

This gorgeous vein of red sandstone (about 290 million years old) appears elsewhere along Colorado's Front Range, but the **Garden of the Gods'** mountain backdrop and exquisitely thin cathedral spires, the result of uplift and erosion, are particularly striking. The best way to admire the central formations like the **Kissing Camels** (pictured right), **Three Graces** and **Montezuma's Tower** is to follow the network of paved trails on foot (figure on an hour or two).

BEST PLACES TO EAT IN COLORADO SPRINGS

Shuga's
This cute little white house is the setting for gourmet sandwiches and cocktails. $

CO.A.T.I.
Hip food hall with pickings that range from Hawaiian and Korean to *paletas* (popsicles) and DJ parties. $$

Marigold
Out by Garden of the Gods is this buzzy French bistro and bakery that's easy on the wallet. $$

Uchenna
You'll love the homestyle cooking and family vibe at chef Maya's Ethiopian restaurant. $$

Rabbit Hole
Downstairs digs and upscale cuisine combine for a most wondrous dining experience. $$$

If you've got a hankering for a bit more adventure, you can explore some 21 miles worth of trails on an e-bike, or sign up for a horseback ride or rock climbing, though we recommend the routes at **Red Rock Canyon Open Space** for the latter.

In summer, don't miss **Rock Ledge Ranch**, a living history museum across from the Visitors Center. Learn about the lives of the Utes and visit a 19th-century homesteaders cabin, blacksmith's shop, the Orchard House, barn and general store.

In summer, visitors must park at the Visitors Center; a free shuttle will then take you the rest of the way.

Museum-Hopping

REGIONAL CULTURE

The expansive **Colorado Springs Fine Arts Center** originally opened in 1936, an offshoot of the once prominent Broadmoor Art Academy. The museum's collection today is one of the best in the state, with some terrific Latin American art and photography, and great rotating exhibits that draw from the 20,000 pieces in its permanent collection. There's a strong focus on Native American, Hispanic and Spanish Colonial art. Other pieces you can expect to see here include Mexican clay figures, Native American basketry and quilts, woodcut prints from social-justice artist Leopoldo Mendez, and terrific abstract work from local artists such as Vance Kirkland and Floyd Tunson. The biggest and most famous work is Richard Diebenkorn's *Urbana No 4*. Be sure to check out the 400-seat theater for its excellent lineup of year-round performances.

Fans of the Olympics and amateur athletes, meanwhile, will likely know that Colorado Springs is home to just one of three **Olympic and Paralympic Training Centers** in the country. Depending on your level of interest, you can either tour the training facility itself and maybe spot a few Olympic hopefuls in action (gymnastics, judo, swimming and volleyball are some of the main sports), or check out the new **US Olympic & Paralympic Museum** 2.5 miles away. At the latter's spectacular and accessibly designed complex, 12 galleries lead visitors through a collection of memorabilia, interactive training exhibits, profiles of athletes and a good overview of Olympic history and technology.

Finally, all the way out by the Springs' small airport is the **National Museum of World War II Aviation**. If you dig aircraft, don't miss this spot: there are 27 beautifully restored planes, plus several others undergoing restoration. Biplanes, B-25 bombers, twin-engine fighters and amphibious craft – they've got it all. Also here are history exhibits that mix archives, maps and interpretive narratives to paint a fuller picture of aviation during the war.

 WHERE TO STAY IN COLORADO SPRINGS

Mining Exchange
Set in a turn-of-the-century bank where Cripple Creek prospectors traded in their gold for cash. $$

Holden House
Three Victorians make up this 1902 bed and breakfast in Old Colorado City. $$

Cheyenne Mountain Resort
Boasting a glorious position overlooking Cheyenne Mountain, this woodsy resort has an air of indulgence. $$$

Cheyenne Mountain Zoo

RICHARD WESTLUND/SHUTTERSTOCK ©

Family Fun

LIONS AND TIGERS AND BEARS

Cheyenne Mountain Zoo, the highest zoo in the country (6700ft), is the Springs' can't-miss destination for families. Launched in 1926 from the private animal collection of Spencer Penrose (1865–1939), founder of the Broadmoor Hotel, the zoo is today home to some 750 animals, including hippos, lions, tigers, Amur leopards and bears. Most famous of all are the reticulated giraffes, which kids are allowed to feed. The hilly setting provides a unique experience, and the Mountaineer Sky Ride will give you a bird's-eye view of the city. Just behind the zoo is the unusual **Will Rogers Shrine of the Sun** (8136ft), a stone tower named after the 1930s Hollywood star.

Back in town, the **Pioneers Museum** has 60,000 regional artifacts on display; particularly good is the Native American collection, which features hundreds of items from the Ute, Cheyenne and Arapaho Nations. It's set in the 1903 El Paso County Courthouse. If the kids (or parents) need to let loose, head to the two-story go-kart racetrack, the **Overdrive Raceway**, for high-speed thrills.

As for accommodations, consider staying at the **Great Wolf Lodge**, a hotel and water park that's only open to resort guests. In addition to the pools, it's got mini-golf, climbing and bowling, as well as more educational pursuits, such as the adventurous 'MagiQuest,' and the take-what-you-make 'Creation Station,' where kids (and adults!) can design and build their own soft toy.

THE BROADMOOR

Founded in 1918, the Broadmoor is Colorado's most famous luxury hotel. Set against the blue-green slopes of Cheyenne Mountain, everything here is exquisite: acres of lush grounds, world-class golf, chichi restaurants and shops, and ubercomfortable guestrooms and a spa. It's no surprise that Hollywood stars, pro athletes and nearly every president since FDR have made a point to visit it.

Visitors can explore the grounds and the free Penrose Heritage Museum (old cars and carriages), but outside of the historic architecture, the real attraction is Seven Falls. This series of tumbling cascades is best experienced as part of the Broadmoor Soaring Adventure: a combination of 10 zip-lines, rickety rope bridges and a 180ft rappel into the canyon.

GETTING AROUND

Colorado Springs is only 70 miles south of Denver, on I-25. As a sprawling city, it is easiest to navigate with your own wheels. However, Pike Ride operates an electric bike share program, and Mountain Metropolitan Transit buses run between Colorado Springs, Old Colorado City and Manitou Springs.

Beyond Colorado Springs

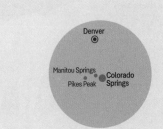

Denver

Manitou Springs
Pikes Peak
Colorado Springs

Whether you drive to the top of Pikes Peak or hike, you'll be rewarded with views that have inspired millions.

It's the most summited mountain in Colorado, and, by some accounts, the country. You can drive to the top, take a cog railway, walk on your own two feet or, if you're feeling particularly masochistic, even cycle. With 7800ft of elevation gain, this is the steepest bottom-to-top ascent in the state, so be prepared for altitude sickness and changes in the weather and temperature.

Regardless of how you ascend, all paths to Pikes Peak leave from Manitou Springs, the small town at the base that's a stone's throw east of Colorado Springs. Walkable and friendly, Manitou is a good alternative to base yourself in.

TOP TIP

Manitou welcomes an estimated 750,000 visitors annually. Free shuttle buses running from the Field's Park lot help ease parking woes.

Garden of the Gods (p259) and Pikes Peak

JOHN HOFFMAN/SHUTTERSTOCK ©

GEORGE BURBA/SHUTTERSTOCK ©

Pikes Peak–Manitou Springs train

Summitting Pikes Peak

PURPLE MOUNTAIN MAJESTIES

Pikes Peak (14,115ft) may not be the tallest of Colorado's 54 fourteeners, but it's certainly the most famous. The Ute originally called it the Mountain of the Sun, an apt description for this majestic peak, which crowns the southern Front Range. Rising 7800ft straight up from the plains, more than half a million visitors summit it every year.

Its location as the easternmost fourteener has contributed heavily to its place in American mythology. Zebulon Pike first made note of it in 1806 (he called it 'Grand Peak,' but never made it to the top) when exploring the Louisiana Purchase, and Katherine Bates, a guest lecturer at Colorado College in 1893, wrote the original draft of 'America the Beautiful' after reaching the summit.

Today, there are three ways to ascend the peak: the Pikes Peak Hwy (about a three-hour round-trip; reservations necessary), which was built in 1915 by Spencer Penrose and winds 19 miles to the top from Hwy 24 west of town; the cog railway (also three hours round-trip; reservations necessary), originally opened in 1891; and on foot via the Barr Trail.

Because the 26-mile **Barr Trail** has so much elevation gain, most hikers split the trip into two days, stopping to overnight at Barr Camp, the halfway point at 10,200ft. Here you can pitch a tent, sleep in a lean-to or bunk in the cabin.

WHY I LOVE PIKES PEAK

Christopher Pitts, writer

'As the first fourteener I ever climbed, Pikes Peak will always hold a special place in my heart. Within days of moving to Colorado, I naively set out to mountain bike to the summit with three dorm-mates. What started out as an enthusiastic joy ride through Colorado Springs soon turned to horror as I found myself pushing the stupid bike up one switchback... and another...and another. Upon reaching Barr Camp, I gratefully ditched the extra weight and slogged on up to the top. By the time we made it back to the camp it was nearly evening, but at least I was able to finally relish the downhill ride home.'

 WHERE TO EAT IN MANITOU SPRINGS

Sahara Cafe
Bustling Mediterranean restaurant with shawarmas, meze plates, falafel and fresh tabouleh. $

Adam's Mountain Cafe
This slow-food cafe includes offerings such as Senegalese veggies and cashew chicken salad. $$

Swirl
Take a seat on the garden patio at this intimate wine bar and sample the sandwiches and flatbreads. $$

AIR FORCE ACADEMY

Founded in 1954, this elite military academy trains a select group of some 4000 cadets to serve in the Air Force or Space Force. Visits to the massive 18,500-acre campus offer a limited but nonetheless fascinating look into the lives of this elite group of students.

From the visitor center, which provides general background on the academy, you can walk over to the rocket-esque modernist chapel (1962) or embark on a driving tour of the expansive grounds. Plane buffs will enjoy the occasional glimpse of aircraft like the B-52 Stratofortress or the sleek T-38 Talon.

The entrance is 20 miles north of Colorado Springs off I-25; ID is required.

Hiking the Manitou Incline

Exploring Manitou Springs

MY OTHER CAR IS A BROOM

The gateway to Pikes Peak, tiny **Manitou** is the unassuming counterweight to Colorado Springs' conservative, evangelical leanings. While there's no truth in the long-running urban legend that it's populated by pagans and witches, you can certainly pick up a few souvenirs while walking through town that will tell you otherwise.

What is true about Manitou is that it gets its name from the mineral springs that bubble up from limestone aquifers beneath Manitou Ave. As they rise to the surface, they pick up minerals and elements such as lithium (a natural mood stabilizer), calcium, potassium and iron. Many springs, such as Shoshone and Cheyenne, have sipping fountains where you can sample the distinctive-tasting naturally carbonated water. Stop by the Visitors Bureau for a map and cup.

Other destinations include the **Cave of the Winds**, which, despite the cheesy entrance, is a real-deal cave (reservations required) full of the stalactites and stalagmites of your dreams. Most visitors opt for the 45-minute Discovery Tour, but the Lantern Tour goes twice as deep, gets twice as dark and lasts twice as long. Above ground is a kids' challenge course.

The **Manitou Cliff Dwellings Site** is a bit confusing – this isn't an actual Puebloan cliff dwelling but a non-Native 20th-century reconstruction with a small museum. Some visitors learn something here; others leave disappointed.

GETTING AROUND

Manitou Springs is 6 miles west of Colorado Springs along Hwy 24.

GREAT SAND DUNES & THE SAN LUIS VALLEY

Denver ◉

● Great Sand Dunes &
the San Luis Valley

For all of Colorado's striking natural sights, the surreal Great Sand Dunes National Park, a veritable sea of sand bounded by jagged peaks and scrubby plains, is a place of stirring optical illusions where nature's magic is on full display.

From the approach up Hwy 150, watch as the angles of sunlight make shifting shadows on the dunes; the most dramatic time is the day's end, when the hills come into high contrast as the sun drops low on the horizon. Hike past the edge of the dune field to see the shifting sand up close; the ceaseless wind works like a disconsolate sculptor, constantly amending the landscape.

Most visitors limit their activities to the area where Medano Creek divides the main dune mass from the towering Sangre de Cristo Mountains. The remaining 85% of the park's area is designated wilderness: its' not for the unprepared or fainthearted.

TOP TIP

Regardless of your chosen activity and where you go in the park, always take a hat, closed-toe shoes, sunscreen, water, and a bandanna to protect your face if the wind picks up; and always check conditions at the Great Sand Dunes National Park Visitor Center before setting out.

Great Sand Dunes National Park

ANDRIY BLOKHIN/SHUTTERSTOCK ©

MOSCA PASS

Lost in all the excitement over the dunes is the park's backdrop: the rugged Sangre de Cristo mountains. The Mosca Pass Trail follows an old Ute path up Mosca Creek, providing fabulous birds-eye views of the dunes. The pass, at 9747ft, offers the lowest passage through the Sangres, and from 1871 to 1911, it was even used as a toll road ($1 horse and rider). It's 7 miles round-trip.

The Montville Store once stood at the foot of the trail. It was built in the 1830s by fur trader Antoine Robidoux, who transported supplies to posts in western Colorado and eastern Utah.

Today, a half-mile nature trail introduces a variety of eco-systems, leading to a grand view.

GREAT SAND DUNES NATIONAL PARK

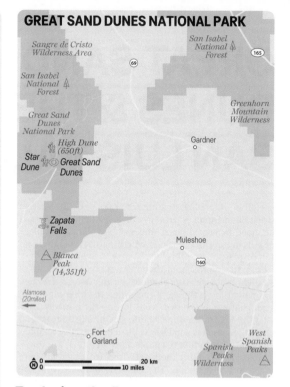

Exploring the Dunes

SAND-TASTIC

Most visitors will want to head straight to the sand, but don't forget to stop in at the visitor center first. From here, a short trail leads to the **Mosca Picnic Area** and ankle-deep **Medano Creek**, which you must ford (when the creek is running) to reach the dunes.

There are no trails through this expansive field of sand – 30 sq miles in all – though two DIY hikes afford excellent panoramic views. The first is a hike to the 700ft **High Dune** (strangely, not the highest dune in the park). It's only about 2.5 miles to the peak and back, but be warned: it's not easy, and it can feel like you're taking a half-step back for every one forward. If you're a glutton for punishment, try pushing on to the second worthy goal, west of the first ridge: **Star Dune** (750ft), the tallest in North America.

 WHERE TO CAMP IN GREAT SAND DUNES

Pinyon Flats Campground
Official park campground, with a great location not far from the dune field. Reserve months ahead. $

Zapata Falls Campground
Seven miles south of the park, up a dirt road, with glorious panoramas from its 9000ft perch. Reserve. $

Great Sand Dunes Oasis
Store, restaurant, campground and motel at the park entrance. Fairly bleak but there are showers. $

In the middle of summer, hikers should hit the hills during the early morning or evening, as the sand can reach 150°F during the heat of the day. Although you might think sandals would be the footwear of choice, closed-toe shoes provide better protection against the heat.

If you are hiking with children, don't let them out of your sight. It's easy to get separated.

Tubing & Sandboarding

ANOTHER WAY TO PLAY

One of the most curious spectacles in the entire park is the snowmelt-fed **Medano Creek**, which flows down from the Sangre de Cristos and along the eastern edge of the dunes. Peak flow is usually in late May or early June, and the rippling water over the sand creates a temporary beach of sorts, which is extremely popular with families. In years when the water is high enough, you can even float down the creek on an inner tube.

Another popular activity is **sandboarding**: the heavy wooden sled may seem like a bad idea when you're trudging out to the dunes, but the gleeful rush down the slopes is worth every footstep. Sand conditions are best after a recent precipitation; when it's too dry you'll simply sink. Also, the best rides are had by those who are relatively light, so if you've been bulking up on microbrews, don't expect to zip down the hill. To rent a board, visit **Kristi Mountain Sports** in Alamosa or the Great Sand Dunes Oasis at the edge of the park.

Hiking Zapata Falls

FAMILY FUN ON THE WAY TO THE FALLS

This short half-mile hike higher up in the Sangre de Cristos provides a refreshing change from slogging through the dunes. **Zapata Falls** (pictured right), though small, are hidden at the end of a slot canyon and the last 150yd to reach them are loads of fun (though not without risk), as you'll need to scramble through ankle-deep ice-cold water and over slippery rocks to get there. This is a good family hike.

Grippy water shoes are a good idea. If you want to make a day of it, you can continue to **South Zapata Lake** (8 miles round-trip). The turnoff for the falls is 7 miles south of the park entrance along Hwy 150. It's a further 3.5 miles up a dirt road from here, from where you'll have an excellent view of the dunes.

WHY ALL THE SAND?

Upon your first glimpse of the dunes, you can't help but wonder: where did all this sand come from, and why does it stay here?

The answer lies in the unique geography and weather patterns of the San Luis Valley. Streams and snow melt have been carrying eroded sand and silt out of the San Juan Mountains (about 60 miles to the west) to the valley floor for millions of years.

There, prevailing winds from the southwest gradually blow the sand into the natural hollow at the southern end of the Sangre de Cristo range, causing the sand to pile up into what are now the highest dunes in North America.

DANIEL MULLINS/SHUTTERSTOCK ©

GETTING AROUND

Great Sand Dunes National Park is 33 miles northeast of Alamosa, the closest town. Be sure to fuel up and buy all your food before arriving. Those with high-clearance

4WD trucks can travel to some of the more remote trailheads in the park; however, remember that getting stuck in sand is all too easy.

Beyond the Great Sand Dunes

The San Luis Valley's agricultural flatland may look monotonous, but it holds troves of history and unexpected sights.

Denver

Grand Sand Dunes
Penitente Canyon
Alamosa
San Luis
Cumbres Pass

The strange and mysterious San Luis Valley is the driest part of Colorado, hemmed in by the San Juan mountains to the west and the Sangre de Cristos to the east. Despite the seemingly barren landscape, however, the valley holds many surprises, including the rippling sea of sand.

The valley was also the first part of Colorado to be permanently settled by non-Natives, when Hispanic pioneers set out from Taos in the mid-19th century to find new homesteads, and their influence still defines valley culture today.

Exploring the southern and western part of the valley will take you to these old Hispanic settlements, while the northeast offers a chance to climb the Sangre de Cristo mountains.

TOP TIP

This is one of the top areas in the world for alien sightings and abductions. Don't say we didn't warn you!

San Luis Valley

MIKE DEMMINGS/SHUTTERSTOCK ©

FAINA GUREVICH/SHUTTERSTOCK ©

Red-winged blackbird, Alamosa National Wildlife Refuge

Wildlife Watching in Alamosa

WILDLIFE AND WETLANDS

The largest town in the San Luis Valley, **Alamosa** (Spanish for 'cottonwood') was built up along the banks of the Rio Grande – the same river that goes on to form the US–Mexico border, some 450 miles to the south. From the highway, its car garages and greasy spoons aren't so different from other towns in the valley, but students at the nearby Adams State College keep the vibe fresh. It's greatest appeal for travelers is as a place to fuel up, buy groceries and, if you'd rather not camp, spend the night. The small **San Luis Valley Museum** has a well-arranged collection of 'then and now' photographs and artifacts from early farm life in the valley.

The main attraction, however, is the **Alamosa National Wildlife Refuge**, 3 miles southeast of town. Located on the banks of the Rio Grande, this special preserve will give you some idea of what the valley must have looked like before it was developed for agriculture. It's best to visit at dawn or dusk, when wildlife is the most active and when you'll hear the amazing soundscape of bird calls and whistles. A 2.5-mile trail along the river and a panoramic overlook on the east side of the refuge give visitors views of the marshes, ponds and river corridor.

UFO WATCHTOWER

Don't panic! The visiting aliens are harmless. Or mostly harmless anyway. And if you're eager for a glimpse (or perhaps want to leave an offering for a weary interstellar hitchhiker), then a stop at the UFO Watchtower is a must.

About 15ft high, the tower will certainly not improve your chances of spotting a flying saucer (though there are two large energy vortexes located here, so...), but the garden and its assorted treasures is truly something to behold.

The watchtower is located off Hwy 17 near Hooper (about 30 miles west of the national park), and is easiest to access if you're driving south toward the dunes from Salida.

🛏 **WHERE TO STAY IN ALAMOSA** ─────────────────────

Dunes Inn
A notch above the cookie-cutter motel experience; better-than-average breakfast and downtown locale. **$**

Rustic Rook Resort
The only glamping experience near the sand dunes: tents, showers, s'mores and breakfast included. **$$**

Fairfield Inn & Suites
The newest and best-kept of the chain hotels west of town. You'll need to drive to downtown. **$$$**

FORT GARLAND

Fort Garland (1858–83) was established to protect early settlers in the San Luis Valley from Ute raids, and Union troops stationed here marched in a campaign against Confederates in Texas during the Civil War.

For a short time, the outpost was under the direction of famed frontier scout Kit Carson. Though Carson successfully negotiated a period of peace with Utes, all hell broke loose after the Meeker Incident in 1879 (p137). After that, the fort became a major base of operations in the forcible removal of Utes from the area.

The town's museum is located in the original fort and contains five of the original 22 buildings.

ANDREAS STROH/SHUTTERSTOCK ©

Cumbres & Toltec Scenic Railroad

Hispanic Heritage in San Luis

THE OLDEST TOWN IN COLORADO

Tucked into the far southeast margin of the San Luis Valley is the town of **San Luis**, which happens to be Colorado's oldest settlement (1851).

Its character – today and throughout history – is largely the result of its isolation. For Spain, the upper Rio Grande was a lost province best left to the nomadic Native American tribes that Spain was unable to dominate. Under the threat of Ute raids, and far from the mercantile and spiritual centers at Taos and Santa Fe, San Luis developed as a self-sufficient outpost and largely escaped the 'progress' that revoked Hispanic tenure in other parts of the valley following the arrival of the railroad; today, the town remains almost 90% Hispanic.

The main attraction in town is the **Stations of the Cross** installation, situated along a 1-mile path up a small hill. Local sculptor Huberto Maestas' 15 dramatic life-sized statues of Christ's crucifixion are a powerful testament to the Catholic heritage of communities near the 'Blood of Christ' Mountains.

 WHERE TO EAT IN ALAMOSA

Locavores
Fresh, casual eatery with a menu that runs from quesadillas and cubanos to salads and fish tacos. $

Cavillo's
The Mexican buffet at this long-standing restaurant is perfect for families, the famished and the indecisive. $

Friar's Fork
Set in a 1926 adobe church; come here for upscale Italian fare in intimate surrounds. $

Six miles west of town is the adobe-walled **Capilla de San Acacio**, one of the oldest churches in Colorado. Built in the 1863, it was dedicated to St Agathius, who is said to have protected the women and children of the Hispanic settlement during a Ute attack in 1853, when the men were away herding sheep.

San Luis is 45 miles south of the Great Sand Dunes, and 40 miles southeast of Alamosa.

Riding the Cumbres & Toltec Railroad

ALL ABOARD!

One of several narrow-gauge trains in Colorado, this impressive ride is a chance to tackle the **Cumbres Pass** (10,022ft) by power of steam.

In 1880, the Denver & Rio Grande Western Rail (D&RG) completed a track over Cumbres Pass, linking Chama, NM, with Denver, and this particular section, running from Antonito to Chama, is now the longest and highest steam railroad in North America. The twisting mountainous terrain was suited to narrow-gauge track, which is only 3ft wide instead of the standard gauge of 4ft 8in, and churning along its track, past hills of pine and aspen and expansive views of the high plains and mountains, makes for an excellent way to spend a day.

Trains run daily, roughly from July to mid-October, from the **Cumbres & Toltec Scenic Railroad Depot** in **Antonito**, 60 miles southeast of the Great Sand Dunes and 30 miles south of Alamosa. Dress warmly as the unheated cars, both enclosed and semi-enclosed, can get quite chilly. Most trips require a full day, and include lunch, though there are also half-day express options.

Alternatively, you can drive a similar route on Hwy 17 west of town, which provides an abundance of hiking, camping and fishing in the remote **South San Juan Wilderness**.

Hiking Penitente Canyon

CONSUELO Y ESPÍRITU

Roughly 55 miles west of the sand dunes, and 45 miles northwest of Alamosa, **Penitente Canyon** offers visitors the chance to climb, hike and mountain bike among a never-ending tumble of strangely shaped giant boulders, spread throughout four separate canyons. This haunting landscape has its origins in one of the largest volcanic explosions in earth's history, which ejected 1000 cubic miles of ash some 27 million years ago.

HIKING THE SANGRES

In a state full of dazzling mountains, the shark-toothed Sangre de Cristo ('Blood of Christ') range certainly holds its own. These steep, jagged mountains rise as much as 6000ft in 4 miles, and three – Kit Carson Peak, Crestone Peak and Crestone Needle – were the last of Colorado's fourteeners to be summitted (Colorado College professors Albert Ellingwood and Eleanor Davis managed the feat in July 1916, after walking here from Colorado Springs).

There are limited access points: the spiritual retreat center of Crestone, halfway between Salida and the Great Sand Dunes and famous for its energy vortexes, is a good jumping-off point. Make for the Willow Creek or North Crestone trailheads for steep but rewarding ascents into the mountains.

WHERE TO STAY NEAR ANTONITO

Elk Creek Campground
Twenty-three miles west of Antonito, off Hwy 17, this is a choice location with 38 forested sites. **$**

Mogote Campground
Shaded spot along the Conejos River, with 41 sites. It's 14 miles west of Antonito. **$**

Rainbow Trout Ranch
For the full dude ranch experience, with horseback riding and fly-fishing adventures. **$$$**

LONESOME SONG OF THE PENITENTE

Of all the groups that populate the early history of Colorado's south, none is more mysterious than Los Hermanos Penitente, a secretive religious sect that thrived in the early 19th century. Some say the Penitente's membership drew from a servant class of Native Americans who worked as housekeepers and shepherds, called *genízaros*.

Gathering in humble meeting houses known as *moradas,* their ceremonies sought spiritual awakening through the suffering of the Passion of Christ.

The songs of Los Hermanos Penitente *(alabados)* are haunting, mournful, unaccompanied hymns that blend Hispanic *folclórica* (folklore) with elements of droning Native song.

Often sung at funeral processions and burials, *alabados* have themes that are, like the group itself, fixated on the suffering and torture of Jesus.

KEN BARBER/ALAMY STOCK PHOTO ©

Penitente Canyon

The main canyon takes its name from Los Hermanos Penitentes and is symbolized by the fading, blue-cloaked mural of the **Virgin of Guadalupe** painted on a canyon wall. Local legend has it that the mural was painted by three men, one of whom descended sitting on a suspended tire; the inscription reads 'Consuelo y Espíritu' ('Comfort and Courage'). Visitors may also spot pictographs on the canyon walls, painted by Puebloans, Apache and Ute, who possibly used the area for game drives. Most will be hard to find, although you can easily spot one at the entrance to the main canyon, near the parking lot.

The surrounding desert landscape makes for some excellent hiking, but be aware that this is rattlesnake country, so watch your step. A great trail is the **Penitente Canyon Loop** (2 miles), which follows the lush canyon, shaded by groves of aspen and thickets of chokecherry, before climbing back up into the desert where you'll be rewarded with glorious views across the valley to the Sangre de Cristo mountains. Along the way you can take a detour to view some old wagon *(carreta)* tracks grooved into the stone.

You'll also spot rock climbers who come here for the bolted sport climbs on the canyon's pocketed rhyolite rock walls. The walls are short – usually ranging from 40ft to 100ft in height – but there are over 300 routes here, some of which are extremely challenging (up to 5.13c) and lots of fun.

Pick up a brochure at the **USFS Divide District Ranger Station** in Del Norte, or stop by **La Garita Trading Post** for good info. The local campground has 13 first-come, first-served sites.

GETTING AROUND

Alamosa, the region's largest city and transport hub, is located at the intersections of Hwy 17, Hwy 160 and Hwy 285. It's 165 miles southwest of Colorado Springs, 80 miles south of Salida and 140 miles north of Santa Fe.

CAÑON CITY & THE ROYAL GORGE

Tucked away in the juniper-and-piñon-dotted scrub of the Arkansas River Valley is the Royal Gorge, a 1000ft gash in the desert landscape where bighorn sheep balance precariously on the sheer walls and rattlesnakes lay coiled in the summer sun. There are only two ways to see the bottom: rafting the rapids or chugging along the historic railway.

Echoes of the Wild West live on along Shelf Rd, the former stagecoach route that runs past limestone cliffs and legendary dinosaur quarries to the one-time gold mines of Cripple Creek.

At the heart of it all is Cañon City, a town that appears sleepy enough until you learn that it's home to 13 prisons. This includes the nearby Supermax, where some of the country's most notorious criminals serve life sentences. Oddly enough, the town does have a prison museum for the curious.

TOP TIP

Cañon City's geography protects it from the worst of Colorado's weather. However, although summer is the high season, remember that the absence of daily thunderstorms means it can get blisteringly hot. We recommend a spring or fall visit for the best temperatures.

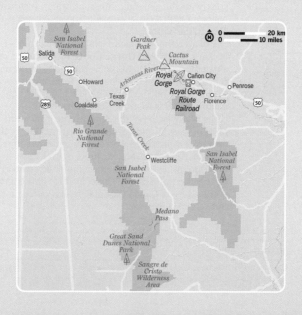

BEST RESTAURANTS IN CAÑON CITY

Bean Pedaler
Great Main St cafe with simple breakfast and lunch options, plus pizzas next door at the Handlebar. $

Brews and Bikes
Come here for the mountain-bike rentals; stay for the nachos and the local beer on tap. $

Whitewater Bar and Gill
Beloved outdoor patio by the turnoff for the Royal Gorge. Rocky Mountain oysters, BBQ and burgers. $$

El Caporal
Family-owned Mexican diner. Think smothered tamales, chili Colorado and chicken en mole. $$$

Nirvana
Maybe not quite the culinary paradise as advertised, but North Indian dishes are delicious all the same. $$

PHOTOFF/SHUTTERSTOCK ©

Royal Gorge Bridge

The Royal Gorge

CHOOSE YOUR OWN ADVENTURE

Most visitors will experience the gorge via the private **Royal Gorge Bridge and Park** up top. Is it a theme park? Yes. But, like most theme parks it is fun, with a gondola, zip-line, skycoaster and via ferrata all upping the ante to see which can provide the most thrills. If walking is more your speed, stick with the general admission, which is focused on the historic 1260ft-long suspension bridge that spans the 1000ft drop to the bottom.

If you have more time to explore, the bottom of the gorge beckons. The **Royal Gorge Route Railroad** makes the trip along the historic D&RG line – the one-time site of explosive railroad wars in 1879. Trips range from simple open-air cars to more eventful journeys with lunch, dinner, wine and even a murder, and leave from Cañon City.

The best way to see the Royal Gorge is on a raft, but the 7 miles of Class IV and V white water are not for the timid. Tour operators typically require rafters to be over 18 years of age in the early season (May to June) or over 12 years when the flow diminishes by midsummer (July to September). There's a large gathering of rafting guides near the Royal Gorge turnoff, 8 miles west of Cañon City, and several others in Salida and Buena Vista upstream.

GETTING AROUND

The Royal Gorge is 8.5 miles northwest of Cañon City along Hwy 50. You'll need a car.

Beyond Cañon City & the Royal Gorge

Drive your trusty steed along the Gold Belt Scenic Byway, which loops to Cripple Creek and back.

Just a 90-minute drive from Cañon City, yet worlds away, Cripple Creek hurls you back into the Wild West of yore. This once lucky lady produced a staggering $413 million in gold by 1952. The booze still flows and gambling still thrives, but yesteryear's saloons and brothels are now modern casinos. A gold mine tour will keep non-gamblers entertained, but the real treasure is the drive here.

A further 15 miles north is the Florissant Fossil Beds National Monument. Although there is little here aside from petrified sequoia stumps, the location is gorgeous and a great place for a hike through wildflower-freckled meadows, boulder-crusted hills and views of the back of Pikes Peak.

TOP TIP

Long sections of the Gold Belt drive are unpaved. You don't need AWD, but it's not for the faint of heart.

Florissant Fossil Beds National Monument (p276)

ZACK FRANK/SHUTTERSTOCK ©

FLORISSANT FOSSIL BEDS NATIONAL MONUMENT

In 1873 Dr AC Peale was on his way to survey and map the South Park area, when he discovered these ancient lake deposits, which were buried by a series of volcanic eruptions.

Located 17 miles north of Cripple Creek and 48 miles north of Cañon City, the site has since been recognized as one of the greatest collections of Eocene fossils (34 million years old) on the planet.

The excellent visitor center contains a small sampling of some of the 50,000 fossils that have been excavated (including the only fossilized tsetse flies in existence), while out in the open is a collection of spectacular petrified sequoia stumps, including one that's 38ft in circumference.

ROUTE THREE PRODUCTIONS/SHUTTERSTOCK ©

Phantom Canyon Road

The Gold Belt

DRIVE BACK IN TIME

This combo former stagecoach road–railroad grade is a drive not to be missed. With its red earth, low-growing piñon pines and juniper, and sheer cliffs, you'll feel like you've entered the set for an old Western. Looping from Cañon City to Cripple Creek and back again, it can be driven in either direction; expect to spend at least half a day.

Start with **Phantom Canyon**, the easier of the two drives. Follow a sinuous old railroad (the Florence & Cripple Creek; 1894–1912) through gorgeous sandstone cliffs and blasted-out tunnels for 35 miles to historic **Victor**, climbing 4500ft in elevation as you go. Although unpaved, you don't need AWD as long as the weather permits.

Coming back from Cripple Creek, try **Shelf Rd** if you're up for the challenge – the first 8 miles of this 26-mile route are also unpaved and definitely not for those with vertigo. This initial narrow section (carved out of the canyon wall) is the 'shelf,' which was originally a toll road ($1.75 stagecoach, 30¢ horse and rider). At the bottom is the **Shelf Road Recreation Area**, home to one of the top sport climbing destinations in the state. The 1000 or so bolted climbs are a fun length (60ft to 140ft), and accessible year-round – although the sun can be scorching in summer.

Don't miss the **Marsh dinosaur quarries** 6 miles past the rock climbing area; these are one of the Jurassic graveyards that spawned the Bone Wars and produced such stars as stegosaurus, diplodocus and allosaurus back in the late 1800s. They're still standing in the Smithsonian today.

GETTING AROUND

Cripple Creek is only 27 miles from Cañon City along the unpaved Shelf Rd, though the fastest route is actually via Hwy 9, which is twice the distance!

TRINIDAD & THE SANTA FE TRAIL

Tucked into a chimney-top mesa, quiet Trinidad sits on the Purgatoire River (sometimes Anglicized as the Picketwire River), which flows down from the heights of the Sangre de Cristo Mountains and the Spanish Peaks in the west. The town's past – from its origins as a Spanish outpost and Santa Fe Trail stopover to its coal-mining period when it played a central role in a groundbreaking labor dispute – is documented in its museums and on the brick-paved streets.

While history buffs may want to take their time here, road trippers will smell adventure on the pine-tinged winds streaming down Rte 12 from Cucharas Pass on the Highway of Legends, the scenic drive that passes through the Spanish Peaks Wilderness, or along Hwy 350, which follows the Santa Fe Trail.

Although the nearby city of Pueblo may be larger, Trinidad has a more dramatic setting and makes for a convenient base.

TOP TIP

Some of the sites along the Santa Fe Trail have limited opening hours or may require advance reservations, such as tours of the Picketwire Dinosaur Tracksite. Even if you're just passing through on a road trip, check ahead to ensure that you are getting the most out of a visit.

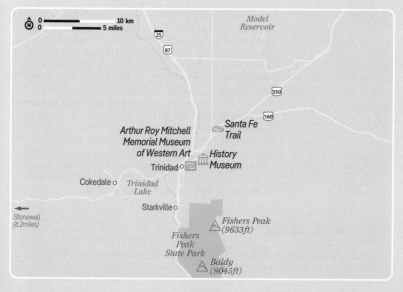

THE SANTA FE TRAIL

The Santa Fe Trail linked Missouri with New Mexico (a Mexican province from 1821 to 1848), bringing manufactured goods west, and Mexican silver and Native American jewelry and blankets east.

The 800-mile route took seven to eight weeks to cross with a covered wagon, and was defined by monotony and hardship.

Near Dodge City in Kansas, the route divided: the southern road (Cimarron Route) cut down into New Mexico, and was shorter but more dangerous. The northern road (Mountain Route) continued through Bent's Fort and Trinidad in Colorado and was longer but safer.

With the expansion of the railroad west, trade along the route eventually diminished, coming to a close in 1880.

JIM LAMBERT/SHUTTERSTOCK ©

ArtoCade festival, Trinidad

Step into Local History

THE NEW MEXICO BORDER

The main attraction in **Trinidad** is the **History Museum**, which takes up a full city block on Main St. There are three sights here: the adobe **Baca House** (1870), the French-style **Bloom Mansion** (1882) and the **Santa Fe Trail Museum**.

Early settlers Felipe and Dolores Baca, who came to Trinidad in the 1860s, bought the unusual two-story Baca House for 22,000 pounds of wool in 1873. But the real prize here is the Santa Fe Trail Museum, set in the Bacas' workers cottage. Displays trace the course of early Trinidad – an interesting mix of Mexicans and settlers from as far off as Nova Scotia – through its heyday during the Santa Fe Trail peak and on to its transformation as a railroad and mining town.

Also in Trinidad is the **Arthur Roy Mitchell Memorial Museum of Western Art**, which displays a collection of cowboys, horses, Western landscapes, more horses and more cowboys. There's a rotating exhibition space and terrific collection of historic Trinidad photos.

The distinctive **Fishers Peak** (9633ft) south of town was named a state park in 2020 and is in now development. Eventually, a trail will lead to the mesa top.

GETTING AROUND

Trinidad is 130 miles south of Colorado Springs, right at the New Mexico border. Amtrak operates a daily Southwest Chief train service between Los Angeles and Chicago that stops here.

Beyond Trinidad

For those who like to walk along the old wagon ruts of history, the Santa Fe Trail beckons.

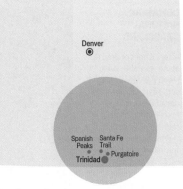

Denver

Spanish Peaks   Santa Fe Trail

Trinidad   Purgatoire

For some people, the Santa Fe Trail is no more than a lonely drive with a series of don't-blink-or-you'll-miss-'em historical markers along the highway. But others will find themselves thrown back to a time when finding yourself in this part of the world meant facing a daily fight for survival.

Either way, this section of Colorado is one of great natural beauty and contrasts. From the wild, sun-drenched prairie around Bent's Fort to the high mesas and billowing clouds on the New Mexico border, and the ancient volcanic walls of the twin Spanish Peaks near La Veta, these long-traveled routes provides a good mix of history and natural wonder.

TOP TIP

If you're camping, look for sites off Hwy 12 in the Spanish Peaks area.

West Spanish Peak, La Veta (p281)

BRENT COULTER/SHUTTERSTOCK ©

COMANCHE NATIONAL GRASSLAND

After an hour of driving along Hwy 350, you'll reach the unassuming settlement of Timpas, one of the gateways to the Comanche National Grasslands.

Walking through the unforgiving wilderness of hip-high grasses here, it's easy to imagine the challenges that traders and settlers faced.

If you're up for some adventure, follow the backroads from Timpas 45 minutes to the Withers Canyon Trailhead, where a 5.6-mile one-way hike along the Purgatoire River leads to the ruins of the Dolores Mission (late 19th century) and the Picketwire Dinosaur Tracksite, where some 1300 dinosaur prints are visible; it's the largest site in North America. Alternatively, reserve a trip with Picket Wire Guided Auto Tours.

Bent's Old Fort National Historic Site

Driving the Santa Fe Trail

TRADING POSTS AND TRAGEDIES

A drive along Hwy 350 provides travelers with a chance to experience the fabled western reaches of the Great Plains through which the Santa Fe Trail passed. Ninety minutes from Trinidad is **Bent's Old Fort National Historic Site**, the central attraction in the region. Built just north of the Arkansas River, the original border between the US and Mexico, the beautifully restored adobe fort (1833–49) was once a cultural crossroads and the busiest settlement west of the Missouri. Built by the Bent brothers, it was a place where information and goods were exchanged, and it provided shelter for every culture and type of person traveling in the West at that time.

Although the Bents are credited with establishing the fort, the local Cheyenne chief, Yellow Wolf, was instrumental in determining its location. Yellow Wolf offered the Bents access to the surrounding land and intertribal trade networks,

 WHERE TO EAT IN TRINIDAD

The Cafe
Gourmet egg wraps and tantalizing sandwiches in the Danielson Dry Goods building. $

Sita's Kitchen
Family-owned vegan restaurant and bakery, with organic bowls (kitchari), salads (falafel) and sandwiches. $

Rino's
Situated in an old stone church, Rino's is where your chicken parmigiana is served by a singing waiter. $$

hoping to forge an important alliance. The Bents, too, saw the wisdom in this, and soon after building the fort, William married White Owl Woman, the daughter of another important chief, White Thunder. Tragically, after the closure of the fort, Yellow Wolf was betrayed by the new settlers and murdered during the Sand Creek Massacre. Today, the old fort is staffed by knowledgeable guides in period clothing."

A further 16 miles east is the **Boggsville Historic Site** (1862), a one-time store, trading post and homestead for frontiersmen Thomas Boggs and Kit Carson.

Nine miles northeast of Boggsville is **Fort Lyon**, where on November 29, 1864, John Chivington led the Colorado Volunteers in a dawn attack on Chief Black Kettle and his band, who had been told they would be safe if they moved to this desolate reservation. Over 150 Cheyenne and Arapaho men, women and children were slaughtered and their corpses grotesquely mutilated, bringing a new wave of conflict to the Santa Fe Trail. The event is commemorated at the **Sand Creek Massacre National Historic Site**, 63 miles northeast of Fort Lyon.

Driving along the Santa Fe Trail will also take you through Granada, where the **Amache National Historic Site** is located. This WWII Japanese internment camp once held 7567 prisoners, most of whom were US citizens, all brought here from the farmlands of central California.

Hiking the Spanish Peaks

HIGHWAY OF LEGENDS

Heading west from Trinidad along the Highway of Legends byway (Hwy 12) is a stunning scenic route that wraps around the west side of the volcanic **Spanish Peaks** (pictured below) for 66 miles before reaching **La Veta**.

The twin Spanish Peaks, which the Ute aptly called *wahatoya* (breasts of the earth), were once important landmarks for travelers crossing the Great Plains and are 2 million years older than the Continental Divide. The East Peak is 12,708ft high, while the West Peak soars to 13,625ft. With hundreds of incredible vertical stone dikes (ancient magma) radiating outward like some kind of primordial fence line, these mountains are ripe for hiking adventures.

Following Hwy 12 from Trinidad will take you to **Cuchara Pass** (9994ft), from where you can take a forest service road 6.5 miles east to the **Cordova Pass Trailhead**. From the trailhead it's a steep 2.5-mile climb to the summit of the West Peak over scree and stones; this is the most popular route up. Figure on 2½ hours up and make sure you're off the summit by noon.

The **Wahatoya Trail** (12 miles one way) traverses the saddle between the peaks. As you approach the peaks, you may still see the remnants of the 2013 wildfire that burned the north side of the East Peak. There are three campgrounds in the area, including reservable sites at **Purgatoire**.

PUEBLO

Those who prefer more urban surrounds may consider staying in Pueblo, 85 miles north of Trinidad.

The one-time railroad hub and steel manufacturing center, which grew up along the Arkansas River, holds a handful of sights, including El Pueblo History Museum. Set at the original site of Fort Pueblo (1842–54), it tells the story of life on the plains in the 1800s. Exhibits include an old cannon, a family tipi and a cut from a massive tree that once stood over present-day Union Ave and was ominously called the hanging tree. Also in Pueblo is the Rosemount Museum, a three-story, 37-room Victorian mansion, constructed in 1893, and the Buell Children's Museum, a fun stop for pre-teens.

TOOLKIT

The chapters in this section cover the most important topics you'll need to know about in Colorado. They're full of nuts-and-bolts information and valuable insights to help you understand and navigate Colorado and get the most out of your trip.

Arriving
p284

Getting Around
p285

Money
p286

Accommodations
p287

Family Travel
p288

Health & Safe Travel
p289

Food, Drink & Nightlife
p290

Responsible Travel
p292

LGBTIQ+ Travelers
p294

Accessible Travel
p295

Cannabis
p296

Nuts & Bolts
p297

Denver International Airport

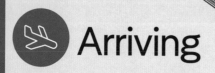

Arriving

Most visitors arrive through Denver International Airport (DIA), 24 miles from downtown Denver. One of the country's biggest and busiest airports, the main terminal has six levels, split between east and west sides. An underground tram links the main terminal to DIA's three concourses; there's also a pedestrian bridge to Concourse A. Expect construction; a massive upgrade project is underway until 2028.

Visas

Many foreign visitors to the US need to have a visa. Exceptions include citizens of Canada and Bermuda and those participating in the Visa Waiver Program (esta.cbp.dhs.gov/esta).

Biometrics

Every person entering the US at DIA has their photo taken by a US Customs & Border Protection agent, which is validated against an existing passport or visa photo.

Cash

ATMs are located throughout the DIA. There are currency exchange booths in Concourses A and B as well as on Level 5 of the main terminal, just outside the international arrivals area.

Wi-Fi & Charging Stations

Free wi-fi is available at DIA; choose 'DEN Airport Free WiFi' on your device (no registration or ad-viewing required). Hundreds of charging stations dot the airport.

Public Transport from Denver International Airport

	Denver	Boulder	Colorado Springs
TRAIN	37 mins $10.50		
BUS	55 mins $10.50	80 mins $10.50	3 hrs $22.50
TAXI	30 mins $60	45 mins $90	75 mins $165
SHUTTLE	varies $30–40	varies $55	varies $54

AIRPORT ART

Thanks to a public-art fund, DIA is draped with a robust collection of murals, photos and large-scale sculptures.

You can't miss *Kinetic Air Light Curtain* in the tram tunnels, a nod to Denver's mile-high elevation, with 5280 tiny propellers that spin with each passing train. Or listen for Native American songs as you walk Concourse A's pedestrian bridge.

As you leave, keep an eye out for the most (in)famous: *Mustang/Mesteño,* nicknamed 'Blucifer,' a 32ft-high blue stallion with gleaming red eyes. In a strange tragedy, the artist, Luis Jimenez, died after the 9000lb structure fell on him during construction.

Getting Around

There are lots of options for getting around Colorado, but a car is essential for exploring beyond the Front Range or ski resorts.

TRAVEL COSTS

Car rental
From $60/day

Petrol
**Approx.
$3.60/gallon**

EV charging
**Free–$0.35/
kWh**

Mountain shuttle
From $69

Car Hire & Costs

Car-rental agencies are available at most Colorado airports. But they don't come cheap! Save some cash by booking off-site, which cuts out hefty airport taxes and fees. A quick cab ride to the nearest town can save you hundreds on a week-long rental.

Road Conditions

City roads and highways are generally paved and well maintained; smaller mountain towns and rural areas often have dirt roads. Some mountain passes close seasonally or when the driving conditions are hazardous. Before heading out, check with Colorado Department of Transportation (codot. gov/travel).

TRACTION LAW

From September to May, along mountainous sections of the I-70, Colorado law requires two-wheel-drive vehicles to have snow tires, all-weather tires or to carry tire chains or autosocks. All vehicles, 4WD and AWD included, have minimum tread requirements of three-sixteenths of an inch. The law is in place to reduce accidents in hazardous winter conditions. Look for electronic signage indicating when the law is being enforced. If disregarded, you could face a substantial fine or, much worse, could injure or kill yourself or others.

TIP

Wildlife often wanders onto roads – deer, elk and moose are common sights, especially in the mountains. Drive cautiously!

DRIVING ESSENTIALS

Drive on the right.

25

Speed limit is 25–35mph in urban areas, 20–40mph on mountain roads and 55–75mph on highways.

.05

Blood alcohol limit is 0.05% (DWI) and 0.08% (DUI).

Mountain Shuttles

Epic **Mountain Express** (epicmountainexpress. com) and **Summit Express** (summitexpress.com) provide door-to-door shuttle service from Denver International Airport to Aspen and major resort towns along the I-70, including Vail, Beaver Creek, Copper Mountain and Breckenridge. Most ski towns provide free bus service around town and to the resort.

Bus

Bustang (ridebustang. com) is the state's regional bus service. It serves cities along the I-70 and I-25 corridors as well as harder-to-reach destinations like Telluride and Crested Butte. In winter, it also runs **Snowstang**, with routes from Denver to several different ski resorts, geared to day trippers.

Plane

Several small commercial airports dot Colorado. Flights tend to be expensive and often involve connecting through Denver. But crunch the numbers! Flying regionally can help you avoid the cost and hassle of renting a car. In winter, many carriers offer direct flights from major US cities to popular ski towns.

Money

CURRENCY: US DOLLAR ($)

Credit Cards

Credit cards are the most common way to pay for goods and services in Colorado, used from corners stores to ski resorts. But consider cash. A 2022 state law allows businesses to offset their credit card processing costs by adding a surcharge to customer bills, typically around 2%.

Sales Tax

Sales tax is added to most goods sold in Colorado, including state tax (2.9%) and a city and/or county tax (averaging around 7% to 8%). There are some exceptions – groceries and prescription medications – but plan on paying as much as 11.2% extra for your mementos.

Tipping

Generally, tipping is expected in restaurants, and anytime a service has been provided.

Breweries	$1–2 per pour
Coffee shops	$1 per drink
Dispensaries	$2 per purchase
Guides	15–20% of the tour cost
Hotel housekeeping	$5 per night
Luggage attendants	$2–5 per suitcase
Restaurants & bars	15–20% of the bill

HOW MUCH FOR A…

museum entry
free–$20

National Park pass (unlimited)
$80

ski-lift ticket
$85–245

Denver CityPASS
adult $39–54
child $32–49

SAVE CASH

Don't be shy about asking about discounts! Children often pay half-price for tours, sights and public transportation. Ditto for students, seniors and military personnel. Museums around the state, too, often offer a free day each month. And if you're traveling to Denver, consider purchasing a CityPASS (citypass.com/denver), a prepaid ticket package that offers significant discounts for some of the city's top attractions.

Scan this QR code for information on Denver CityPASS

LOCAL TIP

Many small businesses like tour companies and B&Bs don't accept credit cards. Be sure you have access to digital cash through Venmo, Apple Pay, PayPal or Zelle to cover your costs.

RESTAURANT SERVICE CHARGES

Hiring and retaining food service workers has become challenging since the pandemic struck. Many quit or were laid off and never returned. To slow the bleed, Colorado restaurants are increasingly adding a 'service charge' or 'cost-of-living' fee' to bills. Added pre-tax, it's typically a percentage of the bill, designated to supplement staff wages or benefits. Often it's directed to non-tipped kitchen staff, but sometimes it's for everyone. Read the menu's fine print or simply ask the server. Typically, if the charge is 12% or less, a gratuity is still expected and appreciated.

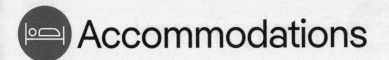

Accommodations

Boutique on a Budget

A growing number of Colorado's cities and mountain towns have modern hostels, still catering to travelers on a budget yet featuring swanky style and boutique amenities. Most offer private rooms (with shared bathrooms) though if you're looking for the ultimate bargain, dorms are where it's at. Most hostels include breakfast and have kitchens for making your own meals too.

Pitch a Tent

Camping is one of the most popular ways to experience Colorado. It's easy, too, with hundreds of established private and public campgrounds spread across the state. Most have shared bathrooms and fire pits; some even have showers and camp stores. Or try dispersed camping, a free back-to-the-basics experience, where you set up camp on public lands, away from the crowds.

Backcountry Huts

Colorado has an extensive system of backcountry huts that are accessible year-round by foot, ski or mountain bike, using trails and fire roads. Some are basic dry cabins while others are nicer affairs with solar-powered lights, wood-burning stoves and even eco-compost toilets. Hut-to-hut travel is a fun option and sometimes includes pre-stocked food. Reserve early for winter stays!

HOW MUCH FOR A NIGHT IN A...

campsite
free–$28

hostel (dorm bed)
$35–85

vacation resort
from $100

VACATION RESORTS

From working ranches to posh alpine lodges, Colorado offers a wide range of resorts. Many are geared to families and include long activity lists that feature guided hikes, horseback riding, fly-fishing, mountain biking, cross-country skiing and more. Accommodations run the gamut from rustic log cabins to cushy suites; meals also range from DIY cooking to four-course tasting menus.

Historic Hotels

Many Colorado cities are home to historic hotels, most dating from the turn of the 20th century. Stepping inside is like stepping back in time, the common areas decked out in antique furnishings and Victorian-era decor and art. Guest rooms feature modern amenities (no outhouses here!) and some occupy modern buildings attached to the original.

COMPETITIVE CAMPING

With the growing number of Colorado residents and the state's popularity among travelers, camping can feel like a competitive sport. Campgrounds fill up fast, especially on summer weekends; some are completely booked months ahead of time, so reserve early. Try recreation.gov for campsites on federal land and Colorado Parks & Wildlife (cpw.state.co.us) for state parks. For dispersed camping near popular destinations like Crested Butte or Aspen, camp midweek or arrive by Friday morning to secure a spot. For more information, stop at ranger stations or a Bureau of Land Management (blm.gov) office.

Family Travel

Colorado is a welcoming place for families, especially for exploring the great outdoors with endless blue skies and adventure galore. But the state is also bursting with history and culture, from prehistoric finds and ancient ruins to modern-day museums. You could spend weeks crisscrossing the state and never truly see it all – but don't let that stop you from trying!

Discounts for Children

In Colorado, discounts for children and youth often apply for tours, admission fees and public transportation; discounts can be as much as 50% off the regular rate, while infants under two are typically free. Restaurants often have kids' menus, with special pricing and kid-oriented dishes. If traveling to Denver, consider purchasing a CityPASS (citypass.com/denver), a bundled ticket package that offers discounts for several family-friendly attractions.

Facilities

- Colorado's cities and ski resorts are well-equipped for traveling kids; small mountain towns and rural areas are hit and miss.
- Most restaurants, diners and cafes offer highchairs for toddlers; many also have kids' menus and offer crayons and coloring books to pass the time.
- Breweries often welcome children, sometimes even offering juice boxes and snacks.
- Hotels have cots and cribs for traveling families.

SKI SCHOOL

Ski and snowboard lessons can be a great way for everyone in the family to make the most of a mountain vacation. Beginners can get quality instruction, while advanced skiers and riders have a few hours to hit the double-blacks. Consider half-day lessons, which allow for a good balance of instruction and family together-time and are available for all ages. If you opt for full days, kids' lessons typically include lunch. Some ski school packages include lift tickets and rentals too – often a great deal. Above all, remember to have fun and keep your expectations reasonable: skiing and boarding are tough to master!

Nursing Rooms

Private nursing or lactation rooms are few and far between in Colorado, but their prevalence is on the rise. Look for them at large facilities like airports, auditoriums and hospitals, as well as at child-centered destinations like children's museums and zoos.

Diaper-Changing Stations

Diaper-changing stations are found in most public restrooms in Colorado. Museums and airports typically have 'family restrooms' – single-user bathrooms with changing tables that are roomy enough for a parent, a couple of children and even a stroller to enter at once.

TOP CHILD-FRIENDLY SIGHTS

The Barn (p169) Practice gnarly moves at Copper Mountain's action sports playground for kids.

Bent's Old Fort (p280) Learn about the Old West at this one-time trading post from staffers in costume and character.

Children's Museum of Denver (p62) Come for imaginative play, maker spaces and even cooking classes.

Dinosaur National Monument (p139) Touch dinosaur skeletons and see thousands of prehistoric bones up close.

Ouray Hot Springs Waterpark (p225) Splash year-round at this water park with geothermically heated water.

RASTKO BELIC/EYEEM/GETTY IMAGES ©

Health & Safe Travel

INSURANCE

Getting basic travel insurance is a good idea, especially for flight cancellations, luggage theft and loss. International travelers should consider adding coverage for medical emergencies, including hospital stays and emergency flights home. While the US offers some of the best-quality healthcare in the world, it can be prohibitively expensive.

High Altitude

Altitude sickness is a serious health risk in Colorado. Stay hydrated, take it easy and allow a few days to acclimatize before going really high – like to the top of a fourteener. A little light-headedness, slight headaches and sluggishness are normal. But if you experience severe and continued nausea, headache and dizziness, consult a doctor and/or get to lower altitudes.

Drinking Water

Colorado has great tap water – you can drink out of the faucet pretty much anywhere in the state. When camping, be sure to purify any water you collect to kill disease-causing viruses, bacteria and parasites. If you choose to boil the water, be sure it's roiling for at least a minute, or for three minutes at altitudes over 6500ft.

THE SUN

High elevation and blue skies mean increased exposure to the sun's rays. Cover up, slather on sunscreen and wear a hat!

WILDLIFE ROAD SIGNS

Bear Crossing

Moose Crossing

Cattle & Livestock Crossing

Deer Crossing

Elk Crossing

WILDFIRES

Wildfires are all too common in Colorado, particularly during summer when conditions are hot, dry and windy. They're often sparked by lightning strikes or unattended campfires, and can spread quickly, causing devastating damage. Even distant communities can be affected by the poor air quality. Always heed fire bans! And if there's a wildfire, follow evacuation orders and road closure signs.

Bites & Stings

Being proactive is effective against bites and stings:

- Use hiking boots to protect from snakes.
- Wear long sleeves and pants, and use bug repellant, to ward off ticks, spiders and mosquitoes; check for ticks at the end of the day.
- If you're bitten or stung, stay calm and seek treatment.

✂ Food, Drink & Nightlife

When to Eat

Breakfast (7–10am) is filling, revolving around eggs, bacon, fruit, orange juice and coffee.

Brunch (9am–1pm) is a leisurely weekend meal, combining breakfast and lunch dishes. Mimosas and bloody Marys are common.

Lunch (11am–2pm) is quick, often sandwiches and salads with iced tea or soft drinks.

Dinner (5:30–9pm) is substantial, varying from takeout to multicourse meals served with wine or beer. Dessert is common.

Where to Eat

Casual dining Relaxed restaurant with moderately priced meals and either counter or table service.

Cafe Unhurried locals' spot that serves breakfast, lunch, pastries and coffee drinks.

Diner Casual, inexpensive eatery, typically lined with booths and serving American staples; open late.

Food truck Kitchen on wheels, serving fast, made-to-order food that's taken to go.

Food halls Collection of indoor eateries offering a variety of cuisines in a classed-up food-court-style setting.

Fine dining Upscale restaurant with gourmet dishes often featuring farm-to-table and ethically raised ingredients.

MENU DECODER

À la carte A menu of individually priced dishes, Colorado's most common.

Blue plate An old-school term meaning 'daily special,' typically used in diners.

Buffet An array of all-you-can eat dishes, typically hot and cold, offered for a set price.

Du jour A French term indicating 'daily special' (eg soup du jour).

Entree The main course of a meal.

Family-style A larger portioned dish, typically enough for two to four people, that is centrally placed for diners to serve themselves.

Prix fixe A set-price meal, including two or more predetermined courses.

Shareable menu A selection of small plates, several of which are ordered and shared to create a meal for two or more diners.

Tasting menu A multicourse meal with small, often bite-sized, portions that showcase the chef's talent.

HOW TO...

EAT AT A FOOD HALL

Food halls are taking Colorado by storm: collections of eateries, and often a bar, surround communal tables. The options can be overwhelming and the process for ordering can be confusing. Here are some tips:

- Before you sit down, peruse the options. It's easy to see what's being made and whether or not the food looks appetizing.

- If you see a menu, order at the counter and find a seat. You'll receive a pager that will buzz when your food is ready.

- If there's aren't any menus visible, find a seat and look for a QR code attached to the table. Scan the QR code for the menus and order from your phone. If you're able to enter a table number, the food will be brought to you; if not, you'll receive a text when your food is ready.

- Occasionally, roving waiters take and bring your drink orders.

- Payment may be taken by mobile scanner or QR code.

HOW MUCH FOR A...

cup of coffee
$3–5

breakfast burrito
$6–8

sandwich
$8–14

scoop of
ice cream
$3–5

dinner for two
(without drinks)
$30–100

pint of craft beer
$6–12

glass of wine
$8–15

ORDER A CRAFT BEER

HOW TO... With over 400 craft breweries, enjoying a glass of beer is a quintessential Colorado experience. Across the state, beer aficionados sip and savor beer as they would wine, and some restaurants even have 'beer sommeliers.' It's not surprising, then, that stepping into a tasting room or brewpub means navigating lots of options. Here are a few tips for handling it like a local:

- Be specific about the type of beer you'd like – IPAs are a Colorado standard but the beer varieties are nearly endless.
- Specify the pour size, typically a full pint or a smaller 10oz glass.
- At breweries with numerous options, consider a 'flight:' a sampler of four to six different beers in 4oz to 7oz pours.
- If you want craft beer to go, buy a six-pack or a 'growler,' a 64oz glass jug.
- Prepare to show your ID. Twenty-one is the legal drinking age but carding happens well into middle age.

Common beers categories:

Ales Full-bodied with complex flavor profiles and a pronounced aroma.

Flavored Brewed with foods that lend unique tastes like raspberry, pumpkin and jalapeño.

IPAs Bitter, hoppy and known for their high alcohol content.

Lagers Light-bodied, crisp and clean tasting.

Stouts and porters Dark, rich and full-bodied. Often brewed with roasted malt and barley, lending a coffee or chocolate flavor.

Sours Tart, crisp and often layered with fruity flavors.

Barrels of Beer

Colorado's first commercial beer was tapped in 1859, to quench the thirst of miners who'd come in search of gold. Today, the state's craft beer industry produces over 1.8 million barrels each year.

COLORADO WINE COUNTRY

Colorado isn't the first place you'd think of when you hear the phrase 'wine country.' But vineyards have been in the region since the late 1800s, when miners planted grapevines to make homegrown wine, a common practice in the era. It wasn't until the 1960s that Colorado produced its first commercial wine. It began with Gerald Ivancie, a Denver periodontist, who started making wine as a hobby in his three-car garage using California grapes and wine-making knowledge he'd gained from his European parents. Ivancie's homemade wine was such a hit with friends and family, he decided to scale up his operation: Ivancie Cellars, in Denver, became the state's first winery. With an eye to growing the business and focusing on Colorado-grown grapes, Ivancie enlisted the help of Warren Winiarski, a rising Californian winemaker. Together, they scouted out and approached farmers in the Grand Valley, near Grand Junction, to plant wine grapes. The red rocks and high desert surroundings seemed unusual, but the fertile soil, sunny days, cool nights and low humidity proved ideal. The vineyards also proved to be record-breaking – growing between 4000ft and 7000ft above sea level, they are the highest vineyards in North America.

Ivancie Cellars eventually folded, but it sparked a movement and an industry. Today, there are 110 Coloradoan wineries, mostly small family-owned estates. Many are in the Grand Valley and the nearby West Elks regions. Winery tours and tasting rooms abound in Palisades (p250) and Paonia (p251), while areas around Cortez and the Front Range are developing.

Responsible Travel

Climate Change & Travel

It's impossible to ignore the impact we have when traveling, and the importance of making changes where we can. Lonely Planet urges all travelers to engage with their travel carbon footprint. There are many carbon calculators online that allow travelers to estimate the carbon emissions generated by their journey; try resurgence.org/resources/carbon-calculator.html. Many airlines and booking sites offer travelers the option of offsetting the impact of greenhouse gas emissions by contributing to climate-friendly initiatives around the world. We continue to offset the carbon footprint of all Lonely Planet staff travel, while recognising this is a mitigation more than a solution.

Support Local

Nibble your way through some of the state's best locally produced food at Boulder County Farmers Market (p94), where vendors adhere to the strict sell-only-what-you-grow-or-make policy. Most only offer organic, non-GMO food. You also can pick up fresh eats at Denver's festival-like farmers markets at City Park (p77) and Union Station (p56). Most mountain towns, especially those on the western slope, have seasonal farmers markets too.

Do Good Outdoors

Join Volunteers for Outdoors Colorado (voc.org) for a day (or more) to help protect and preserve Colorado's public lands. Projects are statewide and include trail construction, habitat restoration and preservation of historic structures.

Give Back

Help with food prep or wash dishes at SAME Café (p79), a donation-based cafe in Denver that strives to provide access to wholesome food for everyone, regardless of their ability to pay.

Geek Out

Learn all about Colorado's delicate ecosystem from scientists at Rocky Mountain Biological Laboratory (p243).

First Place

Colorado is a leader in renewable energy, with more LEED-certified buildings per person than any other state. Standing for 'Leadership in Energy and Environmental Design,' these buildings use less energy and water, ultimately reducing carbon emissions.

Hut-to-Hut Travel Travel through the mountains on foot, ski or bike, staying in off-the-grid huts along the way. Good options include 10th Mountain Division Hut Association (p189), Summit Huts Association (p163) and San Juan Huts (p232). Reserve early!

Get Around Pedal your way around Denver (lyft.com and li.me), Boulder (boulder.bcycle.com), Fort Collins (spin. app) and Colorado Springs (pikeride.org) using their e-bike and e-scooter share programs; most are accessibly priced by the minute or day.

Learn More

Take a free guided hike of Hallam Lake with a naturalist at Aspen Center for Environmental Studies (p189) and learn all about the creatures that call this 25-acre wildlife sanctuary home.

Bottoms Up

Go ahead, have another. Not only is Upslope Brewing Co (p109) a Certified B Corporation, but it also donates a percentage of its sales to protect fisheries and watersheds. And did we mention its award-winning beers?

Stargaze

Take in the twinkling night sky at Black Canyon of the Gunnison National Park (p234) and Great Sand Dunes National Park (p265), two of Colorado's certified Dark Sky Parks, whose light-reduction efforts benefit wildlife and nature conservation. DIY-it or join a ranger-led stargazing program. Or check out Dinosaur National Monument (p139), Hovenweep National Monument (p216) and Mesa Verde National Park (p210), whose Dark Sky efforts help preserve dino fossils and ancient ruins.

Pick Your Own

Pick your own lavender at Sage Creations Organic Farm (p250), a sea of purple on the western slope. Or head to nearby Delicious Orchards (p251) for DIY fruit and veggie picking, from peaches to cucumbers.

RESOURCES

lnt.org
'Leave no trace' resources and volunteer opportunities in Colorado

cpw.state.co.us
Deep dive into Colorado's state parks' offerings

wwoofusa.org
Volunteer opportunities on small-scale organic farms

Choose Sustainable Venues

Enjoy farm-to-table fare at Dushanbe Tea House (p93), a jaw-droppingly beautiful restaurant built entirely by hand.

LGBTIQ+ Travelers

Colorado is a mixed bag for LGBTIQ+ travelers. In general, cities and college towns are more progressive – Denver, Boulder, Fort Collins and Durango are especially accepting. Rural areas and smaller mountain towns are characterized by conservative attitudes and old-school ideas about sexual and gender identity; the more affluent ski towns like Aspen, Telluride and Breckenridge are exceptions.

Pride Festivities

Rainbow flags come out in full force in Denver every June, when the city hosts PrideFest (p66), a two-day celebration with over 500,000 attendees partying in the streets and Civic Park (p68) – Colorado's largest queer fest of the year. Boulder County (outboulder.org), Fort Collins (nocoequality. org), Avon (mountainpride.org) and Colorado Springs (pikespeakpride.org) also host Pride festivals in June and July, celebrations marked with entertainment, food and parades. If you'll be here beyond summer, Durango Pride (durangopride.com) means LGBTIQ+ parties in September and February that include movies, dances and late-night drag shows.

LEGAL PROTECTIONS

Though parts of Colorado are still quite conservative, it consistently ranks as one of the best states for LGBTIQ+ equity. This reflects hard-fought laws that protect the rights of individuals and prohibits discrimination based on sexual orientation or gender identity.

GOINGS ON

For the latest LGBTIQ+ news on what's happening in Denver and beyond, check out the cheeky and smart online magazine Out Front Colorado (outfrontonline.com). For a general overview of LGBTIQ+-friendly events and businesses, check out PrideGuide Colorado (gaycolorado.com).

Rainbow Neighborhoods

Denver's Capitol Hill (p64) is Colorado's best-known LGBTIQ+ neighborhood, with a thriving queer scene from coffee shops and bars to restaurants and LGBTIQ+ friendly hotels. Neighboring Cheeseman Park (p69) is another go-to gathering spot, doubling as ground zero for Denver's annual PrideFest parade. Other LGBTIQ+ inclusive areas include Boulder's Pearl Street Mall (p92) and Fort Collins' Old Town (p141) ,with queer- and trans-friendly locales.

RESOURCES & VOLUNTEERING

The Center on Colfax (glbtcolorado.org) is the largest LGBTIQ+ community center in the Rocky Mountain region, offering programming, resources and events in Denver. **Out Boulder County** (outboulder. org) provides similar services on a smaller scale in Boulder County. Both offer several volunteer opportunities. Beyond the Front Range, IRIS (p237) provides outdoors guiding and instruction catering to women and non-binary and trans people.

Gay Rodeo

Rocky Mountain Regional Rodeo (cgrarodeo.com) is among the country's biggest and best gay-centric rodeos, featuring traditional events like bull riding and barrel racing as well as not-so-traditional events like wild drag racing and goat dressing. Any gender can compete together, a nod to non-binary and trans cowfolk. Held every July in Denver.

Accessible Travel

Travel within Colorado is getting easier for people with disabilities, with accessible facilities, attractions and accommodations plus adaptive outdoors activities. Challenges still exist in off-the-beaten-track places and rural areas.

National Parks

Colorado's national parks have accessible visitor centers, overlooks, campgrounds and picnic areas. Rocky Mountain National Park (p118) also has wheelchair-friendly trails and Great Sand Dunes National Park (p265) loans special sand-friendly wheelchairs. **Scan this QR code for details on accessibility options in the state's national parks.**

RESOURCES

Adaptive Sports Center (adaptive sports.org) provides opportunities for people with disabilities to participate in adventure sports in Crested Butte.

National Sports Center for the Disabled (nscd.org) is a Colorado-based organization providing access to various sports and outdoors activities statewide.

Society for the Advancement of Travel for the Handicapped (sath. org) offers resources for travelers with disabilities.

TrailLink (traillink. com) has a comprehensive list of wheelchair-accessible trails in Colorado.

Denver International Airport is well-equipped for travelers with disabilities, including accessible elevators, restrooms and seating areas, as well as wheelchair assistance. Assistive technology and interpreter services are provided throughout. Ground transportation providers are required to have wheelchair-accessible vehicles.

Colorado offers a variety of accommodations for travelers with disabilities, ranging from wheelchair-accessible campsites to hotels with specially designed rooms. Vacation rental websites often can be filtered by accessibility features like step-free access and wide-width doors.

SKI-RESORT PROGRAMS

Many Colorado ski resorts offer programs specifically designed for visitors with cognitive and physical disabilities. Ski and snowboarding instruction are provided using specialized equipment; some resorts also offer family lessons to teach relatives how to assist with the adaptive equipment.

Public Transportation

Public transportation must be made accessible to all, including priority seating and wheelchair securement. Drivers typically are trained to assist passengers with disabilities to board or exit. Expect braille signage and stop announcements too.

Sidewalks

Generally, Colorado's cities have well-maintained sidewalks with curb ramps; crosswalks are wide and easily visible. Small towns often limit sidewalks to the main commercial areas, while dirt roads and parking areas are common.

The US Olympic & Paralympic Museum (p260) is perhaps Colorado's most accessible museum, with individually triggered features available to visitors, including audio-described video, text-to-speech screen readers, touchscreens with tactile keypads, ASL-guided tours, low-sensory films and more.

All public buildings are required to have braille signage and tactile maps – expect them in places like airports, hotels, restaurants, banks and museums. Many busy intersections also have audible crossing signals.

Cannabis

In November 2012, Colorado and Washington became the first US states – and arguably, the first jurisdictions in the world – to legalize recreational marijuana. But you can't just walk into a restaurant, roll a joint and start puffing away. They want you to smoke at home and certain designated places and, in Colorado, it breaks down like this.

BUY FROM A DISPENSARY

Dispensaries are the only businesses licensed to sell cannabis products. Sales fall into two categories: recreational (21+ only) and medicinal (prescription required). A few things to know:

- With 1000+ dispensaries in Colorado, you're sure to find one near you, especially in cities and ski towns. They often sport a green cross or cannabis leaf image.

- Bring cash. Since the sale of marijuana is illegal under federal law, most banks won't allow their credit or debit cards to be used.

- Dispensaries have ATMs on-site; while convenient, expect a $3 to $4 surcharge.

- Bring government-issued ID. You must prove you're 21+ to even step inside.

- Rely on the budtender. They know the stock. Remember to tip a couple bucks!

RESOURCES

The Cannabist (thecannabist.co) The Denver Post's marijuana news and culture platform.

Colorado Pot Guide (coloradopotguide.com) Statewide cannabis resources.

Bud and Breakfast (budandbreakfast.com) Cannabis-friendly lodging listings.

PARTAKE IN PRIVATE OR SPECIALLY DESIGNATED AREAS

Smoking marijuana in public is not permitted, including in parks, on sidewalks and at concert halls. Other rules to keep in mind:

- Some hotels and vacation rentals are '420 friendly,' but not all. Check before lighting up, or you may face steep clean-up charges.
- Blazing a doobie in a private residence is legal, but not where you can be seen by the public (like on a front porch). Head inside or to the backyard.
- You can partake in specially designated vehicles, like those on a cannabis tour.
- Enjoying MJ in your own car (or even having an open container of it) is illegal.
- Marijuana social clubs were recently legalized but few exist.
- Cannabis remains illegal on federal property, including national parks and some ski resorts.

Cannabis Culture

Though there's plenty of marijuana around the state, Denver is ground zero for everything cannabis. It has around 200 dispensaries alone and hosts the 420 Festival (p70), the largest marijuana fest in the world. It's also home to the International Church of Cannabis (elevationists.org), with guided meditations and laser shows for the general public. Several cannabis tours operate in Denver-metro too, ranging from customized experiences with City Sessions (p68) to raucous party bus excursions with Colorado Cannabis Tours (coloradocannabistours.com).

BE RESPONSIBLE

Don't drive if you're high. You could really hurt someone and face a DUI charge too. Take an Uber or taxi instead.

+ Nuts & Bolts

OPENING HOURS

High-season hours follow. In the mountains and rural areas, many businesses close on Sunday.

Banks 8:30am–5pm Monday to Friday, 9am–noon on Saturday

Breweries noon–10pm Thursday to Saturday, to 8pm Sunday to Wednesday

Bars 4pm–midnight, to 2am Friday and Saturday

Nightclubs 9pm–2am Thursday to Saturday

Restaurants 7am–2:30pm and 5–9:30pm

Stores 10am–6pm Monday to Saturday, noon–5pm Sunday

Cell Phones

Cell phone coverage can be unreliable in mountain regions; use internet-based services like WhatsApp to communicate.

Electricity
120V/60Hz

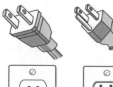

GOOD TO KNOW

Time zone
GMT/UTC minus seven hours early November to mid-March; GMT/UTC minus six hours for the rest of year

Country code
1

Emergency number
911

Population
5.8 million

PUBLIC HOLIDAYS

On the following national public holidays, banks, schools and government offices (including post offices) are closed; transportation and other services operate on a Sunday schedule. Holidays falling on a weekend are usually observed the following Monday.

New Year's Day January 1

Martin Luther King Jr Day Third Monday of January

Presidents' Day Third Monday of February

Easter March or April

Memorial Day Last Monday of May

Independence Day July 4

Labor Day First Monday of September

Mother Cabrini Day Second Monday of October

Veterans Day November 11

Thanksgiving Fourth Thursday of November

Christmas Day December 25

Smoking

Smoking, including vapes and cannabis, is prohibited in all public spaces except in specially designated areas.

Toilets

Public toilets can be hard to find. Try gas stations, libraries, department stores and supermarkets.

THE COLORADO

STORYBOOK

Our writers delve deep into different aspects of Colorado life

Tincup Pass (p202)
LAURENT FOX/GETTY IMAGES ©

A HISTORY OF COLORADO IN

15 PLACES

Colorado's history is written in fossils, petroglyphs, gold dust and ski tracks. It's marked by discovery and domination, vision and modernization, with natural beauty woven throughout. Ultimately, it's a story about change, and how the force of nature and human hands created the Colorado we see today. By Liza Prado

THE NAME 'COLORADO' evokes images of towering mountains, swooshing skiers and fly fishermen. And for good reason: Colorado is a genuine outdoor wonderland. But that's not all – the state has a complex history and rich culture. Knowing how it has developed, and who has lived here and how they have shaped the social and physical landscape, speaks volumes. Context is everything.

Colorado history dates from prehistoric times; it's home to some of the world's best fossil beds, their dinosaur bones telling a story of a once-lush land. Human archaeological sites also dot the state, remnants of ancient communities that whisper about life on the plains, mesa tops and mountains valleys. The discovery of gold brought thousands to this vast wilderness, who built cities, mountain towns, mines and railroads. The native people who'd lived in the Rockies for countless generations were killed or pushed out, relegated to a tiny corner of the state. And still Colorado continued to grow, with the land mined and farmed, parks created and scenic roadways built; along the way, Colorado became a tourist destination.

Today, Colorado is a diverse and thriving state: its population continues to change, as its complex history is revisited and rediscovered, and all the while, its natural beauty is ever present.

1. Dinosaur National Monument
WHERE DINOSAURS ROAMED
Present-day Colorado was a very different place 150 million years ago, during the Jurassic era. It was closer to the equator for one thing, and was mostly low plains, crisscrossed by languid rivers. Dinosaurs of many kinds and sizes lived and died beside those rivers; their bones were covered in successive layers of sediment, creating what became known as the Morrison Formation, arguably the richest dinosaur fossil bed in the world. Its 1877 discovery in Colorado, and the subsequent formation of Dinosaur National Park in 1915, brought world attention to the state. Colorado remains an important center of paleontological research today.

For more on Dinosaur National Monument, see page 139.

2. Mesa Verde National Park
THE FIRST COLORADANS
The incredible cliff dwellings of Mesa Verde National Park were built during the 12th century by the Ancestral Puebloan people. By that time, they had already occupied southwest Colorado for over 1100 years, living and farming the valleys and mesa tops. The dwellings, built in vertiginous natural alcoves and exhibiting sophisticated masonry, were accessed via wood-pole ladders, stairways cut into the cliffs, and narrow tunnels. The site was abruptly abandoned in 1300 CE for reasons still unknown.

Today, Mesa Verde is the largest and best-known archaeological site in Colorado, but by no means the only one.

For more on Mesa Verde National Park, see page 210.

JACOB BOOMSMA/SHUTTERSTOCK ©

3. Santa Fe Trail

WESTERN EXPANSION

The Santa Fe Trail was a 19th-century trade route that connected Missouri to New Mexico. Officially opened in 1821 and used until the arrival of the railroad in 1880, it was lifeline for pioneers and merchants, providing a direct link between the goods of the American frontier and the resources of Mexican and Native American territories. Today, parts of the Santa Fe Trail are protected and preserved along a National Scenic Byway in southeast Colorado. Sights along the route, like Bent's Old Fort National Historic Site (pictured below), provide insights into the cultural crossroads of the Old West.

For more on the Santa Fe Trail, see page 277.

4. Larimer Square

DENVER'S BEGINNINGS

The discovery of gold near the confluence of the South Platte River and Cherry Creek in 1858 sparked the Colorado Gold Rush. Thousands of fortune-seekers descended on the area known today as Confluence Park. An astute land developer from Kansas named William Larimer staked a claim on a square-mile parcel of land near the site, laid out streets and sold plots to settlers. He called it Denver City. Larimer also created the city's first commercial center, with a bank, a jail, a city hall and even a bookstore, and named it after himself. In 1971, Larimer Square became Denver's first historic district.

For more on Larimer Square, see page 59.

5. Sand Creek Massacre National Historic Site

MASSACRE OF NATIVE AMERICANS

On November 29, 1864, around 700 volunteer soldiers attacked a peaceful Cheyenne and Arapaho encampment in southeastern Colorado. More than 150 people, mostly elders, women and children, were killed and mutilated; body parts of the victims were later paraded through Denver in grisly celebration. The massacre reflected the fear of (and utter disregard for) Native Americans held by the US government and, by extension, white settlers. Not surprisingly, it only served to increase conflict in the region. In 2000, the Sand Creek Massacre National Historic Site was established to commemorate the horrors of that day and to raise awareness about the region's history.

For more on the Sand Creek Massacre National Historic Site, see page 281.

6. Durango & Silverton Narrow Gauge Railroad

RAILROADS AND MINING

Railroads were the lifeblood of Colorado's early development, connecting the young state to the rest of the country and greasing the wheels of economic growth. Rails were especially critical to Colorado's burgeoning mining industry. Beginning in 1882, the Durango & Silverton Narrow Gauge Railroad served mines in the San Juan Mountains, carrying over $300 million in gold and silver on its tracks; when gold and silver mining ended, it began hauling coal. The railroad was pivotal to the growth

of the modern-day towns of southwest Colorado and today is a National Historic Landmark.

For more on the Durango & Silverton Narrow Gauge Railroad, see page 218.

7. Matchless Mine

SILVER BOOM AND CRASH

Opened in 1878, Matchless Mine in Leadville became one of the richest silver mines in Colorado, the source of an estimated $7.5 million ($245 million in today's money). It was owned by Horace Tabor, Colorado senator and eventually one of the wealthiest individuals in the state. But his success and that of Matchless Mine didn't last. In 1893, the repeal of the Sherman Silver Purchase Act led to the collapse of the silver-mining industry and Tabor, like many others, lost everything. He died penniless, leaving Matchless Mine to his widow, Baby Doe. She lived out her life impoverished in a small cabin at the mine.

For more on Matchless Mine, see page 182.

8. Colorado Chautauqua

A NEW IMAGE

In 1898, Boulder won the bid to create a 'Chautauqua' for the Texas Board of Regents, which was searching for a desirable summer school locale for its teachers. Part of a nationwide Chautauqua movement, Boulder's location aimed not only to provide a summer school but also to create year-round educational and cultural experiences for its community, with lectures, concerts and social activities, all designed to bridge the perceived cultural gap between urban and rural America. Colorado Chautauqua proved a success. It quickly rose to be the preeminent educational retreat of the West, putting Boulder – and Colorado – on the map as a sophisticated and innovative place.

For more on Colorado Chautauqua, see page 106.

9. St Elmo Ghost Town

THE END OF AN ERA

By the 1920s, hundreds of once-thriving mountain communities, founded during the gold and silver rushes, were abandoned, the mines closed and residents moving to more prosperous areas. St Elmo (pictured above right), a gold-mining town in the Collegiate Peaks, became one of the best-preserved of these 'ghost towns.' Around 40 of the town's buildings still remain standing – a saloon, billiards hall, courthouse, jail and more – with most dating from the 1880s when the town had over 2000 residents. In 1922, the train stopped running and the last mine closed, leaving the town empty.

For more on St Elmo Ghost Town, see page 202.

10. Colorado National Monument

THE BUILDING OF PARKS

The Great Depression had a profound impact on Colorado, with rampant unemployment and families struggling to make ends meet. In 1932, President Roosevelt introduced the New Deal, a series of programs and policies that provided much-needed relief. Colorado National Monument was among many parks where men were put to work, building infrastructure to promote tourism and earning precious wages in the process. Among the projects in the park was the construction of Rim Rd, the epically beautiful 23-mile road that winds through the park, including tunnels and overlooks, offering breathtaking views of the Colorado National Monument's towering red-rock formations.

For more on Colorado National Monument, see page 247.

11. Amache National Historic Site

WWII INJUSTICE

Camp Amache, located on a desolate windy prairie in southeastern Colorado, was one of 10 Japanese internment camps established during WWII between 1942 and 1945. The camps were established under Executive Order 9066, a racist response to the bombing of Pearl Harbor that forced the relocation and incarceration of people of Japanese descent, mostly US citizens. Against all odds, Amache's residents grew enough food to feed the entire camp (which was woefully undersupplied) and provided millions of pounds of surplus produce to the military. What's more, over 400 men from Amache enlisted, and 31 died, in fighting overseas. Amache became a national historic site in 2022.

For more on Amache National Historic Site, see page 281.

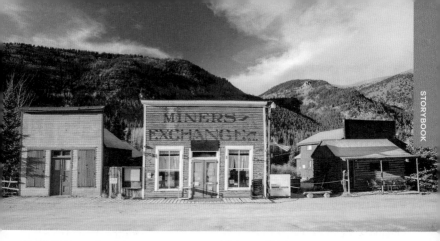

12. US Air Force Academy

MODERN MILITARY PRESENCE

The start of the Cold War highlighted the US' need for more professional and specialized training for its military pilots. In 1954, the US Air Force Academy was opened in Colorado Springs, integrating military training with academic rigor in the sciences. The city was chosen for its central location and favorable climate (and it didn't hurt that First Lady Mamie Eisenhower was from Colorado). It marked the beginning of a major US Air Force presence in the state, which today includes five bases, one of which houses the North American Aerospace Defense Command (NORAD).

For more on the US Air Force Academy, see page 264.

13. Vail

COLORADO'S SKI INDUSTRY

The opening of Vail Ski Resort in 1962 marked the beginning of Colorado's rise as a major ski destination. The brainchild of locals Peter Seibert and Earl Eaton, the ambitious resort quickly became known for its world-class ski slopes, stunning mountain scenery and luxurious amenities. Vail was one of the first ski resorts in the US to offer high-speed lifts, on-mountain restaurants and a wide variety of ski runs for all skill levels. Today, Vail is widely recognized as one of the premier ski resorts in the world, attracting over a million visitors each year.

For more on Vail, see page 172.

14. Coors Field

REVITALIZATION OF DENVER

Downtown Denver's transformation from dreary and dangerous to lively and livable can be traced to one thing: Coors Field. The stadium (a terrific brick throwback) opened in 1995 and was soon followed by a vibrant mix of bars, restaurants, shops and residential buildings. Change was already afoot with artists turning warehouses into lofts in what would become RiNo, and future-governor John Hickenlooper opening Denver's first brewery at 18th and Wynkoop St. Mayor Federico Peña, elected in 1983, worked tirelessly for a stadium downtown, rightly understanding its potential.

For more on Coors Field, see page 57.

15. Colorado State Capitol

PURPLE STATE

The gold-domed Colorado State Capitol houses the Governor's Office, Senate and House of Representatives. Built in the late 1800s, its ornately decorated walls have seen innumerable laws debated and enacted, reflecting the societal attitudes and perspectives of Coloradans over the course of its history. Large portions of Colorado are solidly conservative, but recent state-wide elections and legislation have swung decidedly leftward, including the legalization of recreational marijuana and same-sex civil unions. In 2018, Colorado elected Jared Polis, the US' first openly gay governor, who was re-elected in a landslide victory in 2022.

For more on the Colorado State Capitol, see page 67.

MEET THE COLORADANS

A growing and ever-changing people, most of today's Coloradans were born out-of-state. And while they may not agree on politics, they all love the outdoors. Liza Prado introduces her people.

DRIVING WEST FROM Denver on the I-70, especially on a weekend, there's no doubt Colorado is a fast-growing state. A highway that was a cruiser 15 years ago is now bumper-to-bumper at 8am, packed with city-dwellers headed for mountain fun. Since 2010, Colorado's population has exploded, adding over 800,000 people for a total of 5.8 million – a 15% growth rate, most of it in Colorado's big cities. Denver has repeatedly topped the 'Fastest Growing Cities in the US' lists. With all the new apartment buildings being built these days, it's no surprise. And frankly, neither is the traffic.

The 'Native Coloradan' bumper stickers I so often saw on my commute years ago are now almost a relic. Today, about 58% of Colorado residents were born outside of Colorado, either in another state or another country. Over 160 languages are spoken in the city of Aurora alone. The most commonly spoken language after English is Spanish, of course; it reflects the Latinx population that has immigrated to the state for work as well as those that were here before Colorado even existed (a quarter of the state was once part of Mexico after all). In fact, the Latinx population is the fastest-growing segment of Colorado, projected to hit 26% by 2030. But still, that stereotype about Colorado being really white...? Yeah, it holds water. White Coloradans make up 68% of the population. The percentage of African Americans, Asian Americans and Native Americans are all in the single digits.

Politically, the state is diverse. It has an almost equal mix of Democrats (39%), Republicans (31%) and Independents (28%). A longtime swing state, voters have leaned blue in recent elections. Colorado's progressive policies on issues such as cannabis legalization, environmental protection and same-sex unions are a nod to that. Geographically, Denver and Boulder are the state's liberal hubs. Mountain towns can go either way; ski towns tend to be blue while most others lean red. Colorado Springs, Grand Junction and farming communities are decidedly conservative. As you drive through the state, political billboards and yard signs are prominent. They'll tell you immediately where people stand. Tread lightly. Coloradans value courtesy but can have strong, vocal opinions if pushed, especially on their home turf.

One thing all Coloradans agree on, though, is outdoor recreation. We love it. It's a major reason why people move here. And it's no wonder, with so many people hiking, climbing, skiing and more, that Colorado is often ranked among the healthiest states (if not the healthiest) in the US. Even in big cities, bikers and joggers are a typical sight and green spaces are filled with people playing in the sun.

RELIGION IN COLORADO

Religion isn't a common topic among Coloradans, though the numbers speak volumes: 64% identify as Christian, and of those 41% are Protestants. Only 1% are Jewish, and less than 1% are Muslim or Hindu. Almost 30% of Coloradans have no religious affiliation at all.

A TRANSPLANT WITH COLORADO ROOTS

Like most Coloradans, I was born out-of-state. In Buffalo, NY, to be exact. And like many Coloradans, my parents are Mexican immigrants. I love my parents, I love Buffalo but never, not once, did I think I'd stay in western New York. After college I bounced from coast to coast and lived all over Mexico, but when I moved to Colorado on a whim, I unexpectedly found my home. Like so many other transplants, the mountains called to me. I didn't understand it, but I listened and stayed. About a decade after moving to Denver, I learned my great grandfather had lived here too; Papa Lalo had come with tens of thousands of other Mexican *traqueros* (track workers) to help build the railroads. He'd lived in a shanty town near Union Station. It suddenly made sense. This pull to Colorado had as much to do with snowcapped mountains as with family ties, with my great grandfather who helped build it.

Liza Prado, lead writer

DECLINING SNOWPACK: COLORADO'S CHANGING CLIMATE

In the parched Rocky Mountains, water is everything. How is climate change impacting the region's long-term prospects?
By Christopher Pitts

THE MOST VISIBLE indication of the effects of climate change in Colorado are not in the state itself, but further downstream along the Colorado River. In 2022, water levels at Lake Mead, the massive reservoir formed by the Hoover Dam outside Las Vegas, fell to their lowest level ever, at just one-fourth of the dam's capacity.

The infamous bathtub ring, a chalky white coating on the reservoir's cliffs, is a reminder of just how far the water's surface has dropped in the past two decades. In the summer of 2022, the ring stretched over 150ft from the water's surface to its one-time maximum-capacity mark. If the water in the Colorado River continues to be used at the same rate as today, the US Bureau of Reclamation concluded that the water level in the reservoir will soon drop so low that Hoover Dam will no longer be able to generate electricity. And after that? There remains the possibility that one day, the reservoir could reach 'dead pool,' when the level in the dam drops so low that the river stops flowing entirely,

and Arizona, Nevada, southern California and northwestern Mexico will be cut off from their main source of water.

The Colorado River

But what does all this have to do with Colorado? In a word: snowpack. The Colorado River, whose headwaters lie on the western slope of Rocky Mountain National Park and whose tributaries are scattered across the Rockies, is largely fed by snowmelt. Approximately 90% of all the water in the river comes from the mountains of Colorado, Wyoming and Utah, with the lion's share coming from Colorado watersheds. The equation is simple: the less snow that falls in the Rockies, the less water there is in the river, and the less water is available for one of the most important agricultural regions in the country – not to mention the 40 million people who live in the Colorado River basin (including Los Angeles, San Diego, Las Vegas and Phoenix).

Of course, as any skier will tell you,

snowpack varies from year to year. Some years may be above average, others below. But data from the Environmental Protection Agency (EPA) indicates that, overall, there has been a downward trend over time: across the West, snowpack has declined an average 23% since 1955. More importantly, the date of peak snowpack has been moving steadily backward. That is, the largest amount of snow in the Colorado Rockies used to be measured in mid-April; over the past decade, that date has been inching toward March.

What does this tell us? That because of climate change, winters are slowly getting shorter. Meanwhile, summer temperatures in the Southwest have risen faster than in any other part of the US. In Colorado, they've risen by 2.5°F since the beginning of the 20th century. Higher temperatures mean increased aridity and higher rates of evaporation throughout the landscape. Soils in particular have dried out to such an extent that when the spring runoff begins, much of that snowmelt is sucked straight into the ground, leaving less water to make it into the river system – even in years when snowpack is average.

Factor in the 20-plus-year megadrought that is currently gripping the region (the worst in 1200 years), and a flawed seven-state compact that draws more water from the Colorado River than there is annual flow, and you have all the ingredients for what has become a monumental crisis – albeit in slow motion. At this point, it seems highly unlikely that nature will replenish the Lake Mead or Lake Powell (on the Utah–Arizona border) reservoirs on its own. Barring an end to the drought, the only other way to avoid dead pool is to reduce consumption.

Considering that roughly one-half of all the water that flows out of the spigots in Los Angeles, San Diego and Phoenix comes directly from the Colorado River (in Vegas it's upwards of 90%), drastically reducing consumption in what is one of the fastest-growing regions in the US may seem like a tall order. But city dwellers aren't even the primary consumers. That would be agriculture, which sucks up 80% of the allotted river flow. While there is no sensible argument for growing certain water-dependent crops in the desert – eg cotton and alfalfa – reducing agricultural demand for irrigated water is easier said than done. With only 3in of annual rainfall, Yuma (Arizona) and the Imperial Valley (southern California) might seem like some of the world's most improbable farmland, but they're actually the nation's primary producer of winter fruit and vegetables. When farmland in the rest of the nation is on winter vacation, 90% of all the carrots, lettuce and other greens you find at the supermarket are being grown in the always sunny desert, irrigated directly with Colorado River water.

Climate change is not the only reason the Southwest's most important water source is drying up. Flawed planning, stubborn special-interest groups, outdated water rights and a naturally occurring drought cycle all play their own role. But as in so many other situations, climate change makes an already serious problem that much worse. As the Colorado snowpack continues to decline and summer temperatures continue to rise, eventually, there can only be one outcome. It may not come next year, or the year after that, but sooner or later, cuts to the Southwest's water supply are coming. The only question is: will they be managed with the best possible outcome in mind? Or will the failure to compromise result in a river that stops flowing entirely?

Wildfires

Beyond the consequences for all the people who live downstream, climate change has a direct impact on Coloradans as well. Colorado's mainstay of the tourism economy, skiing ($5 billion in annual revenue), seems to be headed for a day of reckoning, though the impacts of warming weather are less immediately visible for high-altitude ski resorts in the Rockies than in lower-elevation resorts in the Alps or along the East Coast, where winter rainfall is already commonplace. While Colorado ski resorts are nonetheless preparing for shortened seasons and less natural snowfall, there is another less obvious threat on the near horizon: wildfire.

In 2021, just miles from the residential sprawl around Lake Tahoe, California, the Caldor Fire raced through the mountains with such startling speed and ferocity that it's a miracle that firefighters were able to stop the blaze before it reached the lakeside settlements. One of the casualties of the fire, however, was the Sierra-at-Tahoe ski resort, where roughly 80% of the terrain was burned; the shocking photos of empty ski lifts being swallowed up by a raging orange inferno seemed to encapsulate all the fire mitigation challenges the West is currently facing.

While California's fires may get more coverage in the media, this is clearly a region-wide phenomenon. Over the past

> The equation is simple: the less snow that falls in the Rockies, the less water there is in the river, and the less water is available for one of the most important agricultural regions in the country.

GABE SHAKOUR/SHUTTERSTOCK ©

Cal-Wood Fire, Boulder County

decade, unusually hot and dry conditions have led to an increase not only in the number of wildfires per year, but also in their intensity. Warming conditions have stressed forests, making them more susceptible to disease and infestations of spruce, fir and pine beetles. Huge stands of dead trees – anyone who drives up Trail Ridge Rd in Rocky Mountain Park will spot the gray- and rust-colored stands of deadwood – combined with exceptionally dry grasses, low humidity and high winds have resulted in increasingly massive fires. Of the 20 largest fires in Colorado history, 16 occurred after 2011, and the other four took place in the 2000s. The three largest ever – Cameron Peak, East Troublesome and Pine Gulch – all took place in 2020, filling the skies outside several major cities with raining ash and a terrifying red glow.

Another change is that there is no longer a wildfire season. What used to be a late-summer event might now happen at any time of year, as evidenced by the most destructive fire in Colorado history, the Marshall Fire, which sprung up at the edge of Boulder on December 30, 2021. Fueled by 115mph gusting winds and a complete absence of snowfall that year, the grassland fire swept through a dense residential community in a matter of hours, completely destroying over 1000 homes and businesses, taking two lives and causing $2 billion in damages.

There's no question that decades of overly aggressive fire suppression on public lands is partially to blame for the blazes, as the Smokey the Bear strategy resulted in the accumulation of huge amounts of fuel and dense understory vegetation throughout the West. While no one wants unplanned fires to happen (campfires are off-limits in many places throughout Colorado), local officials today are passing on a different sort of message. It's no longer one of fire suppression, but fire adaptation. As the Boulder City Wildfire Preparedness Guide reminds its residents: 'We live in a location where the wildfire threat is real. Wildfires happen frequently. A wildfire that threatens your home is not a matter of if, but when.' Residents in the West are learning to be prepared, because they are now living in an environment where people have to accept wildfires and mandatory evacuations as an inevitable part of their lives. **309**

A KEYSTONE SPECIES: WILL THE WOLF SURVIVE?

An ambitious wolf reintroduction bill aims to have paws back on the ground by 2024, nearly 80 years after *Canis lupus* was declared extinct in Colorado. By Christopher Pitts

PERHAPS NO OTHER animal represents the wilderness more strikingly, for better or worse, than the wolf. Forever untamed yet uncannily familiar, impressively powerful yet hunted to near extinction, fairy-tale villain and howl-at-the-moon hero, wolves will always mean different things to different people.

Thus, in November 2020, when Colorado put legislation to reintroduce wolves to the state on the ballot, it came as no surprise that the vote came down to the wire. The ballot initiative (Proposition 114) ultimately passed, but with a margin of less than 2% (50.9% to 49%, or roughly 57,000 votes).

For political pundits, it was yet another example of America's rural–urban divide (the proposition passed in large part thanks to the overwhelming support along the heavily populated Front Range), but the roots of the conflict go much deeper than contemporary culture wars. The fate of the wolf, it seems, remains inextricably tied to Americans' understanding of public land.

Public Land

Colorado, like much of the West, has enormous tracts of public land: some 36% of the state is owned by the federal government. Of this, just two agencies, the National Forest Service and the Bureau of Land Management (BLM), manage the vast majority. As the US expanded into the arid West, displacing both Indigenous peoples and native species, the development of the vast tracts of new territory became a principal concern. Core industries – mining, logging and ranching – became tied to federal and state land, and their growth was supported by an age-old Western belief: that natural resources were put on earth for us to use.

But even as the government strove to make public land suitable for these industries – by building railroads to facilitate extraction, by driving natural predators like wolves to extinction, by clearcutting old-growth forests and by slaughtering millions of bison and replacing them with cattle – another value system was coming

into being: the conservation movement. Advocates like John Muir argued for the preservation of wilderness for its own sake, for a sustainable way of life that did not necessarily result in the unbridled destruction of the environment.

This core conflict, extraction versus conservation, has been a crucial part of every major debate on land use in the West since the late 1800s. You'll see it in the continuing discussions over new national parks and monuments, endangered species, logging rights, livestock grazing, hunting and fishing, and even recreation.

So when it comes to wolf reintroduction in Colorado, the essential question is this: where is there a protected wilderness area large enough to support a healthy population of wolves? And the answer is: nowhere. The key word in that sentence

is 'protected.' Unlike Wyoming and Montana, which are home to the massive Yellowstone National Park, there are few true wilderness areas in Colorado. When you're hiking through one of the many unspoiled tracts of land here, like the Flat Tops in northern Colorado, this statement may seem hard to believe, but even these areas, which are officially designated as environmentally protected, are still livestock-friendly – that is, ranchers can secure permits and leases to graze cattle and sheep here for a relatively small fee.

This means that as wolves return to Colorado, interactions with livestock are virtually guaranteed, because both groups of animals will be sharing the same public land and wilderness landscapes. Environmentalists argue that these interactions can be minimized through prevention (the removal of dead livestock from the landscape is the easiest and most effective way to prevent wolves from becoming habituated to cattle), though ranchers tend to prefer the easier solution (shoot the wolves). The state government, meanwhile, which Colorado voters have tasked with implementing the reintroduction program, has opted for the most common compromise throughout the West: to financially compensate ranchers for any losses.

Meanwhile, the wolves themselves didn't even wait for the state's plan to go into effect: since the proposition was first put on the ballot in 2018, two packs migrated naturally into the state from Wyoming. The first, in Moffat County, mysteriously disappeared; the fate of the second, in Jackson County, has been watched closely on both sides – local ranchers have continued to lose cattle, while three of the wolves that crossed into Wyoming, where no legal protections exist, were believed to have been shot. Since wolves are naturally migrating to Colorado anyway, some people are questioning why humans need to be involved in the reintroduction at all.

A Keystone Species

The answer, conservationists say, is protection. A carefully managed pack, fitted with radio collars, will be easier to track and study. According to the first draft of the reintroduction plan, Colorado Parks and Wildlife (CPW) will release 10 to 15 wolves per year west of the Continental Divide, at least 60 miles from state borders, beginning in 2024 and extending over the next three to five years. The first release area will be along the I-70 corridor between Vail and Glenwood Springs, and will likely consist of wolves from Wyoming, Montana or Idaho.

Though the CPW plan has been roundly criticized on both sides, it is arguably better than no plan at all. Through feedback from a Technical Working Group (experts in conservation and management strategies) and a Stakeholder Advisory Group (representing the viewpoints of different impacted communities), CPW developed a strategy that aims to take all scientific, social and economic factors into consideration.

Nevertheless, some conservation groups argue that the latest iteration of the plan

is proof Colorado does not actually want the plan to be successful, specifically pointing at the population threshold of 200, after which wolves will be removed from the state's endangered species list and the possibility of wolf hunting might be reintroduced. If wildlife management officials were serious about maintaining a healthy level of wolves, they say, that number would be closer to 750 (for comparison, France, which is much more densely settled, now supports a wolf population of over 600 in the Pyrenees).

And a healthy population level is important not only for the survival of the gray wolf. It may also have a positive impact on their southern cousin, the Mexican wolf, whose gene pool diversity has reached alarmingly low levels. Ecologists hope that the small populations of Mexican wolves will eventually interbreed with gray wolves in the southern Rockies, where there is a natural overlap of territory.

As Michael Robinson from the Center for Biological Diversity stated: 'Simply put, wolves are essential to the balance of nature.' Apex predators do more than just control populations of other mammals, keeping them at healthy sizes and reducing disease and overgrazing. The impact of a keystone species like the wolf ripples outward and has an important impact on the entire ecosystem. In Yellowstone, for example, wolves have demonstrated that they are essential to the restoration of riparian forests, which large herds of elk had previously grazed down to nothing. The simple act of bringing wolves back to Yellowstone resulted in the reappearance of a number of different species: trees (willows and alders), animals (beavers and foxes) and a variety of birds, fish and amphibians. Wolves also keep their cousins the coyotes in check, counterintuitively helping to boost numbers of lynx, snowshoe hares and pronghorn antelope, on which coyotes feed.

The Call of the Wild

It wasn't so long ago that most Americans held a markedly different view of the wilderness. Apex predators were not only viewed as serious threats, capable of killing livestock and even people, but were often depicted as the very embodiment of evil itself – that which challenged humankind's God-given right to dominion over the natural world. Following the large-scale decimation of their natural prey in the 19th century, wolves fulfilled these expectations and turned to cattle and sheep to survive. Spurred on by government bounties, Americans subsequently eradicated the gray wolf from over 95% of its historic range in the US by the 1930s; by 1945, they were gone from Colorado entirely: hunted, trapped and poisoned into local extinction.

But public perception of the wilderness has evolved over the decades: for many of us, it's no longer something to be feared or conquered so much as a place to protect and appreciate. In more than one survey, respondents declared that humans have a moral obligation to restore endangered species to their natural habitat, arguing that animals like the wolf have as much right to live on the land as we do.

But even if Americans are more conservation-minded than ever, there is still plenty of skepticism about whether or not wolf reintroduction is a good thing, as evidenced by Colorado's 2020 vote. Ranchers, of course, have a legitimate concern over the welfare of their cattle, sheep and horses. And ranching is big business: according to the Colorado Department of Agriculture, approximately 60% of the state's $7.1 billion of agriculture-related revenue comes from livestock ($4.26 billion).

And, of course, there are those communities where the buffer between the human and the wild has increasingly disappeared – communities who know first-hand the damage a hungry bear can cause to a house, car or chicken coop, or who have lost a beloved pet to an opportunistic coyote or mountain lion. Many are right to wonder what sort of impact wolves might have on their lives. But the flip side of that question is important, too: ultimately, how will we as a species impact the long-term survival of the wolf?

'Simply put, wolves are essential to the balance of nature.'

Michael Robinson, Center for Biological Diversity

INDEX

Map Pages **000**

Map Pages **000**

**Colorado State
Capitol, Denver
(p67)**

**Reaching the summit
of a fourteener –
Huron Peak
(p203)**

THIS BOOK

Design Development
Marc Backwell

Content Development
Mark Jones, Sandie Kestell, Anne Mason, Joana Taborda

Cartography Development
Katerina Pavkova

Production Development
Sandie Kestell, Fergal Condon

Series Development Leadership
Darren O'Connell, Piers Pickard, Chris Zeiher

Destination Editor
Amy Lynch

Production Editor
Claire Rourke

Book Designer
Dermot Hegarty

Cartographer
Val Kremenchutskaya

Assisting Editors
Peter Cruttenden, Andrea Dobbin

Cover Researcher
Norma Brewer

Thanks
Karen Henderson, Alison Killilea, Jenna Myers, Saralinda Turner

MIX
Paper from responsible sources
FSC™ C021741

Paper in this book is certified against the Forest Stewardship Council™ standards. FSC™ promotes environmentally responsible, socially beneficial and economically viable management of the world's forests.

Published by Lonely Planet Global Limited
CRN 554153
4th edition – August 2023
ISBN 978 1 78701 681 1
© Lonely Planet 2023 Photographs © as indicated 2023
10 9 8 7 6 5 4 3 2 1
Printed in China